CONFLICT AND PEACEBUILDING IN THE AFRICAN GREAT LAKES REGION

CONFLICT AND PEACEBUILDING IN THE AFRICAN GREAT LAKES REGION

Edited by Kenneth Omeje
and Tricia Redeker Hepner

Indiana University Press

Bloomington and Indianapolis

This book is a publication of

Indiana University Press
Office of Scholarly Publishing
Herman B Wells Library 350
1320 East 10th Street
Bloomington, Indiana 47405 USA

iupress.indiana.edu

Telephone orders   800-842-6796
Fax orders   812-855-7931

© 2013 by Indiana University Press

All rights reserved

No part of this book may be reproduced or utilized in any form or by any means, electronic or mechanical, including photocopying and recording, or by any information storage and retrieval system, without permission in writing from the publisher. The Association of American University Presses' Resolution on Permissions constitutes the only exception to this prohibition.

♾ The paper used in this publication meets the minimum requirements of the American National Standard for Information Sciences—Permanence of Paper for Printed Library Materials, ANSI Z39.48-1992.

Manufactured in the United States of America

Library of Congress Cataloging-in-Publication Data

Conflict and peacebuilding in the African Great Lakes Region / edited by Kenneth Omeje and Tricia Redeker Hepner.
    p. cm.
    Includes bibliographical references and index.
    ISBN 978-0-253-00837-4 (cloth : alk. paper) — ISBN 978-0-253-00842-8 (pbk. : alk. paper) — ISBN 978-0-253-00848-0 (ebook) 1. Peace-building—Great Lakes Region (Africa) 2. Peace-building—Africa, East. 3. Postwar reconstruction—Great Lakes Region (Africa) 4. Postwar reconstruction—Africa, East. 5. Conflict management—Great Lakes Region (Africa) 6. Conflict management—Africa, East. I. Omeje, Kenneth C. II. Redeker Hepner, Tricia M.
    JZ5584.G74C66 2013
    303.6096761—dc23

                                                2013002204

1 2 3 4 5 18 17 16 15 14 13

Contents

Acknowledgments   *vii*
List of Abbreviations   *ix*
List of Foreign Terms   *xiii*

Introduction: Conflict and Peacebuilding in the African Great Lakes Region \ Kenneth Omeje and Tricia Redeker Hepner   *1*

Part I. The Great Lakes Region: Challenges of the Past and Present

1. Understanding the Diversity and Complexity of Conflict in the African Great Lakes Region \ Kenneth Omeje   25

2. The History and Politics of Regionalism and Integration in East Africa \ Hannington Ochwada   47

3. Multipolar Politics and Regional Integration in East Africa: Opportunities and Challenges for Nonstate Actors \ Doreen Alusa   65

Part II. Case Studies of Conflict and Peacebuilding in the Great Lakes

4. Historical Dynamics of the Northern Uganda Conflict: A Longitudinal Struggle for Nation Building \ Elias Omondi Opongo   85

5. Kofi Annan's Conflict Resolution Model and Peacebuilding in Kenya \ Alfred Anangwe   106

6. Justice versus Reconciliation: The Dilemmas of Transitional Justice in Kenya \ Ozonnia Ojielo   122

7. Climate Change and Peacebuilding among Pastoralist Communities in Northeastern Uganda and Western Kenya \ Julaina A. Obika and Harriet K. Bibangambah   141

Part III. Social and Cultural Dimensions of Conflict and Peacebuilding in the Great Lakes

8. Media Sustainability in a Postconflict Environment: Radio Broadcasting in the DRC, Burundi, and Rwanda \ Marie-Soleil Frère   161

9   Youth in Transition: The Arts and Cultural Resonance
    in Postconflict Northern Uganda \ Lindsay McClain Opiyo
    and Tricia Redeker Hepner   179

10 Gender Issues in Reintegration: A Feminist and Rights-Based Analysis
    of the Experiences of Formerly Abducted Child-Mothers
    in Northern Uganda \ Eric Awich Ochen   197

11 The "Ambivalence of the Sacred": Christianity, Genocide,
    and Reconciliation in Rwanda \ Janine Natalya Clark   217

    Index   235
    List of Contributors   241

Acknowledgments

WE ARE PLEASED to acknowledge the help we received from different quarters in putting together this book project. Our first debt of gratitude goes to the British Council/Development Partnerships in Higher Education (DelPHE) of the UK government for providing the enabling research grant, without which this project would likely not have been undertaken. Pauline Gangla, George Kogolla, and Dyonis Ndungu of the British Council DelPHE Program Management team in Nairobi, Kenya, deserve a special mention for efficiently facilitating the project grant administration, thereby enabling us to not only accomplish this book project, but to complete diverse capacity-building program activities in the three African project partner universities: United States International University (USIU) in Kenya, Gulu University in Uganda, and the University of Lubumbashi in the Democratic Republic of Congo.

We are exceptionally grateful to colleagues at USIU in Nairobi, especially Moses Onyango, Doreen Alusa, John Mwangi, Prof. Macharia Munene, Prof. Fredrick Iraki, Prof. James Kahindi, and Prof. Munyae Mulinge. At the University of Tennessee we thank Prof. Rosalind I. J. Hackett, Julia Hanebrink, Randal Hepner, and all those involved in Jazz for Justice and the Gulu Study and Service Abroad Program in both Tennessee and Uganda for their professional and moral support.

To all the chapter contributors and manuscript reviewers, we say a big thank you for your commitment and professionalism.

Abbreviations

ABP	Burundi Press Agency
ACP	African, Caribbean, and Pacific Group of States
ACRWC	African Charter on the Rights and Welfare of the Child
ADFL	Alliance of Democratic Forces for the Liberation of Congo
APROSOMA	Association for the Social Betterment of the Masses
ASP	Afro-Shirazi Party
AU	African Union
AU-ACPPDT	African Union's African Charter for Popular Participation in Development and Transformation
BBC	British Broadcasting Corporation
CAR	Central African Republic
CARSA	Christian Action for Reconciliation and Social Assistance
CBOs	community-based organizations
CDR	Comite pour la Défense de la République
CEEAC	Communauté Economique des Etats de l'Afrique Centrale
CEMAC	Communauté Economique et Monétaire de l'Afrique Central
CENI	National Independent Electoral Commission
CEWS	Continental Early Warning System
CMD	Centre for Multiparty Democracy
CNDD	National Council for the Defense of Democracy
CNDD-FDD	National Council for the Defense of Democracy–Forces for the Defense of Democracy
COMESA	The Common Market for Eastern and Southern African States
CEPGL	Communauté Economique de Pays des Grand Lacs
CPA	Comprehensive Peace Agreement
CRC	Convention on the Rights of the Child, 1989
DDR	demobilization, demilitarization, and reintegration
DRC	Democratic Republic of Congo
EAC	East African Community
EACB	East African Currency Board

EACSO	East African Common Services Organization
EACSOF	East African Civil Society Organizations Forum
EACT	East African Community Treaty
EAHC	East African High Commission
ECK	Electoral Commission of Kenya
ECOWAS	Economic Community of West African States
FAR	Rwandan Army
FDD	Hutu Force for the Defense of Democracy
FRODEBU	Front for Democracy in Burundi
GOU	Government of Uganda
HDI	Human Development Index
HPI	Human Poverty Index
HSM	Holy Spirit Movement
HSMF	Holy Spirit Mobile Force
ICC	International Criminal Court
ICGLR	International Conference on the Great Lakes Region
ICTJ	International Center for Transitional Justice
ICTR	International Criminal Tribunal for Rwanda
IDPs	internally displaced persons
IEBC	Independent Electoral and Boundaries Commission
IFASIC	Institut Facultaire des Sciences de l'Information et la Communication
IGAD	Intergovernmental Authority for Development
IGOs	international governmental organizations
IMM	Implementation and Management Mechanisms
IPP	Institut Panos Paris
JED	Journalise en danger
JIG	Joint Liaison Group
KADU	Kenyan African Democratic Union
KALIP	Karamoja Livelihoods Programme
KANU	Kenyan African National Union
KIDP	Karamojong Integrated Disarmament and Development Programme
KPR	Kenya Police Reserve
KPTJ	Kenyans for Peace with Truth and Justice

KPU	Kenyan People's Union
LPA	Lagos Plan of Action
LRA	The Lord's Resistance Army
MINURCA	United Nations Mission in the Central African Republic
MNCs	multinational corporations
MONUC/MONUSCO	Peacekeeping Mission in the Congo
MOUCECORE	Mouvement Chrétien pour l'Evangélisation, le Counseling et la Réconciliation
MPs	members of parliament
NAP	Uganda National Action Plan
NARC	the National Rainbow Coalition
NEMU	the National Election Monitoring Unit
NGOs	Nongovernmental Organizations
NRA	National Resistance Army
NRA/M	National Resistance Army/Movement
NRM	National Resistance Movement
NRT	New Regionalism Theory
OAU	Organization of African Unity
ODM	Orange Democratic Movement
ORINFOR	Rwandan Office for Information
PALIPEHUTU	Party for the Liberation of the Hutu People
PARMEHUTU	Party of the Movement of Hutu Emancipation
PDC	Christian Democratic Party
PNU	Party of National Unity
PP	People's Party
PPRD	People's Party for Reconstruction and Democracy
PRDP	Peace Recovery and Development Plan for Northern Uganda
PSC	Peace and Security Council
PTAs	preferential trade agreements
PTSD	posttraumatic stress disorder
RADER	Rwanda Democratic Rally
RATELKI	Radio Télévision Kimbanguiste
RCK	Katanga Community Radio
RFI	Radio France
RPA	Rwandan Patriotic Army

RPF	Rwandan Patriotic Front
RTDM	Radio Télévision du Diocèse de Matadi
RTLM	Radio Télévision des Milles Collines
RTNB	Radio Télévision Nationale du Burundi
RTNC	Radio Télévision Nationale du Congo
SADC	South African Development Community
SALW	small arms and light weapons
SCiU	Save the Children in Uganda
SFCG	Search for Common Ground
SLPBC	Sierra Leone Public Broadcasting Corporation
SPLA/M	Sudan People's Liberation Army/Movement
TANU	Tanganyika African National Union
TIPRs	trade and intellectual property rights
TJN	Transitional Justice Network
TJRC	Truth, Justice, and Reconciliation Commission
UCC	the Uganda Constitutional Commission
UHRC	Uganda Human Rights Commission
UN-ECOSOC	United Nations Economic and Social Council
UNAMIR	United Nations Assistance Mission for Rwanda
UNLA	Uganda National Liberation Army
UNOMUR	UN Observer Mission for Uganda and Rwanda
UNPC	National Union of the Congolese Press
UPC	Uganda People's Congress
UPDA	Uganda People's Democratic Army
UPDF	Uganda People's Defense Forces
UPDM/A	Uganda Peoples Democratic Movement/Army
UPRONA	Union for National Progress
WASCOF	West African Civil Society Forum

Foreign Terms

Banyarwanda	Rwandan identity
batongole	politico-administrative chiefs
bwola	traditional Acholi dance style
coupage	advertorial news
dingi-dingi	dance
gacaca	a traditional dispute resolution mechanism resurrected by the Rwandan government in 2000 to deal with a backlog of cases from the genocide
ganwa	princely oligarchy
génocidaires	perpetrators of genocide
gucupira	loss of status
Inpuzamugambi	those with a single purpose
Interahamwe	Hutu extremist militia
Interahamwe	those who stand, fight, or kill together
inyenzi	cockroaches, disparaging word used by Hutu to describe Tutsi
kabaka	king
katikiro	powerful administrative assistants
kimbugwe	powerful administrative assistants
lukiiko	a legislative council in a form of a parliament
magendo	petty clandestine trade in items such as cooking oil, soap, flour
mato-oput	Acholi cultural ritual of reconciliation used to mediate disputes between two conflicting clans, "drinking of the bitter herb"
mwami	king
palaver	a cultural, social-political institution with its roots in precolonial Rwanda
rwodi	Luo clan chiefs
sabataka	"the father of all clans"

CONFLICT AND PEACEBUILDING IN THE AFRICAN GREAT LAKES REGION

Introduction

Conflict and Peacebuilding in the African Great Lakes Region

Kenneth Omeje and Tricia Redeker Hepner

THE AFRICAN GREAT Lakes region is one of marked contrasts and striking continuities. Beset by destructive conflicts, it also possesses extraordinary potential for peace and development. From biodiversity to solid minerals and human talents, this geopolitical space is endowed with abundant natural and cultural resources. Some of the world's most ecologically diverse freshwater systems, subtropical rainforests, savannah grasslands, and temperate highlands with immense extractive, agricultural, and touristic value are found in the Great Lakes region. In addition, it is culturally and linguistically diverse, comprising population groups with rich and dynamic historical, religious, economic, political, and legal traditions that have both endured and been transformed by internal and external factors. In defining what constitutes the African Great Lakes region, we must therefore include not only the nation-states that comprise it—Burundi, Rwanda, Uganda, Democratic Republic of Congo, Kenya, and Tanzania—but also the historical, sociopolitical, cultural, and economic geographies that cross and complicate these constructed borders.

Despite its great potential for development—or perhaps because of it—a variety of complex political conflicts at least partly related to the construction of nation-state borders have plagued the African Great Lakes region: genocide in Rwanda; civil wars in Burundi, Democratic Republic of Congo (DRC), and Uganda; flawed democratic elections and violence in Kenya; ethnic hostilities and pastoral conflicts in most states; as well as boundary disputes, cross-border rebel incursions, and interest-driven political interventionism. The loss of life and livelihoods is nothing short of staggering. It is now well known that over 800,000 people were killed in the 1994 Rwandan genocide; less acknowledged are the more than four million who have perished in DRC since the civil war started over a decade ago. The Kenyan postelection violence of 2008 led to at least 1,200 deaths and about 350,000 victims were internally displaced or rendered homeless. The Lord's Resistance Army (LRA) rebel war in northern Uganda and the cross-border pursuit of the rebels by the Ugandan army created millions of internally displaced persons in Uganda, northern DRC, Southern Sudan, and the Central African Republic. Between 1993 and 2005, more than 300,000 people were killed in ethnic violence and civil war in Burundi, while over half a million people were displaced.

Significantly, the Great Lakes region is both defined and surrounded by fragile states marked by varying intensities of instability and complex political emergencies, including Sudan, Central Africa Republic, Ethiopia, Eritrea, Somalia, and Zimbabwe. The sociopolitical and economic crises in surrounding countries are interlocking factors that inevitably aggravate the desperate humanitarian and security situations in different parts of the region. Kenya has been particularly incommoded by the influx of millions of refugees from Somalia. The only country in the region that seems to have been insulated from direct political conflicts is mainland Tanzania. However, election-related violence and separatist agitations have repeatedly arisen on Zanzibar Island, and Tanzania has been heavily weakened by the brunt of hosting hundreds of thousands of refugees, mostly from the DRC. Problems of child soldiering; proliferation of small arms and light weapons; sexual slavery, abduction, abuse, and torture of young girls and women in war zones by rebel fighters; refugees and internal displacement of persons; pastoral and communal violence; rebel and militia insurgencies; and epidemics like HIV/AIDS remain significant problems in different parts of the region. The situation in eastern DRC, where various rebel/militia groups are still fighting the central government, remains extremely dire. Cross-border raids between guerrillas and combatants in the DRC and Rwanda, Uganda and the DRC, Uganda and Sudan, and Somalia and Kenya have occurred repeatedly in recent years, further dislocating vulnerable people and communities.

The interplay of humanitarian catastrophes, political conflict, and insecurity has greatly retarded economic activity and development in the region and further exacerbated the human poverty profile. The natural resource endowments in the region have represented liabilities as well as potential opportunities, as groups have vied for control over resources amid market pressures and the exigencies of neoliberal development and globalization paradigms. While sub-Saharan Africa accounts for 92 percent of the twenty-four countries ranked under the Low Human Development category of the 2009 Human Development Index (HDI), most countries of the Great Lakes region are especially abysmal in terms of the Human Poverty Index (HPI) (Thirlwall 2008, 39; UNDP, 2009). Development infrastructures are generally weak and underdeveloped in most parts of the Great Lakes region, exacerbating political conflict and complicating efforts to create and maintain peace amid persistent structural impediments to social and economic justice.

But conflict, impoverishment, and humanitarian crises are only part of the story of the African Great Lakes region. Local, regional, and international actors, movements, and interventions have also responded by addressing the complex causes and lasting impacts of violence and poverty. Through diverse means and strategies, Africans have actively reshaped their realities in ways that powerfully demonstrate the potential for peace, human security, and development in the Great Lakes region. While some initiatives have been more successful than others, a key feature of conflict situations in the Great Lakes and elsewhere is the very persistence of efforts at resolution and peacebuilding. These have taken place not solely—or even primarily—at the level of states. Often they have occurred in spite of states and national governments, challenging both the logic of sovereignty and the arrogance of political elites who dismiss the capacity of people at the grassroots to effect transformation through their own institutional and cultural resources.

Indeed, with the exception of eastern DRC and, to a lesser extent, northern Uganda, most incidents of political violence, wars, and rebel activities in the region have been practically resolved. This is in part due to the active intervention of regional and international institutions and agencies, including the Intergovernmental Authority for Development (IGAD), African Union (AU), United Nations agencies, and the East African Community (EAC), among others. Donor support for strengthening local and regional stakeholders' capacities (e.g., intergovernmental institutions, states, NGOs, community-based organizations, educational institutions, and the security sector) for a wide range of responsive actions and proactive change have accelerated rapidly. Institution building, democratic reforms, participatory development, and peacebuilding are among the favorite buzzwords of the externally dominated and often petulant conflict and development intervention community active in the region. These interventions have met with mixed results, depending upon how they have interfaced with local needs and sociopolitical dynamics.

But such interventions and their associated buzzwords do not exclusively belong to donors and other external actors and initiatives. They are also mobilized by those most affected, often in contrast to elite-led, top-down efforts. At both the local and national levels, social and cultural resources have been mobilized that promote peacebuilding, conflict resolution, reconciliation, and human rights. Alternatively, they may also fuel conflict. Whether examining the ambivalent role of religion in postgenocide Rwanda, for example, or the therapeutic aspects of the performative arts in Uganda amid ongoing problems of structural violence and political factionalization, both indigenous and hybridized cultural processes are of considerable import when examining the dynamics of political conflict, development, and peacebuilding.

One of the central contributions of this book and its multidisciplinary approach is to illustrate how conflict, intervention, and peacebuilding in the African Great

Lakes region have unfolded in dynamic and kaleidoscopic patterns over time, across state borders, above and below the purview of (often compromised and corrupted) state structures and governments, and certainly in the everyday lives of African citizens, who—contrary to enduring and tenacious popular views, especially in the West—are not programmed by ethnicity or "tribalism." Prioritizing the perspectives and voices of people directly enmeshed in conflict and peacebuilding in Africa challenges us to think beyond, and more critically about, the role of ethnicity, states, supranational institutions, and policies that together still dominate most analyses of conflict in Africa, yet are themselves infrequently or insufficiently problematized. It requires us to remember that—despite seeming to have self-evident lives of their own—states, institutions, policies, and collective identities such as ethnicity are products of human agency, and human lives are the primary grist through which conflict and peacebuilding play out. Finally, prioritizing African perspectives reminds us that essentialized categories like ethnicity are precisely those we must continue deconstructing and demystifying rather than relying on as explanatory frameworks.

The "Conflict Debate" in the African Great Lakes Region

Students and experts of African conflicts have extensively analyzed the African Great Lakes region, focusing on various problems in specific or comparative settings, highlighting certain states or populations, and identifying broader patterns. There is no singular definition of the Great Lakes region or authoritative level of analysis, nor should there be. However, dominant discourses have largely focused on the historiography of the conflicts—notably their complex causalities, nature, and diversity; the nuanced role of external actors; the consequences of conflict for political, social, economic, demographic, and development landscapes; as well as the often fragile nature and politics of conflict intervention, resolution, and peacebuilding in the region. There is a strong recognition among pundits and scholars alike that, in terms of nature and expression, the conflicts in the Great Lakes are multidimensional in spatial and sectoral spread, and multiscalar in institutional and vertical articulation.

In terms of their multidimensionality, dominant narratives have tended to focus on strategic natural resources and the correlated intergroup struggles to control them (Le Pape 2004; Collier 2008); "tribal" antagonisms and "ethnocide" (Lemarchand 1994; Cohen 2007); climate change and its cumulative impact on the interlocking environment, economies, and livelihoods of the region (Juma and Kagwanja 2003; Hoste 2009); political corruption, dictatorship, governance deficits, and warlordism (Bekoe 2006; Mkutu and Sabala 2007); and so forth. Regarding the multiscalar quality, a single conflict is at the same time local, national, regional, and international in character (Roessler 2005; Mkutu 2008, 1–3; Prunier 2009). Intricately connecting the multidimensional and the multiscalar conflict architecture is a complex and often convoluted transhistoricity.

Scholars have portrayed markedly varied perspectives in their analysis of the "conflict architecture" and its constituent elements and pivots. At the center of the debate, however, remain questions about the nature of the state in Africa in both colonial and postcolonial formations and the consequences of the use and abuse of state power for conflict. Most analysts have more or less conceded that the state in the African Great Lakes region has similar characteristics as the state elsewhere in sub-Saharan Africa: inherently pathological, weak, and predatory, largely due to the intervention of essentialist ethnicity and other militarized, collective identities.

The most evocative image of wars in the region and elsewhere on the continent is that of savagery, associated with ethnic differences and rivalries. This unfortunately resonates with popular Western media, cinematography, celebrity humanitarians and activists, and even academia (for some apt examples, see Wainaina 2005). In a pluralistic setting where sovereign states are composed of a multiplicity of ethnocultural groups brought together by colonial diktat to serve imperial interests, age-old animosities based on "primordial" identities are seen as the defining denominator of African politics. The most crucial identity groups for proponents of this view are ethnic groups or more pejoratively, "tribes," which are constructed as premodern, immutable, "mystical" (in the sense of being alloyed with or animated by a spiritist religion), and possessed of an uncanny appetite for vendetta and bloodbath (see Ellis 1995; Ellis and Ter Haar 2004). Dating from precolonial history, African politics are depicted almost exclusively in terms of competition for power, resources, and domination among tribes, whose collective memories of each other are said to be replete with antecedents and mythologies of hate, rapine, pogrom, and inhumanity.

In his analysis of repeated "ethnocide" (largely synonymous with genocide—the wholesale massacre of people on both sides of a socially and legally constructed fault line) in postcolonial Burundi, René Lemarchand (1994, xii) argues that "*ethnocide* in Burundi is about ethnic violence as a mode of discourse and a mode of political action. . . . In *ethnocide*, ethnicity is transformed, mobilized and ultimately incorporated into the horrors and irrationality of genocidal violence." Not much has changed in the way tribes perceive and relate to one another in Africa since precolonial times, many exponents of the tribal vendetta model would argue. The dramatic concomitants of some of the armed conflicts in Africa, such as incidents and allegations of male fighters that wore women's wigs and decorated themselves with human bones, soldiers who stripped and fought as naked brigades, or combatants who used shamanistic charms and other spiritist inoculations in the belief that these magical devices would protect them from the enemy's bullets, are some of the evidence frequently marshaled to buttress this view of atavistic, essentialist violence (for a more detailed discussion and critique, see Omeje 2009).

Exponents of the instrumentalist value of African "tribal" identities, such as Berman and Lonsdale (1992) and Chabal and Daloz (1999), have characterized the dysfunctionality of ethnicity in Africa and its role in armed conflict and genocide in places like the Great Lakes region as "political tribalism." Berman and Lonsdale (1992, 466) contrast political tribalism with its diametrical and more positive opposite, "moral ethnicity." They argue that while the former springs from high political intrigue and constitutes communities through external competition, the latter imagines and creates communities through civic virtues like self-help and mutual support systems. Political clientelism, believed to be widespread in Africa as an element of neopatrimonial governance, is categorized as integral to political tribalism. Similarly, Chabal and Daloz (1999) address why moral ethnicity, a positively functional social tradition coterminous with Goran Hyden's (1980) thesis of "moral economy" in Eastern Africa, is seemingly undercut and superseded by political tribalism as the essence of politics in the region. The answer to this conundrum is the central thesis of the authors' study: namely, political tribalism creates disorder (both institutional and systemic), and disorder is used as a political instrument by African postcolonial elites to entrench and/or perpetuate their patrimonial interests. To wit:

> Why should the African political elites dismantle a political system which serves them so well? . . . Indeed, the current patrimonial and prebendal practices of political elites are most satisfactory, at least from the micro-sociological perspective of the individual and communities they serve. . . . Hence, the notion that politicians, bureaucrats or military chiefs should be the servants of the state simply does not make sense. Their political obligations are, first and foremost, to their kith and kin, their clients, their communities, their regions or even their religions. All such patrons seek ideally to constitute themselves as 'Big Men', controlling as many networks as they can. But to succeed as a 'Big Man' demands resources; and the more extensive the networks the greater the need for the means of distribution. The legitimacy of the African political elites, such as it is, derives from the ability to nourish the clientele on which their power rests. It is therefore imperative for them to exploit governmental resources for patrimonial purposes. (Chabal and Daloz, 1999, 13–15)

Chabal and Daloz hence conclude that Africa works well from the standpoint of the powerful political elites who not only profit from prevailing institutional and systemic dysfuntions, but also conveniently instrumentalize disorder, violence, and impunity for their primordial and self-serving advantages.

Some theorists of the dysfunctionality of the postcolonial state, especially those writing from postmodernist and similar deconstructivist perspectives, tend to present a hybrid imagery of the African state and the conflicts that ravage it. Bayart et al. (1999) and Mbembe (2001) account for African agency in contemporary conflicts as an outcome of an unwholesome blend of colonial legacies, African cultural and institutional norms, as well as the patrimonial interests of postcolonial elites. The African postcolonial state is interpreted as a hybrid between weakly scaffolded colonial structures superficially engrafted on indigenous African structures and normative systems, in which postcolonial elites hypocritically Africanize the former by relying on distorted aspects of the latter. The result is highly politicized institutional and violent conflicts.

Historical materialists like Zeleza (2006, 99), meanwhile, argue that "the legacies of colonialism have apparently not only persisted in the postindependence era but have also been aggravated in some instances, leading to conflicts of varied intensities. Africa is at the same time ravaged by the legacies of colonialism and the ravages of neocolonialism." Perhaps no one has captured the ravages of neocolonialism better than political ecology and resource conflict theorists like Le Billion (2007) and Watts (2008), who focus on the complex intersections of imperialist exploitation and prebendal plunder by governing elites and other local factions (including warlords and insurgents) within the political economy of natural resource rents. Related to a historical materialist and political ecology approach is Patricia Daley's "black feminist geopolitical approach" to the problem of gender and genocide in Burundi. She argues that "the domination and oppression that produces genocide is the outcome of the intersections of race, ethnicity, the patriarchal state, masculinity, the geopolitical economy and militarism" (2008, 7). Focusing on genocidal violence in the region, which she broadly defines "to include those forms of violence with genocidal characteristics (legally defined)," Daley contends that:

> Genocidal violence in the Great Lakes region is neither a post-colonial nor post-Cold War, post-ideological phenomenon. Violence is rooted in the historical experience of the continent and the progressive dehumanization of the African people. Burundi and Rwanda are two states where the struggle for political power led to the refinement of a genocidal state; the socio-political and economic institutions of the colonial state and the drive towards modernity produced the conditions that laid the foundations for genocide. These were reproduced after independence and became enmeshed with global militarism during and after the Cold War (Daley 2008, 7, 8).

The apparent centrality of the genocidal violence in Rwanda (and Burundi to a lesser extent) to some of the most horrendous recent and contemporary armed conflicts in the Great Lakes region have been analyzed by a number of noted commentators, not least the widely acclaimed journalist and former director of the French Center for Ethiopian Studies in Addis Ababa, Gerard Prunier. In his analysis of the implosion of the Congo basin and its periphery (the area more or less defined as the Africa Great Lakes region in this volume) in the 1990s and early 2000s, Prunier (2009, xxxi) argues that the Rwandan genocide and its consequences acted as a catalyst for this regional catastrophe, precipitating a crisis that was latent for many years and later reached far beyond its original Great Lakes locus. "The Rwandan genocide," he continues, "has been both a product and a further cause of an enormous African crisis: its very occurrence was a symptom, its nontreatment spread the disease."

The vigorous "conflict debate" clearly shows the explanatory potency of multiple perspectives regarding the nature and dynamics of armed conflicts in the Great Lakes region. Conversely, the limitations and shortcomings of specific perspectives are equally apparent. For instance, some of the studies conceptually rooted in concepts of "tribal" or ethnic differences and their instrumentalization for armed conflicts have been criticized for casting an inherent pathological slant on African states and politics (Francis 2005; Omeje 2009, 6). Paul Richards (1996), in his critique of the perspective of Ellis (1995) and other scholars that write from a similar perspective—"the new barbarism thesis"—argued that in spite of the efforts by the international community to humanize war, wars still remain inherently uncivil. Mind-boggling monstrosities of various shades, Richards posits, are rampant in wars and are by no means peculiar to Africa. To focus on the evidently sensational neobarbarism episodes and narrative in African wars, according to Richards, is to ignore the underlying causality of the wars—the collapse of the fragile neopatrimonial state that succeeded the colonial state (see Omeje 2009, 8).

As several of the chapter contributions in this volume show, Africa is not as stagnantly trapped in tribal vendetta as many "Afro-pessimist" perspectives and studies highlighted above have portrayed. Despite recurrent hiccups, significant progress continues to be made in both microcommunity and macrosocietal levels in the region and elsewhere on the continent. It is apparent that the conflict literature on the African region, especially in the Great Lakes, is mostly keen to analyze and sometimes exaggerate and magnify problems of conflict. Few studies have yet delved into the analysis of functional remedies, especially some of the unconventional grassroots, conflict resolution, and peacebuilding alternative approaches promoted by nonstate actors and local communities through alternative media that may not be readily adopted or co-opted into political or policy speak, but remain important and vital nonetheless. There are enormously creative and internally self-critical efforts at work among Africans affected by conflict and invested in peace. Whatever theoretical arguments may be made about the "nature" of conflict and the prospects for peace on the continent, these voices must be heard through careful, humanistic, and fine-grained analysis. The investigations and narratives based on this alternative framework are key contributions of this volume. Indeed, as Daley (2007, 5) aptly observes, much of the conflict literature on Africa is focused on pathological factors internal to the state: ethnic hatred, overpopulation, neopatrimonialism, greed, barbarism, retraditionalization—all contributing to a pervasive image of inherent dysfunctionality in African societies. She writes, "The linkage between Africa and the rest of the world; colonialism, neocolonialism, globalization, trade, economic liberalization and aid, are often either under explored in these analyses of warfare or are seen as insignificant to the internal dynamics."

Approaches, Themes, and Perspectives

Adopting a deliberate multidisciplinary approach defined by the perspectives and expertise of mainly African and Africa-based scholars, this book critically explores and analyzes the historical and contemporary dynamics of conflict in the Great Lakes region, as well as the nature, relevance, and efficacy of intervention measures and processes of peacebuilding. Drawing on perspectives from anthropology and sociology, international relations, peace and conflict studies, political science, religious studies, humanitarian studies, and law, we aim to capture the historical depth and complexity of conflict and peacebuilding in the Great Lakes region while simultaneously invigorating the "conflict debate." Recognizing that patterns of violent conflict are rooted in both historical factors and contemporary social, political, and economic arrangements that characterize everyday life, the chapters in this volume collectively demonstrate the continuities and contrasts among various countries, populations, and periods of crisis and transformation.

Beginning with the Great Lakes as a dynamic but discernible region that has changed over time due to internal developments and the shifting trajectories of global geopolitics, we then address specific cases of conflict, interventions, and peacebuilding that render visible the nested dynamics of local, national, regional, and global forces in both the causes of, and responses to, conflict. Complementing and enriching these historical and political-economic analyses that critically interrogate states, political behavior, policy, and governance are social-scientific, ethnographically grounded studies that investigate how cultural patterns are shaped by, and implicated in, patterns of conflict and peacebuilding in the Great Lakes. From media and the arts to religion and reconciliation, social and cultural features emerge as central to public and grassroots engagements with elite institutions, policies, and debates at the national, regional, and international levels. From this angle, several unifying themes emerge, which we further elaborate and anchor to specific chapter contributions, below.

First among these unifying themes is how former colonial powers, and now foreign donors, have played a central role in shaping trajectories of conflict and peace in the Great Lakes region. Relatedly, the chasm between political elites and grassroots, civil society initiatives remains a common issue throughout the countries of the Great Lakes and certainly emerges as a contributing factor to the persistence of conflict, the fragility of peace, and the elusiveness of social and economic justice. Finally, a third unifying theme suggests that bridging this chasm between elites and top-down processes of governance and intervention, on one hand, and the communities and populations most affected by conflict and impoverishment on the other, is absolutely central to securing peace and nurturing development. Through the empowerment of individuals, communities, and local institutions, often via culturally specific and resonant institutions, forms of expression, and modes of conflict resolution, such bridging with top-down efforts may take place.

As noted earlier, there is no single definition of the African Great Lakes region or one authoritative framework for analyzing its features. The different existing conceptions, however, are based in shared historical experience dating from precolonial interactions and trade; common geographical features (especially the sharing of borders with the region's eponymous Great Lakes—Victoria, Tanganyika, Malawi, Turkana, Albert, Kivu, and Edward); a shared lingua franca (in particular, Kiswahili as a neo-indigenous language dating back to precolonial era); interlocking colonial experiences and heritages; and identities, relationships, and cultural formations that cut across modern-day borders of nation-states. Depending on the specific set of factors and perceived common characteristics used, scholars have identified the region as consisting of as few as six states (usually DRC, Uganda, Burundi, Rwanda, Kenya, and Tanzania) to as many as eleven (notably, the above six plus any combination of the following—Southern Sudan, Somalia, Ethiopia, Eritrea, Zambia, Malawi, Zimbabwe, Mozambique, Central African Republic, and Congo Brazzaville).

The formation of the International Conference on the Great Lakes Region (ICGLR) in the aftermath of the civil war in the DRC lends credence to this maximalist definition. Driven largely by Western donor funding and interest in peace and security in the region, the ICGLR was established through the famous Pact on Security, Stability and Development (popularly known as the Pact) signed in December 2006 in Nairobi by eleven heads of the following supposedly stakeholder states—Angola, Burundi, Central Africa Republic (CAR), Democratic Republic of Congo (DRC), Kenya, Rwanda, Republic of Congo, Sudan, Uganda, Tanzania, and Zambia. The ICGLR Pact is guided by some principles that inter alia focus on peace and security, democracy and good governance, economic development and regional integration, humanitarian and social issues, as well as nonaggression and collective defense (Norad 2009, 5). A new secretariat was set up in May 2007 in Bujumbura, Burundi, to help coordinate the implementation of the Pact guiding principles. ICGLR is still a fledgling regional organization, and just one among other comparatively more established and functional regional bodies that more or less straddle the Great Lakes and other adjoining regions, such as the EAC, the IGAD, the South African Development Community (SADC), the Common Market for Eastern and Southern African States (COMESA), Communauté Économique des Pays des Grand Lacs (CEPGL), Communauté Économique des États de l'Afrique Centrale (CEEAC), and Communauté Economique et Monétaire de l'Afrique Centrale (CEMAC) (see Norad, 2009, 11). Only time will tell whether the seemingly donor-driven, maximalist political definition of the Great Lakes region propagated by ICGLR will be able to muster broad-based support among the people of the region and analytical currency among the relevant intellectual community.

Interposed between the minimalist and maximalist definitions is a comparatively minority microdefinition that narrows the region to three core countries of the DRC, Rwanda, and Burundi (see Westerkamp et al. 2009). This volume adopts the minimalist definition and focuses on the six states named above and their combined population of about 201 million people. From the standpoint of long-standing socio-demographic features, and most significantly, the impact of interlocking postcolonial conflicts, we contend that this definition remains most relevant. Given the expertise of contributing authors, however, Rwanda, Uganda, and Kenya receive particular attention within the context of larger regional dynamics central to this book as a whole.

The Great Lakes Region: Historical and Regional Dynamics

In approaching the six constituent countries of the Great Lakes, we begin in the first section of the book by further exploring the factors that define them as a region and the characteristics of individual nations. What are the origins and trajectories of the tension between the region's diversity and complexity, and its historical, cultural, political, linguistic, and ethnic continuities and commonalities? How are these rooted in the colonial past, and how have they been structured over time by shifting political-economic trends regionally and globally? How do these tensions between diversity and continuity map onto the tensions between sovereignty of individual states and the possibilities or incentives for regional cooperation? On what bases has the Great Lakes region been defined as such, and with what consequences and benefits for whom? These questions are productively addressed in the chapters by Kenneth Omeje, Hannington Ochwada, and Doreen Alusa as they seek to identify and critically assess the dynamics of regionalism in the Great Lakes.

Adopting a critical and transhistorical perspective, Kenneth Omeje highlights how the diverse and complex political conflicts in the region have been fluid, multifaceted, and interlocking due to the interconnectedness of socio-demographic factors and histories of the various peoples of the region. "While some of the conflict structures date back to precolonial intergroup animosities," he observes, "European colonial policies and politics most decisively account for the embeddedness and virulence of the conflict structures." He identifies the Bahutu-Batutsi conflict in the Rwanda–Burundi axis as the "metaphoric approximation" of the conflict epicenter because of the direct and indirect historical connections of the conflict with many political events elsewhere in the region. Omeje argues that while colonialism multiplied and aggravated conflicts in the region, different factions of postcolonial elites have deliberately interposed their interests in the exploitative structures inherited from the colonialists as opposed to dismantling and transforming them to serve the public good. Hence, in the postcolonial dispensation, conflict has become even more complex than during the colonial era. Highlighting the two other major themes unifying the volume as a whole—that of the chasm between elite governance and conflict-resolution initiatives driven by the interests and efforts of affected populations, as well as the necessity of bridging such a chasm for lasting peace and development—Omeje submits that the end of armed conflict in most countries and the growing wave of democratization in the region during the last few years present a cautious hope about the possibility of transformative change.

Hannington Ochwada's chapter analyzes the political-economic history of regional integration in Eastern Africa, as well as the associated challenges and opportunities. The author argues that the political leaders of countries in the EAC and larger Great Lakes region "have largely defined the processes of regionalism and integration without considering the local, historical, 'bottom-up' patterns of cooperation that have existed in the region since precolonial times." This skewed approach, Ochwada argues, emphasizes a state-centric model of economic cooperation and commercial gains—an approach that largely benefits the elites and state economies at the expense of populations separated by artificial colonial boundaries and in need of social integration through free movement and residency and citizenship rights for regional immigrants and refugees. Among the challenges Ochwada identifies to postcolonial regional integration in the region are differences in political ideologies, economic orientation, and national identity. The author makes a case for a bottom-up approach to regional integration based on constitutional reforms, civil society engagement, and popular consensus that prioritizes both national and regional social integration as a necessary complement to the aspiration for economic regionalism and development.

Consistent with Ochwada's call for greater popular consensus and the engagement of civil society as a countervailing force vis-à-vis elites and state economies, Doreen Alusa "explores the predicament of regionalism in East Africa with a specific focus on the challenges and opportunities faced by nonstate actors in a multipolar international system." Like Omeje and Ochwada, Alusa traces the history of the politics of regionalism in East Africa to the colonial era, focusing on how British and German authorities established the East African Common Market in 1927 and subsequently created different regional structures to underpin it (e.g., a common currency, a joint income tax board, a joint economic council, and so on). The colonialists, argues Alusa, promoted a Euro-functionalist model of regionalization, "which favored economic integration as a prerequisite for political unity." The EAC was established after independence as a continuation of the colonial regionalist project, although the quest to establish a united East African federation, advocated by pan-Africanists like Tanzania's Julius Nyerere, diminished after independence because of the reluctance of the new states to compromise their sovereignties. Irreconcilable ideological and personality differences among the ruling elites amidst the bipolar politics of the Cold War and politics of neopatrimonialism in East Africa led to the collapse of the EAC in 1977.

The EAC was reestablished in 1999 within what the Alusa terms "multipolar international system" and today comprises five states: Kenya, Tanzania, Uganda, Rwanda, and Burundi. A major innovation embraced by the revived EAC, Alusa argues, is the inclusion of nonstate actors (civil society and business communities) as role players with an observer status in the regional-integration project. However, she also argues that the conferment of observer status onto nonstate actors falls short, as the politics and processes of regional integration within the community remain state-centric. She therefore calls for more concrete statutory and practical steps to be taken towards the democratization of the EAC regionalization process to empower nonstate actors and place them on more equal footing with state-led initiatives.

Conflict and Peacebuilding in Context: Elite Influences and Grassroots Initiatives

In the second part of the volume, the scope narrows from a discussion of regionalism in the past and present to specific case studies in conflict and peacebuilding. Focusing primarily on Uganda and Kenya, as well as cross-border dynamics between the two countries, these case studies further elaborate the unifying theme of how top-down governance and peacebuilding or conflict-resolution approaches interface with the initiatives, interests, and priorities of affected populations. Even more specifically, the chapters collectively illustrate how discourses and institutions associated with the postcolonial and postconflict periods embody implicit traces and explicit legacies of both colonialism and violent conflict, thus reflecting ongoing tensions between transformation and maintenance of the status quo. In their discussions of nation building and conflict in Uganda (Opongo), UN-sponsored conflict-resolution models (Anangwe) and postelection violence and transitional justice in Kenya (Ojielo), and the interrelationship between climate change and militarization among border-crossing pastoralists (Obika and Bibangambah), the authors shed light on a crucial observation made repeatedly by peace and conflict theorists that postcolonial and postconflict discourses and institutions may indeed be transformative agents of change, but can also disguise how patterns of violence (structural and physical) endure long after active conflicts have subsided (see Nordstrom 2004). What appears a break or rupture between the conflict and postconflict moments, then, emerges as both problematic as well as promising in times of transition, highlighting the necessity of critical scholarly analysis and recommendations.

Elias Omondi Opongo's chapter provides a transition from the historical and contemporary dynamics associated with regionalism in the African Great Lakes to analyzing how colonial and postcolonial policies and governance in Uganda underpinned the emergence of protracted conflict in the northern region of the country. Opongo argues that political-economic inequities and the politicization and militarization of ethnicity that began during colonialism and was entrenched by postcolonial governments are at the root of Uganda's infamous north-south conflict. Framing the latter as a "longitudinal struggle for nation building," Opongo explores the tension between ethnonationalism (the state's identification and promotion of a specific ethnic group to the exclusion of others) and nationalism (promotion of interethnic identities into a single national identity) in Uganda's past and present, arguing that "peace negotiations in Uganda, even when deemed successful, have failed to address the historical and political-economic factors at the root of the conflict." That is, as long as Ugandan political elites and international peace and justice brokers address conflict in isolation from its structural and historical dimensions, peace cannot come to its fullest fruition. Critically addressing the International Criminal Court's (ICC) issuing of arrest warrants for top LRA leaders, for example, Opongo notes that "genuine initiatives for political change and improvement in nation-building efforts would be realized more effectively through internal processes of interethnic, political, social, and religious inclusion," as well as mechanisms of restorative, as opposed to punitive, justice.

Alfred Anangwe's chapter shifts the lens from Uganda to Kenya, but retains a critical focus on the relationship between structures of governance and the creation of positive peace. Anangwe analyzes the initiatives led by African Union Chief Mediator and ex-UN Secretary General Kofi Annan in the aftermath of the 2007–8 election violence. Contextualizing his study within the modern political history of Kenya, Anangwe interrogates the protracted struggle for inclusive multiparty democracy and a new national constitution to elucidate why elections in Kenya have too often been marred by violence. Discussing the four pillars of Kofi Annan's conflict resolution and peacebuilding initiative—developing measures aimed at an immediate end to hostilities and restoration of fundamental rights and liberties; dealing with the humanitarian crisis triggered by the conflicts and resettlement of Internally Displaced Persons (IDPs); resolving the political deadlock arising from the disputed election results through formation of a grand coalition government; and examining and proposing solutions for the longstanding issues underlying the conflicts—Anangwe suggests that these interrelated approaches may in fact create an effective bridge between political elites and grassroots popular initiatives and expectations for better governance. By inducing reforms and even transformations in Kenya's grand coalition government in areas like electoral justice, the judiciary, and police and security sectors, Kofi Annan's model explicitly links conflict resolution and peacebuilding with state restructuring. To what extent these changes represent truly radical departures, and thus a clear "break" between structural and physical violence and peace and socioeconomic justice, Anangwe reminds us, remains to be seen.

Continuing the focus on contemporary Kenya, Ozonnia Ojielo addresses how the international culture and political economy of peacebuilding interfaces with transitional justice discourses and institutions following the 2007–8 postelection violence. Problematizing the notion of "transitional justice" from the outset, Ojielo implicitly points out how such popular phrases embody aspirations for change at the same time that they may fall short in their ability to restructure politics and governance as usual. Situating Kenya's effort to create a Truth, Justice, and Reconciliation Commission (TJRC) in the wake of postelection violence within the complex realities of party-politics and international pressures to adopt more retributive models for justice, Ojielo demonstrates the kinds of dilemmas communities and nation-states now face in a world of legal and political pluralism and local, regional, and international pressures. Viewing the TJRC as an important institutional mechanism through which the reforms addressed in Anangwe's chapter took place, Ojielo nonetheless analyzes much of its significance in terms of how transitional justice mechanisms symbolically "demarcate the past from the future to establish a new ethos of governance and of behavior by state institutions and officials." By interrogating how and why Kenyans pursued this form of justice over and above a punitive, criminal prosecution, Ojielo demonstrates the complexity of such justice-seeking measures and their co-optability by contending political players. Moreover, he notes that the international donor community strongly favors a special tribunal or the ICC to the exclusion of the TJRC, thereby casting the terms of the debate as "justice versus reconciliation." Arguing that "the pursuit of justice is not necessarily antagonistic to the pursuit of reconciliation.... Rather than a hierarchy, they each represent elements of a web," Ojielo concludes that "the real issue is cultural." Western donors, he notes, want facts, trials, and prosecutions to show for their investment. Kenyans, however, want truth and better prospects for social justice and harmony, which entails not just a meaningful transitional justice process but a reorganization of the state and political-economic sphere.

The issue of cultural norms, values, and definitions of justice amid the legacies of colonial and postcolonial governance and conflict is also taken up by Julaina Obika and Harriet Bibangambah in their analysis of the interface between changing environmental factors and the militarization of pastoralists on the Kenya-Uganda border. Their chapter introduces yet another dimension to the complexity of conflicts in the African Great Lakes region and the influence of global dynamics: that of climate change. Focusing on the Karimojong of northeastern Uganda and the Pokot and Turkana of western Kenya, Obika and Bibangambah utilize the concept of "eco-conflicts" to examine the relationship between climate change and violent conflict among pastoralists. Of equal importance to their analysis, however, are the culturally and environmentally specific coping and adaptive mechanisms used by pastoralists in the struggle for resources and survival, and how guns and other light weapons have become entangled in these responses.

Noting the shortcomings of past state policies vis-à-vis violence among pastoralists in a changing environment, the authors contend that "human needs and rights-based approaches to problem solving... rather than power-driven bargaining approaches.... [are] suitable for conflict resolution practices because [they] recognize that deep-rooted conflict exists where social structures and institutions are not functioning." Given that pastoralism is often associated in scholarship and policy discourse with armed violence, Obika and Bibangambah argue that "climate change will not undermine human security or increase the risk of violent conflict in isolation from other important social factors." Rather than forcibly de-arming already militarized groups, the authors contend that more effective and culturally appropriate bridges must be constructed as part of an overall process of forging sustainable peace and improving access to resources for pastoralists. Hence, "Fostering the capacity of pastoralists to participate in and appropriate the process of decentralization is a complicated and slow process that has to be driven from within their society if lasting change is to be achieved," which requires policy makers to become actively and responsively engaged with pastoralists themselves. They summarize a key aspect of their argument by noting that "Giving more attention to cultural values and the hierarchical structure within pastoralist communities, their conflict-resolving institutions, and their resource-management and resource-sharing practices, is crucial for peacebuilding in the region."

Bridging the Chasm: Social and Cultural Dynamics

A key unifying theme taking shape in section 2 of the volume, then, is how *culture matters* in both conflict and peacebuilding. While the primary focus is on the problematic disconnect between elite structures of governance and conflict resolution and peacebuilding, and how these contribute to the exacerbation and maintenance of both physical and structural violence, an important subtextual pattern emerges with respect to the meanings and practices associated with conflict, justice, and peace. Implicit in the analyses described above is how cultural meanings, symbols, models, institutions, and practices may be better marshalled as resources in the effort to bridge the chasm between elites and grassroots; civil society and popular actors. Moreover, the rooting of peace, justice, and improved human security in everyday relationships, practices, and meanings may be as crucial—if not more so—for transforming "postconflict" societies as top-down, elite, or internationally backed efforts at conflict resolution and peacebuilding.

Building on this emergent theme, the chapters in section 3 of this volume explicitly address some of the social and cultural dynamics through which conflict and peacebuilding take place. They illustrate how these not only provide possible sites of articulation between elites and popular actors, but also represent an arena in which international, national, and local models of justice and peace become mutually imbricated. They point up how diverse institutions, cultural practices, and forms of social and political organization can be simultaneously, or at different times, mobilized for either conflict or peacebuilding. Thus, they implicitly question the approach to conflict and peace as two poles on a continuum and problematize the related notion that "postconflict" itself is meaningful temporal category by demonstrating how society and culture are ambivalent repositories of relations that can serve both "poles" in various contexts and time periods. Consistent with a longstanding anthropological project to view conflict as an inherent, as opposed to aberrant, feature of human relations, these chapters demonstrate through "close to the ground" analytical methods how the media, music and art, gendered social relations, and religion express the dialectical nature of practices, institutions, and norms that facilitate both violence and reconciliation.

The role of national and local media is of central importance in fueling conflict and peace in the African Great Lakes region. Marie-Soleil Frère's chapter traces the history of media broadcasting in the DRC, Burundi, and Rwanda and "interrogates the capacity of radio stations in three countries of the African Great Lakes region . . . to act as influential independent stakeholders in the postconflict public debate." The author observes that while radio broadcasting was negatively dominated and controlled by the state in the three countries during their prewar years, liberalization of this most popular means of mass communication in the postwar dispensation has resulted in many competing broadcasting stations. Some of the emerging stations are private commercial concerns while others are faith-based (mostly Christian) or community-centered (i.e., dominated by programs appealing to specific ethnic communities). Government-owned national stations have also established many subsidiary broadcasting units at various subnational levels. In a major step towards postconflict peacebuilding, the UN Peacekeeping Mission in the Congo (MONUC, renamed MONUSCO in 2010) established a leading radio station in the DRC in 2002 known as Radio Okapi to promote peace and national integration, while some of the nonstate radio stations are supported by local politicians, business tycoons, and external donors.

Also of great significance as purveyors of popular culture, and therefore promising modes for the promotion of peace and reconciliation, are the performative and plastic arts. The chapter by Lindsay McClain Opiyo and Tricia Redeker Hepner explores the role that music, dance, drama, and painting have played in reconstruction and peacebuilding efforts among war-affected Acholi youth in northern Uganda. They demonstrate how the arts—especially music, song, and dance—have successfully addressed social trauma at both individual and group levels and provided a forum for debate and cultural adaptation of international discourses about human rights, transitional justice, and the ICC. The authors' study is based on two years of ethnographic research in northern Uganda, and draws on ethnographic insights as well as Acholi narratives to investigate the "cross-cultural applicability of key concepts such as suffering, trauma, and mental health on the one hand, as well as human rights, justice, and dignity on the other, in the pursuit of peace and reconciliation." The specific forms Opiyo and Hepner critically analyze play out against a backdrop of proliferating local and international programs that aim to use creative arts as a means to promote peacebuilding, reconciliation, and human rights consciousness since the fragile peace agreement signed in 2006 between the rebel Lord's Resistance Army and the Ugandan government to end the war in northern Uganda.

The study reveals a cultural privileging of peacebuilding approaches based on community reconciliation and harmony over and above those that emphasize justice with a view to securing human rights and dignity. Consequently, community-led peacebuilding approaches and those that are "culturally resonant" with local norms, values, and traditions "tend to be most successful in engaging Acholi youth in artistic expression and contributing to community building and collective healing." The wider implication of these findings, the authors argue, is the need for external donors and champions of peacebuilding in war-affected and bitterly divided postconflict communities to effectively engage local populations and resonant cultural practices in developing and implementing their peacebuilding projects.

Continuing the focus on northern Uganda in the wake of the conflict between the Ugandan government and the Lord's Resistance Army, Eric Awich Ochen's chapter analyzes the challenges faced by formerly abducted young women who became mothers while in rebel captivity and later returned to their former home communities. In exploring efforts at reintegration and the responses to postconflict society by both the formerly abducted child-mothers and their communities and families, Ochen's research highlights a finding of central importance in peace and conflict studies. Ochen argues that "the sociocultural structures, norms, and practices in 'the bush' *mirror—but also markedly differ from*—what obtains in the normal Acholi society" (emphasis added), thus pointing out that while periods of violent conflict may indeed represent dramatic and destructive ruptures, in many ways they are also inherently related to everyday social relations in "normal" or "peacetime" society.

Using a feminist and rights-based approach, Ochen shows how the exploitation and violence suffered by formerly abducted child-mothers while in the bush was not completely distinct from the forms of patriarchy and domination that inhere in Acholi social structure and relationships. Given that conflict is often viewed as an aberration or inversion of normal social relations, such an insight is valuable for understanding how violence is both culturally specific and often more similar to taken-for-granted, everyday realities than we like to acknowledge (Scheper-Hughes and Bourgois 2004). At the same time, however, Ochen shows how child abductees were deprived of the protection and socialization provided to children in "normal" Acholi society, thus compounding their difficulty reintegrating and finding social acceptance upon return from the bush.

The use of a feminist approach in Ochen's work also highlights another important dynamic too often overlooked in studies of violent conflict: although people are certainly victimized and brutalized in situations like that of LRA abductees, they nonetheless maintain both a sense of self and a drive to survive and heal. Ochen writes, "Despite the deeply traumatic experiences and rights violations that the formerly abducted child-mothers underwent, their resilience, fortitude, and agency stand out strongly." Ochen's analysis reminds us that the capacity for human survival and recovery in the midst of violent conflict and its aftermath must not be overlooked when trying to understand the impact of trauma and the potential for rebuilding both individuals and communities when the guns have fallen silent and former captives have returned.

Rebuilding communities and restoring social relations in the wake of violence is a key component of peacebuilding. It is also very often within the purview of religious institutions and actors who aid survivors, victims, and even perpetrators in confronting and making sense of what transpired. Janine Natalya Clark's chapter closes out the volume with a critical analysis of the role of churches and religious actors both during and after the Rwandan genocide. Drawing on R. Scott Appleby's notion of the "ambivalence of the sacred," Clark examines not only the complicity of the churches during the genocide and their failure to protect and aid victims, but also evaluates churches' present efforts and further potential to contribute to peacebuilding and reconciliation. She argues that while "religious peacebuilding *is* occurring.... There are legitimate grounds for questioning whether Christianity can fulfil its peacebuilding potential in today's Rwanda" due to its past complicity and the Catholic Church's active support for clergy who engaged in violence, thus rendering their role as sacred institutions inherently uncertain. "Persistent denial within the Catholic Church and the continuing politicization of religion," in which the Anglican Church has aligned with Paul Kagame in denying that ethnicity was a factor in the violence, remains a central obstacle for religious peacebuilding in postgenocide Rwanda, Clark argues. While both international and culturally specific models for justice and reconciliation in Rwanda, from the International Criminal Tribunal for Rwanda (ICTR) to *gacaca* courts, have received considerable scholarly attention, religious institutions and identities—clearly central features of social and cultural life in Rwanda and elsewhere—have not. Clark's chapter is therefore an important contribution to understanding how social and cultural phenomena play a central role in patterns of violence, reconciliation, and peacebuilding.

Questions of conflict and peace carry perennial weight. Since the formation of complex human societies more than ten thousand years ago, we have mobilized our species' unique genius for purposes of both destruction and harmony, utilizing our capacity for culture and the complex institutions we have created to govern and regulate social norms, to both engage in and reflect on the twin pursuits of violence and peace. Contemporary African societies are especially important for the analysis of these themes: having been overrepresented in media portrayals of conflict, and subject to simplistic and often racist explanations for "innate" or atavistic tendencies, African societies have also been prime targets for the brokering of "conflict deals" in the global economy. Some of these actively feed conflicts, such as the weapons trade and extraction of resources, while others depend upon the ongoing existence of those conflicts to justify a political economy of peacebuilding and development (Nordstrom 2004). Many of these interests, moreover, originate in the powerful financial and political centers of the global North and former colonial metropoles. Conflict and peacebuilding in Africa are therefore global phenomena with deep historical roots and complex ties to both past and present political-economic processes and hierarchies.

This volume aims to shed critical light on conflict and peacebuilding in the African Great Lakes region by examining those deep historical roots and complex ties to colonial legacies and the contemporary political economy. It does so through identifying and prioritizing what constitutes the Great Lakes region in the past and present, training a critical lens on local, regional, national, and international dynamics as they interface with one another, and highlighting the many ways that Africans are actively seeking solutions to the challenges facing their countries, communities, and selves. In adopting an explicitly multidisciplinary approach, the volume embodies the very diversity and complexity of the causes of conflict and efforts to ameliorate the consequences. Given that no single discipline, level of analysis, or set of institutions, policies, or practices can fully capture the range of issues involved, an approach such as this is more than appropriate: it is vitally necessary.

References

Bayart, Jean-François, Stephen Ellis, and Beatrice Hibou. 1999. *Criminalization of the State in Africa*. Oxford: James Currey.
Bekoe, Dorina, ed. 2006. *East Africa and the Horn: Confronting Challenges to Good Governance*. Boulder, CO: Lynne Rienner.
Berman, Bruce, and John Lonsdale. 1992. *Unhappy Valley: Conflict in Kenya and Africa*. Vols. 1 and 2. Oxford: James Currey.
Chabal, Patrick, and Jean-Pascal Daloz. 1999. *Africa Works: Disorder as Political Instrument*. Oxford: James Currey.
Cohen, Jared. 2007. *One Hundred Days of Silence: America and the Rwanda Genocide*. Lanham, MD: Rowman & Littlefield.
Collier, Paul (2008) *The Bottom Billion: Why the Poor Countries Are Failing and What Can Be Done about It*. Oxford: Oxford University Press.
Daley, Patricia O. 2008. *Gender and Genocide in Burundi: The Search for Spaces in the Great Lakes Region*. Oxford: James Currey.
Ellis, Stephen. 1995. "Liberia 1989–1995: A Study of Ethnic and Spiritual Violence." *African Affairs* 94, no. 375: 165–97.
Ellis, Stephen, and Gerrie Ter Haar. 2004. *Worlds of Power: Religious Thought and Political Practice in Africa*. London: Hurst.
Francis, David. 2005. "Introduction." In *Civil Militia: Africa's Intractable Security Menace?*, edited by David Francis, 1–21. Aldershot, UK: Ashgate.
Hoste, Jean-Christopher. 2009. *Climate Change and Security Conference Report*. Paris: CERI. Accessed 27 November 2011. http://www.obsafrique.eu/wp-content/uploads/2011/03/Climate-Change-and-Security-Conference-Report-mars09.pdf.
Hyden, Goran. 1980. *Beyond Ujamaa in Tanzania: Underdevelopment and an Uncaptured Peasantry*. Berkeley: University of California Press.
Juma, Monica K., and Peter M. Kagwanja. 2003. "Securing Refuge from Terror: Refugee Protection in East Africa after September 11." In *Problems of Protection: The UNHCR, Refugees, and Human Rights*, edited by N. Steiner et al., 225–36. London: Routledge.
Le Billion, Philippe. 2007. "Fatal Transactions." In *Violent Geographies: Fear, Terror and Political Violence*, edited by D. Gregory and A. Pred, 133–52. New York: Routledge.
Lemarchand, René. 1994. *Burundi: Ethnocide as Discourse and Practice*. New York: Cambridge University Press.
Le Pape, Marc. 2004. "Democratic Republic of Congo: Victims of No Importance." In *In the Shadow of 'Just Wars': Violence, Politics and Humanitarian Action*, edited by F. Weissman, 209–27. London: Hurst.
Mbembe, Achille. 2001. *On the Postcolony*. Berkeley: University of California Press.
Mkutu, Kennedy A. 2008. *Guns and Governance in the Rift Valley: Pastoralist Conflict and Small Arms*. Oxford: James Currey.

Mkutu, Kennedy A., and Kizito Sabala. 2007. "Private Security Companies and Dilemmas for Security." *Journal of Contemporary African Studies* 25, no. 3: 391–496.

Norad. 2009. *The International Conference on the Great Lakes Region (ICGLR): Review of Norwegian Support to ICGLR Secretariat.* Norad Report 17. Oslo, Norway: Norwegian Agency for Development Cooperation.

Nordstrom, Carolyn. 2004. *Shadows of War: Violence, Power, and International Profiteering in the Twenty-First Century.* Berkeley: University of California Press.

Omeje, Kenneth. 2009. "Introduction: Discourses of the Liberian Civil War and Imperatives of Peacebuilding." In *War to Peace Transition: Conflict Intervention and Peacebuilding in Liberia*, edited by K. Omeje, 1–16. Lanham, MD: University Press of America.

Prunier, Gerard. 2009. *Africa's World War: Congo, The Rwandan Genocide and the Making of a Continental Catastrophe.* Oxford: Oxford University Press.

Richards, Paul. 1996. *Fighting for the Rain Forest: War, Youth and Resources in Sierra Leone*, Oxford: James Currey.

Roessler, Philip G. 2005. "Donor-Induced Democratization and the Privatization of State Violence in Kenya and Rwanda." *Comparative Politics* 37, no. 2: 207–27.

Scheper-Hughes, Nancy, and Philippe Bourgois. 2004. "Introduction: Making Sense of Violence." In *Violence in War and Peace: An Anthology*, edited by N. Scheper-Hughes and P. Bourgois, 1–27. Oxford: Blackwell.

Thirlwall, A. P. 2008. "Development and Economic Growth." In *The Companion to Development Studies*, edited by Vandana Desai and Robert B. Potter, 37–39. 2nd ed. London: Hodder Education.

UNDP. 2009. *Human Development Report 2009.* United Nations Development Programme. Accessed 7 October 2010. http://hdrstats.undp.org/en/indicators/18.html.

Wainaina, Michael. 2005. "The Representation of African-European Relations in Mediated Contemporary Verbal Art." In *Across Borders: Benefiting from Cultural Differences.* Conference Proceedings. Nairobi: German Academic Exchange Service (DAAD).

Watts, Michael J. 2008. "Anatomy of an Oil Insurgency: Violence and Militants in the Niger Delta, Nigeria." In *Extractive Economies and Conflicts in the Global South: Multi-regional Perspectives on Rentier Politics*, edited by K. Omeje, 51–74. Aldershot, UK: Ashgate.

Westerkamp, Meike, Moira Feil, and Alison Thompson. 2009. *Regional Contribution in the Great Lakes Region: A Contribution to Peacebuilding?*, International Alert. Adelphi Paper (June). Accessed September 2010. http://www.initiativeforpeacebuilding.eu/pdf/Regional_Cooperation_in_the_Great_Lakes_region.pdf.

World Bank. 2002. *Greater Great Lakes Regional Strategy for Demobilization and Reintegration.* World Bank Report No 23869–AFR. March 25. Accessed September 2010. http://www.reliefweb.int/rw/RWFiles2005.nsf/FilesByRWDocUNIDFileName/MHII-6AABAW-wb-afr-25mar.pdf/$File/wb-afr-25mar.pdf.

Zeleza, Paul T. 2006. "The Troubled Encounter between Postcolonialism and African History." *Journal of the Canadian Historical Association.* New Series 17, no. 2: 89–129.

PART I
THE GREAT LAKES REGION
Challenges of the Past and Present

1 Understanding the Diversity and Complexity of Conflict in the African Great Lakes Region

Kenneth Omeje

FAR FROM THE influential Western-centric assumptions and international media propaganda that tend to regard African political conflicts as a resurgence of a malignant warrior spirit rooted in precolonial atavism, this chapter elucidates the diversity and complexity of the conflicts in the Great Lakes region. It places the multifaceted and interlocking conflicts and wars that have characterized the postcolonial experiences of the countries of Great Lakes in a historical perspective to illuminate why some have proved recurrent and persistent. I argue that although some conflicts date back to precolonial intergroup animosities, European colonial policies and politics most decisively account for the entrenchment and virulence of the conflicts and their structural underpinnings. With regard to the postcolonial phase, I contend that political conflicts in the Great Lakes region have largely been aggravated by different factions of postcolonial elites deliberately interposing their interests in the exploitative and unjust political, social, and economic institutions and structures inherited from the colonialists, as opposed to revamping the structures to serve the collective interests of the citizens. Furthermore, given the historical and geo-demographic interconnectedness of the people of the Great Lakes region, many of the deep-rooted and protracted conflicts have sprawling regional dimensions. The most significant in this regard is the Hutu-Tutsi imbroglio in the volatile Rwanda–Burundi axis, which I call the "conflict epicenter" on account of its widespread resonance and consequences for regional security.

Colonial Experiences and Structures of Political Violence

The Great Lakes region had mixed colonial experiences that laid the foundation for the nature of political conflicts plaguing the region in the postcolonial dispensation. Following the Berlin Conference of 1885–87 in which Africa was balkanized by contending European powers, three dominant colonizers emerged in the region. Burundi, Rwanda, and mainland Tanzania were colonized by Germany in what was originally known as German East Africa. The Belgians colonized the Democratic Republic of Congo (DRC), originally as a personal fiefdom (known as the Congo Free State) of the brutal Belgian monarch King Leopold II (1885–1908) and subsequently as a colony of the imperial government of Belgium. The British colonized the island of Zanzibar, Kenya, and Uganda. After the defeat of Germany in World War I and the relinquishing of German East Africa to rival European powers, mainland Tanzania (renamed Tanganyika) was ceded to the British as a trusteeship territory under the defunct League of Nations, while Burundi and Rwanda were awarded to the Belgians. The end of World War I in 1918 and its outcome in terms of control of colonies was such a major turning point in the history of the Great Lakes region that some analysts delineate two phases, the first corresponding to the pre-1918 dispensation of three colonial powers (Germany, Belgium, and Britain), and the second phase referring to the post-1918 dispensation of two colonizers (Belgium and Britain).

Notwithstanding the different historical dispensations, the purpose (and to a lesser extent, method) of colonization was essentially the same for all the colonial powers, including those that were not involved in the region, like the French, Spanish, and Portuguese. On the face of it, colonialism was constructed as a necessary humanitarian intervention conceived to save, guide, and civilize the Africans, who were derogatively referred to as the "natives"—a euphemism for inferior, uncultured, and primitive people. Mbembe (2001, 34–35) describes this purported claim of selfless humanitarian intervention as "the fiction of compassion and benevolence." Intrinsic to the latter is a twofold practical objective: The first was obliteration of the natives' "primitive" political, sociocultural, religious, legal, and economic structures. The second was imposition of the colonizers' social, cultural, political, and economic values, and worldviews on the colonized, a process conceived as an upliftment to modernity. The two objectives were deliberately intended to conceal the primary purpose of colonialism—to secure overseas enclaves for natural resource and economic exploitation for the benefit of Western Europe (see Rodney, 1972).

Colonial Land Expropriation

The centrality of resource extraction led the colonial administrations to deliberately expropriate land as they desired. Various imperial statutes were introduced to legalize land expropriated for various purposes: cash crop production, exploration and mining, construction of residential areas for colonial officials, wildlife conservation reserve parks, cattle ranching, and so on. In a settler colony like Kenya, a greater percentage of the country's arable land (mostly in the Rift Valley and Nairobi provincial areas) was expropriated by the colonizers for plantation agriculture and wildlife conservation purposes. In the process, nomadic pastoral groups like the Maasai lost a great part of their lands. In DRC, large scale expropriation was contrived for both mining and plantation agriculture. Throughout the region, the rate of colonial land grabbing was high and almost in all cases pastoral communities suffered the most. Hence, some of the problems of land pressure and related conflicts that have embroiled many pastoral communities in the region—a problem that has evidently been aggravated by climate change—go back to the nature, scale, and externalities of colonial land grabbing. However, among some Nilotic nomadic pastoralists, the history of land pressure and resource conflict goes back to the precolonial era because of their seasonal movements in search of greener pastures and water for their livestock—a lifestyle that seems to have a greater predilection for encroachment on supposedly open territorial lands claimed by other communities, both pastoral and sedentary (see Obika and Bibangambah, this volume).

The colonial land-grabbing policy was in all cases supported by a system that empowered the colonizers to coercively recruit and use the expropriated locals as cheap plantation, mining, and construction labor. Consequently, the bulk of the alienated labor, mostly previous small-scale cultivators of family and extra-family lands, were displaced and squeezed into congested suburbs in the emerging urban economies. These suburbs, which soon developed into deplorable slums, hardly had any cultivable lands. The desperate quest for colonial wage labor engendered by the new liberal market economy, the disproportionate land expropriation among certain communities, as well as the discriminatory preference that the colonizers showed for certain ethnic groups with regard to the scarce colonial casual jobs (e.g., the Baganda in Uganda; see Opongo, this volume) altogether triggered unprecedented mass migration, some of which was encouraged, especially among ethnic communities preferred for colonial service.

The large-scale colonial population displacement, movement, and resettlement had strong implications for land access and interethnic relations. Among these was the resettlement of various groups in the ethnic homelands of others, especially with regard to issues of land access/ownership and rights of indigeneity (an African customary right usually earned by virtue of being a member of an autochthonous ancestral community) as opposed to rights of citizenship (a nationality right acquired by having membership by birth or naturalization in a state) (see Moritz 2004).

Quite significantly, unexpropriated lands were mostly of marginal or no productive value. In a country like Kenya, for instance, these were mainly lands in (semi) arid areas. Colonial intervention was disruptively revolutionary: it unraveled the entire indigenous land-tenure system and distorted the geo-demographic landscape. In many parts of Africa, the injustices created by the colonizers' land intervention were part of the core grievances that catalyzed nationalist struggles for independence and also helped mobilize and sustain the interests of grassroots populations in decolonization campaigns. There was a huge expectation among expropriated and landless peoples that the overthrow of the colonizers, leading to self-rule, would deliver, if not restore, justice on land. This was quickly dashed and scuttled, however; the political elites that inherited power from the colonialists at independence disingenuously replaced the departing colonizers and played up the ethnic card to divert attention and cover up continuing injustice.

Nowhere was this tendency more palpable than in the settler economy of Kenya where the first independence president, the legendary Jomo Kenyatta, usurped a large proportion of the agricultural land vacated by British colonizers and allocated most of the remainder to loyal ethnic Kikuyu aides and some of the veterans of the Mau Mau liberation war (see FIAN 2010, 17). A great part of the reallotted land is in traditional non-Kikuyu homelands, particularly in the lush Rift Valley province—the ancestral homeland of the ethnic Kalenjin and Maasai. The twenty-four-year reign of Daniel arap Moi, who succeeded Kenyatta as president in 1978, was a neopatrimonial dispensation that essentially politicized the land question in a self-serving manner. Moi used his control of state power to directly or indirectly acquire large tracts of land for himself and made similar patronage-driven allocations to members of his ethnic Kalenjin oligarchy. "To restore stolen land, the Kikuyu were evicted from areas where they had earlier settled; associated tensions thereafter had caused thousands of casualties and displaced more than 350,000 persons" (FIAN 2010, 17). Ramifying tension and violence have thus characterized land politics and attempts at reform in postcolonial Kenya.

Ethno-cultural Diversity, Colonial Rule, and Politicization of Identity

In a historical analysis of the conflicts in the Great Lakes region, Rwandan President Paul Kagame (2006) identified three key factors in colonial rule that account for postcolonial conflict. The first was the artificial national boundaries and administrative structures within states created by colonial rule that brought together different ethno-cultural groups unprepared to compromise their diversity, and conversely split apart others that were equally unprepared to compromise their unity. Secondly, the redrawing of the ethno-cultural map of Africa was compounded by the divide-and-rule and discriminatory policy of the colonialists in which certain groups were arbitrarily preferred and privileged over others. In fact, this policy was so efficiently contrived and manipulated that the colonizers used it as an instrument to create different ethnicities within some hitherto homogenous ethnic groups, including groups that had largely neutralized their identity boundaries. For example, in spite of divergent ethno-historical origins, the Hutu and the Tutsi made significant strides in dissolving their ethno-cultural and linguistic differences in the precolonial period. The colonizers not only (re)activated and solidified these boundaries but also split the Hutu and Tutsi into different contiguous states—Burundi, Rwanda, and, to a lesser extent, the DRC. Other examples of arbitrary splitting of homogenous groups across national and provincial boundaries abound. The ethnic Somalis were split into four different colonies that later became sovereign states: Kenya, Somalia, Djibouti, and Ethiopia; this has been the basis for repeated wars of irredentism in the Horn of Africa. The Luo were split into Sudan, Kenya, Tanzania, and Uganda, while the Maasai were partitioned into Kenya and Tanzania. The Karamojong cluster "tribes" were divided into Kenya, Sudan, and Uganda, and the Kakwa were separated into northwestern Uganda, southern Sudan, and northeastern DRC.

In Uganda, the ethnic Baganda, who were ostensibly favored by the British, were used in both the public and security services to subdue all other kingdoms (see Munene 2010). Within Kenya, the Kikuyu had an advantage because of their early contact with the colonizers and Christian missionaries, and their proximity to the administrative headquarters of Nairobi. In the cause of colonial service, however, they were encouraged to migrate from their ethnic domain in Central province to other parts of the country, especially the more strategic Nairobi and Rift Valley areas. This influx had severe implications for land tenure, later exacerbated by postcolonial resettlement of many landless Kikuyu veterans of the Mau Mau independence struggle in the ethnic Kalenjin homeland of the Rift Valley region. Similarly, the Belgian colonizers encouraged a steady influx of Banyarwanda (literally, people from Rwanda) into Congo (DRC) as guest labor in the vast plantations and mines, leading progressively to a large settlement of Kinyarwanda-speaking communities in the North Kivu region of DRC bordering Rwanda (Jourdan 2005, 3).

Within both Rwanda and Burundi, the Belgian colonizers favored the Tutsi over the Hutu, arrogating ethno-racial superiority to the minority Tutsi and setting the context for Hutu reprisals and/or ethnic wars at the dawn of independence and in subsequent years. Political instability in postindependence Rwanda and interethnic feuding between the Hutu and Tutsi both before and during the 1994 genocide aggravated the migratory influx. As a result, the Banyarwanda have greatly outstripped the indigenous Congolese populations in what should be the latter's ancestral homeland. Today, a tripartite conflict faultline exists in North Kivu between the Banyarwanda and the minority indigenous Congolese communities, on the one hand, and within the Kinyarwanda-speaking community (between the Hutu and Tutsi), on the other. The rift between the Hutu and the Tutsi has been exacerbated, especially in the aftermath of the Rwandan genocide.

It is thus evident that colonialism not only dismembered various ethno-cultural groups into different states but also within each state. A characteristic unease was engendered and accentuated among the amalgamated ethnic groups, worsened by the divide-and-rule policy of the various colonial powers. Ethnic identity and discrimination became decisive factors in the allocation of, and competition for, public resources (Nnoli 1989). One deleterious effect in Rwanda, Burundi, Uganda, and Kenya is how the shifting ethnic balance of power was reproduced in the socioeconomic division of labor and access to political power.

The third factor identified by Kagame (2006) was the preoccupation of the colonial administration with exploitation and export of raw materials (extractive minerals and agricultural cash crops) for the economic benefit of Europe and at the expense of developing basic infrastructures and delivery of social services in the colonies. Economic production in the colonies was foremost to satisfy industrial development and consumption needs in the Western metropoles to the utter disregard of local needs and the regional market. DRC and Tanzania, to a lesser extent, mostly produced and exported solid minerals and agricultural resources (copper, diamonds, gold, timber, rubber, coffee, sugar cane, and palm oil) while other Great Lakes countries mainly exported typical colonial cash crops like tea and coffee. Hardly any development infrastructures such as long-distance road networks and railways were constructed either within or among colonies, save those that facilitated evacuation of primary commodities for export (e.g., the Kenya–Uganda railway). The colonial economic structure of producing primary raw materials for exports had overwhelming disadvantages that persisted after independence. It unduly exposed African economies to the volatility of the international commodity market, thereby not only inducing an occasional balance of payment crisis but also fundamentally limiting the options for trade, development, and economic decolonization for most countries (see Omeje 2008).

Throughout colonial history, one factor that contributed to societal fragmentation and conflict was the system of indirect administration using indigenous chiefs, Islamic clerics, and imposed traditional rulers otherwise known as "colonial warrant chiefs." Indirect rule, as it is popularly known, was elevated to the status of a policy by the British but all colonial authorities practiced it to varying degrees because of the limited number of European personnel on the ground and the facade of legitimacy offered by using local surrogates. Indirect rule was preferred for resource extraction (taxes) and maintenance of law and order. But the practice was replete with local oppression and ethnic vendetta. Interethnic feuding was more prevalent in areas where the colonial authorities privileged certain groups and empowered them as indirect administrators and civil servants over others. In securing indirect rule, many chiefdoms were merged or territorially reconfigured for the administrative convenience of the colonizers. Indirect administrators were responsible for widespread acts of impunity, including arbitrary imposition of levies and taxes, land grabbing, unlawful arrest, detention and torture of innocent persons, operation of secret prisons, repression and persecution of subjects using their private (native) police, as well as gun-running and neopatrimonial corruption (see Mamdani 1996; 2001). There was sporadic resistance against indirect administration, especially in various parts of Zanzibar, Uganda, Burundi, and Rwanda.

Decolonization Struggles, Party Politics, and the Legacy of Colonial Divide-and-Rule

One of the most far-reaching consequences of the radicalization of ethnic consciousness and identity during the colonial era was in the evolution of party politics, which was partly tied to decolonization struggles. In most African colonies, multiparty politics was granted as a result of the nationalist struggle for expansion of the political space and ultimately independence. However, anticolonial nationalism either incidentally or by colonial design had profound ethnic dimensions. Similarly, some of the parties that emerged to compete for legislative offices and ultimately form the government at the eve of independence had significant ethnic bias. Even some with a more national reach and scope inadvertently degenerated into ethnic-based parties. In some cases, the colonial masters supported the parochial conservative factions of the elites to the detriment of the more forward-looking (in terms of development ideologies) truly nationalist parties. A few examples can suffice.

Given its huge economic interests in DRC, Belgium was unprepared to grant independence to the Congolese without entrenching a local political faction that would guarantee its neocolonial interests. Both the Belgian colonial authorities and the mining monopolies, some of which were French and American companies, threw their weight behind some of the ideologically compromising and/or local ethnic and regional parties, such as PNP, PSA, ABAKO, Balubakat, Cerea, and Conakat (the acronyms are all French names; see Mpangala 2004, 9). The only truly nationalist party in the race and one that was morbidly disliked by the West, was Patrice Lumumba's MNC, which, to the utter frustration of the colonizers, went ahead to sweep the polls. Unable to scuttle his election as the first prime minister in May 1960, Belgium and the United States supported a secessionist war in the rich mining region of Katanga, backed the conservative President Kasavubu, abetted the arrest and execution of Lumumba, and supported the retrogressive military coup of Joseph Mobutu Sese Seko (see Ngoie and Omeje 2008, 137–50). Mobutu's pro-Western dictatorship plundered the country for the next thirty-two years, thereby setting the context for the civil war of 1997–2005.

In the run-up to Burundian independence in the 1950s, two ethnic-based parties, People's Party (PP) and Christian Democratic Party (PDC), and one more or less progressive nationalist party, Union for National Progress (UPRONA), emerged. The latter tried to ideologically rally and unite the three ethnic groups—Hutu, Tutsi, and Twa—for a higher national cause. UPRONA, which was led by a moderate Tutsi, Prince Louis Rwegasore, won the independence elections of 1961, but Rwegasore was assassinated in a plot allegedly organized by the pro-Belgian rival PDC a few weeks after assuming the office of prime minister (Lemarchand 1996, 53–55). His assassination was followed by fierce interethnic rivalry within UPRONA, repeated massacres, and a protracted cycle of civil conflicts. Most significantly, UPRONA degenerated into an ethnic Tutsi party after the killing of its charismatic founder; Burundi has never had another successful multiethnic nationalist party since.

With regard to Rwanda, all the political parties that led the nationalist struggle for independence were ethnic based. The Rwanda Democratic Rally (RADER) was a Tutsi party while Party of the Movement of Hutu Emancipation (PARMEHUTU) and Association for the Social Betterment of the Masses (APROSOMA) were Hutu-based

(Lemarchand 1996, 9). In Uganda, with the arguable exception of Milton Obote's Uganda People's Congress (UPC), which tried to cross ethnic boundaries in its rhetoric and appeal (although many saw the party as fundamentally anti-Baganda), all the political parties that emerged in the run-up to the country's independence had strong ethnic and/or sectarian followings (notably Catholics and Protestants).

Multiparty democracy in Kenya had a mix of ethnic and multiethnic dynamics. Two of the earliest leading political parties founded in 1960, Kenya African National Union (KANU) and to a lesser extent Kenya African Democratic Union (KADU), could be considered national parties because they mobilized all the people of Kenya but also had ethnic tendencies. While the core of KANU's membership was largely based on the Kikuyu-Luo alliance, KADU was predominantly populated by the Luhya, Kalenjin, Maasai, Turkana/Samburu, and the coastal ethnic groups (Lemarchand 1996). Munene (2009, 2) argues that while KANU was a truly nationalist party at its inception, KADU was actually the brainchild of the white settler minority who, frustrated by the anticolonial stance of the KANU-led nationalist movement, rekindled their divisive politics in the transition to independence. They labeled KANU a party of the "big bad tribes" (Kikuyu and Luo) and persuaded "other small tribes" to join them in KADU. The ethnic balance of power was altered after the arch-Luo leader in the ruling alliance, Oginga Odinga, parted ways with President Jomo Kenyatta to form a new opposition party with a Luo base, the Kenyan People's Union (KPU). KANU struggled with its reputation as a national party after the exit of Odinga, a position that it could only bolster when Kenya was later made a one-party state by Kenyatta. When Moi, an ethnic Kalenjin, succeeded Kenyatta in 1978, KANU continued as a quasi-national party but in reality chiefly pursued a narrow ethnic agenda.

In all of the countries discussed above, it is significant that postindependence political development and party politics have gravitated to ethnic parochialism, often precipitating far-reaching violent conflicts and instability. A typical example was the 2008 Kenyan postelection violence sparked by the disputed multiparty elections of 27 December 2007 (see Ojielo, this volume). But it occurred against the background of actively embedded structures of violence related to land, worsened by deplorable economic conditions and widespread disillusionment (especially among youth populations) with the ruling Party of National Unity (PNU), headed by President Mwai Kibaki. Despite considerable macro-economic development recorded during Kibaki's first term compared to the more decadent regime of Moi, noted for extreme neopatrimonial corruption and authoritarianism, people protested the slow delivery of the long-expected dividends of democracy. Kenya's Electoral Commission (ECK) declared on 30 December 2007 that Kibaki had received 4,584,721 votes against 4,352,993 for his rival and leader of the main opposition party, Raila Odinga of the Orange Democratic Movement (ODM), and proceeded to declare the incumbent president as the winner of the election. Consequently, the president was immediately sworn into office in a polling travesty that all leading international observers (including the European Union election monitoring team) described as flawed for widespread irregularities and vote rigging (EU 2008). The main opposition party rejected the election results and this was followed by violence of unprecedented scale in Kenyan postindependence history.

The postelection violence rapidly degenerated into ethnic vendetta between the Kikuyu (the ethnic group of President Kibaki) and the Luo (the ethnic group of the main opposition leader Odinga). Other ethnic groups prominent in the ODM, notably the Kalenjin and Luhya, fought on the side of the Luo against the Kikuyu and their perceived sympathizers, especially sections of the relatively small ethnic Kisii. When the new power-sharing government appointed Kalonzo Muysoka (an ethnic Kamba and one of the presidential candidates in the controversial election) its vice president, some ODM ethnic loyalists quickly embarked on a reprisal attack against the Kamba in major urban centers. The hitherto more or less neutral Kamba were perceived by the coalition of opposition ethnic groups as spoilers benefiting from a dodgy hegemonic power. In fact, this image of the Kamba was already rife during the election because of Kalonzo's presidential bid, which many conspiracy theorists argued was masterminded by the ruling PNU to diminish ODM's electoral chances.

The changing patterns of ethnic alliance in Kenya are particularly instructive because throughout the twenty-four years of President Moi's regime (1978–2002), the Kikuyu and Luo were in alliance as the leading pro-democracy opposition against the Kalenjin-led neopatrimonial dictatorship. By 2007, that conviviality between the Kikuyu elite and their Luo counterparts had soured, and as is characteristic of elite politics, the masses invariably follow the position of their leaders. More than 1,200 persons were killed in the nearly six weeks of election violence and over 350,000 others became internally displaced (EU 2008). It took a UN-backed panel of eminent Africans led by ex–Secretary General Kofi Annan for peace to be brokered, leading to the formation of a power-sharing agreement and government of National Unity, with Kibaki as president and Odinga as prime minister (see Anangwe, this volume).

A marked exception to ethnic politics in the Great Lakes region is the Tanzanian example. The party founded by the renowned nationalist leader Julius Nyerere, the Tanganyika African National Union (TANU; "Tanganyika" was later replaced by "Tanzania" after the union with Zanzibar), as a platform for championing the independence struggle towered above all other parties in Tanganyika that had ethnoracial and religious undertones. TANU was a genuinely inclusive nationalist movement greatly shaped by Nyerere's personality and ideological values—inclusivity, modesty, equity, simplicity, discipline, transparent accountability, centripetal nationalism, and liberal leftism. Under TANU, the charismatic Nyerere easily won the 1961 independence election to become prime minister, and subsequently president when a republican constitution was adopted in 1962. Being a reputed conciliator, Nyerere brokered the strategic merger between mainland Tanganyika and the offshore island of Zanzibar to form the United Republic of Tanzania in 1964. In contrast with mainland Tanganyika, Zanzibar was a more ethno-racially and politically divided society but Nyerere was able to consolidate the fragile union over his twenty-four years in power (1961–85).

Contrary to the tradition of neopatrimonial rule instituted by many African leaders after independence, Nyerere stands out for his exemplary, detribalized, impersonal rule, which helped to engender a political culture of patriotic national service as opposed to primordial particularism. In the run-up to the famous Arusha Declaration of 1967 that, among other things, introduced *Ujamaa* socialism in Tanzania, Nyerere proclaimed the union a one-party state in 1965, allowing only one party in each part of the republic—TANU in Tanganyika and Afro-Shirazi Party (ASP) in Zanzibar. In 1977 the two parties merged to form the Chama Cha Mapinduzi (Revolutionary Party), which has won every national election even after the restoration of multiparty democracy in 1992.

Remarkably, Tanzania has been able to avoid the centrifugal ethnic wrangles and instability that have characterized most of sub-Saharan African postcolonial states, albeit the Zanzibari Island has been comparatively less peaceful than the mainland. Zanzibar has had a more turbulent political history marked by factional struggles and megaparty alliances that held primary allegiance to competing Arab, Indian, and black African groups claiming ancestral ownership and supremacy over the island. The January 1964 bloody revolution that overthrew the Island's first head of state, Sultan Jamshid Abdullah (an Arab nationalist), and installed the leftist-leaning Abeid Karume (of black African descent) as president, aggravated the ethno-racial polarization and anxiety in Zanzibar. In fact, many scholars have argued that it was fear of a counter-revolution by Arab nationalists loyal to the overthrown national leader Sultan Abdullah that persuaded the junta leader Karume to quickly forge a union government with Nyerere's more powerful mainland Tanganyika a few months after Karume seized power in Zanzibar (see Askew 2006). Karume became the first vice president of the new Tanzania.

Unlike Nyerere, who adopted a relatively mild "Fabian socialist" (i.e., the belief that socialism could be introduced through gradual reforms as opposed to a revolution) approach, Karume opted for a more radical Marxist-Leninist, Soviet-style dictatorship in Zanzibar. Many protesters, especially Arabs and Indians, fled the island to mainland Tanzania, Kenya, and other parts of the world. Preserving the union with Zanzibar has remained a recurrent political challenge to the central government in Dar es Salaam with some dissenting voices on both sides calling for separation. Notwithstanding the challenges posed by the historic union, Tanzanian politics has been relatively stable and inclusive compared to most countries of sub-Saharan Africa. This could be attributed to the strong culture of public service, probity, and centripetal nationalism instituted by Nyerere's regime after independence.

The "Conflict Epicenter" and Contemporary Dynamics

Some theorists posit that seemingly intractable conflicts usually have an epicenter. The "conflict epicenter" is defined as a strategic geo-demographic axis on which the conflicts revolve with antagonistic groups representing contradictory needs, interests, and positions. It is evident from the foregoing analysis that there is not a single conflict in the Great Lakes region but different multidimensional conflicts at various historical stages and with varying degrees of interconnectedness. Hence, a real and typical conflict epicenter seems analytically inappropriate. However, if one were to attempt a metaphoric approximation for some of the most turbulent, ferocious, and persistent conflicts with profound regional resonance, the most apparent location would be the Bahutu-Batutsi conflict in the Rwanda–Burundi axis. The conflict has had direct historical connections with political events in Uganda and DRC and indirect consequences for Tanzania and Kenya, to a lesser extent. To understand the contemporary ramifications of the conflict, it will suffice to delineate and examine its historical context.

The Hutu-Tutsi Imbroglio

The Hutu and Tutsi have their largest homelands in Rwanda and Burundi, although large communities are also found in Eastern DRC and Uganda where different generations of refugees who fled persecution in their homelands have settled. Refugees of the two ethnic communities are also domiciled in Tanzania and Kenya. The Hutu arguably comprise more than 80 percent of the populations of Rwanda and Burundi with the Tutsi numbering only about 15 percent in Burundi and 10 percent in Rwanda. The Twa number between 1 and 2 percent of the populations. The bipolar ethnic antagonism between the numerically larger Hutu and their Tutsi counterparts goes back to precolonial history.

Comparative philologists believe that the Hutu (also called Bahutu) are Bantu-speaking horticulturalists that originated from the Cameroon-Nigeria border areas and migrated to the interlacustrine region surrounding the Great Lakes about 3,000 years ago, bringing with them items like short-horn cattle, goats, sheep, and iron technology to enhance their adaptation (Kashambuzi 2009). Twa hunters and gatherers are said to be the earliest inhabitants (considered aborigines) of the area, and were already in settled forest communities before the Hutu migration.

The historical origin of the Tutsi (also called Batutsi), the last of the three groups to immigrate, is more contested. Originally, many colonial explorers, anthropologists, and missionaries had a priori classified the Tutsi (according to racist classifications of the period) as being of "Hamitic" or "Ethiopid" origin, which was subsequently championed by both German and Belgian colonizers and contrived to concede racial superiority to the Tutsi in accordance with the dominant colonial ideology of white supremacy (Meisler 1973). Two factors accounted for this imperial fraud. Firstly, it credited the Tutsi (and by implication the white race) with the startling technological development, political organization, and civilization the colonizers found in the interlacustrine region, which based on their social evolutionist theory was beyond the intellectual ability of the supposedly inferior "Negro" Bantu tribes. The second was the observed differences in the bodily characteristics of the different groups. The Tutsi were perceived to be tall, slender, and long-nosed, while Hutu were short, stout, and broad-nosed; historically, it has often been impossible to correctly apply this arbitrary distinction. The Twa were identified as having the shortest physical stature. Writing on how the Belgian colonizers approached the different groups in Rwanda (which had a similar colonial history with Burundi), Human Rights Watch (HRW 2004) made the following observations:

> The Belgians believed that Tutsi, Hutu, and Twa were three distinct, long-existent and internally coherent blocks of people, the local representatives of three major population groups, the Ethiopid, Bantu and Pygmoid. Unclear whether these were races, tribes, or language groups, the Europeans were nonetheless certain that the Tutsi were superior to the Hutu and the Hutu superior to the Twa—just as they knew themselves to be superior to all three. Because Europeans thought that the Tutsi looked more like themselves than did other Rwandans, they found it reasonable to suppose them closer to Europeans in the evolutionary hierarchy and hence closer to them in ability. Believing the Tutsi to be more capable, they found it logical for the Tutsi to rule Hutu and Twa just as it was reasonable for Europeans to rule Africans.

Through extensive archaeological studies, postcolonial anthropologists have debunked the myth of (semi)-Hamitic origin credited to the Tutsi. The popular consensus today is that the Tutsi were one of the original nomadic pastoral communities that originated from the Nilotic-Luo speaking groups of southern Sudan. Their precolonial dispersal and settlement in the Great Lakes region is remarkable because of their adaptive capacity. Studies have shown that in most of the new ethnic communities they settled, either by pastoral conquest or migration, the Nilotic-Luo adopted the language of the indigenous population and acquired a different name for themselves, illustrating the historical and social construction of ethnic identity, or what Southall (1970, 28) calls "the illusion of tribes."

Over the years, the pastoral Tutsi were able to dominate other populations by military conquest and by establishing their cattle economy as bases for reckoning wealth over and above the agricultural and livestock economy largely associated with the Hutu and Twa. Consequently, the Tutsi built a strong centralized political system during the precolonial histories of the kingdoms that later came to be known as Rwanda and Burundi. It is significant that Tutsi and Hutu were not originally ethnic but class identities. At the height of their political power during the precolonial era, the governing elites ventured to depict themselves as "Tutsi"—a term that literally described a powerful and wealthy person rich in cattle. The rest of the subjected people were classified as "Hutu," which originally meant an inferior, subordinate, and poor subject of a powerful person. Consequently, the terms represented polar opposites in class and power relations and people could move up or down the social hierarchy (albeit rare in practice). In the course of his feudal-military expansionism, the powerful *mwami* (king) Rwabugiri essentially labeled all the people, groups, and communities he conquered as "Hutu" (see Cohen 2007). Precolonial Rwanda and Burundi were a complex hierarchical system in which Tutsi kings governed with the help of many vassals, which included heads and ruling councils of various communities and lineages. The German colonial authority and subsequently the Belgians used the well-established traditional monarchies to administer the two colonies.

One of the most devastating social policies of German and Belgian colonial rule in Burundi and Rwanda was the unprecedented politicization of "Hutu" and "Tutsi" identities in vicious ethnic terms. Colonial policies and politics deliberately privileged the Tutsi in education (especially higher education), public service, security forces, business-sector employment, Christian missionary orders, and ultimately political power. Compulsory identity cards were imposed by the Belgians on the ethnic hierarchies, a practice that continued well into postcolonial history. A Tutsi monarchy recognized by the colonial administration ruled as regent of the colonial authority, and the Tutsi minority remained politically and economically dominant as independence approached. The Hutu and Twa were relegated and largely consigned to farm labor and other highly exploitative and physically tasking jobs.

These constructions and consequences of ethnicity under colonial rule were profound. Following local protests from the Hutu and pressure from the UN Trusteeship Council, the Belgian colonial authority was forced to relax its policy of Tutsi dominance and to encourage power sharing between the Tutsi and Hutu, especially in Rwanda, in the run up to independence (Cohen 2007). Consequently, Belgium commenced and stepped up Hutu empowerment by increasing their educational access and public-service appointments. A significant but substantially disgruntled Hutu middle class had emerged in both countries during the last decade of colonial rule.

The opening up of democratic space in the 1950s due to decolonization precipitated convoluted ethnic conflicts in both Rwanda and Burundi as the majority Hutu and minority Tutsi competed to lead the country to independence. A bloody Hutu revolution against the Tutsi monarchy occurred in Rwanda in 1959 with reverberating effects over subsequent years. More than 20,000 Tutsi were killed and over 200,000 others fled into exile in neighboring countries (primarily Uganda) between 1959 and 1963 (Cohen, 2007; Magidu 2009). In the midst of the convoluted chain of events characterized by ethnic violence, PARMEHUTU, a coalition party of Hutus of various clans and provinces, won the Rwandan legislative elections of September 1961. The legislative elections were held side by side with a referendum on the monarchy in which the vast majority of Rwandans (disgruntled Hutu) voted to abolish the monarchy. The PARMEHUTU leader Grégoire Kayibanda was overwhelmingly elected president in 1962 when Rwanda obtained independence from Belgium.

The ascendancy of the Hutu majority that had been denigrated, victimized, and marginalized since precolonial days did not abate the vendetta against the Tutsi minority in the country, starting with the 1959 Hutu revolution. A large number of Tutsi became internally displaced and more continued to stream into exile. Throughout the 1960s and 1970s, a series of cross-border attacks were carried out by Tutsi exiles, and the Hutu government frequently responded through military retaliation against the invaders and reprisals against the Tutsi minority in the country, who were always accused of colluding with their kin in exile. Kayibanda's government continued the colonial policy of ethnic discrimination, merely reversing and intensifying the exclusion policy against the Tutsi. Intra-ethnic antagonism and discrimination among the Hutu was also markedly pronounced, partly culminating in the military coup of July 1973 led by General Juvénal Habyarimana. The military leader imposed a one-party state two years later. Every aspect of public life was controlled by government. Great emphasis was laid on ideological mobilization of the populace for military and public service. Consequently, Habyarimana established a personality cult that made him extensively venerated. He commanded the loyalty of the military, the majority of the Hutu populace, public and private institutions, and the church, especially the predominant Catholic institution. Clientelism continued to be an entrenched part of the political culture. A large number of Rwandans, mostly Tutsi and dissenting Hutu, were forced into exile.

In Burundi, the attainment of independence in 1962 was similarly followed by a cataclysmic chain of ethnic violence. Independence witnessed a continued erosion of the traditional Tutsi *ganwa* (princely oligarchy) but not its outright abolition as in Rwanda. The independence election was overwhelmingly won by the young charismatic Prince Louis Rwagasore, eldest son of *Mwami* Mwambutsa, whose nationalist party UPRONA cut across ethnic boundaries. Rwagasore's assassination a few weeks after his election to the office of prime minister triggered a string of ugly events. These included ethnically motivated military coups and counter-coups (including abortive and phantom coups) in the struggle for power by factions of the political elite, intermittent ethnic massacres sometimes masterminded by the minority Tutsi-dominated governments, as well as displacement and exile of persecuted populations, especially the majority Hutu whose exiles formed a large refugee community in neighboring Tanzania. UPRONA lost its nationalist fervor in the ensuing interethnic conflicts and became a Tutsi-dominated party. The British House of Commons Library report (BHCL 2006) aptly described the ethnic vendetta and maneuvering that characterized this crucial phase of Burundian history:

> In January 1965 the Hutu Prime Minister of Burundi, Pierre Ngendandumwe, was assassinated by a Tutsi refugee from Rwanda. New elections produced a Hutu majority in the National Assembly but, following the intervention of the King, the post of Prime Minister was offered to a Tutsi, Leopold Biha. This led Hutu officers to stage an unsuccessful coup in October, killing Biha, which provoked the mass execution of the Hutu elite and a Tutsi monopoly over power for two decades. In 1966 the monarchy was abolished and a Republic declared, led by President Michel Micombero. Burundi had had its own Revolution.

The first systematically executed large-scale massacre of genocidal proportions occurred in 1972 when some exiled Hutu invaded parts of southern Burundi from

Tanzania, killing about 10,000 Tutsi. The Tutsi-dominated Burundian military and Tutsi youth activists responded to the attack by unleashing a systematic massacre of over 100,000 Hutu, forcing even a larger number into exile in Tanzania and elsewhere between 1972 and 1974 (see Lemarchand 1996). Burundi was proclaimed a one-party state in 1974. Intra-ethnic power struggles within the ruling UPRONA precipitated further coups and counter-coups between 1976 and 1990. Following regional and international pressure, multiparty democracy was restored in the country in 1993 after over thirty years of Tutsi-dominated military and one-party dictatorships. The multiparty presidential election was won by Melchior Ndadaye of the Front for Democracy in Burundi (FRODEBU). About three months after he assumed office as president, Ndadaye was assassinated in a plot carried out by the Tutsi-dominated Burundian army, leading to widespread reprisal attacks on the Tutsi and an inter-ethnic war that persisted until the Arusha Peace Accord of 2005 (Kashambuzi 2009). Cyprien Ntaryamira of the ruling Hutu-dominated FRODEBU succeeded the deceased head of state.

Civil War and Genocide in Rwanda

Rwanda was invaded in October 1990 by the Rwandan Patriotic Front (RPF), a rebel movement of Tutsi exiles in Uganda led by Paul Kagame, marking the beginning of a full-scale civil war in the country. Until the RPF invasion, postcolonial Rwanda had maintained a veneer of stability due largely to the exclusion of the Tutsi group from power and authoritarian control by the Hutu military establishment (Daley 2006, 306). "The full-scale war of 1990 to 1994 occurred because of the failure of the Rwandan state to recognise the legitimate right of return of its citizens in exile and to introduce measures of ethnic equity" (Daley 2006, 306). Kagame and many members of his RPF group were resilient combatants that aided Yoweri Museveni to seize political power in the protracted Ugandan bush war. The aim of RPF, which included some dissident Hutu, was to overthrow the Hutu-led Rwandan government.

As the invaders headed to the capital city of Kigali, the country was plunged into a civil war that President Habyarimana branded an "ethnic insurrection." This helped him to attract French and Belgian military deployment to save his regime. With the help of foreign troops, the Rwandan army was able to push the RPF back across the Ugandan border but the war was by no means over. A ceasefire agreement known as the Arusha Accord was signed between RPF and the government, which also recommended the deployment of an Organization of African Unity (OAU) observer mission. Hostilities resumed in February 1993 and the UN Security Council approved the deployment of a UN Observer Mission for Uganda and Rwanda (UNOMUR) to help police the border of the two countries and ensure that the ceasefire was effective. The Arusha peace talk resulted in a comprehensive peace agreement in August 1993 brokered by Tanzania and the OAU. The United Nations Assistance Mission for Rwanda (UNAMIR), originally made up of Belgium and Bangladesh forces, was established to help the parties implement the peace agreement, which, among other things, called for an interim coalition government and power sharing. Meanwhile, Habyarimana's government surreptitiously intensified persecution and elimination of home-based Tutsi and dissident Hutu. Relying on Hutu nationalist war propaganda, the government mobilized and trained youth militias in military combat and used them to unleash terror on the Tutsi and local dissidents. The largest and most vicious of these progovernment militias were the *Interahamwe* (those who stand, fight, or kill together) and the *Impuzamugambi* (those with a single purpose).

A genocidal dimension unfolded in the conflict after unknown assassins shot down a Kigali-bound airplane carrying the presidents of Rwanda (Habyarimana) and Burundi (Cyprien Ntaryamira) in April 1994. The plane crashed, killing the two heads of state as they were returning from a peace talk in Tanzania. It is not clear who is responsible for shooting down the plane. One hypothesis suggests it was Hutu extremists who rejected the Hutu-Tutsi power-sharing plan adopted in the peace agreement and accepted by Habyarimana, a Hutu moderate. An alternative hypothesis attributes the crime to Tutsi extremists. A French judge controversially asserted in 2004 that it was the then-commander of the RPF and current Tutsi president of Rwanda, Paul Kagame, who ordered the shooting. Kagame has denied and dismissed the charge as politically motivated. Two French judges set up a team of French investigators into the cause of the 1994 Rwandan genocide, who released a report in January 2012 exonerating Kagame and his rebel forces from the shooting down of Habyarimana's plane, the event that sparked off the 1994 genocide. The new report blamed Hutu extremists for the atrocity. Many observers see this latest report as a diplomatic move by France aimed at mending its long-battered relations with Rwanda in the aftermath of the 1994 genocide.

A new interim president—the parliamentary speaker and aging and docile pediatrician Dr. Theodore Sindikubwabo—was elected to replace Habyarimana and a new government appointed (BHCL 2006). But the de facto power behind the interim government was the self-appointed Hutu military strongman Colonel Théoneste Bagosora. The genocide not only happened under the watch of the Hutu-dominated interim government but was ostensibly planned and executed by core elements of the government. Daley (2006, 310) argues that the genocide represented the refusal of sections of the Hutu elite to implement the Arusha Peace Accord adopted eight months earlier in August 1993, which would have drastically reduced their claims on power and their attempt to use an extreme militaristic solution to the problem of ethnic plurality. The goal of the Arusha Accord for Rwanda was to stop the war between the Tutsi-led RPF and the Hutu regime and allow Tutsi refugees to return and participate in government (Daley 2006, 310). The full machinery of the state—security forces, ruling party, media, government officials at national and subnational levels, state-sponsored militias—were used to plan, mobilize killers, distribute ammunitions, and execute what quickly became a nationwide genocide (Cohen 2007).

Most confounding was the sheer popularity of the genocidal attacks, which witnessed the involvement of a large spectrum of the population, including judges, civil society actors, medical personnel, friends and spouses of victims, priests, and ordinary citizens (see Cohen 2007; Mamdani 2001; Clark, this volume). Among the first casualties were top Tutsi and moderate Hutu officials in government (including Prime Minister Agathe Uwilingiyimana) and UNAMIR peacekeepers. Within a hundred days an estimated eight hundred thousand to one million people had been slaughtered. UNAMIR was unable to stop the genocide for several reasons: misreading and underestimating of the situation, lack of appropriate mandate, initial casualties suffered, and insufficient troops (Cohen 2007). The UN has been highly criticized for its ineffective handling of the Rwandan civil war and genocide.

The genocide was ended by the RPF who fought their way to Kigali and overthrew the regime. Although originated by and mostly consisting of Tutsi exiles, the RPF tried to portray a detribalized nationalist ideology symbolized by their motto: "Not Hutu, Tutsi, nor Twa." The movement incorporated many Hutu dissidents fleeing the extremist Rwandan regime. To reinforce its claims to a national character, it appointed a leading Hutu dissident of the Habyarimana regime, Colonel Alexis Kanyarengwe, as chairman. The first Rwandan president (July 1994–March 2000) after the overthrow of the genocidal regime, who became head of an RPF-dominated government of national unity, Pasteur Bizimungu, was also a Hutu. The victory of RPF forced hundreds of thousands of Hutu, including genocide protagonists, into exile in neighboring countries.

Events in Burundi and DRC

Ethnic persecution and wars in postcolonial Rwanda have often aggravated tension and violence in Burundi and vice versa. This has been compounded by ethno-political leaders openly inciting their counterparts across the border and the inflow of refugees from one country to the other depending on which side (Hutu or Tutsi) is being attacked. Although Burundi was embroiled in low-intensity ethnic conflict and civil war (1993 and 2005), the country managed to avoid the genocidal implosion following the plane crash that caused the death of Burundian Hutu President Cyprien Ntaryamira and Rwandan President Habyarimana. The civil war was partly contained because of the fragile power-sharing agreement hammered out between the major ethnic-based political parties, FRODEBU (Hutu) and UPRONA (Tutsi) with the help of key regional and international mediators; however, armed Hutu and Tutsi extremist factions were mobilizing against the power-sharing arrangements (BHCL 2006).

The Hutu Force for the Defense of Democracy (FDD), the armed wing of the National Council for the Defense of Democracy (CNDD), and the Tanzania-based Party for the Liberation of the Hutu People (PALIPEHUTU) organized tens of thousands into armed militias to wage a resistance war (BHCL 2006). There were over a dozen other rebel factions and political parties that joined the fray. It took years of multiparty peace talks in Arusha to broker a peace deal—the famous Arusha Peace and Reconciliation Agreement for Burundi signed in 2000—which together with subsequent peace talks in Pretoria and the various ceasefire agreements signed between the government and different rebel movements not participating in the Arusha peace talks, paved the way for the holding of democratic elections in 2005 (ACCORD 2010).

The Arusha peace agreements, among other important provisions, introduced a power-sharing arrangement between the two major ethnic groups in Burundi, a model that despite occasional outbreaks of hostilities and continued tension has thus far managed to maintain the fragile postwar peace in the country. Burundian experts like René Lemarchand (2006, 1) have extolled with cautious optimism the present power-sharing arrangement as one of the most successful examples of consociationalism in bitterly divided multiethnic societies because of the creative adaptation of principles like group autonomy, proportionality, and minority rights. More critical analysts like Patricia Daley do not share this optimism. Daley (2006, 310) condemns what she calls "the Compromise of Pretoria" for giving the 15 percent minority Tutsi group a disproportionate share of the institutions of government: 50 percent of the senate, 40 percent of the government, and 50 percent of the army. Many have blamed this disproportionality for the strong discontent felt by large sections of the Hutu community in and outside Burundi. It is imperative that disproportionality in ethnic power sharing be constructively renegotiated and redressed to ameliorate the Hutu majority's discontent, which has repeatedly boiled over to violent protests and interethnic bloodletting.

The Tutsi-Hutu wars in Rwanda and Burundi, and especially the genocide in Rwanda, had a devastating impact on neighboring DRC. The ascendance of the Tutsi-led RPF in Rwanda forced many refugees and *génocidaires*, including the notorious Interahamwe, across the border to eastern DRC. The influx of more than one million Rwandan refugees into the Kivu region of eastern DRC aggravated the conflict landscape in two major respects. Firstly, displaced Hutu militias and political dissidents used the territory to launch vicious cross-border attacks to destabilize Rwanda and possibly unseat the RPF government. The Rwandan government repeatedly countered with cross-border raids against the renegade militias. Secondly, Hutu rebels in DRC openly targeted and attacked the local Tutsi populations (the Banyamulenge) in eastern Congo. Hence, Hutu rebels fleeing Rwanda waged a bifurcated guerrilla war from their volatile base in the forests and villages of eastern Congo.

It is striking that the Banyamulenge have been marginalized and persecuted in DRC since colonial times. Their Congolese citizenship was a repeated subject of contestational politics under dictator Mobutu Sese Seko, who issued a 1966 decree repealing the citizenship of the Tutsi in eastern DRC and ordering their return to Rwanda. Vehement rebellion by the Banyamulenge in eastern Congo forced Mobutu to rescind this obnoxious decree. Mobutu's prolonged dictatorship and prebendal corruption ruined DRC, leaving the vast majority of people of this resource-rich African country impoverished, marooned, and hopeless.

Mobutu not only demonstrated contempt for the Tutsi minority in his country but also supported Habyarimana in Rwanda and the genocidal regime that succeeded him, both ruthless in their liquidation of the Batutsi. The operation of rebel groups with impunity in eastern Congo and their destabilizing incursions in Rwanda prompted the government of Paul Kagame and his long-time ally President Museveni of Uganda to support an insurgency aimed at overthrowing Mobutu (Vogt 2010). An avowed Congolese adversary of Mobutu, Laurent Kabila, led the Kagame-Museveni backed rebel movement—Alliance of Democratic Forces for the Liberation of Congo (ADFL)—in the proxy war against Mobutu. The seven-month campaign that ousted Mobutu was dubbed "the first Congo war" to differentiate it from the more ferocious "second Congo war" otherwise described as "Africa's world war" (see Francis 2008). The latter, which lasted for five years (1998–2003), was provoked by Rwandan and Ugandan attempts to overthrow President Laurent Kabila with whom Kagame and Museveni had fallen out but whose government they were determined to control.

Consequently, Rwanda and Uganda sponsored Tutsi-dominated (Banyamulenge) rebel and militia movements in eastern DRC to join the anti-Kabila campaign. To protect his fragile regime, Kabila called in external military support. Zimbabwe, Namibia, Angola, Sudan, Libya, and Chad all fought on the side of Kabila and prevailed; more than four million people died in the war. Several peace agreements were signed in cities like Pretoria, Lusaka, and Luanda by various parties to end the hostilities. Nongovernmental militias and rebel forces involved in the war did not sign the peace agreements, however. Consequently, rebel insurgency and attacks on defenseless ethnic minorities have continued sporadically, especially in eastern Congo. Kabila himself was assassinated in January 2001 and his son, Joseph Kabila, was named successor.

There are at least two significant externalities associated with the Congo wars. The first is the predation of Congolese natural resources, casting doubt on the real motive claimed by interventionists. Diamond and timber deposits were regularly exploited (both legally and illegally) by multiple sides in the conflict to pay for their military expenses, resulting in one of the major supplies of "conflict diamonds." The most scandalous episode was in August 1999 when formerly allied Rwandan and Ugandan troops engaged in a fierce confrontation over control of the famous Kisangani diamond and gold mining town in northeastern Congo, a town rescued from rebel occupation and the associated underground trade in gemstones. A special UN report indicated that ex-President Laurent Kabila used the DRC's extensive resources of strategic minerals to obtain military assistance and training, and subsidized the costs of the allies' intervention by granting mining concessions to Zimbabwean and Namibian companies (UN Panel of Experts Report No. S2003/102, quoted in Daley 2006, 306).

The second externality is the staggering incidents of mass rape of women and girls by rebel forces and other armed groups (UN peacekeepers and government forces included). The Congo war is notorious for the systematic use of sexual violence as a weapon of war, second only to the Rwandan genocide in postcolonial history. It is estimated that over 200,000 women and girls have been raped by rebels and combatants since the start of the Congo war while between 250,000 to 500,000 women and girls were raped in the Rwandan genocide (Grignon 2009; Clark-Flory 2010). Statistics on sexual violence in African civil wars remain contested because of the large number of unreported cases, given the traditional stigma associated with rape in various parts of the continent.

This chapter has no pretension to an exhaustive analysis of the multiplicity of conflicts ravaging the Great Lakes region since the imposition of European colonial rule. I have essentially advanced three critical points. The first is that political conflicts in the Great Lakes region are far more diverse and complex than mainstream international media and literature adumbrates. As I have shown, conflicts have been fluid and interlocking due to the interconnectedness of socio-demographic history, identities, and sociopolitical structures. Secondly, while some of the conflict structures date back to precolonial intergroup animosities, European colonial policies and politics decisively account for the embeddedness and virulence of the conflict structures. Thirdly, different factions of postcolonial elites in the Great Lakes region (and Africa in general) have deliberately interposed their interests in the exploitative and unjust political, social, and economic institutions and structures inherited from the colonialists rather than dismantling and transforming them to serve the public good. In many countries, the privileged factions that inherited political power at independence essentially replaced the colonizers to entrench and perpetuate a system of domestic colonialism based on violence. This has aggravated the conflict landscape, precipitating protracted struggles and, in some cases, civil wars to eject corrupt, despotic regimes and push for popular reforms and accountability. In the process, external interveners, both state and non-state parties, have played varied roles, sometimes aggravating the conflicts but at other times supporting progressive change.

In the wake of the major conflicts afflicting specific countries (genocide in Rwanda, civil wars in DRC, Northern Uganda, and Burundi, and election violence in Kenya), most external actors, notably international NGOs and interstate organizations, seem to have adopted a more constructive approach to conflict and development interventions in the region. Significant efforts, attention, and resources have been applied to resolve violent conflicts, rebuild collapsed state structures, and restore or facilitate the transition to multiparty democracy. These efforts have yielded significant dividends: most of the wars that characterized the region in the 1990s and early 2000s have ended or abated. Furthermore, the civilian and military dictatorships and one-party rule prevalent in the region prior to 2000 have been replaced by multiparty democracies. These remarkable features are emblematic of the changing tides, despite monumental state-building and development challenges ahead.

References

ACCORD. 2010. "Burundi Intervention." African Centre for the Constructive Resolution of Disputes (ACCORD), Durban, South Africa, 13th August. Accessed September 2010. http://www.accord.org.za/our-work/peacebuilding/burundi.html.

Askew, Kelly M. 2006. "Sung and Unsung: Musical Reflections on Tanzanian Postsocialisms." *Africa* 76, no. 1: 15–43.

BHCL. 2006. "The African Great Lakes Region: An End to Conflicts?" British House of Commons Library (BHCL) Research Paper 06/51, London. 25 October.

Clark-Flory, Tracy. 2010. "Rape: Weapon of Choice in Congo," 24th August. Accessed September 2010. http://www.salon.com/2010/08/24/congo_rape/.

Cohen, Jared. 2007. *One Hundred Days of Silence: America and the Rwanda Genocide*. Lanham, MD: Rowman & Littlefield.

Daley, Patricia. 2006. "Challenges to Peace: Conflict Resolution in the Great Lakes Region of Africa." *Third World Quarterly* 27, no. 2: 303–19.

EU. 2008. *Kenya: Final Report of 2007 General Election*. Accessed 14 July 1010. http://www.eueomkenya.org/Main/English/PDF/Final_Report_Kenya_2007.pdf.

FIAN. 2010. "Land Grabbing in Kenya and Mozambique." Heidelberg, Germany: FIAN International Secretariat. Accessed September 2010. http://www.fian.org/resources/documents/others/land-grabbing-in-kenya-and-mozambique/pdf.

Francis, David. 2008. "Introduction: Understanding the Context of Peace and Conflicts in Africa." In *Peace and Conflicts in Africa*, edited by David Francis, 3–15. London: Zed Books.

Grignon, Francois. 2009. "Rape as a Weapon of War in Congo." International Crisis Group (ICG). Accessed September 2010. http://www.spiegel.de/international/world/0,1518,629885,00.html.

Human Rights Watch (HRW). 2004. *Leave None to Tell the Story: Genocide in Rwanda*. Human Rights Watch Report (originally published in 1999). Accessed September 2010. http://www.hrw.org/reports/1999/rwanda/.

Jourdan, Luca. 2005. "New Forms of Political Order in North Kivu: The Case of the Governor Eugene Serufuli." Paper presented at the conference Beside the State: New Forms of Political Power in Post-1990's Africa, Milan, Italy, December.

Kagame, Paul. 2006. "Conflicts in the Great Lakes." *The African Executive*, May 17–24. Accessed December 2010. http://www.africanexecutive.com/modules/magazine/articles.php?article=693.

Kashambuzi, Eric. 2009. "History of the Great Lakes Region of Africa." Accessed September 2010. http://www.kashambuzi.com/blog/3-all/259-history-of-the-great-lakes-region-of-africa.html.

Lemarchand, René. 1996. *Burundi: Ethnic Conflict and Genocide*. Cambridge: Cambridge University Press.

———. 2006. *Consociationalism and Power Sharing in Africa: Rwanda, Burundi, and the Democratic Republic of the Congo*. Oxford: Oxford University Press.

Magidu, Nyende. 2009. "Causes and Consequences of Fragility in Africa: The Experience of Countries in the Great Lakes Region." Paper presented at the Economic Policy Research Centre, Makerere University, Kampala, May.

Mamdani, M. 1996. *Citizen and Subject: Contemporary Africa and the Legacy of Late Colonialism*. Kampala: Fountain Publishers / Princeton University Press.

———. 2001. *When Victims Become Killers: Colonialism, Nativism and Genocide in Rwanda.* Princeton, NJ: Princeton University Press.
Mbembe, Achille. 2001. *On the Postcolony.* Berkeley: University of California Press.
Meisler, Stanley. 1973. "Rwanda and Burundi." *The Atlantic Monthly* 232, no. 3 (September): 6-16. Accessed September 2010. http://www.theatlantic.com/past/docs/unbound/flashbks/rwanda/meisler.htm.
Moritz, M. 2004. "Changing Contexts and Dynamics of Herder-Farmer Conflicts across West Africa." *Canadian Journal of African Studies* 40, no. 1 (2006): 1–40. Accessed September 2010. http://www.jstor.org/discover/10.2307/25433865?uid=2&uid=4&sid=21101093897033.
Mpangala, Gaudens P. 2004. "Origins of Political Conflicts and Peacebuilding in the Great Lakes Region." Paper presented at the symposium Ramifications of Instability in the Great Lakes Zone, Command and Staff College, Arusha, Tanzania, 23 February.
Munene, Macharia. 2009. "Politics in Kenya: 1960–2009." Paper presented at the National Defence College in Karen, Nairobi, 1 December.
———. 2010. "Colonization Model and Results." Paper presented at the conference 50 Years of African Independence: Review and Outlook, held at The Observatory about Social Reality in Sub-Saharan Africa, Universidad Complutense de Madrid, San Lorenzo del Escorial, Spain, 5–9 July.
Ngoie, T. Germain, and Kenneth Omeje. 2008. "Rentier Politics and Low Intensity Conflicts in the DRC: The Case of Kasai and Katanga Provinces." In *Extractive Economies and Conflicts in the Global South: Multi-regional Perspectives on Rentier Politics,* edited by Kenneth Omeje, 137–50. Aldershot, UK: Ashgate.
Nnoli, Okwudiba. 1989. *Ethnic Politics in Africa.* Harare: African Association of Political Science.
Omeje, Kenneth. 2008. "Extractive Economies and Conflicts in the Global South: Re-engaging Rentier Politics." In *Extractive Economies and Conflicts in the Global South: Multi-regional Perspectives on Rentier Politics,* edited by Kenneth Omeje, 1–26. Aldershot, UK: Ashgate.
Rodney, Walter. 1972. *How Europe Underdeveloped Africa.* London: Heinemann.
Southall, W. Aidan. 1970. "The Illusion of Tribes." In *The Passing of the Tribal Man in Africa,* edited by Peter C. W. Gutkind, 28–50. Leiden: E. J. Brill.
Vogt, D. 2010. "The History of the Second Congo War." Accessed 2 February 2011. http://www.helium.com/items/1789665-about-the-second-congo-war.

2 The History and Politics of Regionalism and Integration in East Africa

Hannington Ochwada

THIS CHAPTER EXPLORES and analyzes the history and politics of regionalism and integration in East Africa. While the process of forging regionalism and integration entails the establishment of structural conformity, it is important to consider and assess the historical realities that have impacted the process. Cognizant of germane historical conditions shaping the general process of integration in Africa, I analyze the challenges of politically integrating the East African Great Lakes region since the early 1960s, such as the political ideologies, economic orientation, language, and cultural differences. The leaders of Kenya, Uganda, Tanzania, Rwanda, and Burundi have largely defined the processes of regionalism and integration without considering the local, historical, "bottom-up" patterns of cooperation that have existed in the region since precolonial times. Consequently, they have emphasized schemes of economic integration at the expense of social integration.

While economic integration theoretically holds promise for the commercial development of the region as outlined by the East African Community (EAC), I argue that a renewed effort towards integrating the Great Lakes countries ought to emphasize the participation of civil society in debating and popularizing the language and practice of rights—democracy, gender, and social and legal justice. This calls for more participation of individuals in constitutional debates and amendments to enhance regional citizenship and mutual coexistence for stability and security within the region. A move towards integration provides space for a wider terrain of social interaction and self-actualization of individuals and citizenship within the region. Partnership and collective action is crucial for development, and, therefore, enlarging the social terrain of interaction could pay dividends in both economic and political terms.

However, to achieve this as an adequate policy reformulation, new terms of integration should be undertaken to lessen distinctions that ascribe specific characteristics to different states of East Africa, characteristics that define individuals as Kenyans, Tanzanians, Ugandans, Rwandans, or Burundians. That is, the constitutionality of integration must be worked out in terms of a reasonable theory of integration: one that provides for a shared space to pursue sociopolitical and economic activities across national borders and transcends the concerns and interests of top political leaders (see Mutua 2009, 5–9).

The last thirty years have provided scholars with evidence of the collapse of numerous states and the sharpening of ethnic strife globally, from Eastern Europe to Sudan. This has given rise to a searching need for avenues to create and/or reinforce common identities, which would lessen the likelihood of violence and insecurity in subregions worldwide and provide impetus for a framework for cooperation (UNRISD 1994, 1–9). It is my view that East Africans could draw from emerging trends in globalization to make their national borders less obstructive and more open to human interaction, the promotion of human rights, and the provision of security. A "good neighborliness" approach to their affairs could enable the people of East Africa to resolve the insecurity and conflict dogging the politics of the Great Lakes region (Afrika-Studiecentrum 2007, 6–7; Ajulu 2007, 53–56; Salih and Markakis 1998, 7–13). A new attempt towards integration could also enable citizens of the region to stabilize, enhance, and realize the full potential of their human resources for progress and development. This would also lessen the problem of refugees, which has impacted the process of development within the region. East African states have previously concentrated refugees from Rwanda, Burundi, Uganda, Democratic Republic of Congo (DRC), Sudan, and Somalia in the various camps within the region. In other instances, refugees and immigrants have been denied employment because of their citizenship (see Ninsin 2008, 1–19; Mamdani 2001, 1–45; Malkki 1995, 8–25).

Earlier forms of integration emphasized economic factors and the role of the states in alleviating the grave problems of poverty and other social injustices that people experienced. For example, three of the East African countries—Kenya, Tanzania, and Uganda—established interstate parastatals, such as the East African Airways and the East African Railway Services and Ports Authority, in 1967. With such strong state involvement in activities of individuals, the East African leaders perceived economic integration and cooperation as a panacea for the diverse development setbacks that their region suffered. Yet purely state and economic-driven approaches to the problems dogging the region have been limiting and exclusive, to say the least. This is because they focused on the role of the state rather than the welfare concerns of the people. The approach adopted here critiques the emphasis on economic factors and the state in favor of one that encourages the voice of civil society in regional integration.

Precolonial Societies and Integration

The East African nations of Kenya, Uganda, Tanzania, Rwanda, and Burundi share a common historical heritage dating to the precolonial period. The people intermingled freely without inhibition or restrictions of artificial boundaries or country-specific laws, trading among themselves within the region and beyond. They also intermarried and related in various ways, including participating in political affairs of communities within which they resided. Some Arab and Waswahili traders from the eastern African coastal region established chiefdoms and kingdoms in areas as far as the Great Lakes in the nineteenth century, prior to colonialism. Paul Tiyambe Zeleza (1993, 303) confirms that:

> Family, clan and ethnic associations, both real and effective, played an important role in the provision of trading skills, capital and credit, and information. Traders formed alliances in foreign countries through marriage and blood brotherhood. The careers of the famous Swahili and Nyamwezi traders, such as Tippu Tip and Msiri who created commercial empires in Kasongo and Katanga respectively, were built on shrewd alliances with local rulers or people based on either marriage or fictional kinship ties.

Traders therefore created these empires to secure important scarce items and products for daily use that were not available in the areas from which they came. Furthermore, they needed to purchase goods for exchange in the vibrant export and import trade of the nineteenth century. Some areas in present-day Uganda, such as Kibero on Lake Kyoga, and Bunyoro, specialized in salt and iron respectively (Gimode 1996, 3).

The political establishments did not deter movement and the coresidential status of people. Whenever residents found it necessary, and in order to benefit from outsiders, local leaders would levy taxes and tariffs, as was the case in nineteenth-century kingdoms of Mirambo of Wanyamwezi and Kabaka Mutesa I of Buganda. The Akamba of present-day Kenya and Yao of Tanzania were similarly engaged in long-distance trade that took them far away from their homes for several weeks or even months in parts of central and east Africa. Thus the region was integrated by ongoing expanding commercial networks and cooperation.

Adjacent communities, such as the Maasai and Kikuyu of Kenya engaged in local trade activities while the Hutu and Tutsi of Rwanda and Burundi coexisted mutually as well. The system of governance in Rwanda and Burundi gave the Tutsi—who are a numerical minority of 14 percent—a lordship-like license to rule over the 85 percent Hutu majority. Whereas interethnic or intra-ethnic differences, disputes, and sometimes conflicts between groups existed, such as between the Hutu and Tutsi or the Maasai and Kikuyu, they did not deter the people from pursuing wider communal interests. Ali Mazrui (1994, 134–36) has described this system as Africa's culture of tolerance, whereby African communities used their "cultural attribute of short memory of hate" to forgive and build good neighborliness. The existing spirit of accommodation and ecumenism became a valuable asset for integrating communities within the region.

A further illustration of these precolonial ties and the political mechanisms allowing for integration can be found in the Hutu/Tutsi *kwihutura* and *gucupira* institutions, which prevented the hardening of lordship-like distinctions and differences that might give rise to disaffection against the Tutsi rulership, for instance. Mahmood Mamdani (2001, 149–50) argued that in precolonial Rwanda, the institution of *kwihutura* enabled "the rare Muhutu [Hutu person] who was able to accumulate cattle to rise through the socio-economic hierarchy and to shed Hutuness and achieve the political status of a Mututsi (Tutsi person)." Mamdani (2001, 70) added that "the loss of property could also lead to the loss of status summed up in the Kinyarwanda word *gucupira*." This is not to say that the *kwihutura* system or any other inclusive mechanisms designed to establish the realm of governance guaranteed rights in those societies. One can argue, though, that the Banyarwanda upheld citizenship and rights of individuals. Thus, precolonial governance in East African societies emphasized the idea of citizenship and residence in a regional framework.

Lessons from Colonial Integration Efforts

Overlaying the preexisting spirit of cooperation and integration described above, European finance capital opted to give more impetus to colonial integration efforts based on competition and stratification. The late nineteenth century was characterized by colonial merchant capitalism, which established trading networks throughout East Africa. On the other hand, the twentieth century was overwhelmed by the spirit of industrial capitalism for which East Africa was both a market for European manufacturers and a source for raw materials and human resources, and the aim was to create wealth to alleviate the economic problems of metropolitan Europe.

European colonists in East Africa thus embarked on a program of systematic integration of the region for the purposes of economic and political control. For instance, in 1902, the British established the Court of Appeal for East Africa, followed by the East African Currency Board in 1905, and a Postal Union between Kenya and Uganda in 1911. By 1917, the British colonial administration had established a customs union, and by 1920, the East African Currency Board (EACB) was already issuing a single regional currency. When Tanganyika (later known as Tanzania) was transferred from German to British control, the country used the common currency already established (Gimode 1996, 8–9; Secretariat of the Permanent Tripartite Commission for East African Co-operation 1997, 1). Thus the British attempted to harmonize their administration and control of native affairs of the three countries. They argued that a stronger political union would be a prerequisite for the economic integration of East Africa.

Prominent British citizens and parliamentarians also agitated for the Federation of East Africa. Following this, Sir Sydney Henn in 1924 moved in the House of Commons that the East African territories be coordinated. Sir Henn urged the British secretary of state for the colonies to send to East Africa a special commission that would report to him on the workability of the policy and services throughout the territories. He expected the special commission to give him advice on how to run the program of future economic development in East Africa (see Henn 1924, 1–37). Consequently, the British government established an East Africa Commission chaired by Colonial Secretary W. G. Ormsby-Gore. The commission solicited views from Africans, people of Asian descent, and Europeans on the possibility of forming a federation of the British colonies (see Ormsby-Gore 1925, 201–47).

Ormsby-Gore's report confirmed that the African and Asian communities were hostile to the British-induced federation framework. Africans were particularly suspicious of the motives and intentions of the colonists. Instead, they wanted their grievances and their civil rights to be recognized and considered. Thus, instead of pursuing the idea of an East African federation, the Ormsby-Gore Report suggested that regular conferences of governors and responsible officials of the various departments be held in the British East African territories. The conferences would be held on a rotational basis in the territories. The report suggested that governors from Kenya, Uganda, Tanganyika, Nyasaland (Malawi), and Northern Rhodesia (Zambia), and Zanzibar's representative, attend the conferences. The governor in whose territory the conference was held made necessary secretarial arrangements, while the host country was responsible for drawing the agenda of discussion. These governors' conferences dealt with matters of common interest to all territories, including "native" administration, communications, taxation, land policy, and labor, among others, but were interrupted by the outbreak of World War II. Paradoxically, however, the native inhabitants of the region were never consulted about the mode of integration.

The end of World War II revived the debate on the federation question among the colonial administrators. The war had made interterritorial planning a conceivable ingredient in stabilizing colonial control. Britain adopted this strategy in managing its colonies in the post–World War I period, after becoming conscious of the presence of Italy in the Horn of Africa when the latter entered World War II in 1940. Britain could no longer pretend that there was no security threat in its territories from hostile adversaries operating in the Horn of Africa. Consequently, Britain embarked on strengthening government regulation and coordination of its territories, arguing that integration was one way of bringing a wider geographical territory such as East Africa under a central authority (Rothchild 1968b, 47).

In 1944, the Association of Chambers of Commerce and Industry of East Africa criticized the existing system, which vested power in the institutions of individual territories. They argued that decentralization meant that commercial activities in East Africa would be harmonized to speed up development of the territory. After World War II, entrepreneurs and business people called for pursuance of a nonpolitical line in the constitutions of the territories in the interest of colonial capitalism.

Colonial businesspeople were largely dissatisfied with the political institutions and procedures they perceived as inimical to capitalist entrepreneurship. They directed their criticism at the governors' conferences, which they saw as secretive and impotent in the face of new realities of stimulating economic progress in the region. The conferences usually decided upon common legislation in private and then presented identical bills to the three legislative councils (Rothchild 1968b: 47). Naturally, this procedure minimized the role of local, unofficial groups and their representatives, and influenced the legislative council's effective participation in the process of governance. It also locked out the opinion of the majority of Europeans, becoming an object of attack by "citizens" and "subjects" who desired inclusion in the affairs of the colonial state as a profit-making enterprise. The British government took note of this and made efforts to reexamine the inadequacies of the governors' machinery with respect to the capitalist cravings of the European commercial and industrial community. Hence, all reforms were crafted with the intentions of maintaining British colonial economic interests.

Meanwhile, the British Labor Party published its white paper, "Inter-territorial Organization in East Africa," in December of 1945. The British government clarified its position on what a closer political union in East Africa meant for Britain and the general European community. As the secretary of state for the colonies at the time, George Hall, informed the House of Commons in London, this included the provision of a constitutional basis for the operation of common services; the more efficient coordination of policy and action, particularly in the spheres of economic development, communication, and research; the appointment of both British and African public representatives in the management of the common services; and the creation of effective means of enacting common legislation when required (Rothchild 1968a, 48).

However, the British imperial government also stated that the proposal did not mean political unification but rather an arrangement purportedly designed to permit the peoples of East Africa to take responsibility for their own affairs. Despite this rhetoric, all evidence pointed to the colonists' desire to obtain firm control over the three East African territories. The governors hoped to establish a constitution for the common services, which would create both an East African High Commission (EAHC) and a legislative assembly (Rothchild 1968a, 48). The EAHC would consist of the governors of Kenya, Uganda, and Tanganyika, with the governor of Kenya acting as standing chairman. The legislative assembly was vested with power to enact ordinances for the three territories.

The EAHC met regularly during the year to deal with policy matters relating to the supervision of the broad network of common services in the territories and provided the impetus for functional integration of the common services. It facilitated the integration of the system of harbors and railways, the creation of an East African navy, and the expansion of Makerere College into the University College of East Africa (Gimode 1996, 10).

Independence and Integration

On attainment of independence, the East African countries emphasized different development strategies, making the integrative goals stipulated during the colonial era difficult to attain. The interstate integration arrangements inherited from the British colonial administrators dealt mainly with commerce and trade. The idea of specializing in different territorial aspects of production and exportation served British interests best because of the economies of scale. The new, postcolonial specialization entailed forms of transport and communications, and services like reinsurance and tourism, with Kenya specializing in food manufacturing, Uganda producing electricity and processing raw minerals, and Tanzania promoting wildlife tourism.

Even though the political leaders of the newly independent states in the region—Julius Nyerere (Tanzania), Jomo Kenyatta (Kenya), and Milton Obote (Uganda)—realized the limitations of the institutions they inherited, they still hoped to build an East African federation. Their assumption was that integration of the region would lead to pan-Africanism and a closer union of independent African nations. While the leaders recognized the fact that the East African Common Services Organization was an ineffective institution, they nonetheless envisaged the federation of their countries to be the most reasonable way to solve their economic problems. Decolonization of the three territories made it difficult to achieve a supranational unification with clear development strategies. The decolonization process gave rise to different but largely incompatible national ideologies and identities that shaped the political terrain in each country. Thus, debates about integration also emphasized national specificity. Even within countries, divergent views on the form of federation existed, such as the animated debates among the political parties in Kenya, the Kenya African National Union (KANU) and Kenya African Democratic Union (KADU). Adar and Ngunyi (1994, 399) argued that whereas the two political parties accepted the idea of federation in principle, the ideological differences between them posed a setback, given that KADU wanted regional autonomy of different ethnic segments of the country while KANU envisioned a unified entity. The opposing views affected the way Kenya pursued the idea of federation.

There also emerged two centrifugal views in Uganda: the official government position supported the federation as stated in the 1963 Nairobi Declaration, while the Kingdom of Buganda opposed the idea. Buganda favored autonomy for the kingdom as enshrined in the federal constitution of Uganda, thus placing the central government in an awkward position. The government was compelled to clarify the question of federation to its citizens, coming out as a noncommitted party to the process. With the latter's position appearing uncertain, Kenya and Tanganyika considered forming a federation independent of Uganda. For its part, Tanganyika envisaged a closer political federation of the three countries that would alter existing economic disparities within the subregion. Kenya, on the other hand, maintained that a true federation must accommodate provision for the countries to exercise control over their foreign policy and foreign relations.

The federation issue remained daunting in East African integration efforts. As the mid-1960s approached, the warmness with which the leaders had received the idea of federation diminished and general acrimony among the East African states crept into interstate relations. Uganda and Tanzania feared that Kenya would dominate the affairs of the federation, given the country's strong economy. Indeed, Kenya came to dominate economically after inheriting a relatively well-developed infrastructure and considerable property from the colonial British administration and the industrial base established by a relatively large European settler community. This led to an uneasy relationship among the countries. Tanzania and Uganda wanted a more equitable and balanced regional integration program that would promote uniform economic growth in all three countries. Having defined their specific national priorities, it became clear that the national boundaries would remain unchanged, defining the national policies, citizenship, and residence of individuals in the three countries.

In spite of the existing tensions, the political leadership in East Africa nursed the idea of integrating the region and making it sustainable. They realized that economic inducements—the regional comparative advantage, economies of scale, expanded interterritorial projects, and a wider financial base would benefit the inhabitants of the region (Rothchild 1968a, 1). In the years that followed, the countries continued to specialize in different commercial, industrial, and mineral activities. Uganda specialized in mining and electric production, Kenya continued to manufacture household products, while Tanzania tried to jump-start its poor economy in industrial production as opposed to tourism.

Ideological differences among the leaders solidified because of the economic disparities of their countries. By the mid-1960s, it became clear that some of the gains towards integration had been lost, compelling the leaders to initiate meetings in Kampala and Mbale in 1964 and 1965 to resolve their differences. During the meetings, not only did they agree to embark on a robust program for industrialization in Tanzania but also sought to correct trade imbalances between their countries. In June 1965, Tanzania proposed that each country should establish separate currencies and banks because its leaders were not convinced of the benefits of integration. Kenya, which was experiencing a positive interterritorial trade balance over the rest, warmly embraced the idea. However, the sharp competition among the countries would signal the collapse of the East African Common Market.

Because East African political leaders still believed in integration, they set up another commission in September of 1965 that recommended a common market and common services for the region. They appointed Kleid Philip, a United Nations leading economist, to look into ways of making the federation work. He proposed the transformation of the legal and institutional structures so as to promote the objectives of regional integration. Philip's team comprised three ministers from each of the countries in a working partnership. This culminated in the Treaty for East African Co-operation in Kampala on 6 June 1967 (effective 1 December 1967), which in turn established the East African Community (EAC) with headquarters in Arusha, Tanzania. Yet the EAC was not different from earlier programs of integration.

Whereas the formulations of the 1967 treaty laid down new strategies for integration of the region, the new political leadership did not abandon the structures they had inherited from the colonial state but instead added new elements to them. They hoped to correct trade disequilibria between the territories and promote a more viable economic development strategy through harmonization of fiscal incentives offered by each country. These included the transfer tax system (a transaction fee imposed on the transfer of title property in the different countries) and the establishment of the East African Development Bank. The assumption was that a more equitable distribution system of industrial resources and benefits would diversify wealth and bring about economic equilibrium in the region.

They assumed that by putting into place a series of financial and administrative structures, they would regulate the functioning of the Common Market services (Mutere 1996a, 6–7). But the blueprints did not facilitate the process of integration that the leaders had anticipated. Eventually, the East African Common Market, which was perhaps one of the most advanced institutional structures in Africa's attempts at regional integration, collapsed in the mid-1970s. The collapse was largely due to lack of political goodwill and economic vision on the part of the leaders of member states (Gathii 2011, 182–202). Apparently, there was little or not enough commitment to implement the economic policies that were promulgated. Absolom Mutere correctly observed that the institutional machinery of the EAC was ineffective and overly dependent on the goodwill of the national leaderships. Lacking autonomy, the regional institutions failed to create mechanisms to harmonize the interests of the different states and steer them away from political controversy. Little wonder, then, that ideological and personal rivalry between the leaders persisted and undermined the EAC (Mutere, 1996b:8).

Obviously, East African political leaders were not ready to forfeit their political ambitions and the personal fortunes they framed in the language of national economic sovereignty. Their trust in state involvement and the emphasis they laid on commercial and trade gains from integration militated against the success of the EAC. Strident economic competition and strong feelings of nationalism became a recipe for the growing spirit of acrimony that seemed to spread within the region. The antagonism also spread from the governmental level to the mass media, creating an atmosphere of immobility and enmity among East African residents. Ostensibly, however, the ideological differences and personal rivalries among leaders were largely a reflection of the separate political and economic paths the East African partners had chosen to follow against the backdrop of postindependence Cold War dynamics. Tanzania chose to follow a socialist path, while Uganda contemplated moving towards the left, and Kenya embraced free market capitalism that was paradoxically disguised as African socialism. The different political philosophies and economic policies conflicted with each other and rendered the federation idea a spent force.

The divergent ideological differences among the East African leaders translated into the economic practices adopted, leading to the collapse of the EAC, as the process of distributing assets and liabilities proved. For instance, the Kenyan media subtly described Tanzania's socialism as a euphemism for laziness. As early as 1975, Kenya's attorney general, Charles Njonjo, had advised the government to withdraw from the EAC. Some senior Tanzanian government officials described Ugandan leader Idi Amin as a "primitive fascist." Following the strained relations of the three heads of state, Julius Nyerere of Tanzania, Idi Amin of Uganda, and Jomo Kenyatta of Kenya, parted ways and the EAC collapsed in 1977, dashing the efforts towards integration.

Even with the collapse of the EAC, the residents of East Africa needed each other, given their shared cultures and borders. Cooperation between the countries continued at various levels of social and economic interaction. For example, following the expulsion of the Asian business community and the sharp decline of manufacturing in Uganda from the mid-1970s onwards, the Kenyan business class intensified trade in Uganda. Consumer goods and other imports from Kenya increased in markets in Uganda. Mamdani (1983, 97) noted that in 1971, imports of animal oil and fats, cotton fabric, and sugar valued in Uganda shillings at UgSh24 (US$168) million, UgSh12.3 (US$86) million, and UgSh11 (US$77) million respectively, streamed into Uganda from Kenya. By 1976, Uganda imported from Kenya products valued at UgSh94.99 (US$912) million, UgSh41.68 (US$400) million, and UgSh76 (US$730) million. Concomitantly, some of the multinational corporations (MNCs) operating in Kenya extended their commercial undertakings to Uganda. These included Cooper Motors, Leyland Paints, East African Industries, Robbialac Paints, and Shell Chemical Company.

Kenya continued to make economic inroads into the Ugandan market—a move Uganda largely ignored because of the country's shattered economy from Idi Amin's misrule. For example, in 1980, Kenya won a contract of 110.6 million British pounds sterling to supply Uganda with buses, trucks, and Land Rovers. The business that went on between the two countries appeared to convince economic and political analysts that Uganda and Kenya were moving closer again, despite the earlier political misunderstandings (Okoth 1994, 374). Similar agreements existed between Kenya and Tanzania.

Numerous MNCs operating in Kenya extended their commercial activities in the Tanzanian market. The Phillips electronic manufacturing plant, for instance, spread its trade network to Tanzania. But while this business was going on between well-established MNCs, the ordinary people of East Africa were restricted by their governments from crossing the national borders to trade, work, or visit relatives. Only prominent business people were allowed to cross the national borders for trade. The restriction created a security issue on the common borders of the East African nations. Using the ethno-demographic and cultural contiguity of most borderline communities, the masses violated the border restrictions in various ways in search of better living standards by engaging in *magendo*—petty clandestine trade in items such as cooking oil, soap, flour, and toothpaste, among others (Kasfir 1984, 84–103). In some cases, women engaged in prostitution on either side of the border for economic gain. The security problem became real with the increase in refugees, especially Ugandans fleeing the tyranny of the misrule of Idi Amin into Kenya and Tanzania.

The security problems compelled the East African countries to rethink regional cooperation. Although Tanzania and Kenya were not on very good political terms, when Idi Amin made a flagrant claim on a part of Kenya's territory in 1976, President Nyerere sharply criticized him in apparent support against a common foe. Similarly, when Tanzanian troops invaded Uganda, ostensibly to "discipline" Amin in 1979, Kenya remained silent as if nothing happened. Tanzania's invasion of Uganda was a direct response to the latter's brief provocative occupation of Tanzanian territory. It would appear the mood among the ruling elites in Kenya was jubilant with Amin's ouster; explaining Kenya's silence, Godfrey Okoth (1994, 373) observed that within a few days of Yusufu Lule's taking leadership in Uganda, there was a positive move to improve the relationship between Kenya and Uganda. Lule's ascendance to the presidency redefined Uganda's foreign policy initiatives regarding its relations with Kenya. Kenya and Uganda revived bilateral relations that included economic assistance and extradition of fugitives.

The spirit of East African integration lingered on, despite the intermittent misunderstandings among the East African heads of state. What was not clear about the whole matter was the kind of integration they would pursue. For example, in 1980, President Apollo Milton Obote of Uganda had strong political and ideological differences with President Daniel arap Moi of Kenya. In the following years, however, the two presidents warmed up to each other. In fact, following an agreement signed between the two presidents, Uganda's debts were rescheduled and Ugandan railway wagons carrying coffee were allowed to proceed up to the Kenyan seaport of Mombasa instead of unloading them at the Kenyan/Ugandan border town of Malaba, as had previously been case. Moi and Obote also agreed to tighten the border security to curb cross-border cattle rustling and smuggling by ethnic communities residing on the frontier, such as the Karamoja, Turkana, and Sebei.

The events and realities in the three countries during the first two decades of independence prompted a rethinking of the philosophy of integration. In the early 1980s, East African leaders started warming up to each other, perhaps because of the realization of the futility of continuing their seemingly undeclared "cold war." Real or imagined threats to the political interests of the ruling elites compelled them to adopt strategies they assumed would guarantee state security. For example, in the 1982 attempted coup by members of the Kenyan air force, the Tanzanian government cooperated with Kenya to repatriate the coup leaders who had fled to Tanzania in order that they might face trial in Kenya. The coup leaders, Hezekiah Ochuka and Pancrass Okumu Oteyo, were subsequently tried and hanged in Kenya. The Kenyans exchanged the coup leaders for Tanzanians who were also believed to have hatched a plan to overthrow Nyerere's government and who had sought political asylum in Kenya.

Towards Integration or Cooperation? A Strategic Rethinking

Following a resurgence of efforts towards cooperation, East African leaders reexamined the policies they had put in place in the late 1960s and with which that had toyed in the following decade. Clearly by the mid-1970s, the overall economic performance of African countries had slowed down considerably. Some of the basic socioeconomic infrastructure inherited from the colonial administration in East Africa was rapidly deteriorating. The stagnation of national economies militated against the thought of establishing cooperation in basic areas, such as education and training, research, transport, production, and marketing of strategic industrial products like chemicals, metal, and engineering goods, as well as money and finance.

By the late 1970s, African leaders were already redefining strategies to manage their affairs, seeking appropriate solutions to their dire economic and social problems. On the other hand, African intellectuals and policy specialists met in Monrovia in February of 1979 to discuss development prospects in Africa. They were chiefly concerned with the type of development and the means that would transform the functionality of African social and economic systems as they approached the twenty-first century. Other meetings followed, with perhaps the most important of them being the sixteenth session of the Assembly of Heads of State and Government of the Organization of African Unity (OAU) in July of 1979. The outcome became known as the "Monrovia Declaration of Commitment." The adopted strategy emphasized three basic principles: namely, self-reliance, self-sustainment, and economic cooperation and integration. It was envisaged that this would help Africa to solve its social, political, and economic problems.

In April of 1980, the second extraordinary summit of the OAU was held in Lagos, Nigeria, and adopted what was known as the Lagos Plan of Action (LPA)—a translation into specific actions of those basic principles of the Monrovia strategy. The East African leaders followed up on the LPA as a new source of inspiration for greater regional integration and pan-Africanism. For instance, in his speech at the summit meeting to sign the formal winding up of the East African Community in Arusha on 14 May 1984, Julius Nyerere offered an alternative framework for integration. Nyerere argued that even though they were formally signing an agreement to end the EAC, they had learned from their past mistakes and should moot new forms of cooperation. In essence, he urged the three countries to leave the door open for a fresh start in integration (Nyerere 1984, 1–2).

According to Nyerere, the reasons for the breakup of the EAC could not be sought in organizational faults or the different ideologies adopted in the three countries; rather, the breakup occurred through a general lack of political will. It is true that there had been a weak disposition for cooperation and a lack of appreciation of national independence. The three countries ran mixed economies and traded with both capitalist and communist countries. Yet the same countries could not trade among themselves.

The leaders realized that they needed to trade with each other and signed the East African Mediation Agreement in 1984 to pave the way for a new form of cooperation. Presidents Nyerere, Moi, and Obote signed the East African Community Mediation Joint Communiqué, which heralded a new era in the East African cooperation. However, political developments in Uganda and the ouster of President Milton Obote in 1985 slowed down the process of close cooperation and integration in East Africa. But on a different level, scholars and lawyers in East Africa began to rethink alternative frameworks for integration. They proposed a move away from exclusively emphasizing state structures (statism) and economic affairs to reexamining the constitution of the countries of East Africa with a view to empowering civil society in the management of affairs. They envisaged a new approach that would consider politics and the role that civil society played in strengthening the newly found spirit of integration among East Africans. In 1996 lawyers and social scientists from the East African states met in Mombasa, Kenya, to debate an appropriate constitutional framework for a civil society-based mode of integration. They came up with eight resolutions on how to integrate the social and economic spheres. One of the proposals was to establish legal institutes in different countries to legislate and promote human rights within the region.

In the past, schemes to integrate East Africa had been considered in purely economic terms, giving little attention to the social aspect of cooperation. A great deal of energy had been expended in erecting economic institutions to foster development within the region. The 1920s, 1940s, and even the 1960s and 1970s schemes emphasized commercial and economic forms of integration (Collaborative Centre for Gender Development 2006, 18–19). Whereas economic cooperation and integration and the building of institutions are plausible approaches that could give impetus to progress and development in East Africa, a need to shift focus and reconsider how civil society could participate in reforming institutions of governance in the region became increasingly important. For example, with the new wave of democratization in the early 1990s, various groups were involved in discussion on the question of East African integration (see Njenga 2009, 1–3). Scholars in public universities, women's groups, youth groups, transnational and diaspora communities, and different ethnic groups across borders demanded freedom of association and movement within the region (Shivji 2009, 80–92). They underscored the importance of adhering to constitutional reforms as the way towards long-term integration.

Cognizant of the common cultural heritage throughout East Africa that could be harnessed in the integration scheme, the leaders of the subregion called a meeting in Arusha on 14 March 1996. At this meeting Presidents Moi, Benjamin Mkapa, and Yoweri Museveni signed an accord that brought into being the Secretariat of the Tripartite Commission for East African Cooperation (Asaminew 2009, 10–11). The problem with this accord, however, was that it emphasized economic structures and the centrality of the state as the principal organizational unit for the affairs of the inhabitants—the proverbial old wine in a new wineskin. Hence, it did not take into consideration the place of civil society and individual citizens in shaping their own destiny. Without tackling the issue of constitutionalism, the process of integration remained a far-fetched dream for East Africans.

Even with the numerous meetings that have been held at different levels under the auspices of institutions, such as those of the East African Judicial Committee, Environmentally Sustainable Development, and The Promotion of Trade and Defense and Security in the Sub-region, integration efforts have not laid the foundation for mitigating country-specific nationalist sentiments. Economic considerations and statism continue to define efforts towards integration of the region. While it is a good idea to rely on economists as consultants to implement integrative efforts, there is a need to cast the net wide to involve relevant policy consultants, actors, and practitioners of other backgrounds.

Since the early 1990s, East Africa has witnessed a resurgence of constitutionalism to reexamine the constitutions of the countries with a view to imposing limitations on the exercise of state power and delegating some power to citizens. The process has encouraged people of the subregion to redesign their own forms and modes of governance. The limitation of government involvement and the protection of fundamental human rights and freedoms have been the underlying tenets of political, civil society-driven initiatives (Nanok 2009, 8–9).

Recent media reports provide evidence that East Africans are keen on reviving regional integration (Nalo 2011, 13; *The East African*, 16–22 November 2009, 1–12). This will require the nurturing of a common political environment in the entire Great Lakes region, including Rwanda and Burundi. A responsive civil society-friendly political culture in East Africa will help to mitigate the problems of insecurity and political instability that have affected the African Great Lakes region. This type of integration is also likely to go far in solving the current refugee problem. For example, the impoverished peasants who have outmigrated from Rwanda and Burundi since the early 1950s, who now form the Banyamulenge of the eastern Congo and a significant proportion of the population of Uganda, will not be considered aliens or immigrants but citizens committed to the progress of the region. This proposal quickly brings into focus the need to redefine and unify the criteria for citizenship and residence within the various countries in the region. Citizenship, for instance, could be tied to membership in a political community while residence requirements for supposedly nonindigenous or alien communities and immigrants could emphasize direct or indirect provision of labor in the economy over a stipulated number of years.

The current notion of residence, perceived in terms of border surveillance by the leaders of the different countries, appears to strip the same people they are "protecting from the external economic predators" of their basic rights and dignity. This kind of approach, while appearing to contribute to institution building and the economic development of the countries in which the so-called foreigners reside, is an abuse of human rights. Rwandan refugees suffering injustices in Uganda fall within this category. Successive Ugandan governments have considered them aliens with no rights of citizenship despite the role they played in installing the ruling National Resistance Movement (NRM) at the political helm. During the early days in the NRM constitution of villages, anyone, whatever their birth or descent, could be elected to Resistance Committees responsible for running village affairs during the guerrilla war. The criteria of birth and descent were largely ignored and, instead, residence and labor were emphasized. Nevertheless, these political ideals were abandoned once the war was won and Ugandan citizens began to nurse leadership ambitions (see Mamdani 2001, 159–84).

Various segments of the East African population have received the idea of the bottom-up approach to civil matters and regional management with mixed feelings. For example, the political leadership has preferred to maintain the status quo, whereas various groups of people have sought a political order with broader-based participation of individuals in shaping their destiny. In this context, several social movements have been emerging in the East African subregion. They have included associations of the media, lawyers, women's movements, business people, and university lecturers and students, among others. These groups have embraced a grassroots as opposed to state-organization approach to underscore the importance of civil society in the process of governance. There is no doubt that such an approach will ensure a political culture that would render national boundaries more porous. This in turn would lead to new perceptions and ways of governing the affairs of the region by empowering the people.

This chapter has provided an historical explanation of the politics of integration among the states and peoples of East Africa. I have examined how individuals mutually coexisted and cooperated without regard to rigid political boundaries in "premodern" history, as well as the various integration schemes deployed since colonial times. There are growing conversations about issues of individual rights and citizenship among different ethnic groups and states in Eastern Africa, which provide a solid basis for regional integration. The mutual recognition of individual rights among ethnic groups and states would guarantee and nurture security, in turn enabling the free movement of people and other interactions for better economic wellbeing in the region.

The advent of colonialism altered social relations by emphasizing residence instead of citizenship and rights. The colonial administrators dichotomized society into two domains—the citizen and subject. These actors were organized within the state structure and governed by constitutions that stripped civil society of the power to influence decisions. This is because African "subjects," who constituted the majority, were under the control of the colonial administrative machinery that gave more power to the few European "citizens." As a result, state power became synonymous with European power and presence. The integrative efforts that were forged at the beginning of the twentieth century were patterned after and adopted an exclusive top-down approach, which was why grassroots populations in the East African region initially rejected them.

It is common knowledge that the independence schemes of integration were both formal economy based and government enforced. Consequently, they were authoritarian in nature and did not take into consideration the civil and political issues and experiences that confronted Africans. Although the intentions of postindependence political leaders may have been good, they were based on unworkable premises and were therefore inadequate. The preponderant statist and economistic approach to integration contributed to the collapse of the East African Community barely ten years into its existence.

These previous approaches to East African integration need to be more carefully thought through in order to better emphasize the much-needed bottom-up orientation. This entails grounding debates in constitutionalism and the possibility of constitutional consensus. The assumption is that, if consensus can be achieved as part of a regional political process, the established social, political, and economic boundaries will be rendered less consequential over time and integration can naturally take place. This would also mean greater respect for human rights in the region. It is thus possible that the much-sought economic development might be finally realized, as human resources and capital could be harnessed more effectively.

References

Adar, K. G., and M. Ngunyi. 1994. "The Politics of Integration in East Africa since Independence." In *Politics and Administration in East Africa*, edited by Walter O. Oyugi, 1–60. Nairobi: East African Educational Publishers.

Afrika-Studiecentrum. 2007. *DPRN Report No. 7: Regional Expert Meeting West, East and Central Africa & the Horn of Africa*. Leiden: The African Studies Centre.

Ajulu, Rok. 2007. "The Case for State-Led Developmental Regionalism." In *A Changing Global Order: Eastern African Perspectives*, edited by Sebastian Sperling, 53–56. Nairobi: Friedrich-Ebert Stiftung, Kenya.

Asaminew, Emerta. 2009. "Who is Afraid of Regional Integration?" *New Path* 4, no. 3: 10–11.

Collaborative Centre for Gender Development. 2006. *Women and Cross Border Trade in East Africa: Opportunities and Challenges for Small Scale Women Traders within the East African Customs Union*. Nairobi: Friedrich-Ebert Stiftung.

The East African, no. 785 (16–22 November 2009): 1–12.

Gathii, James Thuo. 2011. *African Regional Trade Agreements as Legal Regimes*. Cambridge: Cambridge University Press.

Gimode, E. 1996. "Attempts at Economic Integration in East Africa: Memories, Problems and Prospects." Paper presented at the 4th Historical Association of Kenya Symposium at Kenyatta University, Nairobi, 6–8 December.

Henn, S. 1924. "Motion on Co-ordination of the East African Territories." In *House of Commons Debates* (United Kingdom), Fifth Series, Vol. 172, April 8th. Cols. 351–53.
Kasfir, Nelson. 1984. "State, *Magendo*, and Class Formation in Uganda." In *State and Class in Africa*, edited by Nelson Kasfir, 84–103. London: Frank Cass and Company Limited.
Malkki, L. H. 1995. *Purity and Exile: Violence, Memory, and National Cosmology among Hutu Refugees in Tanzania.* Chicago: Chicago University Press.
Mamdani, M. 1983. *Imperialism and Fascism in Uganda.* Nairobi: Heinemann.
———. 2001. *When Victims Become Killers: Colonialism, Nativism, and the Genocide in Rwanda.* Princeton, NJ: Princeton University Press.
Mazrui, A. A. 1994. "Development in a Multi-Cultural Context: Trends and Tensions." In *Culture and Development in Africa*, edited by I. Serageldin and J. Taboroff, 125–48. Washington: The International Bank for Reconstruction and Development.
Mutere, A. 1996a. "Unfinished Business." *Southern Africa Political and Economic Monthly* 9, no. 7: 5–7.
———. 1996b. "Regional Cooperation and Anatomy of Conflict." *Southern Africa Political and Economy Monthly* 9, no. 7: 8–9.
Mutua, M. 2009. "Introduction." In *Human Rights NGOs in East Africa: Political and Normative Tensions*, edited by Makau Mutua, 1–9. Philadelphia: University of Pennsylvania Press.
Nalo, David. 2011. "After Sad Collapse, EAC Now on Right Path of Growth." *The East African* (31 January–6 February): 13.
Nanok, Tutui. 2009. "EAC: It's Been a Decade of Mixed Achievements." *New Path* 4, no. 3: 8–9.
Ninsin, K. A. 2008. "West Africa's Integration: The Logic of History and Culture." In *The African Union and New Strategies for Development in Africa*, edited by Said Adejumobi and Adebayo Olukoshi, 123–40. Amherst, NY: Cambria.
Njenga, John. 2009. "Bumpy Road to Regional Integration: The Numerous Hurdles That Make Political Federation a Mirage," *New Path* 4, no. 3: 1–3.
Nyerere, J. 1984. "President Nyerere's Speech and the Summit Meeting to Sign the Formal Winding Up of the EAC." Arusha: 14th May 1984. In *The East African Community Mediation Agreement 1984*, 14. Arusha: Government of Tanzania.
Okoth, G. P. 1994. "The Foreign Policy of Uganda toward Kenya and Tanzania." In *The African Union and New Strategies for Development in Africa*, edited by S. Adejumobi and A. Olukoshi, 360–85. Nairobi: East African Educational Publishers.
Ormsby-Gore, W. G. 1925. *Report of the East Africa Commission.* Cmnd. 2387. London: His Majesty's Stationery Office, 7–9.
Rothchild, D. 1968a. "From Federation to Neo-Federalism." In *Politics of Integration: An East African Documentary*, edited by D. Rothchild, 1–16. Nairobi: East African Publishing House.
Rothchild, D. 1968b. "Politics of Integration: The Second Attempt." In *Politics of Integration: An East African Documentary*, edited by D. Rothchild, 47–65. Nairobi: East African Publishing House.
Salih, M. M. A., and J. Markakis, 1998. "Introduction." In *Ethnicity and the State in Eastern Africa*, edited by M. M. A. Salih and J. Markakis, 7–13. Uppsala: Nordic Africa Institute.
Secretariat of the Permanent Tripartite Commission for East African Co-operation. 1997. *East African Co-operation Development Strategy* [EAC/DS/4/97] (1997–2000).

———. 2009. *Where Is Uhuru? Reflection on the Struggle for Democracy in Africa*. Nairobi: Fahamu.

Thisen, J. K. 1989. "Alternative Approaches to Economic Integration in Africa." *Africa Development* 24, no. 1: 19–60.

UNRISD. 1994. *Social Integration: Approaches and Issues*. Geneva, Switzerland: United Nations Research Institute for Social Development.

Weggoro, N. 1997. "The Way Ahead for the East African Cooperation." *The East African* 114: 3–33.

Zeleza, Paul Tiyambe. 1993. *A Modern Economic History of Africa*. Vol. 1, *The Nineteenth Century*. Dakar, Senegal: CODESRIA.

3 Multipolar Politics and Regional Integration in East Africa

Opportunities and Challenges for Nonstate Actors

Doreen Alusa

This chapter explores the predicament of regionalism in East Africa with a specific focus on the challenges and opportunities faced by nonstate actors in a multipolar international system. For slightly over a hundred years, formal regionalization has been part of the East African political landscape. Regionalization commenced during the colonial period as an effective tool of colonial management. During that time, Britain and Germany perceived the region as one economic unit and sought to coordinate it as a regional bloc. They did this through the creation of the East African Common Market, which became fully functional in 1927 and stipulated the terms of a customs arrangement between British East Africa and German East Africa. Within this common market, the three East African states shared a common currency, a joint income tax board, a joint economic council, and a single East African high commission. There were also over forty East African institutions in the fields of research, social services, education, training, and defense (Kasaija 2006, 4).

As independence loomed, African leaders from the three East African states supported deeper integration in the region. For instance, President Julius Nyerere of Tanganyika (Tanzania) was willing to delay the country's independence for a year so that the East African states could simultaneously gain independence and establish an East African Federation. In June 1963, discussions were held to map a way forward for the creation of a political federation in East Africa. During the meeting, the support for a unified East Africa was evident when key leaders of the region emphatically issued a joint declaration that "we believe a political federation of East Africa is desired by our peoples. There is throughout East Africa a great urge for unity and an appreciation of the significance of federation" (Kasaija 2006, 5).

The enthusiasm for political unity and its subsequent appeal for an East African federation diminished dramatically after independence. This was mainly because the newly independent states were reluctant to dissolve their sovereignties into the supranational regional scheme. In addition to this, ideological differences that emerged as a result of the alignment of African states with either the pro-capitalist West or the pro-communist East derailed and eventually led to the collapse of the East African Community (EAC) in 1977 (Delupis 1970; Mitelman 1975; Best 2008, 417).

Regionalization in East Africa reemerged in the wake of the end of the Cold War and the remodeling of the study of regionalization as "new regionalism." This new approach is characterized by several changes. While earlier studies focused on formal state initiated regionalization, new regionalism incorporates the role of nonstate actors in regionalization processes. Furthermore, unlike previous studies that fell within the framework of a bipolar world, recent studies factor in the multipolar transformation that is taking place in international politics (Schultz et al. 2001, 3; Hettne & Söderbaum 2002, 32–33). This transformation has given rise to new security concerns, resulting in the assimilation of new regionalism and security studies (Turner 2009, 64; Fawcett et al. 1998, 1–6). Within this context, new regionalism is seen as a strategy through which actors can cope with global security and development transformations, given that threats and challenges in today's complex and diverse world cannot be adequately addressed within the framework of the state-centric Westphalia system. In addition to this, the evolving multipolar international system has empowered all stakeholders involved in regionalization processes in Africa. The end of the Cold War ushered in a new era of freedom that enables both state and nonstate actors to freely engage with those whom they could not have comfortably dealt with inside of the confining ideological and political constraints of the bipolar world. Regionalization actors can therefore look beyond their traditional economic and political allies and cultivate or revive relations with emerging players, such as those in the Asia-Pacific region, who form part of the pillars of the multipolarized international system. In spite of the post–Cold War developments, integration in East Africa has been at best lethargic and to a large extent manifests the characteristics of an anachronistic, state-centric, Cold War regionalization process.

An Overview of the Application of Mainstream Regional Integration Paradigms to Africa

The term "integration" is commonly used to describe the process through which different parts are combined into a whole. In the context of state and territorial collectivity, regional integration is usually conceptualized within the framework of classical and neoclassical political and economic theories. The key assumption behind these approaches is that integration is a voluntary process through which two or more states link their economic and/or political domains and cede authority over key areas of domestic regulation and policy to a supranational institution (Mattli 1999, 41). The incremental and gradual transfer of authority and legitimacy to a supranational organization is often done in response to interdependence—a condition in which actors in the international system are sensitive and vulnerable to the acts of other entities that include governments and transnational actors, such as multinational corporations and even terrorist groups (Kasaija 2006, 4).

In Africa, there have been several conceptions and prescriptions that denote both empirical and normative differences on the strategies and paths to integration schemes on the continent. These differences reflect the preferences of various stakeholders in support of either political and/or economic activities as foundations for integration. Proponents of political integration date back to colonial times and included the "founders" of independent African states, such as Kwame Nkrumah, Sekou Touré, Julius Nyerere, and Patrice Lumumba. The underlying argument that permeates this school of thought is derived from the philosophy of pan-Africanism, which advocates a politically united Africa as a necessary and inevitable prelude to the economic and social empowerment of its people (see Hanchard 2010). Within this context, several incremental stages of political unification are envisaged. These stages are similar to those conceptualized by Karl Deutsch in 1957. According to Deutsch's model, political integration is a natural outcome of the various processes of modernization. He argued that incremental processes of economic development, urbanization, structural differentiation, and communication would eventually reduce group distinction and lead to the development of stable politically integrated societies (see Sbragia 2008, 36–37).

Building on Deutsch's model, Kasaija (2006) outlines four stages of political integration. At the basic level, a process of political cooperation is established whereby institutions that monitor and facilitate mutual policy arrangements among member states are created to achieve common interests and objectives. With time, political cooperation evolves into political integration—a stage in which member states retain their identity while joining an organization that transcends nationality. Through political integration, actors in the distinct member states are persuaded to shift their loyalties, expectations, and political activities towards a new center, whose institutions possess or demand jurisdiction over the preexisting states. Further assimilation takes place in the third stage, referred to as political federation. During this stage, the regional political organization establishes institutions that develop and implement procedures that fall within the framework of hard security, such as defense and foreign policy. Lastly, the ultimate stage of political integration is the creation of a political union in which all members surrender most or all of their sovereignty to a supranational political unit.

Throughout the 1950s and 1960s, African politics was dominated by debates about the continent's political unification. These debates gave rise to a clear rift between those who preferred political integration at a continental level and supporters of economic, cultural, and ultimately political integration at subregional levels. It is during this dispensation that ideological and personality clashes were witnessed between those who supported continental unification and those who preferred regional integration. While pro–continental unification adherents led by Kwame Nkrumah and Sekou Touré called for the creation of a strong United States of Africa, the pro-regionalism group, speaking through the Nigerian head of the delegation to the Addis Ababa conference, Mataima Sule, cautioned that although "Pan-Africanism is the only solution to our problems ... we must be realistic. It is for this reason that we would like to point out that at this moment the idea of forming a union of African states is premature.... At the moment, we in Nigeria cannot afford to form a union by government with any African state by surrendering our sovereignty" (Yoh 2008, 135). The above sentiments were reinforced when, on 20 August 1960, Prime Minister Tafawa Balewa of Nigeria, in his address to Nigerian parliamentarians, warned that "it will be the greatest threat to peace in Africa if any country sets out to undermine the authority of the properly chosen leaders of another state with a view of imposing political union" (Yoh 2008, 135–36). It was as a result of the charged political tension that the gradualist approach to African unity in terms of economic and cultural cooperation at the subregional level was endorsed as the most feasible path to integration on the continent. Consequently, the expectation was that integration schemes in Africa would be a replica of European integration, which is modeled on classical and neoclassical frameworks. Whereas classical approaches, such as functionalism, primarily focused on how to maintain order in international relations after various catastrophic wars in Europe, it is the neoclassical approaches, including neofunctionalism and regional economic integration theory, that provided the impetus for postcolonial integration schemes in East and West Africa.

Neofunctionalism is primarily a response to the need to relate and apply functionalist ideas to the integration experiences in Western Europe and other regions (Senghor 1990, 20). Functionalist ideas were popularized by David Mitrany in his 1943 essay, "A Working Peace System." In this essay, Mitrany argued that political division was the main cause of conflict between states and that peace and state welfare could be achieved through cooperation among states. He called this the "pragmatic functional approach," whereby states would gradually build peace by ascribing authority to activities in areas of agreement rather than making treaties to ensure national coexistence. The key assumption of this approach was that the successes of joint activities would lead to greater cooperation and the creation of a "working peace." Since the "working peace" was to be based on functional cooperation, it would begin not from political activities but from low-key economic and social tasks such as the harmonization of labor standards, the provision of common services, and the joint management of scarce resources. Through such functional development, the system would gradually set up a solid foundation for political cooperation and, hence, international peace.

In spite of Mitrany's compelling arguments, functionalism was deemed an inadequate approach to regional integration for two reasons. First, it described the steps that states should undertake in order to achieve peaceful coexistence without specifying fully the conditions necessary for such an achievement. Second, its rationalization of integration as a peace project was not compelling. This is because there are numerous examples of states that have either joined or opted out of regional agreements for reasons that are not related to the achievement of peace. As a result, neofunctionalism was developed as an improved analytical framework for the study of regional integration (Mattli 1999, 22–23; Schulz et al. 2001, 9).

Neofunctionalism was first systematically analyzed and elaborated on by Ernst Haas in his pioneer study *The Uniting of Europe* (1958). It is in this work and later writings that Haas developed a framework for neofunctionalism that explains how and why political actors from several distinct states shift their "loyalties, expectations and political activities towards a new and larger center whose institutions possess or demand jurisdiction over the pre-existing state" (Mattli 1999, 24). According to the framework, the integration process is controlled by the activities of two categories of actors. The first category is made up of supranational regional institutions that operate from above the state to promote integration through their official structures and activities. The second category is made up of actors who operate from below the state, including political parties and interest groups through which citizens' interests can be collectively expressed. Within this system, governments are perceived as the custodians of ultimate political power who can accept, bypass, and disregard or sabotage the decisions made by supranational regional institutions. Nevertheless, because of actors' interests within the region, governments may opt to give in to the decisions made by supranational institutions.

Another important analytical attribute in neofunctionalism is the concept of interest politics. Unlike functionalism, which evaluated the harmonization of actors' interests as unselfish acts of good will, neofunctionalism postulates that the process of regional integration is motivated by selfish interests and aims. Therefore, the success of the integration process is ultimately dependant on whether actors' interests can be better achieved within the structures of a supranational authority. Neofunctionalism also elaborates on the processes that facilitate integration: namely, functional spillover, political spillover, and upgrading of common interests. The underlying hypothesis of functional spillover is that sector integration occurs when different segments of a modern industrial economy are highly interdependent such that overall goals can only be achieved if any action in one sector of the economy is accompanied by actions in other sectors of the economy. Political spillover refers to the incremental shifting of expectations, the changing values, and coalescing at the supranational level of state interests that may occur in response to sectoral integration. The upgrading of common interests occurs when member states experience challenges as they seek common policy. States overcome this challenge by using the services of an institutionalized autonomous mediator to seek compromises that strengthen the power base of the supranational institution (Mattli 1999, 24–26; Schulz et al. 2001, 9).

The functionalist approach to economic integration is usually reinforced by regional economic integration theory, which looks into the welfare effects of integration in terms of trade creation, trade diversion, and terms of trade. The first elaborate account on the welfare of integration was made by Jacob Viner in 1950. Viner stated that the creation of a customs union involves the removal of intra-area trade barriers and the equalization of tariffs on imports from states that are not members of the union. There are at least two possible outcomes of the creation of a union. The first is that it might result in trade creation because the output of insufficient industries would be replaced by cheaper imports from more efficient industries within the union. Trade creation is desirable because it results in lower prices that increase the consumer's surplus and permit production gains. The second is that a customs union may result in trade diversion. This would occur if suppliers outside the integrated area choose not to supply their products to the union because of the competitive disadvantage in prices after the creation of the union. Trade diversion is undesirable if it reduces a country's economic welfare by discouraging imports from outside the union and encouraging imports from less efficient sources of supply within the integrated area (Mattli 1999, 31–32).

Two additional arguments have been used by economists to further explain why states are motivated to create customs unions. According to the first argument, states that produce competitive goods with high price-elasticities of demand may find the terms of trade creation, as members of a customs union, preferable to welfare loss as a result of trade diversion. The second motivating factor is related to efforts by states to boost and protect domestic industrial and agricultural production without going against international trading agreements (Mattli 1999, 33–34).

Because of its focus on gradual economic cooperation as opposed to swift political unification, the functionalist approach was quickly adopted by postcolonial regional schemes on the continent, including the East African Community (EAC). However, the enthusiasm that accompanied the creation of functionalist regional bodies waned dramatically as they failed to live up to grand expectations of economic growth and poverty reduction. In fact, since the 1980s, there has been a plethora of criticism about regionalization processes in Africa, with a majority of the critics arguing that the blatant mimicking of dominant Eurocentric integration models is the key reason for the dismal performance of African regional organizations (see Muchie et al. 2006). Other scholars have also cited concurrent membership in multiple regional organizations, lack of revenue, poor infrastructure, security issues, and lack of political will as additional shortcomings facing regional integration institutions on the continent (see Economic Commission for Africa 2010; Omoro 2008, 150–58).

Although these factors are important, the disappointing performance of regional integration in Africa can also be attributed to the transplantation and prolongation of colonial and Cold War state-centric strategies in regionalization processes on the continent. Consequently, whereas international relations is abreast with changes and opportunities that have been brought about as a result of the tectonic shift from bipolar to multipolar politics, most regional organizations in Africa, including the EAC, have yet to embrace opportunities offered by the evolving multipolar international system. Their failure and reluctance to do so is a key contributing factor to their poor performance in international relations in the twenty-first century.

The Colonial Paradox in Regional Integration

According to Kasaija (2006), the process of regional integration in East Africa was advertently set in motion in 1895 when Britain embarked on the construction of the Kenya–Uganda railway to facilitate the transportation of raw materials to British industries. By 1927, Britain and Germany perceived East Africa as one economic unit and sought to coordinate it as a regional bloc. They did this through the creation of the East African Common Market, which stipulated the terms of a customs arrangement between British East Africa and German East Africa. Within this common market, the three East African states shared a common currency, a joint income tax board, among other institutions and structural facilities. Several commissions were also appointed to explore the possibilities of East African federation. They included the Ormsby-Gore Commission in 1924, the Hilton-Young Commission in 1927, and the Joint Selection Committee of both Houses of the UK Parliament in 1931 (Kasaija 2006). As independence loomed, various actors were optimistic that after slightly over sixty years of successful integration, the region had evolved to a level of functionality that made political unity inevitable. Indeed, the mood among the parliaments of the three countries at the time was for the countries of Tanganyika, Kenya, Uganda, and Zanzibar to federate immediately after they had attained independence. These strong reactions were captured in March 1963, when President Nyerere declared that "a federation of at least Kenya, Uganda and Tanganyika should be comparatively easy to achieve. We already have a common market, and run many services through the Common Services Organization—which has its own Central Legislative Assembly and an executive composed of the Prime Ministers of the three states. This is the nucleus from which a federation is the natural growth" (Kasaija 2006, 3). These sentiments were strengthened through the creation of two key committees. The first was a Working Party Committee on East Africa Federation that drafted a constitution for the region. The second committee, referred to as the East African Common Services Organization (EACSO), was created in 1961 to review the structures of East African cooperation with a view of maintaining the momentum of the integration process in the postcolonial era (Kasaija 2009, 4).

In spite of the optimism that East Africa was on its way to establishing the first postcolonial political federation in Africa, it soon became clear that colonial practices had drastically altered the essence of regionalism in East Africa. Paradoxically, while the East African states had inherited an organization that appeared to have sound functional organs that would facilitate deeper integration, they had also inherited norms, values, and practices that were incompatible with the process of regionalization. In fact, colonial state policies that were manifested through the indiscriminate treatment of indigenous populations, the privileging of some groups over others, the uneven distribution of wealth, and the formation of nonparticipatory governmental systems were replicated at the regional level. Therefore, the East African regionalization processes, throughout the colonial period, were dominated by centralized autocratic structures that were skewed to serve the interests of the settler community who were the political elite. These structures were inherited by African leaders and their advisors, who proceeded to entrench the culture and structures of autocratic processes, leaving little room for grassroots participation or bottom-up feedback through nonelitist actors. Consequently, the EAC was "owned" by the region's heads of states whose personal differences, as opposed to the interests of the region's populace, determined the fate of the EAC.

Indeed, these differences were played out during the Cold War. During this time, the alignment of Tanzania and, to a much lesser extent, Uganda, to the pro-communist East at a time when Kenya identified itself with the pro-capitalist West, to a large extent led to the eventual collapse of the East African Community (EAC) in 1977 (Delupis 1970; Mitelman 1975; Best 2008, 417).

Regionalism in an Age of Multipolarity

Regionalization in East Africa reemerged in the wake of the end of the Cold War with the revival of the EAC in July 2000, which somehow coninicided with the emerging intellectual focus on new regionalism. This new approach is characterized by several changes. While earlier studies such as those by Ernst Haas (1964) and Leon Lindberg (1966) focused on formal state-initiated regionalization, new regionalism, which includes studies by Michael Schultz et al. (2001), and Hettne and Söderbaum (2002), has increased in scope, diversity, and fluidity by addressing the role of nonstate actors in regionalization processes. These nonstate stakeholders comprise members of the civil society that include, but are not limited to, community-based organizations (CBOs), nongovernmental organizations (NGOs), business organizations, trade unions, and the academic community.

Furthermore, unlike previous studies that fell within the framework of a bipolar world, recent studies factor in the multipolar transformation that is taking place in international politics (Schultz et al. 2001, 3; Hettne et al. 2002, 32–33; Katzenstein 2002, 104–5). This transformation has led to the assimilation of new regionalism and security studies (see Krishner 1998, 64; Fawcett et al. 1998, 1–6). Within this context, state and nonstate actors have been ushered into a new era of freedom that enables them to actively form new patterns of interregional alliances in international relations. The impetus for the shift in international relations is, to a large extent, driven by a broadly liberalizing international trading environment that has made it necessary for geopolitical systems to adapt to the rise of emerging giants from the developing world (O'Rourke 2009, 26).

The multipolar dispensation in international relations has also challenged traditional functionalist approaches to regional integration. Within the framework of New Regionalism Theory (NRT), regionalism in the twenty-first century is conceived as a worldwide phenomenon that reflects the deeper interdependence of today's global political economy and the relationship between globalization and regionalization. It argues that although previous literature on interdependence, such as those by Keohane and Nye (1998), and Keohane (2009), correctly identify the simultaneous involvement of state and nonstate actors at the global, regional, national, and local levels, they fail to coherently explain how the world order transformation and the emergence of a multilevel pattern of governance makes regionalization processes possible and necessary (Hettne and Söderbaum 2002, 33–35).

In an attempt to bridge this gap, NRT uses global social theory, social constructivism, and comparative regional studies as its metatheoretical building blocks to explain the essence of regionalism. Through the use of global social theory, NRT examines regionalization schemes not only as activities that transcend state-centric structure but also as social processes that are delinked from national space and are affected by globalization. Indeed, Susan Strange (1999) argued that analysis in international relations should not be bogged down by attempts to defend or excuse the "Westfailure" system. NRT combines social theory with social constructivism. The latter is a critique of neorealist and neoliberal institutionalism. It criticizes these theories because they focus on the pursuit of power and wealth by states without factoring in how ideas influence and transform international relations. Constructivists argue that political communities are not exogenously given but constructed by historically contingent interactions. These interactions are done in the pursuit of interests that are derived from the ideas of actors, in particular, social structures. Understanding how interests, identities, and social structures change over time enables one to discover the emergence of new forms of cooperation and community (Wendt 1999, 92–138; Barnett 2008, 160–73). Therefore, regionalization is socially constructed by those who participate in it, those who are affected by it, as well as those who observe and describe it. In this sense, regions do not develop through natural processes but rather through processes of conscious or unconscious construction, deconstruction, and reconstruction by actors. The behavior of actors in these processes is also shaped by their norms and beliefs, as well as their reactions to challenges imposed by the actions of others and the changes in their social environment (Schultz et al. 2001, 14; Hettne and Söderbaum 2002, 35–37). For instance, during the 1960s and early 1970s, African elites, the key actors in the regionalization process, based the EAC's construction on inherited colonial structures that were designed to consolidate power and maintain the status quo. Hence, the perception was that the EAC was "owned" by heads of state who made decisions about the regionalization process based on their personal misconceptions rather than the needs of the region's people.

Lastly, proponents of NRT, including Axline (1994), and Hettne and Söderbaum (2002) argue that the understanding of regional integration is enriched through methods that incorporate comparative studies. Hence, in a nutshell, regionalization processes in the twenty-first century can no longer, and should not, take place within state-centric confines.

The EAC Framework for Nonstate Actors

In Africa, the involvement of nonstate actors in regionalization processes is largely derived from two models. The first is the United Nations Economic and Social Council's (UN-ECOSOC) statute for nongovernmental organizations created through Resolution 1996/31. Established on 26 July 1996, the statute builds on the first UN consultative framework that was created in 1950 (United Nations 1996). The second is the African Union's African Charter for Popular Participation in Development and Transformation (AU-ACPPDT), which was formulated in Arusha, Tanzania, in February 1990 after the International Conference on Popular Participation in Recovery and Development Process in Africa (OAU Secretariat 1990). Both the UN-ECOSOC statute and the AU-ACPPDT provide models on how international governmental organizations (IGOs) and regional organizations can enhance the participation of nonstate actors in their activities. The frameworks not only lay out guidelines on how organized representation of citizens in decision making through nonstate actors such as civil society organizations can be enhanced, but also suggests ways in which capacities and skills can be shared and harnessed between nonstate actors and regional organizations.

Borrowing from the UN and AU frameworks, the heads of government of Kenya, Uganda, and Tanzania revived the defunct EAC by ratifying the East African Community Treaty (EACT) on 30 November 1999. The EACT, which came into force on 7 July 2001, maps out an ambitious plan to create an East African political federation that will be preceded by a common market and a monetary union. To this extent, the EAC member states established a customs union in 2005. This was followed by the signing of a common market protocol in November 2009 between the EAC's old members Kenya, Uganda, and Tanzania, and its new members Rwanda and Burundi. The EACT also opened up various avenues for the participation of nonstate actors in the regionalization process through four key provisions. Article 5.3 (g) provides for the participation of civil society by stating that "the Community will ensure, inter alia, the enhancement and strengthening of partnerships with civil society, so as to achieve sustainable socio-economic and political development" (EAC Secretariat 2001). Through this article, the EACT recognizes that lack of participation of nonstate actors in the integration process was an impediment to integration efforts in the past. Support for the participation of the civil society is further captured in Articles 127.1 and 127.3, which respectively provide that "the Partner States agree to provide an enabling environment for the participation of the civil society in the development activities within the Community, and... the Partner States undertake to promote a continuous dialogue with civil society at both the national and the Community level" (EAC Secretariat 2001). The involvement of the private sector is pledged in Article 127.4, which states that "the Secretary General shall provide the forum for consultations between civil society organizations, the private sector, other interest groups and appropriate institutions of the Community" (EAC Secretariat 2001).

In line with the above statutory provisions, the EAC Secretariat has granted Observer Status to members of the civil society and business community in the region by allowing them to have representatives in selected meetings and committees. This provision enables nonstate actors to participate, upon invitation, in specified meetings of the Permanent Tripartite Commission or any other organs and institutions of the EAC without a right to vote (EAC Secretariat 2002). The provisions that provide for Observer Status are in line with the tenets of neofunctionalism, which recognizes the role of nonstate actors in various functional areas in the integration process. In his study of the EAC, Teun van Dijk (2003) identified key functional areas through which the involvement of nonstate actors could be enhanced and sustained. These areas include the preparation, operationalization, implementation, monitoring, and evaluation of policies.

In spite of the provisions for the participation of nonstate actors in the EAC, only a handful of organizations have been granted Observer Status because of the restrictive nature of the rules that govern the process. Indeed, the rules stipulate that organizations must demonstrate that they have been registered and have had an active track record of operations in all EAC member states for a minimum period of three years (EAC Secretariat 2001). Furthermore, organizations that have been privy to the process experience a number of challenges. This is because their participation in the functional processes of the EAC are restricted by Articles 6 and 7 of the EACT, which state that all organizations that have been granted Observer Status have to, among other things, accept the fundamental principles underlying the EAC and structure their objectives in line with the operational principles of the EAC. As a result, neither civil society nor the business community can fully vet the decisions made by the organization. This goes against the current trends in new regionalism that place emphasis on the democratization of integration structures such that nonstate actors are not simply invited to join existing state-dominated regional arrangements but to participate in their democratic transformation (Muchie et al. 2006, 10).

In the light of this, the goals and objectives of the EAC cannot be achieved and sustained within the old functionalist framework. Diversity in the regionalization process through the participation of nonstate actors will promote advocacy, dialogue, and transparency, thus contributing to the success of the EAC. Hence, the power distribution among the units forming the integrative power has to be renegotiated. If this is done, the power to set agendas, define issues, and determine the path will no longer be the monopoly of governments, but will belong to a new partnership of people with governments.

A Critique of the EAC Framework for Nonstate Actors

Due to the limitations imposed by the rules and procedural practices of the EACT, various attempts have been made to create a consultative status as an alternative to granting Observer Status to nonstate actors. These attempts are in line with statutory provisions in the EACT that mandate the Secretary General to oversee the creation of a consultative structure that "will provide the forum for consultations between the private sector, civil society organizations, other interest groups and appropriate institutions of the Community" (EAC Secretariat 2001).

One such attempt led to the establishment of the East African Civil Society Organizations Forum (EACSOF) with a steering committee made up of representatives who are members of civil society organizations from the five EAC states. To this end, three key workshops for civil society organizations of the EAC were held in 2005, 2007, and 2009. The key objective of these workshops was to facilitate the involvement of civil society in the operations of the EAC. In spite of the efforts that have been made so far, the process of mapping a way forward that will enable the EACSOF to become fully functional has been marred by suspicions between state and nonstate actors. While state actors are concerned about the sources of influence and agendas of nonstate actors, nonstate actors perceive state actors as entities that must be taken to task over policies and activities related to human rights and governance. In addition to this, the success of the EACSOF has been affected by financial constraints (see Kinyua 2009).

In addition to structural challenges, nonstate actors are faced with the challenge of operating in an environment that has a miasma of political leaders who either relapse into old practices of neopatrimonial politics or put up barriers that curtail political pluralism. These trends are a threat to integration in the region as elite political actors are able to manipulate the decision-making organs of the regional organization and enact policies that may be detrimental to constituents at the grassroots level. This trend has been witnessed in the EAC through the controversial negotiations of preferential trade agreements (PTAs) between the regional body and key developed states. Although the PTAs are supposed to enhance trade between developed and developing states, these agreements are often used to discriminate against some of the latter's most competitive products through the use of nontariff barriers. For instance, the United States' PTA initiative, the African Growth and Opportunity Act (AGOA), excludes exported tobacco and peanuts from Africa, yet these products are part of the industrial crops that are produced within the East African region.

Currently, questions have been raised about the EAC's willingness to enter into an economic partnership agreement (EPA) with the European Union (EU). EPA is an instrument of trade partnership required by the Cotonou Agreement to replace the trade component of Lomé IV. The Cotonou Agreement, signed in 2000, is a partnership pact between the EU and the African, Caribbean, and Pacific Group of States (ACP). Before the Cotonou Agreement, European-ACP trade relations were facilitated by the Lomé Convention. The Lomé Convention facilitated ACP trade access to Europe in preference to goods from other countries. It was renewed and renegotiated successively through four agreements—Lomé I, Lomé II, Lomé III, and Lomé IV. The Cotonou Agreement, therefore, is the successor to Lomé IV (see Woolcock 2007). The key objective of EPA is to have closer economic ties with developing states by encouraging regional blocs, such as the EAC, to liberalize the economies of their member states. Indeed, the EAC has signed an interim agreement with EPA that gives preferential treatment to consumer goods from the EU. Whereas this may provide consumers in the EAC with a greater variety of goods at lower costs, it will threaten the growth of manufacturing industries across the region. For instance, according to the terms of the agreement, its full implementation will be realized when EU imports to the EAC rise from 65 percent to 82.6 percent by 2033 (see European Commission 2009; Flint 2009, 79–82). The EPA framework is, therefore, perceived by nonstate actors as a diktat rather than an agreement.

Notwithstanding the difficulties that have been experienced by nonstate actors in their quest to become participants rather than observers in the regionalization process, it is possible for them to become key players alongside state actors in the EAC. One strategy that may be used to ameliorate the situation is the reconfiguration of the structures of the EACSOF so that they may resemble those of the West African Civil Society Forum (WACSOF). WACSOF, which was created in 2003, is an autonomous civil society initiative that is recognized by members of the Economic Community of West African States (ECOWAS). WACSOF's key strength, which could be adopted by the EACSOF, is that it was established as an autonomous body that is formally recognized, but not entrenched, within the organs of ECOWAS. It can therefore freely give recommendations that are processed through the council of ministers so as to influence decisions made during the meetings of the Summit of Heads of State of ECOWAS partners (WACSOF 2010).

Nonstate actors in the region can also use alternative avenues within the framework of the multipolar environment in international relations to enhance their role and participation in the regionalization process. One of the most effective avenues through which nonstate actors have been empowered to air their views is the use of new horizontal communication channels that permit the exchanges of technical knowledge and capacity building. Within the context of regional integration, horizontal communication channels refer to avenues that make state borders more porous and allow nonstate actors to directly interact with each other. Horizontal communication has been facilitated by the EACT through the milestones that have been made in regional integration between 2005 and 2008. These milestones include the introduction of a customs union in 2005, the endorsement of free movement in 2008 and the establishment of the Protocol for a Common Market that came into effect in 2008. These channels have been used by the business community to make cross-border investments in the region, which in 2010 was estimated to have slightly over 116 million people with a GDP of US$31.1 billion (Alvensleben and Kurz 2010, 9).

The horizontal communication channels have also enabled nonstate actors from the developing world to have a unified voice against unfair international trading policies. Indeed, this method was used to lobby against trade and intellectual property rights (TIPRs) that would have put the lives of millions of HIV-infected persons in Africa at risk by banning the manufacture of generic drugs. In this regard, a similar strategy can be employed by the business community in East Africa to voice their concerns over the EU-EAC EPA.

In spite of the milestones that have been gained through the use of horizontal communication channels by the business community in the regionalization process, there are two key challenges that need to be addressed. First, although regional trade has substantially grown since the existence of the customs union in 2005, trading across the region is often undermined by tariff disputes. For instance, some of the industrial groups in some of the member states actively lobby for protectionist barriers to be put up against goods from other EAC member states. Examples include lobbying by Ugandan manufacturers for tariff barriers against raw materials from Kenya. This is because Ugandan manufacturers prefer to buy raw materials from other players in the world market at cheaper prices. Second, EAC member states have created nontariff barriers in attempts to protect their nascent industries. Nontariff barriers are defined as quantitative restrictions and specific limitations that act as obstacles to trade; they appear in the form of rules, regulations, and laws that have a negative impact on trade. In East Africa, nontariff barriers are usually camouflaged under the umbrella of "Nationalistic Compensation Measures." They include immigration procedures that curtail movement within the region, bureaucratic licensing procedures, weighbridges, and police roadblocks, among others (see Alvensleben and Kurz 2010, 10).

The foundations for regional integration in East Africa were laid when the colonial powers in the region established various political, social, and economic structures to facilitate the management of their colonies. For slightly over sixty years, Britain, and to a lesser extent Germany, structured integration in the region on the functionalist European model, which favored economic integration as a prerequisite for political unity. Indeed, at the eve of independence, the East African region had a common market, a nucleus through which services within the region were jointly coordinated, as well as a central legislative assembly with an executive composed of the prime ministers of the three states. The expectation, therefore, was that postcolonial states in East Africa would easily gravitate towards each other and create a political federation of at least Kenya, Uganda, and Tanganyika. Contrary to these expectations, the East African region quickly disintegrated after independence and was officially dismantled in 1977. Although many authors cited ideological differences and the lack of political will as reasons why the EAC collapsed, its rapid demise could also be attributed to the state-centric and patrimonial norms and practices that were inherited from the colonial masters by the African elites.

Whereas regional integration reemerged with the ratification of the East African Community Treaty in 1999, I am of the view that it is unlikely for the EAC to succeed if the state-centric and anachronistic practices that are part of the colonial legacy are not dismantled. Two key areas that were cited as challenges that have contributed to the perpetuation of state-centric regionalism in East Africa are the EACT provision on Observer Status and elitist neopatrimonial political strategies that have permeated the process of regionalization in East Africa. It was noted that although the provision for the Observer Status was established as a framework that would facilitate the participation of nonstate actors, the criteria and rules that govern the implementation of the framework are limiting to both civil society and the business community.

It is not sufficient for the promulgation of the EACT rules to demonstrate an impetus towards greater participation by nonstate actors. Instead, there should be deliberate attempts by state actors to dismantle structures that stifle the involvement of nonstate actors. The first and most important step towards the dismantling of these structures would be the democratization of the regionalization process such that nonstate actors in the region become facilitators, with similar privileges as state actors, rather than observers of the regionalization process.

In addition to efforts by state actors to restructure the process, nonstate actors should initiate mechanisms that will facilitate their involvement in the regionalization process. For instance, regional bodies for nonstate participation, such as EACSOF, can be strengthened if its members supplement the funding that the organization gets from EAC governments by lobbying for funding from external sources. Nonstate actors should also continue to make use of various horizontal channels of communication that have emerged as a result of multipolar politics in the twenty-first century.

References

Alvensleben, Busso, and Sonya Kurz. 2010. *Business Environment Reform in Regional Integration through Public and Private Sector Institutions in Southern and East Africa*. Accessed 28 January 2011. www.businessenvironment.org/dyn/be.

Axline, Andrew. 1994. *The Political Economy of Regional Cooperation: Comparative Case Studies*. London: Associated University Press.

Barnett, Michael. 2008. "Social Constructivism." In *The Globalization of World Politics: An Introduction to International Relations*, edited by John Baylis and Steve Smith, 160–73. 4th. ed. Oxford: Oxford University Press.

Best, Edward. 2008. "Regionalism in International Affairs." In *The Globalization of World Politics: An Introduction to International Relations*, edited by John Baylis and Steve Smith, 44–56. 4th ed. Oxford: Oxford University Press.

Delupis, Detter. 1970. *The East African Community and Common Market*. London: Longman.

Dijk, Teun van. 2003. *Civil Society Participation within the East African Community*. Arusha, Tanzania: EAC.

EAC Secretariat. 2001. *The Treaty for the Establishment of the East African Community.* Accessed 28 January 2011. http://www.eac.int/treaty/.

EAC Secretariat. 2002. *Procedure for Granting Observer Status in the East African Community.* Accessed 28 January 2011. www.eac.int/advisory-opinions/doc.

Economic Commission for Africa. 2010. *Assessing Regional Integration in Africa IV: Enhancing InterAfrican Trade.* Accessed 15 October 2010. http://siteresources.worldbank.org/INTAFRREGINICOO/Resources/1587517-1271810608103/UNECA-4th-Africa-RI-Assessment-May2010.pdf.

European Commission. 2009. "The Fact Sheet on the Interim Economic Partnership Agreement: The East African Community (EAC)." Accessed 28 January 2011. http://trade.ec.europa.eu/doclib/docs/2009/january/tradoc_142194.pdf.

Fawcett, Louise, and Andrew Hurrell. 1998. "Introduction." In *Regionalism in World Politics: Regional Organizations and International Order*, edited by Louise Fawcett and Andrew Hurrell, 1–12. Oxford: Oxford University Press.

Flint, Adrian. 2010. "The End of a 'Special Relationship'? The New EU–ACP Economic Partnership Agreements." *Review of African Political Economy* 119: 79–92.

Haas, Ernst. 1958. *The Uniting of Europe: Political, Social and Economical Forces, 1950–1957.* Stanford, CA: Stanford University Press.

———. 1964. *Beyond the Nation State: Functionalism and International Organization.* Stanford, CA: Stanford University Press.

Hanchard, Michael. 2010. "Perspective Contours of Black Political Thought: An Introduction and Perspective." *Political Theory* 38, no. 4: 510–36.

Hettne, Bjorn, Andras Inotai, and Osvaldo Sunkel, eds. 2000. *The New Regionalism and the Future of Security and Development.* Basingstoke: Macmillan.

Hettne, Bjorn, and Fredrick Söderbaum. 2002. "Theorizing the Rise of Regionness." In *New Regionalism in the Global Political Economy: Theories and Cases*, edited by Shaun Breslin, Christopher Hughes, Nicola Phillips, and Ben Rosamond, 32–45. London: Routledge.

Kasaija, Phillip. 2006. *Fast Tracking East African Federation: Asking the Difficult Questions.* Paper prepared and presented at a Development Network of Indigenous Voluntary Associations (DENIVA) Public Dialogue on Fast Tracking East African Federation Dialogue, Hotel Equatoria Kampala, 24 November 2006.

Katzenstein, Peter. 2002. "Regionalism in Asia." In *New Regionalism in the Global Political Economy: Theories and Cases*, edited by Shaun Breslin, Christopher Hughes, Nicola Phillips, and Ben Rosamond. London: Routledge, 46–65.

Keohane, Robert. 2009. "The Old IPE and the New." *Review of International Political Economy* 16, no. 1: 34–46.

Keohane, Robert, and Joseph Nye. 1998. "Power and Interdependence in the Information Age." *Foreign Affairs* 77, no. 5: 81–94.

Lindberg, Leon. 1966. *The Political Dynamics of European Economic Integration.* Stanford, CA: Stanford University Press.

Mattli, Walter. 1999. *The Logic of Regional Integration: Europe and Beyond.* Cambridge: Cambridge University Press.

Mitelman, James. 1975. *Ideology and Politics in Uganda: From Obote to Amin.* Ithaca, NY: Cornell University Press.

Muchie, Mammo, Adam Habib, and Vishnu Padayachee. 2006. "African Integration and Civil Society: The Case of the African Union." *Transformation* 6, no. 1: 3–24.

OAU Secretariat. 1990. "African Union's African Charter for Popular Participation in Development and Transformation." Accessed 28 January 2011. http://www.apic.igc.org/./charter3.htm.

Omoro, Mariam. 2008. *Organizational Effectiveness of Regional Integration Institutions: A Case Study of the East African Community*, M. Phil. Dissertation, Pretoria, University of South Africa.

O'Rourke, Kevin. 2009. *Politics and Trade: Lessons from Past Globalizations*. Brussels: Bruegel Essay and Lecture Series.

Sbragia, Alberta. 2008. "Review Article: Comparative Regionalism: What Might It Be?" *Common Market Studies* 46: 29–46.

Schulz, Michael, Fredrick Söderbaum, and Joakim Öjendal, eds. 2001. *Regionalization in a Globalizing World: A Comprehensive Perspective on Forms, Actors and Processes*. London: Zed Books.

Senghor, Jeggan. 1990. "Theoretical Foundations for Regional Integration in Africa: An Overview." In *Regional Integration in Africa: Unfinished Agenda*, edited by P. Anyang' Nyong'o, 15–22. Nairobi: African Academy of Sciences.

Strange, Susan. 1999. "The Westfailure System." *Review of International Studies* 25, no. 3: 34–54.

Turner, Susan. 2009. "Russia, China and a Multipolar World Order: The Danger in the Undefined." *Asian Perspective* 33, no.1: 159–84.

United Nations. 1996. NGO-Related Resolution 1996/31. Accessed 28 January 2011. http://www.unog.ch/80256EDD006B8954/(httpAssets)/C7E95770B97058CEC1256F5D003D82C3/$file/Eres96-31.pdf.

WACSOF. 2010. *The West African Civil Society Forum*. Accessed 28 January 2011. www.wacsof.net/inde.php?option=com_content.

Wendt, Alexander. 1999. *Social Theory of International Politics*. Cambridge: Cambridge University Press.

Woolcock, Stephen. 2007. "European Union Policy towards Free Trade Agreements." ECIPE Working Paper, no. 03/2007. Accessed 28 January 2011. www.ecipe.org/./PDF.

Yoh, John. 2008. *The Institutional Role of the Organization of African Unity in Conflict Resolution in Africa*. PhD diss., Pretoria, University of South Africa.

PART II
CASE STUDIES OF CONFLICT AND
PEACEBUILDING IN THE GREAT LAKES

4 Historical Dynamics of the Northern Uganda Conflict

A Longitudinal Struggle for Nation Building

Elias Omondi Opongo

THE NORTHERN UGANDA conflict can be characterized as part of a longitudinal struggle for nation building that both precedes and postdates the twenty-two-year civil war between the Lord's Resistance Army (LRA) and Government of Uganda (GOU). Although military interventions and peace talks (most recently in 2006–8) have resulted in a ceasefire and relative stability, the war cost close to 200,000 lives and dramatically increased poverty and insecurity. The northern Acholi region remains the most affected by both the conflict and perfunctory postconflict rehabilitation measures. It also faces the challenge of designing an effective transitional justice framework that reconciles the model of retributive justice favored by the International Criminal Court (ICC) and models of restorative justice based on cultural mechanisms supported by some members of local communities and nongovernmental organizations (NGOs). Northern Uganda has therefore been considered both one of the worst humanitarian crises in the world, as well as a laboratory for postconflict transitional justice and peacebuilding.

Despite the degree of international attention currently focused on northern Uganda and the appearance of some important critical analyses (Branch 2010; Finnström 2008), many have persisted in characterizing (and politicizing) the conflict as a north-south struggle for power with profound ethnic dimensions. I argue, however, that the concept of nation building represents a more effective framework for analyzing the conflict and its aftermath. Four major factors are especially crucial.

First, this is not simply a regional conflict between the largely Acholi-based LRA and the GOU, but reflects a much deeper, historical tension between competing ethnonationalisms, or the promotion of ethnic identities, and an overarching Ugandan national identity. The creation of the Ugandan state, as in most African countries, was hurriedly undertaken as a conglomeration of ethnic groups that were themselves constructed incongruently during the precolonial, colonial, and postindependence periods. This has led to persistent tensions between ethnonationalist and nationalist dynamics. Such tensions have been exacerbated by a second factor: namely, militarization and the proliferation of small arms and light weapons (SALW) in the region. Third, persistent conflicts *among* ethnonational populations have weakened internal nation-building efforts and destabilized neighboring regions. This implies that peace negotiations in Uganda, even when deemed successful, have largely failed to address the historical and political-economic factors at the root of the conflict and their cross-border or regional ramifications. Peace negotiations have mainly focused on ending the militarized conflict between the LRA and GOU without fully addressing broader implications. Finally, the fourth crucial factor relates to a critical assessment of how international intervention and especially the role of the ICC has precipitated debates about restorative and retributive justice and how to reconcile local, national, and international models of postconflict transformation.

The LRA Insurgency

The LRA has claimed over the years to be fighting against the marginalization of northern Uganda, particularly the Acholi people, while the GOU dismisses the rebels as a disorganized group without any agenda (Finnström 2008). Historically, the conflict is one among many insurgencies since Uganda's independence in 1962. President Yoweri Museveni came to power in 1986 after National Resistance Movement (NRM) rebels overthrew the government. However, since then Museveni's government has been faced with multiple insurgencies, the longest of which has been the conflict with the LRA.

The LRA has fought the government for more than twenty-two years and "has become infamous for massacres, maiming, and the forced recruitment of thousands of Acholi, many of them children" (Branch 2007, 180). Hence, the conflict's psychosocial impact on the local population has been immense and has further impoverished the northern region. The social fabric has been weakened and Acholi communities divided by the violent activities of the rebels. According to a 2007 World Development Report entitled "Development and the Next Generation," more than 66,000 children have been abducted in the last two decades of LRA insurgency. Among these, two-thirds "are severely beaten, a fifth are forced to kill and nearly 10 percent are forced to murder a family member or friend to bind them to the group" (World Bank 2007, 82).

The resistance in northern Uganda began in August 1986 when the Uganda Peoples Democratic Movement and Army (UPDM/A) launched a struggle for multiparty democracy. Also in late 1986, the Holy Spirit Movement (HSM) and the Holy Spirit Mobile Force (HSMF), led by a spiritual and charismatic figure named Alice

Lakwena, emerged. She had a large following in the north and advanced her army towards the capital Kampala in the south, but was defeated in 1987 in Jinja town by the GOU forces. In the same year, the UPDF/A entered into an agreement with the government to end the conflict, but some of the discontented soldiers joined the HSM and eventually became the LRA, led by Joseph Kony.

The LRA maintains that their aim is to overthrow the government and institute a system of governance based on the Biblical Ten Commandments (Oola 2008, 67). They also claim to be fighting for the end to political and economic marginalization of the north by the southern government, a return to multiparty politics, the introduction of constitutional federalism, and the promotion of national and regional peace and security (Finnström 2008, 122). However, the spiritual dimension of the conflict has dominated most of the analysis on northern Uganda. Finnström (2008, 115) points out that the overemphasis on the religious aspect of the LRA's objectives has marginalized other important and legitimate social, political, and economic concerns. Chabal and Daloz (1999, 86) assert that the LRA does not have a strong political agenda to justify their cause, concluding that the crisis is much more humanitarian than political. Moreover, while the LRA may be dominated by members of the Acholi ethnic group, it is not an ethnic conflict. Extreme violence on the northern population through abductions, killings, and stealing has compromised the LRA cause among none so much as the Acholi themselves, and in 2004 led to the indictment order on the rebel leaders by the International Criminal Court (ICC).

I contend that while the conflict in northern Uganda emerged as a resistance to military repression by the NRM and later the GOU forces, it gradually developed into a political agenda. As I have stated elsewhere, changes in events, historical perspectives and leadership have engendered new agendas in civil conflicts (Opongo 2006, 76–77). What began as resistance to Museveni's rule has developed into a claim for equitable distribution of the national resources and an end to the marginalization of the north. The ugly face of the LRA tactics that target the northern population has also meant that the real causes of the LRA-GOU conflict have remained unclear in recent years. A historical and political analysis of the conflict in terms of larger problems of nation building and competing ethnonationalist and nationalist dynamics, and how these relate to contemporary peacebuilding initiatives, provides a more thorough understanding of the nature of the conflict in northern Uganda.

Nation Building and the Colonial Period

Ethnic polarization and ethnonationalist tendencies have dominated both the LRA-GOU conflict and most analyses of it. In fact, it has often been referred to as a north-south conflict (Finnström 2008) or a Nilotic-Bantu conflict. These patterns date to the colonial era, when British attempts to conglomerate different ethnic groups into one national entity induced even greater fragmentation as groups played to the "ethnic differentiation constructs" (Kisekka-Ntale 2007, 423) created by the British.

Prior to colonization, the region known today as Uganda was mainly dominated by the expanding Buganda kingdom. Bantu-speaking groups inhabited the southern territories with the kingdoms of the Buganda, Banyoro, Banyankole, and Toro in central, eastern, and western parts of the country, and the Nilotic-speaking, largely pastoral and agricultural groups now known as the Karamojong, Iteso, Lango, Acholi, Mahdi, and Lugbara inhabited the northern and northwestern parts of the country.

The British interest in Uganda was mainly to safeguard the Suez Canal, the Nile River, and the Cairo–Cape corridor, which ensured a business link with the Cecil Rhodes Company in South Africa (Kisekka-Ntale 2007, 423–24).[1] This was to counter the earlier German treaty of friendship with the *kabaka* (king) of the Buganda kingdom. Hence, following the Anglo-German agreement of 1886, the British acquired the territory and hurriedly "bundled the different ethnic groups together to create a single administrative colonial entity that later became Uganda" (Kisekka-Ntale 2007, 424). In fact, the British colonial legacy of forced unification of multiple independent nations with different forms of political, economic, and social organization into a single nation has been highlighted as one of the major root causes of the northern Uganda conflict (Mamdani 1984). The Buganda and the Banyoro kingdoms had autocratic monarchs that were supported by a hierarchy of chiefs and advisors. On the other hand, "the Lugbara, Bakedi and Acholi political organizations, by contrast, were characterized by a more or less extreme form of acephalous social and political organization" (Sathyamurthy 1986, 71). These Nilotic-speaking groups from the north were viewed as less sophisticated in their social and political organization than the Buganda and Banyoro. The Acholi of Luo origin, for example, had clan chiefs referred to as *rwodi* who controlled decisions on land possession and transfer, as well as facilitated harmonious co-existence. There were also rivalries and conflicts among the different clans of the Acholi, as well as with the Mahdi, Teso, and Langi. The key point is that these "ethnic nations" were thus already well established, with their own independent systems of governance. The concept of nation was parallel to ethnic identity. Equally important is the fact that some of these groups had a more centralized system of governance while others were decentralized. These factors took on new significance in the context of the colonial nation-building project.

The Central Role of the Buganda Kingdom

Buganda dominance during the precolonial, colonial, and postcolonial periods is at the heart of the struggle for nation building in Uganda. As Low (1962, 66) observes, whatever happened in Buganda "was bound to influence what was to happen or not happen" in other provinces of the protectorate. When colonialists arrived in the nineteenth century, the Buganda kingdom was the most powerful and best organized in the region. Contact in the 1830s with Arab traders meant that Buganda was advanced in commerce and ammunition and at one point had a standing army of more than

6,000 men who engaged neighboring ethnic groups in search of slaves and political expansion (Gukiina 1972, 43).

The Buganda kingdom's system of governance allowed clan chiefs some autonomy beneath the control of the *kabaka*. The *kabaka* was very powerful and rewarded chiefs with land and wealth for their loyalty (Sathyamurthy 1986, 75). In fact, by 1856 when Mutesa I came to power, the Buganda kingdom had expanded and was composed of ten counties. There was a sophisticated system of government: a royal court attached to the *kabaka*; a military; powerful administrative assistants known as *katikiro* and *kimbugwe*; a legislative council in a form of a parliament known as the *lukiiko*; a clan system of governance under the *bataka* chiefs; and politico-administrative chiefs referred to as *batongole*. The *kabaka* was "the father of all clans" and hence referred to as the *sabataka*.

Predictably, the British chose to govern by means of indirect rule through the Buganda kingdom and engaged political elites in negotiations as a strategy to conquer the region. The privileged status of the Baganda in the colonial system led to what Kisekka-Ntale (2007, 424) refers to as "Buganda sub-imperialism." The close collaboration between the British colonialists and the Buganda kingdom legitimized the rule of the former, increased the political domination of the latter, and created animosity among the other ethnic groups. Furthermore, the 1900 agreement between the British colonialists and the Buganda kingdom, also known as the "Uganda Agreement," privileged the latter as a ministate within the region. Even though this agreement was between Buganda and the British, it had ramifications for the rest of Uganda, creating unequal relationships between Buganda and the rest of Uganda.

The position of the Buganda kingdom within the Ugandan nation has remained a bone of contention to date, sometimes leading to calls for secession. This, in turn, has heightened north-south tensions and similar calls for secession from other ethnic groups. For example, as recently as May 2009, a member of parliament and leader of Greater Northern Uganda, Felix Okot-Ogong, in his complaint in parliament against the government's nepotism and tribalism, was quoted as saying: "If the state of Uganda cannot accommodate the people of Greater Northern Uganda and treat them as equal citizens, then these people will one day find where to belong" (Ladu and Naturinda 1 May 2009). The "dream secessionist nation" of northerners has been referred to by their proponents as the "Nile Republic."

Ethnic Categorization and Implications for Nation Building

The colonial definition and administration of ethnic groups, as well as missionary education systems that used local languages as media of communication, further confined these groups to their respective territories, creating tensions and animosity between them and further undermining the prospects for national cohesion in the postindependence period.

In his discussion of ethnicity, Barth (1969, 15) observes that the conceptualization of boundaries based on ethnic identity implies that broader ethnic constructs within a particular region are given priority in the definition of a group rather than the internal variation in subjective cultural values and activities. For example, Young (1976, 229–30) observes that in the drawing of the colonial administrative districts, the British put several ethnic groups under the Busoga ethnic designation, whereas smaller chiefdoms came under Ankole jurisdiction; fifty clans that were independent units were merged to become the Acholi; and the Bakiga identity was formed out of the residents of the Kigezi districts. Okot p'Bitek (1970, 12) posits that in the early twentieth century, "Acholiland was divided into thirty politically independent units. But these have not been called tribes. . . . It was the new political unit set up by the British colonial administration which was labeled Acholi District, which became known as Acholi tribe."

Under the leadership of Fredrick Lugard, one of the major architects of British colonization in Africa, the British protectorate attacked the Bunyoro kingdom, reduced its size, and established the hitherto rebellious section of the kingdom, the Toro, into a separate entity. The kingdom of Toro was legitimized by Lugard as an independent state under British protection (Sathyamurthy 1986, 105). Five other districts were taken away from the Bunyoro kingdom and given to Buganda in a formal treaty in 1900 in return for levies that were to be paid to the British (Sathyamurthy 1986, 106). These came to be known as the "lost counties" and have led to the persistent claims of the Banyoro to reclaim their counties.

The colonial attempts to both define and categorize ethnic groups and simultaneously recombine them into a single identity ignored the fact that these ethnic groups often had stronger affiliations among them and were bound in solidarity despite their expansive nature. Ayoob (1995) argues that colonial governments conglomerated different ethnic groups regardless of their preexisting ethnic, linguistic, or sociopolitical loyalties and affiliations, weakening some groups and elevating others, disbanding or manipulating systems of governance, and economically impoverishing communities by introducing new economies of cash-crops. Such a pattern also obtained in Uganda. In a study of political boundaries in Africa, Englebert et al. (2002, 1095) demonstrate how the notion of territoriality was a European import that contrasted "the relative survival of local traditions of political authority and social interaction." They further assert that many ethnic groups have maintained their affiliation and social organization across political boundaries. For example, the Mahdi, Acholi, Kakwa, Lugbara, and Alur live in both northern Uganda and South Sudan, and some as far as Democratic Republic of Congo (DRC). Yet despite the distances, some families and clans have maintained stronger ties and share greater similarities in cultural practices across state borders than within them. These challenges for nation building have persisted well into the postindependence period and any analysis of the conflict in northern Uganda must account for this deeper historical and political context. As Finnström (2008, 46) notes, "colonial boundary marking by no means froze the play of collective identities."

The North-South Divide

Economic disparities among different ethnic groups in Uganda, while rooted in colonial policies, have contributed to a corresponding north-south divide over the years (Kisekka-Ntale 2007, 427). The south, through the Baganda, had earlier access to commercial activities due to favorable climatic conditions, and cash crop plantations such as coffee, cotton, and sugar cane. They also represented the seat of colonial power through indirect rule, as noted earlier. In order to safeguard their economic interests, the British colonial government chose to recruit its army from among the Acholi, who were labeled as warriors given their persistent combat with their Karamojong neighbors in the east, the Langi in the south, and the Mahdi in the west, as well internal conflicts between the Acholi subclans (Byarugaba 1998; Kisekka-Ntale 2007). Other northern populations were also recruited into the army. For most, "a military career was their first introduction to Uganda as a national entity" (Mazrui 1975, 39). The continuous provision of unskilled military labor led to the impoverishment of the north during both the colonial and the postindependence periods (Kisekka-Ntale 2007, 427). It also contributed to hardening ethnic stereotypes that were later implicated in analyses of the LRA-GOU civil war.

Such ethnic and regional balkanization has continued to mark postindependence Uganda, leading to identity politics in competition for the national cake. As in other African countries, successive governments have linked political support to respective ethnic groups rather than promoting national consciousness (Allen 1994, 125), leading to a situation in which "politics is ethnicized and ethnicity is politicized" (Kanyinga 2002, 40). Utilizing the power of ethnicized politics, a succession of key figures from the northern ethnic groups intermittently ruled the country for the first twenty-four years of independence (1962–85). Milton Obote, from the northern Langi ethnic group, was the first president of Uganda following independence in 1962, but was overthrown in 1971 by his army general, Idi Amin, a northern Kakwa, who was in turn overthrown in 1979 through the aid of Tanzanian troops. The Tanzanian invasion of Amin was provoked by Amin's attempt to annex part of Tanzanian territory (Mudoola 1988, 285). As a result, northern rule was briefly interrupted and Y. K. Lule, a leader of the Uganda National Liberation Army (UNLA) took over power from Amin. Even though he was anti-Obote, the UNLA was pro-Obote; and Godfrey Binaisa took control as the interim leader, but he was in turn removed by the Military Commission, which installed Obote's political associate, Paulo Mwanga. Mwanga paved way for the return of Obote, hence commencing the Obote II regime. However, in yet another coup d'état, Obote was overthrown in 1985 and Tito Okello, also a northerner, took over until driven out by a military insurgency led by Museveni, a southerner, in 1986. The period of "northern rule" was marked by military repression of the south, though there were also intranorthern conflicts, which led to deaths and extreme violations of human rights.

President Museveni has thus been accused of retaliating against the north for the past repressions of the south and furthering the ethno-political divide by referring to his war against the LRA as a fight by the Bantu in the south against the Nilotics in the north. He has also stated that the Acholi were particularly responsible for the violent history of Uganda (Okuku 2002, 22–23; Behrend 1998). On the other hand, previous northern governments, particularly Obote's, referred to Museveni's NRM as Tutsi or Rwandan invaders (Finnström 2008, 75). And as Mamdani (2001, 168) argues, "the more the repression of the Banyarwanda was stepped up, the more Banyarwanda soldiers joined Museveni and the NRA in the bush." In its 2002 report, the Uganda Human Rights Commission (UHRC) affirmed that most people from central Uganda perceived the LRA-GOU conflict much more as the government's war against the northerners than a war for democracy (Allen 2006).

Hence, the situation in Uganda has been characterized by a weak state plagued by politicized ethnonationalisms. This "ethnocratic heritage," as Mazrui (1975, 51) would refer to it, has trapped the country into a vicious circle of violence. In Uganda, as in many African countries, both politicians and local people are held hostage by the ideological ethnic entrapments that are used to claim recognition and justify violent resistance. In the north, such resistance is linked to increased poverty and poor quality of life in the region. According to a progress report on Uganda's Millennium Development Goals (United Nations 2007, 12), there is an obvious economic imbalance between the north and the rest of the country: "The northern region has maintained the highest incidence of poverty of 61 percent. This is largely attributable to the nineteen-year-old conflict in the region, coupled with the cattle rustling problem that has traditionally plagued Karamoja and the surrounding subregion." The Acholi population has been victim of both the GOU violent military activities and the LRA brutal violence. Yet, my historical and political analysis has shown that this violence is linked to a deeper process of ethnic differentiation and inequality that originated in the colonial project. In many ways, the LRA conflict has entrenched the very conditions that northerners were ostensibly resisting when the HSM, and later the LRA, took shape.

One stark example can be found in the GOU's decision in 1996 to confine the Acholi population in "protected camps" that made it extremely difficult for the people to cultivate their land and rear their animals, while at the same time rendering them even more vulnerable to rebel attacks. As a result, out of the 87.4 percent of potentially arable land, less than 10 percent was cultivated during the years of the conflict (Acker 2004, 343). The major source of capital investment in the north is cattle. Successive armed insurgencies, including the GOU's response to the LRA, have robbed the Acholi of their main source of livelihood through cattle rustling. For example, Weeks (2002, 35) asserts that by 2001 there were only 3,000 head of cattle left in both Gulu and Amuru districts in the north, compared to 123,375 in 1983. This has meant that many families can longer afford to take their children to school, further reinforcing the circle of poverty.

The claims by the LRA that the north has been systematically marginalized therefore have deep historical roots. With largely unskilled labor, limited economic industrialization, and poor infrastructure, compounded by the psychosocial and economic impact of the conflict, the north finds itself in what Sachs (2006) refers to as a "poverty trap."

Militarization and Proliferation of Small Arms and Light Weapons

The militarized approach to confronting conflicts has undermined the use of dialogue and mediation as means to mitigate conflict and enhance nation-building processes. Kabwegyere (1972, 303) hypothesizes that "any agent of change *alien* to the people whose way of life this agent is determined to change radically, always uses violence as a main means to bring about the change." Such a pattern is again rooted in the past: certainly the colonial government used violence to amalgamate ethnic groups into larger entities in order to form administrative districts, empowering groups in certain ways over and above others (Kabwegyere 1972). As is well known, postindependence Uganda experienced a series of coup d'états and military resistances that arguably expressed already institutionalized ways of expressing grievances. The state was politically weakened and nation-building processes interrupted, leading to the mushrooming of resistances both legislatively in parliament and militarily in different regions.

The protracted nature of the Ugandan conflict and regional instability has meant that Uganda has been faced with the challenge of controlling the proliferation of small arms and light weapons (SALW). The instability in Burundi, Democratic Republic of Congo (DRC), and Somalia has facilitated the movement of SALW to rebel groups. One of the major challenges faced by Uganda in controlling the transfers of SALW is policing the extensive and porous borders with its neighbors (Safer World 2008, i), made even more difficult by the cross-border affiliations among ethnic groups noted earlier (see Obika and Bibangambah, this volume). The northern region has been the most susceptible to this proliferation. The interclan cattle rustling between the Karamojong and neighboring groups both in Uganda and across state borders has meant that different ethnic groups have armed themselves for self-protection. The GOU has also made several attempts to counter the proliferation of SALW, including the Karamojong Integrated Disarmament and Development Programme (KIDP), the Peace Recovery and Development Plan for Northern Uganda (PRDP), and Uganda National Action Plan (NAP) on Small Arms and Light Weapons. However, these initiatives are yet to bear significant results, and both the proliferation of weapons and the use of military intervention have continued to dominate the GOU's approach to addressing the LRA and other conflicts in the north.

Regional and Cross-Border Implications and Interventions

The LRA conflict has led to regional destabilization in countries that have been struggling with their own nation-building processes. For example, the LRA was long at the center of political tensions and distrust between the governments of Uganda and Sudan. In the 1990s, the Sudanese government, in a bid to fight its own rebel insurgency led by the Sudan People's Liberation Army/Movement (SPLA/M), provided the LRA with a base in Sudan in addition to support with logistics and military equipment. The LRA "functioned as a buffer between the central Sudanese army and the south Sudanese rebels" (Finnström 2008, 84). In retaliation, the GOU supported the SPLA/M rebels and equally supplied them with military equipment. It was not until 1999 that the US-based Carter Center facilitated a dialogue between the two countries that led to cessation of hostilities and restoration of diplomatic relations (Finnström 2008, 85).

A further shift in regional relations occurred in 2005 when the Sudanese government and SPLA/M signed a Comprehensive Peace Agreement (CPA). This led to the stabilization of relations between the two countries. The Sudan government allowed Uganda to pursue the LRA rebels into their bases in Sudan. This military offensive, known as "Operation Iron Fist," weakened the LRA. Consequently, the LRA was pushed into peace negotiations with the GOU. The talks were held in Juba, the capital of what is now South Sudan. In 2006, the two parties agreed to a cessation of violence, pending the signing of the peace agreement; prior to this, all other previous peace initiative attempts had failed (Lucima 2002). However, the two parties could not ultimately reach a peace agreement and to date the stalemate maintains. The GOU further pursued the LRA in December 2008 in the ninety-day "Operation Lightning Thunder," which also failed to end the conflict but left many civilian casualties.

The Ugandan situation reflects the challenge that many African nations have been facing in dealing with insurgencies. These insurgencies, in turn, represent problems associated with nation building more generally throughout the region. In fact, the expansive spread of the LRA into the unstable Democratic Republic of Congo (DRC) and conflict-affected Central African Republic (CAR) raises concerns over the destabilizing effect of the rebel movement throughout the region. These countries, like Uganda, have been struggling with their own nation-building processes. Most insurgencies have emerged out of a historically rooted claim for political or economic participation in national structures of governance, themselves bedeviled by colonial legacies of politicized ethnonationalisms and inequalities. For example, such struggles for inclusion have been witnessed by the twenty-one-year-old conflict between SPLA and the northern Sudan government that ended in the 2005 CPA, and later in a referendum in January 2011 and South Sudan's independence in July 2011. In the DRC and CAR, several regional insurgencies have emerged, further weakening both nations. The instability in affected countries tends to affect the regional peace, as has been demonstrated by the case of the LRA expansion into the DRC, Sudan, and CAR.

Ending militarized conflicts sustained by arms proliferation and historically politicized ethnic grievances is therefore crucial to the nation building-process. The African Union has taken this into account and in May 2004 launched its new Peace and Security Council (PSC), which aims at addressing conflicts regionally. The PSC Protocol defines itself as "a collective security and early-warning arrangement to facilitate timely and efficient response to conflict and crisis situations in Africa" (African Union 2002). This protocol allows for intervention of conflicts before they escalate into a crisis. The Continental Early Warning System (CEWS) is the body charged with the responsibility of defining moments and methodological processes to intervention. However, Wane et al. (2010) observe that the challenge for CEWS is to work out mechanisms that will respond to the diverse conflicts in Africa. The African Union initiative is in line with the principle of responsibility to protect, a UN protocol calling on the state's responsibility to protect its citizens against all forms of human rights abuses.

While still in its nascent stage, the PSC demonstrates the awakening call to strengthen internal mechanisms for nation building by countering potential situations of conflict that could destabilize both individual countries and whole regions. As such, it is a supranational response to problems of nation building generally. As a boost to these efforts, in May 2010, the United States government signed the LRA Disarmament and Northern Uganda Recovery Act, which stipulates an express commitment to eliminate the LRA. However, unless there are more concerted efforts like the PSC to contain and end the violent activities of the LRA, the rebel group could destabilize Uganda further, prolonging and igniting new conflicts in the unstable countries in the Great Lakes and central African regions.

Peacebuilding Initiatives

Despite the depth and complexity of the LRA conflict in Uganda, the GOU has carried out several attempts to end conflict and create a positive atmosphere of peace and mutual understanding. When the NRM came to power it proposed a Ten Point Program as a guiding principle for governance and national cohesion (Dicklitch 2001, 183).[2] The program cited politicized ethnicity as the core of the Uganda conflicts and attributed this to "ethnicized" political parties (Dolan 2009, 63). Subsequently, Museveni's NRM temporarily banned political parties' activities (Dicklitch 2001, 183) and instituted a "no party system" that favored the NRM's monopoly of power (Dolan 2009, 63). However, in 2005, a multiparty system was reintroduced and political parties were again allowed to compete in elections.

The major challenge for the government and other stakeholders has been ending insurgencies through conflict mediation and the successful fostering of peacebuilding processes. Thus, efforts towards peacebuilding have included the institution of a constitution-making process that brings back the rule of law and citizen participation in the affairs of the state; peace negotiations with different armed groups; and introduction of the Amnesty Act, Human Rights Commission, and National Reconciliation Bill 2009.

In order to enshrine a robust and broadly consultative constitution, the government put into place in 1989 the Uganda Constitutional Commission (UCC) (Hansen and Twaddle 1995, 10). The UCC collected views from the population and came out with a comprehensive report with diverse proposal on what the Ugandans wanted in the constitution (Waliggo 1995). In describing the constitution making process, Waliggo (1995, 28) opines that the UCC succeeded in laying the ground for democratization process and produced a report that was "centered on the aspirations and concerns of the Ugandan people and a draft constitution based on principled compromise." Moehler (2008, 41) equally confirms that the constitution-making process was participatory and widely consultative. Efforts at enhancing democratization are intended to encourage nation building by working in tandem with peace negotiations.

There have been several attempts to peace negotiations; I focus on three of the best documented, which took place between 1985 and 2008. These are the 1985 Nairobi Process; the National Resistance Army (NRA)-Uganda People's Democratic Army (UPDA) Peace Talks; and the LRA-GOU peace negotiation attempts between 1993 and 2006. Each of these instances illustrates the persistent and historically rooted problems of ethnic polarization and north-south divides that are critical to understanding the LRA conflict as a whole.

The Nairobi Peace Talks took place in 1985 for four months following General Tito Okello's coup d'état against President Milton Obote (Okuku 2002, 24). There were two major parties to the conflict: on the one hand, Yoweri Museveni's National Resistance Army/Movement (NRA/M), and on the other, the Military Council under the chair of General Tito Okello, which was a coalition of former rebel groups (Kiplagat 2002).[3] The peace negotiations resulted in a power-sharing agreement in a coalition government. Under this agreement, "a military council would govern and priority would be given to the reconstruction of a national army" (Doom and Vlassenroot 1999, 9–10). However, the peace agreement collapsed within a year when Museveni's National Resistance Army launched an attack on the Ugandan army in 1986.

Also in 1986, peace talks took place between the predominantly Acholi UPDM/A and the new government under Museveni's NRM. The parties reached an agreement in what came to be known as the Gulu Peace Accord, which essentially "meant the final end of the armed struggle of the UPDA" (Doom and Vlassenroot 1999, 15). The talks were therefore fruitful: the parties made an agreement to end the conflict; provide jobs for the former UPDM/A combatants; work out a joint military operation against Alice Lakwena's HSM; and disarm the Karamojong cattle rustlers. Despite this success, Okuku (2002, 34) notes that less than two years after the peace agreement some of the UPDM/A generals who had been integrated into the army were charged with treason, further raising suspicion over the Museveni government's commitment to peace.

The most recent peace talks have been between the LRA and GOU in Juba between 2006 and 2008. The Juba Peace Talks started early 2006 under the UN Secretary General Special Envoy President Joaquim Alberto Chissano and the Chief Mediator for the Host Government Dr. Riek Machar Teny Dhurgon, the vice president of the government of Southern Sudan (Lucima 2002). There were hopes that the talks could lead to an end to conflict, particularly following the signing of the cessation of violence agreement by the two sides. The parties also agreed to have a clear program for the demobilization, demilitarization, and reintegration (DDR) of the former LRA combatants through a process of Implementation and Management Mechanisms (IMM); Joint Liaison Group (JIG); and an Oversight Forum. Another key agenda in the agreement was on accountability and reconciliation, which aimed at seeking ways of addressing human rights violations (both inside and outside the country) that took place during the war. The agenda explored both judicial and culturally based forms of justice as well as reconciliation and healing in all the affected communities (Oola 2008, 68). While the talks went on for two years and made some positive progress, they did not culminate in a signed peace agreement (Schomerus 2007, 34).

Importantly, the government has undertaken a number of institutional reforms as a means of addressing some of the causes and consequences of the conflict. These include the Amnesty Act 2000, the Human Rights Commission Act, and the Land Act. The National Reconciliation Bill is yet to be passed by parliament. In an attempt to incentivize peace, in January 2000 the government of Uganda, under the Amnesty Act 2000, offered an official pardon to all rebel groups (McDonnell and Akallo 2007, 119). The Preamble of the Amnesty Act (Government of Uganda 2000) underscored that the objective was to "provide for an Amnesty for Ugandans involved in acts of a war-like nature in various parts of the country and for other connected purposes." The Preamble further adds that the Amnesty Act is seen as "the expressed desire of the people of Uganda to end armed hostilities, reconcile with those who have caused suffering and rebuild their communities . . . the desire and determination of the Government to genuinely implement its policy of reconciliation" (Government of Uganda 2000). The 2000 Amnesty Act offered amnesty for alleged crimes committed after the law was passed. Children over twelve and adults who had spent more than four months of fighting in the bush were eligible to apply (Allen and Schomerus 2006, 37).

The larger objective of the Amnesty Act was to reconcile Ugandans, particularly those in the north, to reintegrate excombatants through provision of basic needs, and to prepare the community to receive those who had been pardoned. The amnesty was extended to those living outside the country as long as they renounced any military action again the government. The amnesty provisions indicate that once an excombatant has received amnesty, such a person cannot be subjected to the prosecution of war crimes unless the person commits other crimes. This provision could well clash with the ICC proceedings in situations where the ICC investigations show that some of the people that had been granted amnesty might have been among those bearing the greatest responsibility for crimes against humanity (Eichstaedt 2009, 60). However, as the ICC cases stand so far, arrest warrants have only been issued against the top LRA leadership.

To some extent the Amnesty Act achieved its objectives, though it still faces challenges such as lack of sufficient funding, hesitance on the part of some excombatants to present themselves for amnesty, and misunderstandings on the benefits and implications of the Amnesty Act (Refugee Law Project 2005; Eichstaedt 2009, 168). Allen (2006, 122), in his interviews with northern Ugandans, found that opinions on the Amnesty Act were divided: while some people welcomed amnesty for the LRA perpetrators and subsequent culturally based reconciliation rituals, others called for justice against those implicated in the killings.

Additionally, the enactment of the new constitution in 1995 led to the founding of the UHRC under Constitution Article 51 (Bouckaert 1999, 43). This was officially ratified under the Uganda Human Rights Commission Act of 1997. The UHRC has substantial independence with similar powers as the judiciary (Schmitz 1999, 69) and has been active in advocating against human rights abuses.[4]

The GOU, in collaboration with civil society and cultural elders, has also advocated for national reconciliation. The National Reconciliation Bill 2009, which has been drafted but not yet passed by parliament, aims to address the historical legacy of violence by instituting a national reconciliation process. Given that the final version of the bill is not yet out, it would be premature to speculate possible impact of the initiative.

Another effort towards peacebuilding has been initiatives to resolve numerous land disputes in the north (Rugadya 2008, 7). Uganda has attempted several land reform decrees since independence; however, these have been faced with resistance and misunderstanding. According to Branch (2007), land justice in Acholiland entails, among other things, compensation for property lost during the war, fair land policies, and integration of the formerly abducted or returnees.

There is generally a high level of distrust among the Acholi population about the government's intention to commercialize and privatize Acholi land (Branch 2005, 3). There have also been suspicions that the government intends to displace the Acholi in the north and replace them with the southerners or Tutsis from Rwanda (Jackson 2009, 324). The government's invitation to private investors to purchase Acholi land before all the IDPs return to their ancestral lands has heightened the suspicion about the government's intentions (Branch 2005, 3).

The problem of land disputes, like many other issues associated with the conflict in the north, has deep roots. The 1995 constitution made clear some of the key provisions on land ownership, giving rights to individuals or groups to own land or property (McAuslan 2003).[5] The 1998 Land Act took away from the courts the monopoly on the settlement of land disputes and made provisions for land dispute resolutions through a "District Land Tribunal consisting of a chairperson, who is qualified to be a magistrate grade I, and two other members" (McAuslan 2003, 8). Further, the land disputes can be settled by cultural leaders or a mediator appointed by the District Land Tribunal. In 2009, however, the government drafted a controversial National Land Policy that was hurriedly passed by parliament but failed to resolve the historical problems of land tenure ownership, land disputes, women's right to land ownership, and uncontrolled state power over land ownership. The National Land Policy has not adequately addressed the issue of resettlement of IDPs and resolution of land disputes (Rugadya 2008, ii). The postconflict land disputes have mainly been attributed to disagreements over land boundaries and perceptions of increased value of land (Rugadya 2008, 34). In order to fund these institutional reform initiatives, the government has relied on external donors who have in turn put stringent conditions on accessing the aid.

The above discussion illustrates the challenge of peacebuilding in Uganda, while highlighting the multidimensional realities of the conflict, its historical and political roots and impacts on society, and the need for appropriate transitional justice mechanisms in addition to governance reforms and negotiations for sustainable peace. Yet, these too, are fraught with challenges.

The ICC Intervention and Transitional Justice Debates

The conflict took on an international dimension when in 2005 the ICC issued warrants for the arrest of LRA rebel leaders. Officially instituted in 2002, the ICC's main stated objective is ending impunity and prosecuting crimes against humanity. The LRA arrest warrant was consequent to President Museveni's request in 2003 that the ICC prosecutor investigate the criminal activities of LRA (Allen 2006, 1). The ICC warrants obligate regional and international countries to cooperate in the arrest of the LRA top leadership. Oola (2008, 69) maintains that the LRA leadership refused to sign the peace agreement due to the fear over "personal safety and the ICC warrants" of arrest as well as lack of clarification on "the operational linkages between traditional *mato-oput* systems, [and] the newly created Special Division of the High Court which is to be Uganda's domestic war crimes court and the International Criminal Court." According to Allen's (2006, 126) analysis, despite the fact that the LRA may want to see an end to the war, they would equally prefer a negotiated settlement that would guarantee their security and comfort.

Mato-oput is an Acholi cultural ritual of reconciliation that has traditionally been used to mediate disputes between two conflicting clans, particularly in cases where there have been killings caused by one member or members of a clan against another. In recent years, there have been calls for the application of this ritual to welcome back the LRA rebels by traditionally cleansing and reconciling them with the community. When applied as a local initiative, the culturally based mechanisms of peacebuilding can be effective in mitigating conflict but "they may lose much of their value when encouraged and programmed by the state or by international institutions" (Andrieu 2010, 546). However, at the same time reconciliation rituals in transitional justice processes tend to create opportunities for dialogue and exploration of possible ways of mitigating the negative impacts of conflict and reconstructing relationships. Hence, there continues to be interest in the role that these restorative justice mechanisms can play.

To return to the central argument, one must ask to what extent is the ICC intervention relevant to ending impunity and encouraging the nation-building process in

Africa? I view the ICC as a deterrent to impunity and crimes against humanity through the exertion of external pressure, especially if this has a larger international backing. However, genuine initiatives for political change and improvement in nation-building efforts would be realized more effectively through internal processes of interethnic, political, social, and religious inclusion. These are precisely the historic fault lines that have contributed to so much conflict in Uganda and elsewhere.

Within the context of debates about the proper mechanisms for transitional justice, the ICC indictment cannot directly be attributed to the failure of the Juba Peace Talks, as some would have it. Contrary to the general expectation, in a survey conducted in eight districts in northern Uganda by Tulane Initiative on Vulnerable Populations (2007), 68 percent of the respondents believed that the ICC contributed to the pressure on LRA to participate in the peace talks. In research I conducted in northern Uganda (January–May 2010) on NGO peacebuilding activities, I learned from the respondents that the majority preferred traditional mechanisms of reconciliation, which they described as restorative in contrast to the punitive ICC approach. Further, the restorative approach was seen as a means to the rebuilding of severed relationships between parties.

Just as the root causes of the LRA conflict lie in problems of longitudinal nation building, the root causes of the failure of the peace talks lies in the lack of institutionalization of a common aspiration towards the promotion of a national identity with the respect of the diverse ethnic groups, political participation among citizens, and commitments to social justice. Economic and political marginalization of certain groups, and the fragmentation and polarization caused by ethnonationalism, as already noted, is at the root of the Ugandan conflict. Unless these issues are addressed, the ethnic card may always be used to create new grievances. In fact, as Schoenbrun (1993) contends in his discussion on ethnic manipulation for political gains, failure to address the real issues affecting people could engender new forms of oppression masked as ethnic liberation. The reordering of the power relations nationally and regionally will have to take into account the fact that nation building has to be inclusive and participatory.

Most analyses of African conflicts tend to limit themselves to the postindependence reality of the continent. African conflicts such as that between the LRA and GOU have often been inaccurately diagnosed by reductionist statements such as: "Ethnic identities and hatred are . . . the cause of violent conflict" in Africa (Elbadawi and Sambanis 2000); or that "Africa's civil wars conform to a global pattern that is better explained by political and economic factors, as well as by the extent of ethnic, cultural and religious diversity in the society" (Collier and Hoeffler 2002, 1). Other scholars like Haynes (2007) have argued that the homogeneity or diversity of ethnic identity could be at the foundation of most African conflicts.

While my analysis of the historical and political roots and trajectories of the LRA-GOU conflict in Uganda supports elements of these observations, I have also shown how the situation is much more complex than the above reductionist characterizations. At the root of the conflict is the struggle for nation building. I have argued that colonial policies contributed to the rise of polarizing ethnonationalisms, which were then embodied by successive leaders who failed to build a cohesive national identity and state that allows for inclusive political participation, equitable distribution of resources, and social integration. Attempts to marginalize certain sections of the society in order to gain support from one's own region have polarized ethnic communities and weakened national identity.

Political processes of peace negotiations in view of nation building therefore have to take into account four key factors. The first is the critical assessment of the historical residue of unresolved grievances and the recognition that the current conflict in Uganda is much more complex than the LRA-GOU nexus or the ethnic and north-south characterization. While the immediate goal of negotiations may be to end the LRA-GOU conflict, Uganda must work out a long-term proposal for dealing with other historical grievances such as land distribution, the "lost counties" of the Banyoro, and integration of all ethnic communities into a national identity. The second task is to address economic and political marginalization, particularly of the northern region, through initiatives for equitable distribution of resources and wider political participation. The third is to engage in a long-term process of the de-militarization of conflict and to stem the use of violence and SALW as the primary means of resolving disputes. The fourth, which is in line with Kanyinga's (2002) observation, is to address the ideology of ethnicized politics and politicized ethnicity by developing an alternative political and economic ideology with an objective of national unity.

The signing of the peace agreement is inadequate for realizing sustainable peace in northern Uganda. Monitoring the peace agreement, ensuring peace and security, and effective positive policy changes are critical to the sustainability of peace. Every conflict has what Lederach (1997, 131) terms the "polychronic simultaneity" dimension in which different events and players have multiple effects on the conflict. As such, for peace to be sustainable in northern Uganda, there have to be sustained efforts towards inclusion of different ethnic groups into political and economic structures of nation building. In the long-term, a more inclusive approach to nation building would ensure sustainable peace, economic development, and social cohesion. On the other hand, exclusivist approaches through ethnic marginalization in political and economic structures would continue to weaken the state, thereby rendering it susceptible to insurrections, violence, and instability.

Notes

1. Cecil Rhodes Company was one of the most powerful economic enterprises in South Africa towards the end of the nineteenth century (Legassick 1974, 260). The company controlled large resources of diamond and gold mines. The British colonial agents hoped to make lucrative business by securing links with Cecil Rhodes.

2. The Ten Point Program referred to ten guiding principles: promotion of democracy; security of all persons and property; promotion of national unity, and bringing an end to sectarianism; consolidation of national independence; economic sustainability; improved social services and postconflict reconstruction; elimination of corruption and abuse of power; addressing root causes of dislocation of different section of population; pan-African cooperation in defense of human and democratic rights; and establishing a strategy for a mixed economy (Mutibwa 1992, 180).

3. These included the UNLA; Federal Democratic Movement of Uganda (FEDEMU); Uganda Freedom Movement (UFM); Uganda National Rescue Front (UNRF); and the Former Uganda National Army (FUNA).

4. For example, it reported that since 2006 "the right to personal property and freedom from torture" had been violated and subsequently topped the list of abuses (Kobusingye 2010, 81). Further, between January and September 2009, the commission reported that "there had been about 5000 human rights violations reported against the police and 3000 of them had been substantiated. The officers involved either faced disciplinary action, or had been handed over for prosecution" (Kobusingye 2010, 81). The commission has thus prosecuted a number of human rights abuse cases.

5. For example, "Article 26 of the Constitution provides that every person has a right to own property either individually or in association with others and further provides limitations on the state's power to compulsorily acquire private property."

References

Acker, Frank V. 2004. "Uganda and the Lord's Resistance Army: The New Order No One Ordered." *African Affairs* 103, no. 412: 335–57.

African Union. 2002. *Peace and Security Council (PSC) Protocol*. Addis Ababa: African Union.

Allen, Tim. 1994. "Ethnicity and Tribalism on the Sudan-Uganda Border." In *Ethnicity and Conflict in the Horn of Africa*, edited by Katsuyoshi Fukui and John Markakis, 112–39. Oxford: James Currey.

———. 2006. *Trial Justice: The International Criminal Court and the Lord's Resistance Army*. London: Zed Books.

Allen, Tim, and Mareike Schomerus. 2006. *A Hard Homecoming: Lessons Learned from the Reception Center Process in Northern Uganda. An Independent Study*. Washington, DC: United States Agency for International Development (USAID).

Amnesty International. 1997. "Breaking God's Commands: The Destruction of Childhood by the Lord's Resistance Army." *Amnesty International Country Report*. London: Amnesty International.

Andrieu, Kora. 2010. "Civilizing Peacebuilding: Transitional Justice, Civil Society and the Liberal Paradigm." *Security Dialogue* 41: 537–58.

Ayoob, Mohammad. 1995. *The Third World Security Predicament: State Making, Regional Conflict and the International System*. Boulder, CO: Lynne Rienner.

Barth, Fredrick. 1969. "Introduction." In *Ethnic Groups and Boundaries: The Social Organization of Cultural Difference*, edited by Fredrick Barth, 9–38. Oslo: Scandinavian University Press.

Behrend, Heike. 1998. "War in Northern Uganda: The Holy Spirit Movements of Alice Lakwena, Severino Lukoya and Joseph Kony (1986–1997)." In *African Guerrillas*, edited by Christopher Clapham, 245–43. Oxford: James Currey.

Bouckaert, Peter. 1999. *Hostile to Democracy: The Movement System and Political Repression in Uganda*. New York: Human Rights Watch.

Branch, Adam. 2005. "Neither Peace nor Justice: Political Violence and the Peasantry in Northern Uganda. 1986–1998." *African Studies Quarterly* 8: 1–31.
———. 2007. "Uganda's Civil War and the Politics of ICC Intervention." *Ethics & International Affairs* 21: 179–98.
———. 2010. "Exploring the Roots of LRA Violence: Political Crisis and Ethnic Politics in Acholiland." In *The Lord's Resistance Army: Myth and Reality*, edited by Tim Allen and Koen Vlassenroot, 25–44. London: Zed Books.
Byarugaba, E. G. 1998. "Ethnopolitics and the State: Lessons from Uganda." In *Ethnicity and the State in Eastern Africa*, edited by M. A. Mohamed-Salih and John Markakis, 180–89. Uppsala: Nordic Africa Institute.
Chabal, Patrick, and Jean-Paschal Daloz. 1999. *Africa Works: Disorder as Political Instruments*. Oxford: James Currey.
Collier, Paul, and Anke Hoeffler. 2002. "On the Incidence of Civil War in Africa." *Journal of Conflict Resolution* 46: 13–28.
Dicklitch, Susan. 2001. "Action for Development in Uganda." In *NGOs and Human Rights: Promise and Performance*, edited by Claude E. Welch, 82–201. Philadelphia: University of Pennsylvania Press.
Dolan, Chris. 2009. *Social Torture: The Case of Northern Uganda, 1986–2006*. New York: Berghahn.
Doom, Ruddy, and Koen K. Vlassenroot. 1999. "Kony's Message: A New Koine? The Lord's Resistance Army in Northern Uganda." *African Affairs* 98, no. 390: 5–36.
Eichstaedt, Peter H. 2009. *First Kill Your Family: Child Soldiers of Uganda and the Lord's Resistance Army*. Chicago: Lawrence Hill.
Elbadawi, Ibrahim, and Nicholas Sambanis. 2000. "Why Are There So Many Civil Wars in Africa? Understanding and Preventing Violent Conflicts in Africa." *Journal of African Economies* 9, no. 3: 244–69.
Englebert, Pierre, Stacy Tarango, and Matthew Carter. 2002. "Dismemberment and Suffocation: A Contribution to the Debate on African Boundaries." *Comparative Political Studies* 35, no. 10: 1093–1118.
Finnström, Sverker. 2008. *Living with Bad Surroundings: War, History, and Everyday Moments in Northern Uganda*. Durham, NC: Duke University Press.
Government of Uganda. 2000. "The Amnesty Act, 2000." Kampala: Ugandan Government Ministry of Internal Affairs.
Gukiina, Peter M. 1972. *A Case Study in African Political Development*. South Bend, IN: University of Notre Dame Press.
Haynes, Jeffrey. 2007. "Religion, Ethnicity and Civil War in Africa: The Cases of Uganda and Sudan." *The Round Table* 96, no. 390: 305–17.
Jackson, Paul. 2009. "'Negotiating with Ghosts': Religion, Conflict and Peace in Northern Uganda." *The Round Table* 98, no. 402: 319–31.
Kabwegyere, Tarsis B. 1972. "The Dynamics of Colonial Violence: The Inductive System in Uganda." *Journal of Peace Research* 9, no. 4: 303–14.
Kanyinga, Karuti. 2002. "Leadership and Governance in Post-colonial Africa." In *East Africa in Transition: Communities, Cultures and Change*, edited by Judith M. Bahemuka and Joseph L. Brockington, 36–46. Nairobi: Acton.
Kiplagat, Bethuel. 2002. "Reaching the 1985 Agreement." *Conciliation Resources*. Accessed 15 October 2012. http://www.c-r.org/accord-article/reaching-1985-nairobi-agreement-2002.

Kisekka-Ntale, Fredrick. 2007. "Roots of the Conflict in Northern Uganda." *The Journal of Social Political and Economic Studies* 32, no. 4: 421–52.

Kobusingye, Olive. 2010. *The Correct Line?: Uganda under Museveni*. Central Milton Keynes, UK: Authorhouse.

Ladu, I. L., and S. Naturinda. 2009. "Anger, Secession Calls Follow Onen's Sacking." *The Daily Monitor*. 1 May, Kampala: The Nation Group.

Lederach, J. 1997. *Building Peace: Sustainable Reconciliation in Divided Societies*. Washington, DC: United States Institute of Peace.

Legassick, Martin. 1974. "South Africa: Capital Accumulation and Violence." *Economy and Society* 3, no. 3: 253–91.

Low, Donald A. 1962. *Political Parties in Uganda*. London: Published for the Institute of Commonwealth Studies by Athlone.

Lucima, Okello, ed. 2002. *Protracted Conflict, Elusive Peace: Initiatives to End the Violence in Northern Uganda*. London: Conciliation Resources and Kacoke Madit.

Mafege, Archie. 1998. *Class and Ideology of Ethnicity in Africa: Proposals for a New Paradigm*. Dakar, Senegal: CODESRIA.

Mamdani, M. 1984. *Imperialism and Facism in Uganda*. Trenton, NJ: Africa World Press of the Africa Research and Publications Project.

———. 1995. "Indirect Rule, Civil Society and Ethnicity: The African Dilemma." In *From Post-traditional to Post-modern? Interpreting the Meaning of Modernity in Third World Urban Societies*, edited by Preben Kaarsholm, 63–64. Roskilde, Denmark: International Development Studies, Roskilde University.

———. 2001. *When Victims Become Killers: Colonialism, Nativism, and the Genocide in Rwanda*. Princeton, NJ: Princeton University Press.

Mazrui, Ali A. 1975. *Soldiers and Kinsmen in Uganda: The Making of a Military Ethnocracy*. Beverly Hills, CA: Sage.

McAuslan, Patrick. 2003. "A Narrative on Land Law Reform in Uganda." In *Urban Land Markets in Transition*, edited by Gareth A. Jones. Conference paper presented at Comparative Policy Perspectives on Urban Land Market Reform in Eastern Europe, Southern Africa and Latin America, July 1998. Cambridge, MA: Lincoln Institute of Land Policy.

McDonnell, Faith J. H., and Grace Akallo. 2007. *Girl Soldier: A Story of Hope for Northern Uganda's Children*. Grand Rapids, MI: Chosen Books.

Moehler, Devra C. 2008. *Distrusting Democrats: Outcomes of Participatory Constitution Making*. Ann Arbor: University of Michigan Press.

Mudoola, Dan. 1988. "Political Transitions since Idi Amin: A Study in Political Pathology." In *Uganda Now: Between Decay and Development*, edited by Holger B. Hansen and Michael Twaddle, 280–98. London: James Currey.

Mutibwa, Phares Mukasa. 1992. *Uganda since Independence: A Story of Unfulfilled Hope*. London: Macmillan.

Okuku, Juma. 2002. "Ethnicity, State Power and the Democratization Process in Uganda." *Discussion Paper 17*. Uppsala: Nordic Africa Institute.

Oola, Stephen. 2008. "Conflicting Justice Systems and the Search for Peace, Justice and Reconciliation in Northern Uganda." In *Activating Human Rights and Peace: Universal Responsibility*, edited by Robert Garbutt, 66–72. Lismore, Australia: Southern Cross University, Centre for Peace and Social Justice.

Opongo, Elias O. 2006. *Making Choices for Peace: Aid Agencies in Field Diplomacy.* Nairobi: Paulines Publications Africa.

———. 2011. *NGO Peacebuilding in Northern Uganda: Interrogating Liberal Peace from the Ground.* PhD thesis submitted at Department of Peace Studies, University of Bradford, UK.

p'Bitek, Okot. 1970. *Song of Ocol.* Nairobi: East African Publishing House.

Refugee Law Project. 2005. *Whose Justice? Perception of Uganda's Amnesty Act 2000: The Potential for Conflict Resolution and Long-Term Reconciliation.* Kampala: Refugee Law Project.

Rugadya, Margaret A., Eddie Nsamba-Gayiiya, and Herbeter Kamusiime. 2008. *Northern Uganda Land Study: Analysis of Post-Conflict Land Policy and Land Administration: A Survey of IDP Return and Resettlement Issues and Lesson: Acholi and Lango Region.* Kampala: World Bank.

Sachs, Jeffrey D. 2006. *The End of Poverty.* London: Penguin Books.

Safer World. 2008. *Uganda and International Small Arms Transfer: Implementing UN Programme of Action Commitment.* London: Safer World.

Sathyamurthy, T. V. 1986. *The Political Development of Uganda: 1900–1986.* Hants, UK: Gower.

Schmitz, Hans P. 1999. "Transnational Activism and Political Change in Kenya and Uganda." In *The Power of Human Rights: International Norms and Domestic Change,* edited by Thomas Risse-Kappen, Steve C. Ropp, and Kathryn Sikkink, 39–77. Cambridge: Cambridge University Press.

Schomerus, Mareike. 2007. *The Lord's Resistance Army in Sudan: A History and Overview.* Geneva, Switzerland: Small Arms Survey, Graduate Institute of International Studies.

Schoenbrun, David L. 1993. "A Past Whose Time Has Come: Historical Context and History in Eastern Africa's Great Lakes." *History and Theory* 32, no.4: 32–56.

United Nations. 2007. *Millennium Development Goals: Uganda's Progress Report.* New York: United Nations.

Waliggo, John M. 1995. "Constitution-Making and the Politics of Democratisation in Uganda." In *From Chaos to Order: The Politics of Constitution-Making in Uganda,* edited by Holger B. Hansen and Michael Twaddle, 18–40. Kampala: James Currey / Fountain Publishers.

Wane, El-Ghassim, Charles Mwaura, Shewit Hailu, Simone Kopfmüller, Doug Bond, Ulf Engel, and João Gomes Porto. 2010. "The Continental Early Warning System: Methodology and Approach." In *Africa's New Peace and Security Architecture: Promoting Norms, Institutionalizing Solutions,* edited by Ulf Engel and João Gomes Porto, 91–110. Aldershot, UK: Ashgate.

Weeks, Willet. 2002. *Pushing the Envelope: Moving beyond "Protected Villages" in Northern Uganda.* New York: Report submitted to United Nations Office for the Coordination of Humanitarian Affairs (UNOCHA).

World Bank. 2007. *The 2007 World Development Report: Development and the Next Generation.* Washington, DC: World Bank.

Young, Crawford. 1976. *The Politics of Cultural Pluralism.* Madison: University of Wisconsin Press.

5 Kofi Annan's Conflict Resolution Model and Peacebuilding in Kenya

Alfred Anangwe

KENYANS WENT TO the polls in December 2007 to elect their leaders amid rumors and fears of a possible rigging by the incumbent government. These fears were informed by three factors: First, President Kibaki appointed commissioners to the Electoral Commission of Kenya (ECK) without consulting the opposition. Second, he announced the election date too late. Third, he went on to appoint judges to the High Court just days before the election. It was feared that the ECK commissioners would facilitate the rigging while the judges would rule in favor of the president in the event of an election petition. After the elections, these fears seemed to have been substantiated when independent election observers declared that the elections were not free and fair (Murunga 2009). Worse still, the chairman of the Electoral Commission of Kenya, Samuel Kivuitu, remarked that it was not possible to tell who actually won the presidential race. All these factors triggered the political violence that took place minutes after the winner of the presidential polls was announced. It was also apparent that youth unemployment, regional development imbalances, and the results of the 2005 constitutional referendum—which aggravated the country's polarization along ethnic lines—catalyzed the violence (see Ojielo, this volume).

The former United Nations Secretary General, Kofi Annan, assisted by other eminent African personalities, facilitated the mediation process that ended the crisis. The Annan team considered certain apparent causes and key issues of the crisis and grouped them into four agendas that formed the basis of Kofi Annan's peacebuilding model. Issues that were initially considered before selecting the four agendas included immediate stoppage of violence, restoration of fundamental rights and liberties, humanitarian intervention aimed at resettling internally displaced persons (IDPs), constitutional/legal and institutional reforms, tackling poverty and inequality, consolidating national cohesion and unity, undertaking land reform, and addressing transparency, accountability, and impunity (Sihanya 2009). Most of these agenda items bordered on establishing, strengthening, and reforming democratic institutions, which likewise requires the promotion of peace and stability, prosperity, freedom, good governance, and rule of law.

Since the postelection political violence experienced in Kenya was triggered by a flawed electoral process, this chapter examines how the instrumental approach to promoting democracy in the country through various constitutional, legal, and institutional reforms can help restore order in the short term and sustainable peace in the long run. In the years since independence, Kenyans have advocated for comprehensive constitutional reforms that guarantee restoration of genuine democracy. These struggles have often been characterized by episodes of political violence.

Background to Kenya's Political Violence

Among the numerous challenges Kenya's political leaders faced at independence were building democratic institutions and processes while at the same time embarking on nation building. Historically, the British colonial regime was authoritarian in nature and decolonization of the Kenyan state required opening up of democratic space based on a sound legal and constitutional framework. Shortly after independence, Kenya's leaders emphasized nation building in the face of shrinking democratic space, thereby preventing the will of the people from prevailing. Notions of nation building were invoked to mask personalized, ideological needs and the centering of power around the president (Kiangi 2001; Keane 1991). This was the case in most African countries where post independence leaders became infatuated and preoccupied with state security to promote authoritarianism (Nyon'go 1992; Chazan et al. 1992; Mandaza and Sachikonye 1991; Ergas 1987; Chabal 1986). Thus instruments of domination such as the army, the police, secret services, and the presidential guards grew much faster and bigger than civil society organizations. Kambudzi (2001) has observed that Africans' mistake was the assumption that real freedom would necessarily and with little trouble follow political liberation from colonial rule. This was a disastrous misinterpretation both of the struggle for, and the management of, independence.

The crisis of governance in Kenya and other African countries has been prompted in part by excessive centralization of power in the president, or what might be called "imperial presidency." Kenya is among those African countries that, according to Dogbey (2001), have suffered a series of political setbacks resulting from the emergence of civilian dictators in the postindependence period. Since 1963, Kenya's successive regimes have generally been characterized by "one-party dictatorships, powerful presidency, authoritarianism and limited freedoms for the people, massive violation of human rights, increased repression, criminalization of thought and expression, crackdown on free association and assembly, emasculation of parliament, control and intimidation of the judiciary, political detentions, killings and disappearance of key political figures and a complete negation of elections through outright rigging" (Akivaga et al. 2001, 1).

According to Shivji (1990), democracy should be a strategy of resistance and struggle against domination. When periodic elections are held freely and fairly, they enable the citizens to vote out dictators while at the same time meaningfully influence the political and economic institutions that affect their lives (Arias 2000). The absence of credible democratic channels for resisting domination has led citizens to resort to violence as an avenue through which to challenge authoritarianism. Dogbey (2001) has observed that many of the conflicts witnessed in Africa have roots in long years of suppression by rulers who proclaimed themselves as revolutionaries, redeemers, and even emperors.

Incidences of election rigging have become common in African countries and have triggered postelection violence as means of resistance and a challenge to the suppression of democracy. Kenya, Zimbabwe, and Cote d'Ivoire have all experienced postelection violence between 2008 and 2011; moreover, there have been many incidents in Kenya's history where elections have been manipulated to generate results that favor the incumbent president. Indeed, the Kenyan constitution has, since independence, been mutilated in order to repose absolute power in the presidency. This power was used to adulterate election outcomes, as the president had the prerogative to appoint commissioners to the ECK without consulting his opponents, as well as to appoint High Court judges who preside over election petitions, enabling the manipulation of institutions that ideally should ensure free and fair electoral outcomes.

Andersen and Olsen (1996) and Mandaza and Sachikonye (1991) have held that African states became patrimonial shortly after independence as centralized executive authority was personalized in a charismatic president who attempted to control the state. Political leaders who promoted patrimonial and clientelistic structures did so arguing that the presidency of a nation was metaphorically equivalent to fatherhood in a family. The unfortunate result was the establishment of dictatorial governments in Kenya. Abutudu (2001) asserts that patrimonialism led to a crisis of governance, which then became the central problematic in contemporary Africa. Instead of being fathers, African presidents became dictators who resorted to material inducement as a mechanism of buying support rather than seeking genuine political legitimacy. This had a profoundly negative impact on electioneering and other democratic processes.

In the early 1990s, Kenyans arose to challenge their domination by the political class. Akivaga et al. (2001, 2) have noted that "Kenyans risked and lost their lives while resisting the one party oppressive regime because they were fighting to restore their human dignity and to recapture their aspirations of self-rule which they had embraced at independence." The ruling clique, for their part, resisted a return to democratic politics; the general perception within official circles of the ruling Kenya African National

Union (KANU) government was one of fear of losing power. This is because African leaders "yielded to democratic pressures (both internally and externally) in the early 1990s more out of convenience than of conviction. This happened at a time when the international community was waving the 'stick and carrot' bait to African countries reluctant to swallow multi-party democracy" (Ngwane 2004, 20). The incumbent regime thus employed various strategies for the sole purpose of convincing Kenyans that multiparty politics was bad for the country.

Despite the protracted struggles between those bent on sustaining the status quo (authoritarian rule) and those opposed to it, the ruling establishment ultimately bowed to both internal and external pressures. This paved way for the repeal of Section 2A of the constitution, which had declared Kenya a one-party state, thus ushering in multiparty politics.

The Era and Challenges of Multiparty Politics in Kenya

In 1992, Kenyans held their first multiparty elections in twenty-six years. Great hope surrounded these elections based on the understanding that multiparty politics serve as a forum for the free flow of competing ideas in a democracy. Ideally, political parties criticize and check each other, and by so doing, offer citizens the opportunity to choose. In addition, parties tend to become more responsive to public opinion, thereby enabling the citizens to influence government policy and effectively participate in the affairs of their country. The benefits of multiparty politics were not to be realized in Kenya, however, because political parties did not operate under a democratic constitution nor observe internal party democracy. Nor did they have a vision of government that exhibited a national outlook opposed to mere capturing of power (Akivaga et al. 2001).

It is in light of the lack of these crucial factors in Africa's democratic transition, among others, that Kambudzi (2001), after observing a decade of multiparty politics in Africa, warns of the danger of reducing democracy to multiparty elections. There was no political will on the part of the ruling elite to embrace true democracy because they were not prepared to lose their hold on power (Mentan 2009; Ngwane 2004; Jalang'o 2010). Just before the first multiparty elections in Kenya in 1992, politically instigated ethnic clashes erupted, resulting in the death of thousands of innocent Kenyans and widespread destruction of property. This was subsequently used to prove the official government argument that multiparty politics would divide the country along ethnic lines and consequently cause hatred and bloodshed through ethnic wars. The political class thus floated the argument that one-party rule and a powerful presidency were instrumental in holding the nation together.

Promoting ethnic violence just before the first elections in 1992 served to demonize multiparty politics. Kenyans became gripped in a general environment of ethnic suspicion and insecurity. Some parts of the country were declared ruling party (KANU) zones, with the effect that entire populations perceived to be sympathetic to the opposition were evicted from their farms. Provincial administrations, state resources, security operations, and the state-run media were all mobilized to campaign for the ruling party through spreading propaganda and intimidation. The electoral administrative system was solely appointed by the president without reference to even the parliament or opposition political parties. Money was printed and pumped into the economy through open bribery of potential voters. Not surprisingly, the elections resulted in a KANU win, and due to the politicization of ethnicity, took on a fairly ethnic pattern. The National Election Monitoring Unit (NEMU) in its conclusion judged the 1992 elections as neither free nor fair (Akivaga et al. 2001).

After the 1992 elections, Kenyans embarked on agitation for constitutional review that would create a level field for all political players in the anticipated 1997 elections. Jalang'o (2010, 3) has observed that "the history of the demand of the new constitution can be traced to the 1992 General Election when the Ruling party KANU won the elections with a tally of 34 percent of the total votes cast." These demands were captured by the call of "no reforms no elections" (Akivaga et al. 2001). Once again, these reforms were resisted by the KANU government. The political elite (within the ruling KANU party) feared that such reforms would eventually lead to political defeat. As a result, KANU politicians continued to issue politically inflammatory statements in several parts of the country prior to the 1997 elections. It became evident that both the opposition and civil society organizations were losing out on the reform agenda as the elections approached. Their demands then took the form of street protests, strikes, and boycotts that invited government brutality, as evidenced by the violence unleashed by security forces on the protesting but unarmed public. As the situation deteriorated, the security forces did not hesitate to shoot and kill in a bid to quell the riots. Many innocent people lost their lives or livelihoods. This situation is not unique to Kenya; Ngwane (2004) has observed that multiparty democracy in Cameroon, for example, has remained a façade and charade, promising much and delivering nothing.

After the 1997 elections, the structures of dictatorship remained intact and human rights violations by the government only increased. According to Akivaga et al. (2001) the postelection period was characterized by a range of problems, including a lack of comprehensive reforms, the manipulation of parliament and opposition parties, ethnic conflict and dictatorship within political parties, orchestrated calls for the president to continue beyond 2002 (contrary to the constitution), and fear of a snap general election. Increased insecurity (crime and violence), continued polarization according to ethnic differences, and irresponsible and inflammatory utterances by public officials were also widespread. Such postelection problems in Africa have led scholars like Mentan (2009, 23) to conclude that "elections, usually taken to be a hallmark of democracy, have become a tool for predatory authoritarian kleptocrats seeking to legitimate their rule."

After the 1997 elections, political conditions in Kenya remained the same as before the 1990s, and the call for constitutional reforms continued and intensified until 2002. This provided fertile ground for the National Rainbow Coalition (NARC) party to exploit as it trounced the ruling KANU party during the 2002 elections. The NARC administration was elected on its promise of carrying out comprehensive constitutional reforms in the first one hundred days in power. However, failure by the NARC administration to fulfill this promise contributed to the political violence witnessed after the 2007 elections.

The NARC Government, Constitutional Review Process, and Political Violence

It is no wonder that the agenda for constitutional reforms enabled the opposition NARC political party to win the 2002 elections after promising to realize these reforms within the first one hundred days in power. Political divisions within the ruling NARC coalition government, however, ultimately undermined efforts to realize a new constitution. Kenyans lost confidence in the popularly elected NARC government and consequently rejected the constitution provided during the 2005 referendum. In the absence of a new constitution, many Kenyans who had voted against the constitution sided with other antigovernment forces and formed a formidable opposition determined to push through a new constitution after the 2007 elections.

The results of the 2005 constitutional referendum made it clear that the incumbent government had lost political legitimacy, which would not be restored through winning elections alone. Like many other Kenyans, Ng'ang'a (2008) and Nderitu (2010a) have held the view that marked tension before and during the December 2007 elections resulted from the 2005 constitutional referendum that deeply polarized the country and contributed to the 2007 political violence. The referendum left the president, his cabinet, and his region isolated because they had all voted in favor of the proposed constitution. Six out of the eight provinces of Kenya voted against the proposed constitution. It is with this political isolation and intense emotion that the country went to the polls in December 2007, leading to sharper polarization along ethnic lines in the postelection period; as a result, neither of the two leading political parties, Orange Democratic Movement (ODM) and Party of National Unity (PNU), could have formed a truly legitimate government. Thus, the crisis was partly caused by the failure of the political class to understand the management of ethnic affairs. Ethnicity has long been used for political mobilization, and even though this feature was clearly manifested at independence, it has especially been visible since the restoration of multiparty politics in 1991 and the subsequent elections of 1992, 1997, 2002, and ultimately in 2007.

Having considered the ethnic factor in relation to the 2005 constitutional referendum and its role in precipitating political violence, it is important to note that the conduct of the ECK in the 2007 general elections helped trigger the mayhem. The president, exercising his constitutional powers and mandate, went ahead to unilaterally appoint commissioners to the ECK and High Court judges shortly before the elections, as well as choose an election date close to the expiry of the president's mandate. All of these created great suspicion.

To a large extent, however, the postelection crisis exposed the larger national crisis. Although remarkable economic gains had been realized over the previous four years, the failure to effect political reforms had divided the country sharply. It was on the basis of the need for political reforms that the government, featuring a coalition of the PNU and the ODM-K, was locked in a confrontation with the ODM. The latter held that the immediate solution to the crisis lay not in legal or judicial remedies, but on political settlements that entailed undertaking comprehensive constitutional, legal, and economic reforms aimed at addressing poverty, regional development imbalances and restoring political legitimacy through improved democracy. This view was adopted by players in the mediation process.

Kofi Annan's Peacebuilding Model: Path to Democracy

An agreement ending Kenya's postelection violence was signed between contending political parties on 28 February 2008 after the Kofi Annan–led team's successful mediation (Ng'ang'a 2008). The mediation team, through consultation, came up with four main agenda items that were to be the guiding principles for bringing about sustainable peace. Agenda 1 was intended to immediately end the violence and restore fundamental rights and liberties. Agenda 2 was intended to deal with humanitarian crisis and resettlement of IDPs. Agenda 3 was intended to resolve the political crisis occasioned by the contending political parties through formation of a grand coalition government. And finally, agenda 4 was meant to examine and propose solutions for the longstanding issues. Momanyi (2010, 9) states that "after the violence, Kenyans agreed that there were some things that could not wait any longer to be changed." These changes amounted to what Kambudzi (2001) calls "political renewal," which entails rebuilding collapsed systems of governance, administration, and public conduct by putting in place well-defined rules, limits, and controls to guide political and electoral behavior and thereby restore democracy through well conducted elections.

In the realm of electing political leaders, well-defined rules and controls help to ensure free and fair elections, which in turn enable citizens to participate in decision making and hold their representatives accountable. Elections confer legitimacy on political leadership and provide a crucial mandate to the government; they can also serve as an egalitarian method of participation. However, regular elections must be supported by functioning institutions; otherwise they cease to be avenues for establishing legitimate governments. The peacebuilding team led by Kofi Annan drafted fundamental proposals aimed at restoring legitimacy in Kenya's governance structure after the latest flawed electoral process. These fundamental proposals, when effected, will lead to establishing and maintaining a "governance realm" that guarantees interaction between the rulers and the ruled based on legitimate authority and reciprocity. Such systems are admired because they ensure a measure of bargaining, compromise, and tolerance among competing interests and between those who exercise political authority and those subject to it (Andersen and Olsen 1996). Parliament is an important arm of government that plays important roles in any political system: namely, legislative, oversight, and watchdog. These roles can be adequately carried out within a functioning democratic constitutional environment. Kenya's authoritarian constitution has hindered the parliament from carrying out these roles adequately. It is against this background that the Kofi Annan–led team proposed the meaningful and relevant parliamentary and constitutional reforms that are discussed in the next section.

Parliamentary and Constitutional Reforms

Most of the proposed reforms by the Kofi Annan-led team required parliamentary legislation and therefore depended on the political will of members of parliament (MPs) as lawmakers. In this regard, the Parliamentary Service Commission expanded its secretariat to ensure that relevant and adequate skills were made available to MPs to enable them carry out their work (Nderitu 2010b). With an expanded secretariat, the legislature recruited legal experts to assist in the drafting of new laws, thereby enhancing its capacity and efficiency in realizing these reforms. This has enabled the Kenyan parliament to carry out its three functions of oversight, legislation, and acting as a watchdog (Nderitu 2010b). In addition, this also enabled parliament to amend its standing orders and procedures to enrich the quality and output of parliamentary debate and strengthen multiparty democracy. In the aftermath of parliamentary reform, there has tended to be greater flexibility in the processing of bills, responding to citizen's concerns, and providing live coverage of parliamentary proceedings. Parliamentary reforms have fostered and helped to realize a new constitution and political culture for Kenyans.

After the 2007 postelection violence, reforming the Kenyan constitution in order to strengthen democratic institutions of governance was considered of utmost importance. Although this need had been identified twenty years prior, the process accelerated following the successful mediation process around the 2008 postelection political violence (Momanyi 2010). In fact, fears had been expressed that if a new constitution was not in place before the 2012 general elections, there could be serious chaos and anarchy (*Katiba News* 2010; Sihanya 2009).

Many Kenyans were delighted to see that the constitutional review process, down to the referendum, proceeded smoothly despite a few court cases challenging it. Sixty-seven percent of Kenyans who took part in the referendum voted in favor of the new constitution. The new constitution proposes the establishment and creation of legislative and institutional frameworks that will go a long way in reforming the electioneering process in the country and thereby contribute to promoting democracy and minimizing ethnic tensions. Ethnic tensions generated around elections are likely to lessen because, according to the reforms, the president must win with more than 50 percent of the total votes cast, forcing presidential aspirants to seek the support of all Kenyans. The new constitution has also created accountability mechanisms designed to mitigate acts of impunity often perpetrated by powerful politicians.

Electoral Reforms

New electoral laws have been enacted within the new constitution that addresses eight important dynamics. First among these is that the counting of votes should take place at every polling station to minimize tampering while ballots are in transit to tallying centers, as happened in the past. Second is the promotion of gender and age-related parity and inclusivity. The new constitution, unlike the old one, makes provision for the election of a woman for each county in the national assembly. This will inevitably increase women's representation. Also, the old constitution only allowed candidates for elective positions from among those nominated by political parties. Junior candidates and women, then, experienced difficulties being nominated by strong and popular political parties. Political parties are now required to observe gender parity in nominating candidates for elective positions at various levels of representation. In addition, the new constitution provides for independent candidates, thus benefiting those who may not secure political party nominations (Korir 2011).

Third among the new procedures is the establishment of an electoral-dispute resolution framework. While the old constitution lacked prescription of the time frame within which an election petition challenging a presidential run must be heard, the new one sets time targets. There was also no allowance for challenging a presidential election before the president was sworn into office. In some circumstances, a president elect would steal a match by immediately being sworn in, and once in power, using the means at his disposal to frustrate the petition (Kipsang 2011a). Fourth, issuance of electoral documents to all those who qualify is now guaranteed under the new constitution (Korir 2011). Potential voters perceived to be sympathetic to the opposition were previously denied identification documents and subsequently a chance to participate in elections as voters or potential candidates for elective offices.

Fifth, voter bribery has been curbed through devolution of national resources. The old constitution failed to allow for equitable distribution of national resources, leading to regional economic imbalances. Areas where the president received overwhelming political support were poised to receive large allocations of national resources in order to induce voters (Korir 2011). In addition, the new body charged with managing elections in Kenya (Independent Electoral and Boundaries Commission) is mandated to check cases of voter bribery. The commission limits the amounts that candidates or political parties may spend in an election campaign.

A sixth measure is that the arbitrary arrest of voters and candidates for elective offices around election times has been curtailed (Nderitu 2011a). For example, arrested persons shall not be remanded in custody if they are charged with offenses punishable by a fine or by imprisonment for not more than six months (Nderitu 2011). The old regimes had organized arbitrary arrests the night before elections to deny opposition supporters from participating in voting processes. These included arresting on trumped-up charges those candidates for elective office deemed to be popular.

Seventh, the new constitution and accompanying legal provisions now demand that political parties maintain "political hygiene" by observing accountability, transparency, and loyalty. Political parties are now required to maintain proper records, democratically elected office bearers, and physical addresses. Furthermore, parties are proscribed from establishing a militia and engaging in bribery and other forms of corruption (Kipsang 2011b). In addition, the Political Parties Act makes the Office of Registrar of Societies and Political Parties independent from political interference, allowing for expediency and efficiency in maintaining order and discipline within and between political parties.

Other important reforms in electoral conduct include the outlawing of hate speech and incitement, which are some of the ultimate triggers of political violence (Nderitu 2010b). This has been achieved through setting up of the National Cohesion and Integration Commission under the National Cohesion and Integration Act. A number of Kenyans, including MPs and politicians, have been prosecuted in a court of law for making hate speeches during election preparations. The key issue here is that the process of national healing is unlikely to succeed as along as Kenyan society is polarized. Hence, all electoral reforms have been strengthened by reforms in the judiciary, which plays the role of determining disputes relating to election results (Momanyi 2010).

Establishment of a Reformed Electoral Management Body

In addition to the laws discussed above, new institutions that promote democracy in the country have been established. The most important of these is the Independent Electoral and Boundaries Commission (IEBC), which replaces the defunct ECK whose dismal performance contributed, to a larger extent, to the violence witnessed after the 2007 elections. In its analysis of the constitutional and legal framework governing elections in Kenya, The Kriegler Commission pointed out that ECK's problems were due to weaknesses and inconsistencies in the constitutional and legal frameworks, which in turn weakened its effectiveness in guiding the electoral process. Moreover, the lack of independence and inefficiency on the part of the ECK was attributable to problems in its organizational structure, appointment criteria, composition, and management systems. Finally, the ECK maintained a poor system of electoral law enforcement and dispute resolution.

The reforms recommended by the Kriegler Commission have been factored into the IEBC. The IEBC thus marks a point of departure in the history of election management in Kenya for several reasons. First, the act establishes an IEBC fund from which the commission will draw its salaries, allowances, and other benefits, thereby cushioning it from undue financial constraints, which dogged the defunct ECK. Second, commissioners and other staff are subject to stiffer penalties in the event that they flout provisions of the act to undermine credible, free, and fair elections. The penalties include a three-year jail term, fine of up to one million Kenya shillings, or both; and upon conviction, commissioners or staff becoming ineligible to hold public office for a period of ten years following the conviction. To enhance accountability and transparency, the commission is also now required to present its annual report to the president and parliament within three months after the end of each financial year. This renders the commission open to public scrutiny. In addition, the commission is required to observe and promote the principle of public participation and consultation with stakeholders (citizens, political parties, and civil society organs), and as noted earlier, candidates or political parties are limited in the amount they may spend in an election campaign. This is in order to curb voter bribery.

Most importantly, commission members are now appointed through an open and transparent process. Positions are advertised in national daily newspapers and applicants are supposed to be cleared for integrity by bodies such as the Kenya Revenue Authority and the Criminal Investigation Department. Interviews of short-listed candidates are conducted in public and names of selected candidates are forwarded to the president and parliament for final approval. Criteria for appointments in the past lacked clarity and merit and did not allow for participation of all key stakeholders, thereby undermining the legitimacy and credibility of the constitution and the office bearers (Kipsang 2011a).

The issue of the appointment of public servants is critical in determining their performance and that of the institutions to which they are appointed (Wendoh 2011). Whereas the old constitution gave enormous unilateral and discretionary powers to the president to appoint senior government officers to bodies such as the defunct ECK, the new constitution opens a novel chapter regarding public appointments.

The New Dawn of Appointing Public Officers

The new constitution no longer allows the executive appointment of public servants with questionable credibility, competency, and integrity (Irungu 2011). In the past, such executive appointments ultimately led to widespread corruption and mediocrity in public service sectors. Appointees furthered the interests of the appointing authority, which were not necessarily in conformity with the wishes of the citizens. As a result, the public lost trust and confidence in public institutions, including electoral and judicial bodies. So far, the appointments to the judiciary and IEBC have been undertaken fairly through a competitive and consultative process like that of South Africa during the transition from apartheid regime (Wendoh 2011).

While this is cause for celebration, there have been attempts by the executive to undermine constitutional requirements regarding public appointments (Thuita 2011). A case in point is the president's attempt to nominate a chief justice through a shortcut process. This was hotly contested by key institutions and officials, including the High Court, Parliament, the Judicial Service Commission, the attorney general, the minister of Justice and Constitutional Affairs, and key civil society groups. The argument was that the appointments were unconstitutional due to lack of consultation between the president and the prime minister, who are equal partners in the coalition government. Ultimately, the president withdrew the nomination and let the Judicial Service Commission restart the search for the next chief justice. This withdrawal was the first indication of a new dawn with respect to appointments of key public officers and presented a new opening for Kenya to create an independent, legitimate, and credible justice system in line with the checks and balances established under the new constitution.

The position of the chief justice is of utmost importance and at the center of realizing sustainable electoral and judicial reforms in Kenya. Anything short of an open and transparent process is likely to erode public trust in the judiciary and other public institutions. The people of Kenya are fearful of returning to the old dark days when public officers, including judges, were beholden to their appointers and therefore not independent, fair, and impartial. The new constitution promotes the principles of international best practices on judicial appointments, which require that appointments are made based on well-defined criteria that include public advertisement of vacancies, equality of opportunity for all who are eligible, merit-based eligibility, and gender equity. Such a process is important because any perceptions that the chief justice appointed will simply further and protect the interest of the appointing authority can have a negative effect on public confidence and trust in the institution.

In a nutshell, public officers now have to undergo vetting before being cleared to assume public duties (Kipsang 2011a). Vetting of public office holders is intended to reinforce adherence to the national values and principles of governance as required under Article 10 of the new constitution, which requires a competitive recruitment exercise based on the principles of equality, participation of the people, good governance, and transparency and accountability. Competitive recruitment ensures that every Kenyan with the relevant qualifications shall have the opportunity to be considered for any suitable appointment. Appointments were hitherto carried out behind the scenes, in boardrooms; this bred cronyism and stifled independence of institutions concerned (Kimondo 2010; Kipsang 2011a). Vetting procedures by parliament can hopefully help in inculcating the culture of responsibility, professionalism, and accountability by persons thus appointed (Okello 2011).

The vetting of judicial officers has been undertaken within the framework of international best practices. This was done in order to correct perceptions that it was corrupt, inefficient, and incompetent. Judicial appointments need to mirror the principles of independence (Kwengu 2011). One of the major challenges to securing judicial independence and accountability the world over has been the process of selecting, appointing, and removing judges. Many commentators have argued that clear, predictable, and transparent criteria free from political interference are the best antidote to redeeming this important institution. The new constitution entails provisions that can help address some of the inherent challenges that have bedeviled the judiciary for decades. For example, Chapter 10 of the constitution expressly provides for vesting judicial power in the judiciary; bolstering the powers and securing the independence and autonomy of the Judicial Service Commission; outlining comprehensive provisions on the appointment and removal of judges; enhancing security of tenure; and enhancing budgetary and administrative autonomy and the creation of a Judicial Fund. In the old constitutional dispensation, members of the Judicial Service Commission were composed of presidential appointees. Therefore, the manner in which public servants have been appointed to the judiciary has contributed to the much awaited judicial reforms that are so necessary for promoting democracy.

Judicial Reforms

In reference to Cameroon, Mentan (2009) and Ngwane (2004) have observed that African dictators have not only undermined all remnants of their countries' legal and political institutions to perpetuate their personal rule, but have also amputated the legislative and judiciary branches of government and totally ignored input from opposition parties and civil society. In the judicial sector, the Kenyan courts have a terrible history of being used by the state to fight prodemocracy advocates. "Indeed, the height of Daniel arap Moi's authoritarianism was accompanied by his enlisting the courts to give 'judicial legitimacy' to his dictatorship" (Murunga 2009, 19).

Since elections denote competition for power, disputes routinely arise on the conduct and outcome of elections. In Kenya, the power to determine election disputes with regard to presidential and parliamentary elections is vested in the High Court. The electoral dispute resolution system deals with political issues that should be settled expeditiously, efficiently, and fairly. Over the years, the argument has been that "since the judiciary is the final arbiter in electoral disputes, Kenya must seek to enhance its independence, efficiency and impartiality" (Nderitu 2010a:16). In the past, the High Court has been slow in determining electoral disputes. For example, the High Court's final ruling on the petition for the 2002 elections for the area represented in parliament called Magarini constituency was determined in November 2006. It took four years for the Court to make the decision to nullify the election results and order a repeat of the parliamentary election, which the petitioner won. This signified a delay in the administration of justice when one considers that parliamentary elections are held every five years.

The 2008 political crisis in Kenya was escalated by the ODM's view that the judiciary was incapable of independently, efficiently, and impartially determining the electoral dispute. The winner-takes-all political system heightened the stakes. ODM said that it could not file an electoral petition since the courts were manned by judges appointed by the Judicial Service Commission, whose members are presidential appointees. The fact that five judges of the High Court had been appointed just days before the elections heightened the suspicion. Where a president is serving a second term, a petition on his elections might be heard by judges who were appointed during his first term, casting doubt on their impartiality (Nderitu 2010a). Bearing in mind the fact that justice delayed is justice denied, the new constitution proposes laws that will ensure speedy determination of electoral disputes. The election court can sit daily to exclusively hear the election petition, or the chief justice can administratively set up an Election Petition Division in the High Court, which can be activated in the period following an election with the mandate of hearing and determining the election petitions. The chief justice has the alternative of setting up an independent Electoral Disputes Court or Tribunal to deal exclusively with election petitions and render decisions. Aware of the impending judicial reforms, the High Court has proved that it can independently determine electoral disputes with regard to petitions filed after the 2007 elections. Results for election petitions for two areas represented in parliament called the Dagoretti constituency and the Matuga constituency, filed after the 2007 elections, were determined in a record time of nine months and two years respectively. In the past, it took four years to make a final ruling on election petition cases. The new constitution recommends fresh vetting of all serving judges who wish to remain in office (Nderitu 2010b). This is intended to clean up the judiciary of ineffective and corrupt judges. The police are an important extension of the judiciary since they are charged with enforcing law and order. In this case, police reforms as suggested by the new constitution are equally important in promoting democracy in the country.

Police Reforms

The Kenya police force is the primary organ mandated to maintain law and order, especially before, during, and after elections in the country. The police force has not been impartial in carrying out these functions, however. The commission of inquiry into postelection violence, chaired by Justice Philip Waki, proposed necessary and urgent police reforms in order to restore public confidence in the force. As a result, the government appointed a task force chaired by Justice Philip Ransley to review the constitutional and legal framework regulating the police and identify key reforms required to increase the effectiveness of the force. The task force came up with more than two hundred reform measures that an implementation committee, chaired by Titus Naikuni, is supposed to implement within one year (Momanyi 2010). The new constitution will enhance reforms in the police force through provision of adequate equipment, legal reforms, reasonable remuneration, and retraining of the force to enhance its respect for human rights (Momanyi 2010). So far, since the postelection violence, the police force has shown improvement in maintaining law and order during by-elections and the constitutional referendum held in August 2010. During some elections and the referendum, incidents of violence have subsided, especially following the clampdown on armed youth gangs like the Mungiki, which have since been outlawed.

This chapter has not by any means exhausted the evaluation of Kofi Annan's peacebuilding framework because implementation of the new constitution is ongoing. As such, it is still too early to conclude whether or not the proposed framework for rebuilding the country's democratic institutions will significantly contribute to stemming future election violence in the country. However, several critical observations stand out. Firstly, an investigative analysis of the root causes of the political violence that erupted after the December 2007 elections was carried out through a consultative process involving both contenting parties under the leadership of Kofi Annan. Secondly, the analysis laid the proper framework upon which short-term, medium-term, and long-term frameworks for resolving the crisis have been based. Thirdly, reviewing the constitution in order to create functional institutions and legislative framework with checks and balances was the most important contribution towards ensuring the establishment of true democracy and stability.

However, transforming this moment of calm into sustainable peace depends on the will and commitment of the political class to undertake implementation of the proposals in the new constitution, especially making legislation proposed by the new constitution within the stipulated time frame. The political will and commitment so far realized in the completed constitution review process needs to be sustained. Kenyans on their part need to sustain pressure on the political class in order to demand the will and commitment necessary for realizing desirable reforms that promote democracy. The need for exerting this public pressure is informed by the fact that democracy promotion agendas tend to become overloaded, with many proposals to be fulfilled within a limited time frame.

While faced with all these expectations and challenges, Kofi Annan's conflict resolution model and peacebuilding framework presents Kenyans with a sense of optimism as they face the 2012 elections. The model and framework also presents positive lessons for conflict-affected African countries. Unlike in countries such as Angola where elections have been hurriedly held under undemocratic conditions, Kenya's peacebuilding process is working on establishing a democratic culture before the 2012 elections. In the past, Kenyans and opposition political players went to elections with a sense of preelection pessimism, making it difficult for political competitors to accept election results. Elections held under a democratic culture serves to arrest postelection tensions, which sometimes spill into violent conflicts, by putting in place democratic institutions involved in electioneering processes.

References

Abutudu, Musa I. M. 2001. "Africa: Visions of the Future." In *African Voices, African Visions*, edited by Olugbenga Adesida and Arunma Oteh, 19–30. Uppsala, Sweden: Nordic Africa Institute.
Akivaga, Kichamu, Smokin Wanjala, and Jephthah Gathaka. 2001. *Multipartism without Democracy!: A Challenge to the Voter.* Nairobi: Ecumenical Center for Justice and Peace.
Andersen, Elin W., and Ragnhild K. Olsen. 1996. *Press Freedom and Democracy in Zimbabwe.* MK Report No. 22. Oslo: University of Oslo, Department of Media.
Arias, Oscar. 2000. "Confronting Debt, Poverty, and Militarism: A Humane Program of Support for the Developing World." *Journal of Third World Studies* 17, no. 1: 13–20.
Chabal, Patrick, ed. 1986. *Political Domination in Africa: Reflections on the Limits of Power.* Cambridge: Cambridge University Press.
Chazan, Naomi, Robert Mortimer, and Donald Rothchild. 1992. *Politics and Society in Contemporary Africa.* Boulder, CO: Lynne Rienner.

Dogbey, Godwin Y. 2001. "Towards a Strategic Vision for a Continent in Distress." In *African Voices, African Visions*, edited by Olugbenga Adesida and Arunma Oteh, 37–52. Uppsala, Sweden: Nordic Africa Institute.
Ergas, Zaki, ed. 1987. *The African State in Transition*. New York: St. Martin's.
Irungu, Albert. 2011. "Vetting of Public Officers." *Katiba News* 7/8: 13–15.
Jalang'o, Dennis. 2010. "The Political Will Yardstick." *Katiba News* 1.10: 3–9.
Kambudzi, Admore M. 2001. "Issues and Problems of Political Renewal in Africa." In *African Voices, African Visions*, edited by Olugbenga Adesida and Arunma Oteh, 53–66. Uppsala, Sweden: Nordic Africa Institute.
Katiba News. 2010. "Juggling Parallel Reform Initiatives." *Katiba News* 1.10: 13–15.
Keane, John. 1991. *The Media and Democracy*. Cambridge: Polity.
Kiangi, Geoff. E. 2001. "Africa: Problem, Challenges and the Basis for Hope." In *African Voices, African Visions*, edited by Olugbenga Adesida and Arunma Oteh, 67–83. Uppsala, Sweden: Nordic Africa Institute.
Kimondo, Maina. 2010. "Of Senate and County." *Katiba News* 2.10: 5–7.
Kipsang, Moses. 2011a. "Meeting the Deadlines: The Challenges of Filling up Constitutional Offices." *Katiba News* 1/2: 3–6.
———. 2011b. "Countdown 2012." *Katiba News* 3/4: 17–20.
Korir, Mark. 2011. "The Gains for the Youth in the New Constitution." *ADILI* 122: 1–7.
Kwengu, Jane. 2011. "Judicial Independence and Accountability in Kenya: Which Way the Judicial Service Commission?" *Katiba News* 1/2: 10–13.
Mandaza, Ibbo, and Lloyd M. Sachikonye, eds. 1991. *The One Party State and Democracy*. Harare: SAPES.
Mentan, Tatah. 2009. "Cameroon: Gambling with Democracy." *CODESRIA Bulletin* 1/2: 23–28.
Momanyi, Dorothy. 2010. "What Agenda?" *Katiba News* 1.10: 9–16.
Murunga, Godwin Rapando. 2009. "The Kenya General Elections: Troubling Political Propaganda in an Intellectual Garb." *CODESRIA Bulletin* 1/2: 16–22.
Nderitu, Macharia. 2010a. "Electoral Justice in Kenya." *Katiba News* 2.10: 13–16.
———. 2010b. "The Constitutional Minefield." *Katiba News* 1.10: 5–6.
———. 2011. "Does the New Constitution Guarantee Democracy?" *Katiba News* 3/4: 9–12.
Ng'ang'a, Jeremiah. 2008. "Post-election Crisis in Kenya: A Regional Perspective." *New Path* 3, no. 1: 5–11.
Ngwane, George Mwalimu. 2004. "Cameroon's Democratic Process: Vision 2020." *CODESRIA Bulletin* 3/4: 20–26.
Nyong'o, P. Anyang', ed. 1992. *30 Years of Independence in Africa: The Lost Decades?* Nairobi: African Academy of Science.
Okello, Johnson. 2010. "A Comparative Analysis of the Proposed and Current Constitution of Kenya." *ADILI* 118: 1–5.
Shivji, Issa G. 1991. "State and Constitutionalism: An African Debate on Democracy." *Southern African Political and Economic Monthly (SAPEM)* 2: 27–54.
Sihanya, Ben. 2009. "Is There Political Will towards Achieving Agenda Four?" *ADILI* 109: 1–7.
Thuita, Guandaru. 2011. "Like It or Hate It, Implementation of New Law Inevitable." *Katiba News* 3/4: 13–16.
Wendoh, Peter. 2011. "Appointments to Public Office under the New Constitution." *Katiba News* 3/4: 5–8.

6 Justice versus Reconciliation

The Dilemmas of Transitional Justice in Kenya

Ozonnia Ojielo

THIS CHAPTER EXAMINES the contradictions and challenges inherent in the efforts of the government of Kenya to establish criminal accountability of the masterminds of the postelection violence of 2007 and 2008. I argue that any expectation of criminal prosecution was misplaced as a result of the structural and political context that underpinned the 2007 election and the consequent postelection violence. I further interrogate the work of the Truth, Justice, and Reconciliation Commission (TJRC), and the opportunities offered by such a domestic restorative justice mechanism, versus the international criminal justice accountability mechanism embodied in the trials of the four alleged masterminds of the violence before the International Criminal Court (ICC).

On 30 December 2007, the Uasin Gishu district of Kenya exploded into an orgy of violence and destruction:

> Large marauding gangs of 1,000–2,000 Kalenjin youth, brandishing machetes, bows and poisonous arrows, occasional firearms, matches and projectiles filled with petrol... blocked and manned a variety of roads with tree trunks and huge rocks, some of which were transported by tractors, throughout the district. They burned vehicles and tyres while refusing to allow anyone to pass. They also engaged in killing, rioting, and looting of Kikuyus and their property. This included numerous simultaneous attacks and cutting off all five entrances to Eldoret town, other roads and highways, as well as the main artery to Kisumu and Uganda, and beyond from Timboroa to Turbo. The violence was so overwhelming that for some time, long term trade was at a standstill with no supplies going in or out of Uganda and Eastern Congo. There was arson, looting, the destruction of property and livestock, maiming and gang raping of defenceless civilians. (Waki Commission Report 2009, 53)

Uashin Gishu district was not alone. Across the country, in parts of the Rift Valley, Nyanza, Nairobi, and Western and Eastern provinces, violence erupted in many towns and communities as people expressed rejection of the results of the presidential election of December 2007 and attacked Kikuyus and other supporters of the Party of National Unity (PNU). According to the commission of investigation into the postelection violence (known as the Waki Commission), more than 1,000 persons were killed and more than 350,000 displaced. Of the victims of the postelection violence in the Rift Valley, the majority were young people; 50 percent were Kikuyu, 22 percent Kalenjin, four percent Luo, nine percent Kisii and Luhya, and ten percent came from other ethnic groups (Waki Commission Report 2009, 49). There were also revenge attacks by PNU supporters. In parts of the Central province and the Kikuyu-dominated areas of the Rift Valley, the Mungiki militia was deployed to organize retaliatory attacks against Kalenjins and Luos.

The reasons why Kenya imploded in 2007–8 have been documented in a number of texts (Mute, Akivaga, and Kioko 2002; Task Force on Establishment of TJRC 2003; Waki Commission Report 2009). First, the growing politicization and proliferation of violence led to the institutionalization of violence following the legalization of multiparty democracy in 1991. Second, the deliberate use of violence by politicians to obtain power since the early 1990s and the decision not to punish perpetrators led to a culture of impunity and escalation of the use of force. This, in turn, has caused a further diffusion of violence in the country that now is largely outside of the control of the state and its security agencies. Violence in Kenya has become a factor not just of elections but in everyday life. The Waki Commission Report (2009) therefore concluded that violence is widespread and can be tapped for a variety of reasons, including but not exclusively to win elections.

The Waki Commission Report identified the centralization and personalization of power around the presidency as a factor in the violence. This has had a twofold impact. One the one hand, it has given rise to the view among politicians and the general public that access to state resources and goods is dependent on sharing the same ethnic identity as the president. One the other, it has led to a deliberate denudation of the authority and legitimacy of other oversight institutions that could check abuses of power and corruption and provide some accountability, and at the same time be seen by the public as neutral arbiters with respect to contentious issues, such as disputed elections results. As a result, in many respects the state agencies are not seen as legitimate.

The third factor identified by the Waki Commission Report in sustaining violence is a feeling among certain ethnic groups of historical marginalization, arising from perceived inequities concerning the allocation of land and other national resources as well as access to public goods and services. This feeling has been tapped by politicians to articulate grievances about historical injustices that resonate with certain sections of the public. This has created an underlying climate of tension and hate and the latent potential for explosive violence.

An additional problem is a growing population of poor, unemployed youth, both educated and uneducated, who agree to join militias and organized gangs. These gangs have been alleged to intersect with parts of the government and security forces and have become "shadow governments" in the slums and in other parts of the country and have been used by politicians to attack their opponents and to enhance their own power and security. Furthermore, these proliferating militias tend to reduce the state's capacity to control the violence, and they increasingly threatening the integrity of both the state and the nation. This underlying endemic situation has created a climate where violence is increasingly likely to be used, and where its use is increasingly unlikely to be checked.

International mediation by the Kofi Annan–led Committee of Eminent African Personalities led to a number of agreements to end the violence, address the humanitarian situation, and establish a coalition government comprising the two main factions in the dispute: the Party of National Unity (PNU) and the Orange Democratic Movement (ODM) as a solution to the political crisis. The committee also worked towards addressing the structural issues that fed into the violence, including proposing institutional reforms and a new constitution. No serious prosecution of the masterminds of the violence had taken place. In addition, it would be practically impossible to prosecute the thousands of youths who had taken part in the violence across the country. While some victims could identify their perpetrators, the majority only knew their attackers by their ethnic or other affiliation, making prosecution impossible. As a result of the historical injustices, the inability and/or unwillingness of the state to deal with previous cases of impunity, violence, and violation of human rights, and the challenge of prosecuting all the perpetrators of the violence, the parties further agreed to establish a Truth, Justice, and Reconciliation Commission as a vehicle for national healing and reconciliation (KNDR 2008).

It was hoped by the parties that the TJRC would document the historical and systemic factors underlying the inability of the state to deal with the previous cases of impunity and the role of state institutions in exacerbating or perpetuating violence. The recommendations of the TJRC would then provide a new normative framework for institutional reforms and a new ethos of behavior among state officials, as well as contribute to eliminating interethnic tensions and promote reconciliation in the country. This would help mark the departure between the past and the future and therefore provide a good foundation for a future based on the rule of law, equity, and social justice—fundamental elements of a transitional justice outcome.

The foregoing provides the context for this chapter. While majority of the perpetrators were unknown, many of them were well known to their victims. It is therefore reasonable to expect that the government would take measures in keeping with its obligations to the citizen to bring the culprits to punishment. In order to contextualize how the state has dealt with the postelection violence and its impact, it is now appropriate to examine the obligations of the state in relation to victims of mass violence.

Obligations of the Kenyan State

The constitution of Kenya contains very progressive and robust human rights provisions and protections. It promises the citizen all the rights that are part of the international human rights regime to which Kenya has subscribed, including the right to life, freedom, and security of the person; and freedom of association, assembly, and expression. In addition, the penal code contains strict punishment for felonies such as murder, manslaughter, kidnapping, abduction, wrongful detention, and for other offenses such as arson, unlawful assemblies, riots, other offenses against public tranquillity, incitement to violence, offenses relating to property, malicious injury to property, and attempts to commit any of these offenses. The punishment for a conviction for murder is a sentence of death.

The government of Kenya (2009), under the constitution and the penal code, was obligated to investigate, prosecute, and punish the perpetrators of the postelection violence and all previous cases of mass violence in the country. It does not need a special tribunal to do so. The constitution of Kenya and other domestic legislation provide sufficient basis for any prosecution. In addition, the government was obliged to disclose to the victims, their families, and the society all that can be established about the violence. Further, it was under obligation to offer victims adequate reparations and to separate the known perpetrators from law enforcement bodies and from other positions of authority. In addition, the government was supposed to prosecute those responsible for gross violations of human rights and for other human rights abuses. It is obliged under international law to deal in a meaningful way with grave violations of human rights regardless of current constraints and to take steps to prevent or to bring to justice those responsible for crimes against humanity. International law imposes these obligations on states in response to massive and systematic violations of fundamental rights.

With the elaborate provisions and protections offered by both national and international law, the choice of approaches for dealing with both the past and with the postelection violence should have been obvious. That the approach to adopt is still in dispute brings to the surface the need for conceptual clarity about transitional justice mechanisms.

In deciding whether to start with criminal prosecutions or a restorative justice mechanism like a truth commission, every society looks at its political history, the nature of the conflict, the nature of the violations that occurred, and the political context that brought about an end to the conflict or violence, and should construct a process that benefits from both retributive and restorative approaches. There may be a question of timing or sequencing, but the solution to the question should arise from a dialogic process that acknowledges the importance of the two approaches and leverages the opportunities presented.

Transitional Justice

In countries undergoing a shift from repression, despotism, authoritarian rule, and inconclusive political transitions to democracy, the question of transitional justice presents the first real test for the establishment of genuine democracy and the rule of law, and articulates the very principles that will hopefully distinguish the new regime from the old. Strong political pressure for victor's justice in dealing with those who served the former regime and the need to demonstrate a separation between the old and the new governments may call for immediate and harsh retribution against a large number of individuals. If handled incorrectly, such action may deepen rather than heal the divisions within the nation. Trial and punishment of those who committed violations is not only essential to achieve some degree of justice, but a public airing and condemnation of their crimes is the best way to draw a line between the old government and the new. In cases where abuses were committed both by the former government and by its opponents, some have argued that the best approach is to forgive both sides (Kritz 1995).

There may also be noncriminal approaches to the transitional justice process. Such approaches contribute to interrogating the past and laying the foundations for the future. For example, administrative penalties may be imposed on the officials of the former regime. These may include lustration, or the purging from the public sector (especially from security sector and justice institutions) of officials found culpable of committed human rights violations. This serves to restore public confidence in the institutions of government and to remove obstacles to reform that may be presented by these officials.

A third transitional justice approach is represented by the deliberate efforts made to acknowledge the past through the development of a full account of what happened, and to seek to restore the dignity of the victims of the violations. Truth commissions represent this approach. They may also be accompanied by efforts to reaffirm history, such as memorials and remembrances, and the payment of reparations to the victims.

Transitional justice is constructed on the notion of temporariness and accommodation. The characteristics of a transitional justice situation include the collapse of institutions of accountability and of oversight; the erosion of capacity and resources of the state and its institutions to perform their officially sanctioned responsibilities; and acknowledgement that sufficient time is required to fully develop the capacity of the state and its institutions to deliver justice and peace dividends to the public. At the same time, victims demand justice and accountability for the wrongs they suffered. Others want to find closure and to move on with their lives. In this situation, the state (often through a peace agreement and at other times based on public consultations) develops and implements temporary or transitory arrangements to respond to the demands of justice and accountability while efforts continue to be made to develop the capacity of the institutions. The type of mechanism developed determines the length of the transitory arrangements. Criminal trials usually take time and on the average last from three to seven years. Truth commissions, being short-term, officially sanctioned investigating bodies, often last for about two years, with the possibility of extension of their mandate. These arrangements are necessary because it is important to fully demarcate the past from the future to establish a new ethos of governance and of behavior by state institutions and officials and to demonstrate that all official malfeasance will be challenged and punished (Ojielo 2004).

Following the postelection violence, there was no policy decision by the new coalition government on why a transitional justice process had become necessary or on why it settled for a Truth, Justice, and Reconciliation Commission. This lack of policy clarity is exemplified by the contradictory interpretations being given about the TJRC. At one point, in the heat of the national debate on the role of the ICC in the postelection violence, the cabinet issued a public statement that the TJRC would further prosecute the masterminds of the postelection violence, a role that completely derogates from the mandate and work of truth and reconciliation commissions. What emerges therefore is confusion in terms of the larger objectives for an appropriate transitional justice mechanism for Kenya. As a result, there seems to be incoherence in terms of what should be achieved and what mechanisms should be used. Since a national transitional justice mechanism has been established—a Truth, Justice, and Reconciliation Commission—the government and all the relevant stakeholders, such as the political parties, civil society, community groups, and organizations, are proceeding along in the hope that the process will generate the right results.

The Choice of a Transitional Justice Mechanism

As part of the Kenya National Dialogue and Reconciliation Process, agreement was reached in February 2008 on the establishment of a Truth, Justice, and Reconciliation Commission. The commission is charged with compiling an accurate, impartial, and historical narrative and with investigations of violations and abuses of human rights and international humanitarian law in Kenya from 1963 to early 2008. Its mandate includes investigating economic crimes and grand corruption, identifying those responsible for the violations, making recommendations for amnesty for crimes other than violations of international humanitarian law, and making recommendations for preventing the recurrence of the violations and abuses so as to promote healing, reconciliation, and unity. The TJRC was expected to work with civil society, the faith community, and other actors in the discharge of its mandate.

The parties to the negotiations on ending the postelection violence also agreed to the establishment of a commission of inquiry (Waki Commission). The Waki Commission Report recommended the establishment of a special tribunal that should seek accountability against persons bearing the greatest responsibility for crimes committed during the postelection violence. The commission recognized that the government may resist this process by refusing to sign an agreement to establish a special tribunal, by failing to enact a statute for the tribunal, or by obstructing its functioning as an independent or autonomous entity. In anticipation, the commission developed a list containing the names and relevant information on those suspected of bearing the greatest responsibility for the violence, which it handed over to the Committee of Eminent African Personalities with a further request that upon the expiry of a deadline set by the commission for the government to establish the special tribunal, the panel should hand over the list to the prosecutor of the ICC to analyze and determine whether to proceed with investigations and prosecution of the suspected persons (Kofi Annan Foundation and Africa Union 2010). The recourse to the ICC was a default action arising from the failure of the state to act on the recommendations of the Waki Commission Report. While officially professing support for trials by the ICC, the state and leading sections of the coalition government have continued to show their discomfort with the possibility of international prosecution. An unsuccessful attempt was also made to have the parliament endorse a proposal to withdraw from the ICC.

Why did the negotiators at the Kenya National Dialogue and Reconciliation Process (otherwise known as the Serena Process) choose a Truth, Justice, and Reconciliation Commission rather than criminal prosecution? Why is the government unwilling to prosecute the masterminds of the violence? This question goes to the root of the type of transitional justice mechanism chosen by the government—a Truth, Justice, and Reconciliation Commission. There are a number of reasons why the current government cannot prosecute the perpetrators of the postelection violence.

The first consideration of the type of transitional justice mechanism chosen, and by whom, is the nature of the political transition in Kenya. The discourse on criminal prosecutions in transitional societies acknowledges that there is usually a formal political transition that establishes a basis for a successor regime to work towards putting the leaders of the previous regime on trial. As Mue (2010) argues, Kenya after the 2007 elections has not gone through a "transitional moment" in the same way as other societies coming out of armed conflict. In addition, there was no regime change, and Kenya's politicians are adept at recycling themselves in power. A transitional moment would require a political transition or a radical alteration of the political, economic, or social foundations of the society. The Kenya National Dialogue and Reconciliation Agreement amounted to a ceasefire that resulted in a coalition government comprised of the two antagonistic groups: the PNU and the ODM. Such a negotiated peace is an accommodation of the various interests and hardly provides the framework for radical societal transformation. In the absence of a political transition or radical alteration of society, it would amount to the same players investigating themselves. It is therefore not surprising that there is no motivation to pursue criminal accountability for the postelection violence. The next opportunity for a real political transition would be the March 2013 presidential and general elections. The election of a president with overwhelming public acceptance and legitimacy could provide an enabling environment for revisiting the desire for criminal accountability for the postelection violence.

The second consideration is the control of the security forces and the potential for resumption of hostilities. In the absence of a political transition, the security forces are still under the control of the same key actors and groups in government, many of whom are perceived to have been complicit in committing violations during the postelection violence. In addition, while the violence has ended, fear of insecurity still pervades some of the communities where the violence was most severe. In parts of the Rift Valley, internally displaced persons remain in transit sites because they still consider their original homes to be insecure. While internal displacement has officially ended, there are tens of thousands of Kikuyus in the Rift Valley who have no confidence in the ability of the security agencies to protect them if they return to their original communities, and who are afraid that their neighbors and former friends would mete out violence against them if they returned home.

The fear of insecurity by the internally displaced is tied to the nonresolution of some of the structural factors that fed into the postelection violence. Key among these is the land question, which has become part of what is generally referred to as "historical injustices." Many communities in the Rift Valley are opposed to the return of the displaced persons because the displaced are perceived as the embodiment of the injustices done to these communities by previous governments, further reflected in the inability or unwillingness of the current government to address the historical or structural issues. Part of the polarization that affected the internal workings of the coalition government during its first eighteen months in office was the continued detention and prosecution of some of the youths who allegedly participated in the violence. A majority of the youth come from the Kalenjin community and were perceived as affiliated to the ODM. The Kalenjin community leadership felt that the continued detention of the youths was an attack on their community when the youth were "fighting for the rights of their community." The failed attempts by the state to prosecute some of the youths were received in the community with celebratory public rallies and processions led by politicians and other public officials from the community. A certain unspoken assumption seemed to have been adopted by state officials, who released the remaining detained youths out of fear that any further prosecution might result in continued polarization among the Kikuyu and Kalenjin, and potentially in violence.

A third consideration of the type of transitional justice mechanism is the duration of the conflict. The violence in Kenya lasted for not more than eight weeks. In cases where the violence is of short duration, there is more permissibility to prosecute the masterminds, as the violence tends to be restricted and does not involve large numbers of people. Where the violence is of sustained duration, large numbers of persons are typically involved and it is difficult to engage in criminal prosecution of all them. In such societies, truth commissions become the most appealing option. While the violence in Kenya was short lived, it was also widespread. Six out of the eight provinces in the country were widely affected. In testimonies to the Waki Commission and to the Kenya National Commission on Human Rights, many of the victims clearly knew their perpetrators as friends and neighbors. Prosecution would have been straightforward. Yet, the government has been unable to utilize the penal code as a basis for prosecuting the perpetrators and instead seemed to adopt a negative public policy approach that it would be more destabilizing to prosecute all the middle and low-level persons who engaged in the postelection violence.

Given the inability of the executive to prosecute the masterminds of the violence, it is surprising that it has not substantively supported the TJRC, which is supposed to focus on the broader social inquiry into the trends, patterns, and systemic foundations for the violence. Through reforms proposed by the TJRC, the basis for further violence may be eliminated. Some of the intense opposition to the TJRC by leading human rights groups, such as the International Centre for Policy and Conflict and the International Center for Transitional Justice, emanate from this interpretation of the state's intentions. The TJRC is inadvertently presented to the public as lesser justice: a platform for "hugging and kissing" where the facade of "all is well" could be presented while impunity continues to reign in the country.

A fourth reason for the choice of a Truth, Justice, and Reconciliation Commission as the appropriate transitional justice mechanism stems from the perception that the state is pandering to political and economic allies and trying to conceal the involvement of its leaders in human rights violations. On 15 December 2010, the prosecutor of the ICC, Luis Moreno-Ocampo, announced the names of six Kenyans (now popularly dubbed the "Ocampo Six") whom he accused of being behind the postelection violence. He requested the Trial Chamber of the Court to issue a "Summons to Appear" to the six. Five of the six persons are very prominent leaders of the coalition government and held senior public offices. When the Kenya National Commission on Human Rights published the report of its investigations into the violence (2008), it had named four of the six as some of the ringleaders of the violence and recommended that they be further investigated. With such leading members of the government alleged to have participated in the postelection violence, it was not surprising that any attempt at criminal prosecution would not be well received. Following the report of the Waki Commission, the state made two half-hearted attempts to have the parliament approve legislation to establish the special tribunal, which failed as expected. A private members' bill for a special tribunal introduced by Hon. Gitobu Imanyara (2009) similarly failed when members of parliament (MPs) conspired to walk out of parliament while the bill was being debated, denying the parliament of the quorum to continue with the debate.

The same MPs tried to obfuscate the debate by claiming that they had no confidence in the local judiciary and would prefer that the ICC conduct prosecution of the masterminds of the violence. The phrase "Don't be vague, go to The Hague" became part of the political lexicon to justify a preference for the ICC. The preference for the ICC was based on the false assumption that international prosecution would take forever and that by the time the ICC came around to issuing indictments, some of the alleged perpetrators would have been safely ensconced in State House Nairobi.

Earlier, I alluded to the obligation of the state under national and international law to protect the human rights of victims and to offer them reparation for violations and to prosecute those responsible for the violations. The unwillingness of the executive and the parliament to enact legislation on the special tribunal and to cooperate with the ICC flies in the face of the state's obligations. It seems obvious that the political elite had no intention of holding themselves accountable for the violations that occurred during the postelection violence.

In settling for a Truth, Justice, and Reconciliation Commission, many Kenyans expected that substantial progress would be made in working towards reconciliation, in accordance with the Kenya National Dialogue and Reconciliation Process. It seems clear, however, that the political actors have literally left the job of reconciliation to the Truth, Justice, and Reconciliation Commission, the faith community, and civil society organizations. In a context such as Kenya, where the causative factors of the violence were political, though accompanied and fed by other factors, the foundation for a sustainable national reconciliation process must also be political. Political reconciliation does not just occur at the national level. It cascades to other levels of society and provides a framework that encourages and sustains other levels of reconciliation such as intercommunity and interpersonal reconciliation between victims and offenders. While political reconciliation at the national level might be said to have partially occurred, evidenced by the formation of the coalition government, the mistrust, infighting, and rivalry that still characterize transactions within the government continues to send negative signals to the rest of the country, and undermine the possibility of reconciliation at other levels.

With the state unable or unwilling to prosecute the masterminds of the violence, leaving the TJRC as the only mechanism for interrogating the past and constructing the future as well as ensuring justice to the victims, it is now necessary to examine the commission and its prospects for contributing to healing and reconciliation in the country.

The Truth, Justice, and Reconciliation Commission

The task force on the establishment of a Truth, Justice, and Reconciliation Commission, after traversing the country and seeking the views of Kenyans, recommended in 2003 that such a commission be established by presidential fiat. The task force was convinced of the goodwill and integrity of the then government and of its desire to establish a new regime based on the rule of law and the independence of state institutions. In recommending a Truth, Justice, and Reconciliation Commission, the task force echoed and acknowledged the overwhelming public desire, championed by civil society groups for more than a decade, that the nation depart from a past marked by state impunity and commission of human rights violations. Moreover, the task force criticized the undermining of state institutions and the concentration and personalization of power and authority by the president. It therefore hoped that a Truth, Justice, and Reconciliation

Commission would be the national catharsis that would lead to strengthening democracy, economic prosperity, and development in the country. It argued that a ravaged state like Kenya could not be reconstructed without an agenda for transitional justice that would end public corruption and prevent human rights abuses. It concluded that Kenyans had overwhelmingly decided that the truth about the past (before 2003) must be known, that the perpetrators must be identified and punished, and the victims accorded justice. The task force concluded that reconciliation is only possible after the truth is known and justice done to victims.

Efforts between 2003 and 2008 to establish the TJRC failed. What became clear was that the promise of a new dawn offered by the political transition of December 2002, in which President Kibaki came to power, seemed to have been aborted. By 2007, the expected new dawn was being regarded as being eclipsed by politics-as-usual.

The 2007 postelection violence provided additional impetus. Given the urgency of the times and the desire to move speedily to establish the commission as mandated by the Agenda Item 4 Agreement, parliament quickly passed the Truth, Justice, and Reconciliation Commission Act in 2008 over and above the complaints by civil society organizations that there had been very limited consultations on the legislation before it was presented to parliament and then enacted (Government of Kenya 2008). While there were full consultations in 2003, this was quite limited in 2008. The justifications offered by the task force in 2003 were even more valid in 2008 when the Truth, Justice, and Reconciliation Commission Act was finally enacted. Between 2003 and 2008, in the absence of fundamental reforms to the state and its institutions, the state was perceived as continuing to act above the law, entrenching impunity and corruption, with the security agencies engaging in human rights violations.

The establishment of the TJRC in 2008 had become an absolute necessity. The implementation of the agreements reached under the Kenya National Dialogue and Reconciliation (KNDR) process and the construction of a "new nation" would be impossible unless the country engaged first in a cathartic process of national reflection, acknowledgement, and cleansing; it must lay bare, confront, and bury the ghosts of the past and establish a new ethos for the country. Kenyans hoped that the new Truth, Justice, and Reconciliation Commission would be the vehicle for achieving these purposes.

There were many problems with the TJRC Act that was approved by parliament and assented to by the president in 2008. In detailed comments submitted to the parliament, the International Centre for Transitional Justice (ICTJ 2008) outlined a number of conceptual, strategic, and substantive issues that the legislation ignored or failed to address. These included confusing and missing definitions: while crimes against humanity and genocide were defined, other international crimes were not. Gross human rights violations were defined, but human rights violations were not, although they were referred to throughout the Act; victims were defined, but perpetrators were not; and the Act provided for granting of amnesty for economic crimes, but the crimes were not defined. The Act further required a perpetrator of economic crimes to make restitution before he or she could benefit from amnesty, meaning that such perpetrators were likely to wait until there was a good prospect of prosecution before making restitution. Since there is little prospect of effective prosecutions taking place few, if any, corrupt persons will come forward. There were also issues with the contradictory powers of the commission in relation to amnesty processes, including the power to grant amnesty to persons who make full disclosure before the commission.

The civil society Multi-Sectoral Task Force on the TJRC (2008) also issued detailed criticisms of the legislation, largely adopting those leveled by the ICTJ. In addition, comments submitted by the Office of the United Nations High Commissioner for Human Rights raised concerns over several provisions of the proposed bill and urged legislation that would grant the TJRC clear operational independence so that it could carry out its work without political interference. It insisted that the commission must be seen to operate free of direct or indirect influence or control by government in relation to the appointment of commissioners, hiring of staff, budgetary decision-making and in relation to research and investigation, report writing and formulation of recommendations. The draft bill, in the opinion of the Office of the High Commissioner (2008), contained several provisions that could be contrary to these principles.

In protest against perceived official exclusion from participation in the debate and finalization of legislation on the TJRC, the Kenya Transitional Justice Network (TJN), Kenyans for Peace with Truth and Justice (KPTJ), and the Centre for Multiparty Democracy (CMD) issued what they called a "Model Bill on the TJRC" that embodied all the elements of what a truth commission represents. The civil society groups forgot the fact that truth commissions are negotiated political processes. As a result of Kenya's long history of struggle to confront impunity, the TJN and other civil society groups assumed that political actors had been sufficiently mortified by the postelection violence and would be willing to seek accommodation with civil society and other actors in framing legislation on the TJRC. The perceived underhanded approach of the government in the enactment of the legislation contributed to an atmosphere of suspicion of the Truth Justice and Reconciliation Commission.

This situation was not mollified by the fact that in composing the commission, the government deferred to civil society groups such as the Law Society of Kenya, the Kenya Private Sector Alliance, the trade union movement, and the faith community organizations to identify members of a selection committee that would vet applications and nominations and make recommendations to parliament on the persons to be appointed to the commission.

The national and international commissioners that were finally appointed to the commission are persons of substance in their respective spheres. They include Betty Murugi, renowned human rights activist and former vice chair of the commission, who has since resigned. Others are Tom Ojienda, a former president of both the Law Society of Kenya and of East Africa; General Ahmed Farah, who had a distinguished career in the armed forces of Kenya; Margaret Shava and Tecla Wanjala, both of whom were renowned for their work in civil society; and the chairperson, Bethwel Kiplagat, who after a career in the public service acquired even greater recognition as an international peacemaker. He also led the civil society efforts to end the postelection violence, and provided advisory services to the Kofi Annan–led mediation efforts. Among the international commissioners are Berhanu Dinka, renowned Ethiopian former diplomat who subsequently served as special representative of the UN Secretary General in several posts, including Sierra Leone and the Great Lakes; Professor Ronald Slye, professor of law from Seattle in the United States; and Justice Gertrude Chawatama, a judge of the High Court of Zambia.

However, no sooner had the commission been appointed than allegations began to surface about the chairperson and his association with President Daniel arap Moi's regime (1978–2002) and of a potential conflict of interest. The conflict of interest was in relation to his having benefited from allocation of land during Moi's regime, a subject that the commission was also charged with investigating. The cynicism around the commission was not helped by the delay of the government in addressing the complaints from civil society organizations. A 2010 petition by the commissioners, calling for a tribunal to investigate the chairperson, went unheeded. Ultimately, the vice chairperson of the commission resigned, complaining that the cloud of suspicion hanging over the chairperson—and by inference the commission—would prevent the commission from discharging its mandate. Even the Parliamentary Committee on Justice and Legal Affairs threatened to present a bill in parliament to dissolve the commission because of the nonresolution of the issues around the chairperson. Finally, the chief justice formally established the tribunal, and the chairperson felt compelled to step aside to face his accusers at the tribunal. Unfortunately, official indifference to the complaints against the chairperson fed into and reinforced the perception that the state had an agenda to plant its sympathizers within the commission and to skew whatever report the commission might eventually produce.

While the commission has tried to recover lost ground, cynicism within the human rights community remains strong. The KTJN issued a public statement in May 2009 calling for the commission to be disbanded. In early 2011, not satisfied that the chairperson had stepped down, they wanted the commission dissolved and the process started afresh. At the time of writing, victims' networks and different community groups across the country, such as the various ethnic councils of elders, continued to see the commission as an opportunity to have their stories told and to have the state formally acknowledge the multiple violations to which they were subjected by the Kenyatta and Moi regimes and by various other institutions of the state, such as the military and the police.

The role of the state remains ambiguous. Senior members of government continue to publicly pledge support for the commission. Some of them criticize the commission publicly and then turn around to defend proposed budgetary allocations to the commission before the departmental committees of the parliament. However, the commission remains grossly underfunded and almost closed shop in December 2010 due to its inability to pay staff salaries.

The commission has completed taking statements from Kenyans across the country, collecting more than 40,000 testimonies. It is also well into the most important aspect of its work: the public hearings. Public hearings by truth commissions are opportunities for national dialogue and national catharsis. Nothing equals how national attention can be riveted by testimonies of victims describing their hurt and pain and of perpetrators recanting their behavior and asking forgiveness from their victims. If well managed, public hearings can catapult national sentiments towards an environment of accountability, healing, and reconciliation. For a country like Kenya that is in the midst of difficult reforms, public hearings can propel a groundswell of national opinion and consensus towards the agreed reform agenda. It is therefore unfortunate that official proclamations of support of the commission by senior ministers in government remain hot air.

At the beginning of the chapter, I explored Kenya's 2007 postelection violence and the state's obligations under domestic and international human rights instruments to deal with the violations. I further analyzed why it is impossible for the current government to prosecute the masterminds of the violence. This left the Truth, Justice, and Reconciliation Commission as the only transitional justice mechanism that could address the experience of the violence and lay the foundations for a new nation and state based on equity, fairness, and justice. The preceding discussion captures the challenges the commission has faced in discharging this expectation, and elaborated how the state contributes to this by failing to respond in a timely manner to the internal problems of the commission and by not providing sufficient funding. If the TJRC fails, the entire transitional justice agenda in Kenya will have failed. The implications of this could bring more violence during the next general elections in 2012.

However, the commission could still make an important contribution to confronting impunity and enthroning the rule of law in Kenya. The best way it can rebut the cynicism is to ensure that it delivers an authoritative historical narrative of the issues forming part of its mandate, and a credible report about the violations, abuses, and crimes, as well as the trends and patterns of the violations suffered by the victims who testify before the commission. It must strenuously shed any perception that it was established to do a whitewash job for some people in government and deliver a report that becomes the reference point on this epoch in Kenya's history.

Justice versus Reconciliation

A certain mindset currently exists in Kenya where support for the TJRC is perceived as eroding or undermining support for the special tribunal or to the ICC. Therefore, among donors, the predominant view is to support the ICC to the exclusion of the TJRC. The argument among the donors and their civil society supporters is that impunity has proliferated for so long in Kenya that only a mechanism like the ICC can work; moreover, this should contribute to showing that no one is above the law. While the executive has not endeared itself to Kenyans for effective and timely prosecution of cases, especially where the alleged perpetrators are big-time and well-heeled politicians, it is a false argument that one transitional justice mechanism is more important or preferable to the other.

Musila (2009) correctly notes that the discourse on transitional justice in Kenya has been bereft of a clear policy articulation and occurs within a polarized political environment, making consensus on approaches improbable. In addition, the discourse is shaped by competing notions of justice that themselves dictate different approaches. At the beginning of the coalition government, the view of the ODM was that the many youth who were arrested for their roles in the postelection violence were protesting against the theft of their votes and therefore should not be punished. In addition, it argued that the real perpetrators of the postelection violence were the commissioners of the former Electoral Commission of Kenya (ECK) who had allegedly manipulated the election in favor of President Kibaki. The commissioners of the ECK were the ones who should be prosecuted, the ODM argued. In addition, it claimed that what was needed was to heal and reconcile the nation rather than to engage in punishment of the youth who were simply exercising their legitimate rights of protest.

On the other hand, leading members of the PNU insisted that the ringleaders of the postelection violence were the leadership of the ODM who had called for "mass action" to protest the presidential election results, instead of taking their dispute to the judiciary for arbitration. According to the PNU, any call to mass action is an invitation to violence. ODM leaders, including Prime Minister Raila Odinga, should be prosecuted for the violence. These discordant voices continued to dominate and overlap each time there was tension within the coalition government. With these competing notions of justice, and the unwillingness of the two factions in the coalition government to effectively deal with the violence as a result of the factors mentioned earlier, it is reasonable to assume that no action would have been taken against anyone.

The report of the Waki Commission into the postelection violence dramatically changed the notions of justice to individual responsibility when it submitted to Kofi Annan its list of names of the secret masterminds of the violence. It further invited the participation of the ICC through recommending investigations if the state failed to act on its report. Two leading politicians with presidential ambitions, from the Kikuyu and Kalenjin communities respectively and fiercely opposed to each other, found common ground through being adversely mentioned in the Waki Commission Report. For the first time in Kenya's recent political history, the Kikuyu and Kalenjin political elite, rather than being antagonistic to each other, have become bedfellows. Individual guilt has suddenly been transformed into community guilt, creating a siege mentality within the affected communities as well. While the desire for justice in Kenya is widespread, it is shaped by ethnic-based contestation for group interests and advantage.

The combined strength of the Kikuyu and Kalenjin gives them huge numbers in parliament, and through their ethnic alliance they can actually determine political succession in Kenya in 2012 as well as the direction of government. This overwhelming strength is now being put to use in the control of executive powers, including the composition of public bodies and in parliamentary processes. It has huge implications for any transitional justice mechanism, such as the creation of the special tribunal, and for the success of the TJRC.

At the time of writing, the opposition to ICC criminal trials is framing them as an invasion of the sovereign right of Kenya that can undermine peace and stability as well as the new state institutions provisioned by the new constitution. By implication, the dominant view among the political elite, or at least within the new majority in the coalition government, is that the leaders of the violence should not be prosecuted. The discourse does not mention any obligation of the state to the victims of the violence, or the need to confront and end impunity. The direction of transitional justice is being largely shaped by the political aspirations of the leaders in the government.

The debate over the supremacy or importance of justice versus reconciliation is a false one. The victim in the village wants the neighbor next door who was responsible for her violation to be punished. She also wants to be able to sleep peacefully at night knowing that neither he nor his family can attack her again. The pursuit of justice is not necessarily antagonistic to the pursuit of reconciliation. Both are stages in a process of sustainable peace and neither is more important than the other. Rather than a hierarchy, they each represent elements of a web.

Current Responses to the Transitional Justice Process

It might be easy and convenient to dismiss the transitional justice process in Kenya as destined for failure, perhaps with the exception of the ICC trials. This would be a hasty conclusion. In January 2012, the ICC by majority decision ruled that four of the six Kenyans accused of being the masterminds of the postelection violence should stand trial. Many commentators argued that the Kenyan case before the ICC did not meet the threshold of crimes against humanity. One of the judges of the ICC chamber agreed. However, most Kenyans felt that, given the long history of efforts to tame impunity and to establish an accountable human rights regime in Kenya, it is sufficient that some persons are "tarred with the brush of indictees" by the ICC. Even if some or all of the four persons to stand trial at the ICC are not convicted, it is sufficient and necessary for Kenya's political development that some of them would be tried in the court. According to this view, the trial will go a long way in establishing that crimes will be punished and that no one is above the law. This is seen as a necessary ingredient in reforming the Kenyan state, making it accountable to Kenyans and consolidating the possibilities and gains of transitional justice in the country.

It should be noted that the Kenyan case is groundbreaking. It is the first time in the history of the ICC that the prosecutor has utilized one of the mechanisms for catalyzing investigations and prosecution by applying to the court to have certain persons charged and tried for international crimes. More importantly, Kenya does not fit the types of cases that have been subject to international justice in the past: it was not a protracted armed conflict marked by very serious violations of human rights, such as Rwanda, the former Yugoslavia, and Sierra Leone, among others; rather, it lasted about eight weeks at the most. It is therefore telling that the pretrial chamber of the ICC decided that this is a case worthy of international justice. It sends a clear and powerful signal to leaders all over the world that if they try to manipulate and suppress accountability in their domestic courts, they could always be held accountable through international mechanisms. A clear entry point has therefore been opened for civic actors and other interested parties to catalyze international prosecution for events that are essentially domestic.

The announcement by the prosecutor in December 2010 of the names of the six persons who should be held accountable for the postelection violence also generated a counterreaction, with calls for the enactment of a special tribunal. These reactions came largely from the supporters of the named persons. They argued that there were other "deserving perpetrators" who should have been charged before the ICC for the same crimes. The desire for a special tribunal was to exact some form of revenge by having these other perceived perpetrators charged before the special tribunal. These emotions soon wore off, however. As a result of the increased public awareness of the issues around the postelection violence and international accountability, parliament could not unilaterally enact legislation on a special tribunal that would be targeted at certain people.

Public opinion in Kenya is certainly in favor of a special tribunal, because while the ICC would have "taken care" of the masterminds of the violence, there were many other actors at high and middle levels who many Kenyans genuinely believe should be tried before such a tribunal. However, were any such intentions by some members of parliament to be subjected to public input, the emerging legislation would be so robust and strong that it would not offer comfort to the supporters of the indictees who were hoping to use the tribunal as a form of retribution against their opponents. Clear evidence of this conclusion is provided by the draft legislation on a special tribunal produced by the Ministry of Justice in 2010. The draft provides for a trial chamber comprised of three judges, with a Kenyan as chair and two other international judges, and for an international prosecutor with prosecutorial and investigative staff drawn from within and outside Kenya. This is quite robust already and with additional safeguards, it is possible to have a legislation that meets the threshold of international justice.

It is debatable whether the Kenyan political elite will continue to call for a special tribunal given the above background. As parliamentarians prepare for a general election in 2013, the debate is expected to die quietly and parliament can conveniently claim that it did not get around to enacting legislation for a special tribunal because of its congested legislative agenda.

The international community has been hasty in its abandonment of the TJRC. This is not surprising. In all parts of the developing world where the possibility of a truth commission and a criminal tribunal have co-existed, the international community has been quick to rush to the criminal tribunal at the expense of the truth commission. Some of the arguments advanced for this are banal: that the criminal tribunal puts people in prison, stops impunity, and holds people accountable, hence the evidence of its work is easily visible. In contrast, a truth commission is composed of so much "to-ing" and "fro-ing" that it is difficult to appreciate its work.

The real issue is cultural. The members of the international community who subscribe to this view are mostly Western donors. Factual processes like criminal tribunals are very easy to understand, and can provide easy justification for their financial investment. Yet, factual processes are only one element of the wider search for truth. Truth commissions, on the other hand, are focused on broader societal inquiry, underpinned by a need to repair relationships at all levels so as to preserve and protect cohesion, and are a foundation for sustainable development. When Western donors therefore refuse to provide financing for truth commissions, it should not be seen as indication that such commissions do not work. Rather, if a state and its people believe in the importance and relevance of their truth commission, they must grant it the resources it needs to do its work successfully.

While the Kenya Truth, Justice, and Reconciliation Commission has had many challenges, the motivation of its commissioners and staff remains high. If the state misses the importance of the ongoing hearings as a platform for national dialogue and fails to provide the funds needed by the commission, the TJRC will be irretrievably damaged and will add little value to the discourse on accountability in the country. Given the uncertainty over the establishment of a special tribunal, the TJRC may turn out to be the only domestic accountability mechanism for the foreseeable future. If the state provides the resources and the commission manages to win over the skeptics, to deliver public thematic hearings that lead to national reflection, and to produce a solid report with actionable recommendations, it may ultimately salvage its reputation and make an important contribution to national development. The jury is therefore still out on the contribution of the commission to societal transformation, accountability, healing, and reconciliation in the country.

References

Government of Kenya. 2008. Truth, Justice, and Reconciliation Commission Act. Nairobi: Government of Kenya Printer.

———. 2009. *The Penal Code, Laws of the Republic of Kenya*. Rev. ed. Nairobi: Government of Kenya Printer.

Imanyara, Gitobu. 2009. "Statute for the Special Tribunal for Kenya." 1–26 January, Nairobi.

ICTJ. 2008. "Comments by the ICTJ on the TJRC Bill." International Centre for Transitional Justice. ICTJ Briefing Paper 3, November.

Kenya National Commission on Human Rights. 2008. *On the Brink of the Precipice: A Human Rights Account of Kenya's Post-election Violence*. August. Nairobi: Kenya National Commission on Human Rights.

Kenya Transitional Justice Network. 2010. "Petition on the Establishment of a Tribunal on the Chairperson of the TJRC." 8 September. Nairobi: Kenya Transitional Justice Network.

KNDR. 2008. "The Kenya National Dialogue and Reconciliation Monitoring Project." Kenya National Dialogue and Reconciliation, (KNDR). Accessed 4 February 2011. http://www.dialoguekenya.org/docs/Project%20context%20and%20summary%20of%20findings.pdf.

Kofi Annan Foundation. 2010. *Kenya National Dialogue and Reconciliation: Basic Documents*, Geneva, Switzerland: Kofi Annan Foundation.

Kritz, Neil. 1995. "Dilemmas of Transitional Justice." In *Transitional Justice: How Emerging Democracies Reckon with Former Regimes*, edited by Neil Kritz, xix–xxx. Vol. 1. Washington, DC: United States Institute of Peace Press.

Mue, Njonjo. 2010. "Kenya Case Study." African Transitional Justice Research Workshop on Advocating Justice: Civil Society and Transitional Justice in Africa. Accessed 5 January 2011. www.transitionaljustice.org.za/docs/2010.

Multi-sectoral Task Force on the TJRC. 2008. "Analysis of the Approved TJRC Bill." 1–12, Nairobi: 4 November.

Musila, Godfrey. 2009. "Options for Transitional Justice in Kenya: Autonomy and the Challenge of External Prescriptions." In *International Journal of Transitional Justice* 3, no. 3 (October): 445–64.

Mute, Lawrence M., Kichamu Akivaga, and Wanza Kioke, eds. 2002. *Building an Open Society: The Politics of Transitional Justice in Kenya*. Nairobi: Clarion.

Office of the High Commissioner for Human Rights. 2008. "Comments on the Draft Bill to Establish a TJRC for Kenya." April:1–10.

Ojielo, Ozonnia. 2004. "How Much Truth, How Much Reconciliation: Commissions, Coalitions and Other Solutions." Paper presented at the Wilton Park Conference of the British Foreign Service, Sussex, UK, July.

Truth, Justice, and Reconciliation Commission. 2010. "Petition Pursuant to Section 17 and Section 10 of the Truth Justice and Reconciliation Commission Act No. 6 of 2008 as Amended on the Establishment of a Tribunal on the Chairperson of the TJRC," Nairobi: April.

Task Force on the Establishment of the Truth Justice and Reconciliation Commission (TETJRC). 2003. *TETJRC Report*, Nairobi: August.

Waki Commission Report. 2008. *Report of the Commission of Inquiry into the Post-election Violence (CIPEV)*, September. Nairobi: Government of Kenya Printer.

7 Climate Change and Peacebuilding among Pastoralist Communities in Northeastern Uganda and Western Kenya

Julaina A. Obika and Harriet K. Bibangambah

The link between climate change and conflict is a continuously debated subject that has attracted a growing body of research. In the developing field of eco-conflicts, many scholars focus on assessing whether climate change increases the risk of conflict. Drawing on a wide range of literature and using the cases of the Karimojong in Uganda and the Pokot and Turkana in Kenya, this chapter examines climate change, conflict, and peacebuilding among pastoral societies in the Great Lakes region of East Africa. Building on Homer-Dixon's (1999) theory of eco-conflicts, we argue that climate conditions and change have impacted the political, economic, and social characteristics of pastoralism, and exacerbated conditions for conflict. Pastoralist communities of East Africa are faced with the challenge of a declining natural resource base that impinges on their survival and that of their herds. This has become a structural cause of violence in the region as well as a sustaining factor for conflict.

Pastoralism in the Great Lakes Region of East Africa

Pastoralists are people whose livelihood depends on their livestock; in East Africa, this mode of production is accompanied by a nomadic or seminomadic lifestyle. Harsh environments of very high spatial and temporal variability in rainfall have been responsible for the evolution of pastoralism over the years (Tarekegn 2007, 170–71). However, pastoralism still remains the most capable traditional land management system in regions with scanty vegetation, erratic rainfall, increasing droughts, and other climatic uncertainties (Mulugeta and Hagmann 2008, 73).

The Kenya-Uganda border is ethnically diverse, forming the boundary that traverses the homelands of the Samia, Teso, Pokot, and Turkana, dividing them from the Ugandan Karimojong, Dodoth, and Jie (Mkutu 2006). The Pokot are situated in the Rift Valley, along Kenya's western border, and are divided into three groups, the smallest of which lives in Uganda (Upe Pokot). The Turkana are nomadic pastoralists and the second largest pastoral community in Kenya next to the Maasai. They occupy the northwestern part of Kenya, an area of about 67,000 square kilometers in the Rift Valley. Karamoja occupies approximately 27,200 square kilometers in northeastern Uganda, bordering Sudan and Kenya (Mkutu 2008; Stites and Akabwai 2009). The region is known to be "one of the most inhospitable ecozones in Africa," where rainfall is generally unpredictable, making agriculture an unreliable subsistence strategy (Jabs 2007, 1501); the environment is so fragile that no other group of people has ever wanted to occupy it (Knaute and Kagan 2009, 6).

Pastoralist zones in the Great Lakes region have been described as wracked with conflict, the conventional explanations for which are said to be the competition for scarce resources, including water and pasture (Jabs 2007; Markakis 2007). It is pertinent to note that extreme weather conditions such as drought bring about additional shocks and stresses, particularly for poor communities who must find ways of coping, recovering, and adapting. These adaptation mechanisms vary as the extreme climatic conditions worsen.

As a result of environmental degradation, shrinkage of the natural resource base, and armed confrontations over grazing land and water, pastoralism is therefore increasingly associated with uncontrolled violence (Hagmann and Mulugeta 2008, 19). This "pastoralist violence" discourse is gaining popularity among researchers, media, donors, and state officials. In the 1990s there were devastating conflicts between the Pokot and the Turkana over land and other resources (Österle 2007, 202). In Uganda, Karimojong warriors have had violent interactions with the Toposa of Sudan, and have often attacked the agriculturalist Iteso in an ongoing conflict for over fifty years (Mkutu 2008, 29). The Pokot, who live on both sides of the Kenya-Uganda border and cross over frequently, have clashed with their neighbors, the Karimojong, because—as Mkutu (2008, 22) believes—the Pokot are trying to keep their land while the Karimojong want possession of it.

The preceding examples comprise conflicts among pastoralists, as well as between pastoralists and agriculturalists; higher incidents of violent conflict seem to be found among ethnic communities and groups whose main source of survival is directly linked to the environment. Indeed, pastoralists have been largely blamed for environmental degradation with little attention or regard to their circumstances (Thebaud and Batterbury 2001, 69). We argue that the conditions pastoralists experience as well as the dynamics of conflict and cooperation among them and other neighboring groups are strongly linked to the complexity of activities used to secure resources and the inconsistent role of the state in assisting or regulating pastoralist livelihoods. However, we concur with Barnett and Adger (2007, 644) that climate change will not undermine human security or increase the risk of violent conflict in isolation from other important social factors.

Climate Change and Theories of Violent Conflict

Recent scholarship has examined how conflict might be stimulated by climate change, and conversely, "changes in social systems [are] driven by *actual* or *perceived* climate impacts" (Barnett and Adger 2007, 640). Many scholars agree that the link between climate change and conflict, in spite of its popularity, must be treated with caution. Despite a general concern that the environmental effects of climate change, especially the depletion of natural resources, will create conditions that increase the risk of violent conflict, many researchers have been cautious about drawing such a definite link. A debate clearly exists in the scholarly literature. For example, Carius and Imbusch (1999, 18–23) point to the "triggering and accelerating effect" of environmental degradation and resource depletion on conflict, while Schwartz (2002, 137) argues that environmental stress is a "relatively distant factor" that should be analyzed within the context of political, economic, and social factors. However, he acknowledges that environmental stress should not be ignored, as it plays an important role in causing conflicts.

Over millennia, pastoralists have been faced with harsh conditions and have adapted through nomadism and other strategies to secure food and water resources for themselves and their animals. Conflicts may arise due to competing demands for a resource but may not always result in violence. The plausibility of a singular "conflict trigger" declines when analyzing cases at the micro-level where site-specific variables become apparent (Castro 2007, 343). In fact, Homer-Dixon (1999) cautions against adamant claims about the causal role of environmental scarcity that subordinate other contextual factors. However, the degree of environmental scarcity a society experiences is not, as it turns out, entirely the result of economic, political, and social factors (such as failed institutions and policies), but is also partly a function of the particular physical characteristics of the environment. It is widely recognized that developing countries like Uganda and Kenya are more vulnerable and stand to suffer disproportionately from the effects of climate change, including threats to food security, health, and economic growth. Faced with multiple stresses such as poverty, hunger, low literacy levels, gender inequality, limited technological means, and lack of good governance, it is evident that developing countries are in the weakest position to mitigate the adverse effects of climate change (Osman-Elashaand El Sanjak 2007, 33; Reuveny 2007, 657).

Tänzler et al. (2002, 4–5) and Brauch et al. (2002) addressed key questions on climate change, environmental stress, and conflict, by presenting scientific evidence on the linkages between the three variables. Brauch et al. focused on six causes of global environmental change that contribute to both degradation (e.g., of soil and water) and scarcity (e.g., of water and food), thus adding to environmental stress. Taking the specific global and national conditions into account, these causes may lead to several outcomes, including distress migration, and internal or international conflicts. Reuveny (2007) discusses the climate change-migration-conflict link by postulating that the process leading up to conflict after migration occurs when certain dynamics—such as competition, ethnic tension, distrust, fault lines, and auxiliary conditions—are at play. Studies of civil war reiterate that political and economic factors are the strongest indicators of conflict risk (see Raleigh 2007) rather than environmental ones. Many scholars thus agree that long-term environmental and climatic conditions have a limited role in generating civil or international wars, and argue that the propensity for increases in communal conflict are speculative at best (Nordas and Gleditsch 2007, 2).

Impoverishment and migration have been identified as important social effects of environmental scarcity, which in turn serves as an important cause of violent conflicts—a situation that is evident in Africa (see Homer-Dixon 1999, 6). Although the very nature of the pastoralists' lives depends on moving from place to place, climate change has now increased the frequency and distance of those migrations, forcing groups to encroach on the territories of others in order to find land for grazing. The change in mobility patterns is likely to trigger conflict, especially when a group encroaches on an area where resources are already scarce and tensions already exist. Moreover, such environmental scarcity conflicts can be expected to have more influence in coming decades because of population growth and higher subsequent resource consumption.

The two causal intersections between environmental scarcity and violence we highlight as especially significant for the Karimojong, Pokot, and Turkana are: ethnic clashes arising from population migration and deepened social cleavages (including impoverishment) due to environmental scarcity; and civil strife (including insurgency and banditry) caused by environmental scarcity that affects economic productivity, and in turn, people's livelihoods (see Homer-Dixon 1999, 5). We believe that while it is essential to be cautious, we should not underestimate the role that climate change plays in conflict. Such an underestimation would negate the importance of climate change and its impacts, and prevent peacebuilding processes in pastoral societies from making headway. Climate change is a global phenomenon; an offshoot of this dynamic has been an increase in violent conflicts, especially for communities that depend entirely on the environment for their survival.

Accounting for Complexity in Pastoralist Conflicts

The lived situation for pastoralists can perhaps be described as complex. It is claimed that pastoralism as a way of life is threatened by the impacts of climate change mainly in the form of drought cycles and associated pressures like famine and competition over resources (Tarekegn 2007, 172; Birch and Grahn 2007). Some links have been made between environmental stress and pastoral conflicts, though explanations of pastoral conflicts build upon different disciplinary traditions and schools of thought. One such school of thought, characterized by "primordialist" thinking, emphasizes the ritualistic and traditional dimensions of pastoralist violence, suggesting this was an integral part of the herders' life, acting both as a means of conflict regulation and of shaping individual and collective subjectivities. According to Hagmann and Mulugeta (2008, 23), the "war-like," "aggressive," and "belligerent" nature of pastoralists is stereotypical of primordialist and essentialist thinking and discourse, and has been challenged by a younger generation of anthropologists, ecologists, and pastoralist activists. For example, Homer-Dixon (1999) emphasized the environmental conflict paradigm by predicting that unfulfilled demands and competition for grazing land and water trigger tension and disputes among pastoral groups. This sentiment has been shared by Nordås and Gleditsch (2007, 6), who believe that the prolonged drought cycles—that have caused famine, population displacement and migration, disease outbreaks, and a reduction in resources such as water and food—will create disputes among groups affected by the increasing resource scarcity. Climatic changes have also led to desertification and to the narrowing of the belts of pasture upon which the pastoralist mode of production depends, thus drastically reducing access to rangeland. We therefore contend that the increased frequency of droughts among the pastoralist societies has aggravated the risk of conflict within the communities and their neighbors.

Mkutu (2006, 61) affirms the complex interplay of environmental, cultural, historical, and governance issues in pastoral conflicts at the Kenya-Uganda border, noting how scarcity, mobility, and competition are aggravated by climatic conditions. Another factor is the variety of actors who are both directly and indirectly involved; these include the pastoralists themselves, businessmen, politicians, mercenaries, security forces and warlords, and the state, among others. Indeed, there are multiple causes of pastoral conflicts in the Great Lakes region. Vadala (2003, 632) observed that marginalization coupled with geographical conditions has contributed to the exacerbation of conflicts among pastoralists, the state, cultivators—and most of all—other pastoralists. Mulugeta and Hagmann (2008) also argue that the regulation of violent conflicts in areas marked by a weak state presence and lack of state legitimacy must be understood as the outcome of interactions among multiple social orders, actors, and norms within a particular spatial setting. The authors have further argued that the phenomena of inter- and intracommunal conflicts in arid and semiarid ecosystems are largely a response to a shrinking natural resource base (Mulugeta and Hagmann 2008, 23-24). Indeed, many scholars agree that climate change may not necessarily be a direct cause of violent conflicts but must be analyzed in relationship to other salient anthropogenic factors within the context. We agree with Raleigh (2007, 64) that the risk of adverse consequences due to climate change is related to the preexisting political, economic, and physical vulnerability of communities. Pastoral conflicts are not reducible to resource-based conflicts alone, but consist of by a host of different conflicts that may also change over time. In general, whether it be conflicts of interests, scarcity driven by inequalities, marginalization, poverty, the environment, or some other trigger that results in disputes or violence—this all depends on multiple other factors within the economic, social, and political context. Pastoralists have been marginalized since colonial times, and attempts at development have not given adequate consideration to the social and ecological realities of these arid areas. We assert that while pastoral conflicts are not new, they have intensified as the aspirations of pastoralists are increasingly under threat. The existence and way of life of these pastoralist communities are tied to their cattle. As pastoralists struggle to survive the increasingly prolonged droughts, competition over grazing lands and water for their livestock also increases. With the disruption of their social networks, their source of livelihood is being threatened and they are finding it difficult to cope. This threat to their very existence leads them to come up with methods to adapt and preserve their way of life.

Adaptation and Coping Mechanisms

Faced with challenges of recurring droughts, reduced pasture and water reserves, competition for scarce resources and violent raids (Mkutu 2008, 13), pastoralists have acquired the ability to adapt to their harsh environment, using complex strategies for their own survival and that of their animals. Adaptability refers to "the degree to which adjustments are possible in practices, processes, or structures of systems to projected or actual change in climate" (Tarekegn 2007, 173), and can be spontaneous or planned to minimize the potential damages or to take advantage of opportunities associated with climate change (IPCC 2001a).

Pastoralism is by its very nature a form of adaptation to climate change and hostile environments that has demonstrated its success over millennia. Archeological evidence indicates that pastoralism developed in response to long-term climate change and has provided food security for many communities through the optimal utilization of elusive resources (Thebaud and Batterbury 2001, 70; Birch and Grahn 2007, 1; Leroy 2007, 167).

Documented coping mechanisms include leaving land fallow, splitting families to better manage herds, pooling resources, creating alliances with other groups, and raiding (Mkutu 2006, 2008; Jabs 2007). Pastoralists also apply principles of flexibility and opportunism in managing their environments, as well as herd stratification in order to spread risk and manage scarce resources that vary both spatially and temporally (Birch and Grahn 2007, 2). The pressures on the way of life of many pastoral communities discussed earlier—population growth, loss of pasture land, drought, famine, and violent conflict—are collectively threatening a system that has proved highly adaptive to harsh conditions in the past (Fratkin and Mearns 2003, 112). Thus, pastoralism is not without risks and downsides (Mkutu 2008; Vadala 2003, 632). Jabs (2007, 1501) observed that a multiyear drought can decimate a herd, just as an epidemic can wipe out an entire cattle population. In spite of their coping abilities, it is becoming increasingly difficult for pastoralists to survive. Changes due to both natural and human factors have arguably altered or even eroded the adaptive capacity of pastoral communities to changing climatic conditions. A perceived environmental threat may force communities to violate traditional resource-sharing norms and boundaries, and even pursue violent means (Tarekegn 2007, 174; Leroy 2007, 167), because coping strategies during lean times tend to become more specialized and directed towards survival (Raleigh 2007, 64). Other factors, unrelated to environmental change that are known to influence resilience, include the availability of markets and access to infrastructure and aid, which increase people's ability to withstand the effects of environmental hazards such as droughts (Raleigh 2007).

Nonetheless, in spite of their resilience and their effective coping strategies to the environmental challenges, pastoralist communities in the Great Lakes region of East Africa are faced with other threats to their way of life, existence, and livelihood. These include the proliferation of small arms and light weapons, cattle rustling, and marginalization by their governments, which we discuss in the following section.

The Proliferation of Small Arms and Light Weapons

The proliferation of small arms and light weapons (SALW) among pastoralists in East Africa has escalated in recent decades to unprecedented levels. The evidence is insurmountable and the effects devastating. The UN Secretary General noted that "The accumulation of small arms and light weapons continues to be a serious threat to peace, stability and sustainable development" (Mkutu 2008, 1). According to the UN, the category of "small arms" includes self-loading pistols, carbines, assault rifles, submachine guns and light machine guns, whereas that of "light weapons" includes heavy machine guns, handheld underbarrel and mounted grenade launchers, and portable antitank and antiaircraft guns (Mkutu 2008, 4).

The armament of the Pokot and the influx of modern firearms such as automatic guns in other nomadic regions in East Africa began in the context of both colonialism and the Cold War, as the rival superpowers fought battles for domination of the region (Mkutu 2008; Österle 2007). Many other accounts are given for the infiltration of firearms in the region; for example, the Turkana and Karimojong are said to have traded ivory for arms (Mkutu 2006, 51). Arms acquisition was augmented in Karamoja when Ugandan leader Idi Amin was overthrown and the Matheniko, a Karimojong group, broke into Moroto barracks and looted firearms that had been left behind by the retreating regime. Significant numbers of Karimojong warriors were also recruited into the Uganda National Liberation Army (UNLA) to fight for the Obote II regime, and in 1986, when the National Resistance Army (NRA) defeated the UNLA, many demobilized Karimojong soldiers fled back to Karamoja with their arms (Kopel et al. 2003, 8; Mkutu 2006, 52). Research has also shown that along the Kenya-Uganda border pastoralists have acquired arms from legal sources such as Local Defense Units and paramilitary groups whose primary purpose is to supplement the police in maintaining security within communities. The Karimojong are also reported to have captured weapons from the Uganda People's Defense Forces (UPDF) (see Eavis 2002, 251–52; Mkutu 2006, 52–53, 62).

Today, the acquisition of arms by pastoralists is more complex and the actors varied. Arms are acquired through raiding neighboring communities as well as through porous international borders (Österle 2007, 195), creating a localized intercommunal arms race in northern Uganda, Somalia, and Sudan. The governments of Kenya and Uganda have also been responsible for arming various groups. After a botched disarmament process in Karamoja in 2001–3, insecurity increased and some communities became more vulnerable to others. In Kenya, the Kenya Police Reserve (KPR), whose activities augment those of regular police in the pastoralist areas, have been armed to tackle insurgents and cattle rustlers; according to Mkutu (2006, 55–56), they are supposedly volunteers with no salaries and very minimal training.

The increased access to small arms and light weapons has been associated with the escalation of conflicts, insecurity, trauma, violence, and crime, on the one hand, and the disruption of families, infrastructure, and development, on the other—all these increasingly becoming endemic problems (Jabs 2007, 1499). The nature of the conflict is therefore local, national, regional, international, and global. Interethnic conflicts become a national issue when they are manifested between communities. When pastoralists cross borders to neighboring countries, and raids impinge on security (such as in the case of the Pokot incursions against Karamoja), then conflicts take on an international dimension (Eavis 2002, 255; Mkutu 2008, 3).

The proliferation of SALW among the Karimojong, Turkana, and Pokot may not cause conflict directly, but is a major contributing factor that fuels and sustains conflicts, increasing their destructiveness and making reconciliation more difficult (Eavis 2002, 251). When asked what factors have transformed a once-adaptive cultural practice into a violent, intractable conflict (Jabs 2007, 1502), we suggest that one way to answer this question is to analyze the complex interaction between climate change and the sociopolitical context in which it unfolds. For instance, where governance structures are weak and can be exploited, accessibility to guns is likely to increase as a means of securing livelihoods, even though it is also responsible for a series of adverse effects on the pastoral populations.

It is imperative to understand and appreciate the complex reasons behind the demand for small arms among the pastoralist communities (Mkutu 2006, 47). Automatic rifles have a double function as they are used, on the one hand, for defense (protection of households and herds) and, on the other, for staging attacks in order to enlarge existing herds or establish new ones. Österle (2007) argues that pastoralists have to protect resources such as water, cattle, and pasture against competitors, and the affordability, robustness, and handiness of the AK-47, compared to the traditional spears or bows and arrows, makes it part and parcel of everyday life. He describes how a "gun culture" contributes significantly to the disintegration of belief systems that tend to emphasize a sense of interlocking security among neighboring communities and mutual respect and self-help, and to the reorganization of patterns of action and communication, leading to the "militarization of beliefs and identities," in which male identity is inextricably bound to the possession of guns. Although it is debatable as to how far weaponry can act as a "change agent," Mulugeta and Hagmann (2008) assert that there is reason to believe that the widespread availability of SALW among pastoralists like the Karimojong, Turkana, and Pokot is partly to blame for the challenges they face. By arming themselves for defensive as well as offensive purposes, pastoralist communities' animosities continue to increase. We, however, contend that while the proliferation of small arms seems symptomatic of a failed state, it actually provides survival and coping strategies for many pastoralist groups who have to struggle against all odds for their daily survival. The proliferation of SALW puts a strain on the already existing tensions among the pastoralists as they seek to survive and protect their cattle. However, it is perhaps prudent to note that it has also provided a new, albeit deadly, avenue for the attainment and [re]distribution of the already existing scarce resources.

Cattle Raiding and Rustling

Today, as in decades and centuries past, cattle remain at the center of pastoralist communities. They are prized possessions, inextricably tied to pastoralists' identities (Jabs 2007, 1500). Cattle hold a central place and are a basis of association in a network of social, political, and religious institutions. In Karamoja, for instance, animals are vital for survival in a harsh environment and have intrinsic cultural value as the means on which the entire social fabric depends. The Karimojong believe that all the cattle in the world belong to them and herding is "a way of life" and not just a mode of livelihood (Mkutu 2008, 12).

For the pastoralist Turkana, Pokot, and Karimojong, interethnic cattle raiding has been a long-standing tradition (Jabs 2007, 1499). Cattle rustling is a collective term loosely used in reference to illegal dealings in livestock or a forceful attack by an outside pastoralist group with the purpose of stealing cattle (Mkutu 2008, 17; Mulugeta and Hagmann 2008, 74). Raiding has cultural and historical connotations and raiders are driven by both symbolic and economic motives, including retaliation for prior attacks (Mkutu 2008; Mulugeta and Hagmann 2008, 74), restocking cattle after reduction by drought or disease, obtaining cattle for bride price, demonstrating bravery, initiating boys into manhood (Markakis 2007, 57), and competing for social status and prestige (Österle 2007). It can also be seen as a quasi-legitimate sharing of resources, permitting groups on the verge of economic ruin, and even starvation, to replenish their systems of food production and natural resource management (Jabs 2007, 1499).

In the past, deaths caused by raids were treated seriously and compensated with cattle. Raiding expeditions had to be sanctioned under strict rules of preparation, engagement, disengagement, and conflict resolution (Österle 2007, 74) in a manner that provided for mediation and compensation rather than punishment (Markakis 2007, 57). Warriors rarely harmed women, children, and the elderly, who were said to be protected by special norms and rules (Österle 2007, 200). But those norms that once existed to protect vulnerable people have been eroded, leaving them as targets of indiscriminate violence. In the context of Karamoja, access to SALW has led to a shift in the status quo that has had far-reaching cultural effects. The proliferation of SALW (discussed in the previous section) is inextricably linked to cattle raiding and rustling and thus should not be discussed separately. Among the Pokot in Kenya, Österle (2007, 196) notes that such firearms—besides being vital for the management of resources such as pasture,—are now also used for economic activities such as cattle rustling and car jacking, which are considered criminal acts under Kenyan law.

Jabs (2007, 1511) cites Coleman (2003) who noted that arms proliferation can create a sense of deprivation, ambiguity, and the opportunity for norms to shift. The younger armed warriors become instantly powerful, tipping the balance of power in their favor against their elders. With the influx of firearms, intra-ethnic conflicts occur constantly. The elders, "seers," and "diviners" who used to bless raiding expeditions, are now consulted less frequently, because raiders are able to undertake raids without the approval of their communities (Jabs 2007, 1513). Cattle raiding therefore has undergone a major transformation in the last four decades from the customary raids after droughts to an illicit, violent, and deadly commercial activity maintained by SALW and benefiting only a few. Conflict is now an integral part of pastoral life (Mkutu 2008), leading to the entrenchment of stereotypical views of primordial or essentialist violence. The purpose of cattle raiding in the volatile Sudanese-Ugandan-Kenyan-Karimojong cluster has mutated from herd restocking and accumulation to selling livestock for money or for more weapons. A new phenomenon of "cattle warlordism" has emerged due to the increasingly sophisticated weaponry and military tactics employed by raiders, and widespread looting with indiscriminate killings now take place during cattle rustling in northwest Kenya (Mulugeta and Hagmann 2008, 75; Osamba 2008). Cattle raids have thus been transformed from an adaptive and redistributive activity to a maladaptive, violent, and predatory strategy responsible for the increase of famines, epidemics, and male adult mortality among pastoral groups in the Great Lakes region of East Africa.

The Role of the State

With imperialism and the process of colonization in East Africa came the creation of boundaries to maintain law and order where territorial organization rarely existed. Boundaries in Africa as a whole are reflections of imperial rivalries rather than a genuine pattern of population settlement along geographical or ethnic lines (Vadala 2003, 628). The colonialists were selective in their rule, favoring some communities and marginalizing others. The scars of imperialism are still evident today, perhaps because some of the conflicts in the area can be traced back to the colonial period. Moreover, colonialism added two significant variables important to understanding pastoralist conflicts: boundaries and military repression (Mkutu 2008, 14). These boundaries have had the devastating effect of interfering with social systems, disrupting mobility, increasing cross-border conflicts, limiting access to grazing land and water, increasing vulnerability to drought, dividing kin groups, and creating conflicts between the authorities and the pastoralists (Jabs 2007, 1510; Mkutu 2008, 22; Vadala 2003, 631) as well as between pastoralists and their agricultural neighbors. For example, the Karimojong in Uganda did not recognize a central governing authority, but operated with a decentralized self-government based on territorial units instead (Mkutu 2008).

A severe imbalance in the distribution of wealth and power also caused scarcity and resulted in the disproportionate distribution of resources that sustained people's livelihoods (Homer-Dixon 1999). Such unequal distribution, or "structural scarcity," in Homer-Dixon's terms, is often deeply rooted in institutions and ethnic relations inherited from the colonial period, and is a key factor in virtually every case of scarcity contributing to conflict.

Besides being poorly endowed in terms of natural resources, pastoralist communities have long been neglected by the states that rule them. Markakis (2007, 57) opines that the state believed that pastoralism did not have any market, profit, or revenue value, which led to their underdevelopment, purposeful abandonment, marginalization, brutalization, and dehumanization. Many national governments and development policy makers have carried a negative attitude towards pastoralism as an irrational, wasteful, and shortsighted system (Fratkin and Mearns 2003, 113), and have progressively closed off the pastoralists' options through spatial barriers and obstacles inherent in their development models (Birch and Grahn 2007, 2). Tarekegn (2007, 174) also believes that political factors have exacerbated the tension between groups with competing livelihood strategies. National politics are dominated by politicians who favor their own ethnic groups and their client networks—a fact that reflects an important aspect of Kenya's political reality (Österle 2007, 203).

Peacebuilding Processes and Opportunities

Climate change undermines human security by reducing people's access to the natural resources that sustain their livelihoods. It also undermines the capacity of states to provide opportunities and services as well as to maintain and build peace. In peacebuilding processes among pastoralists, it is important to ascertain the complex causes of the conflict and not just deal with the symptoms. When dealing with eco-conflicts and the escalating tensions that amount to violence, it is vital to identify unequivocally those who own and have access to the resources, and to know what is being done about resource scarcity. By doing so, we believe one can discern the violent consequences of environmental stress that has been worsened by climate change, and identify various stakeholders to mitigate its impacts.

Homer-Dixon (1999, 10) argues that there is no "magic bullet" to resolve environmental influences on violent conflict. Many variables are at play and therefore policy makers must act quickly and proactively through interventions at the community, national, regional, and international levels to avoid escalation of conflicts. This is important to note when implementing peacebuilding interventions among pastoral communities where conflict threatens national and international security. It is also pertinent to point out that conflict, especially eco-conflicts, may not be one-time events. They may develop over time, following various stages that may result or escalate into violence.

The way in which policy-makers view pastoralism affects the discourse around it as well as the ways in which issues surrounding pastoralist conflicts are addressed. While pastoralism can be a productive, rational, and even essential way of utilizing scarce resources, when it is viewed as backward and irrational, the logical response is to "modernize" it (Birch and Grahn 2007, 3). Global discourse on climate change should make space for pastoralists, who are directly affected by it, and avoid the top-down technical solutions that fail to comprehend the multiple factors at work and do not appropriately engage affected communities. Attempts at making pastoralists in East Africa practice "modern" agriculture and "controlled" grazing have failed because they were in direct conflict with the long held tradition of transhumance (Moyini 2004).

These interventions need not be capital-intensive or expensive. One example of an expensive project is the Karamoja Livelihoods Programme (KALIP) that supports massive agriculture development among the Karimojong (*Daily Monitor* 2011). The Uganda government embarked on this program with support from the European Union in 2011. The program is estimated to cost €15 million and supports agriculture diversification and capacity building, encouraging agro-pastoral production and setting up small-scale water infrastructure. However, the community leaders do not support the project but regard it as an attempt by the government to undermine pastoralism. Homer-Dixon (1999) suggests effective yet inexpensive strategies, such as greater support for nongovernmental organizations (NGOs) that are involved in rehabilitating local environmental resources. Finding integrated solutions to vulnerability, food and human insecurity, porous borders and the easement of arms flows, resource management and the diversification of livelihoods, would generate significant rewards in terms of economic and social development and would expedite the peacebuilding process.

Based on our analysis of conflicts among the Karimojong, Turkana, and Pokot, we argue that this can be achieved by employing human needs and rights-based approaches to problem-solving—which states and many NGOs have the capacity to integrate in their programs—rather than power-driven bargaining approaches. The human needs approach is suitable for conflict resolution practices because it recognizes that deep-rooted conflict exists where social structures and institutions are not functioning, meaning that human needs such as food, shelter, security, community, identity, and recognition are not met (Bremner 1994, 4). The drive to meet such basic human needs is so profound that where parties are unable to satisfy them within societal norms, they will move outside these norms (Anstey 1999, 17). Conflict resolution then becomes the process of reforming or restructuring social institutions so that human needs can be satisfied. Empowering pastoralists by providing them greater access to resources will minimize sporadic conflicts. Measures must be put in place to address inequalities in access to land and water, and investments must be made in human, social, and natural capital (Fratkin and Mearns 2003, 113). The long-term hope for resolution lies in building accountable national institutions that can meet the basic needs of citizens (Mkutu 2006, 69). Additionally, the enhancement of indigenous technical capacity necessary to produce rapid economic development (Homer-Dixon 1999, 11) must be encouraged. To address conflicts over natural resources, Osman-Elasha and El Sanjak (2009, 27) recommend five strategies. These include the incorporation of climate change concerns into peacebuilding processes and national policies; the use of bottom-up approaches to involve all the stakeholders; the strengthening of national and regional collaboration in resolving trans-boundary disputes; and the building on the strengths of local institutions.

Furthermore, in order to proceed with the development of pastoral communities, a major reconsideration of dryland ecology has to be made, taking into account that livelihoods are derived from environments that are intrinsically at disequilibrium (Fratkin and Mearns 2003, 114). Pastoral production and sustainability depend on the mobility of herds; therefore, land tenure policies, social service provision, rural infrastructure, and other policies, all need to support this basic requirement. State efforts at intervention should improve the understanding of the predicaments that pastoralists currently face. This would be the first step in assessing conflict causation and finding meaningful and lasting solutions (Markakis 2007, 58).

Governance and development policies need to take into account the distinctive situation of pastoralists and their marginalized position in society (Thebaud and Batterbury 2001, 76). Mkutu (2008) and Markakis (2007) have claimed that a majority of interventions attempted in pastoralist communities have tended to deal with symptoms rather than underlying causes. Disarmament, for instance, has usually been coercive. This has been true in the case of Karamoja, where the process of disarmament in the last decade has generated much criticism (Stites and Akwabai 2009). During the disarmament process, the Karimojong, for instance, were first promised effective protection by the UPDF, as well as oxen, ploughs, and building materials in exchange for their guns (Kopel et al. 2003, 8). As a result, the Karimojong were said to have had a positive attitude towards disarmament, and voluntarily surrendered guns prior to the forced disarmament process (Mkutu 2008, 128). However, the UPDF's method of selective disarmament created a situation of insecurity as some communities were left vulnerable to attack by those that had not been disarmed. One of the many unanimous points of agreement is that disarmament as an intervention has exacerbated the insecurity in the region instead of bringing peace. (Österle 2007; Stites 2007; Kopel et al. 2003; Mkutu 2008). Mkutu (2008, 124) asserts that the approach needs to address the root causes of the demand for arms, recognizing that arms have become an economic asset. He argues that unless alternatives are provided, disarmament will not work.

Whatever approach is emphasized, it is essential for any intervention in pastoralist communities to proceed with an openness to learning their customs and norms, and to listen more than talk, in order to gain people's trust and a clear understanding of a complex situation (Jabs 2007, 1516). Fostering the capacity of pastoralists to participate in and appropriate the process of decentralization is a complicated and slow process that has to be driven from within their society if lasting change is to be achieved. It involves not only acquiring information but also changing the perceptions, beliefs, attitudes, and behavior (Hesse and Thebaud 2006, 20) of policy makers, peace and development actors, and wider communities towards pastoralists engaged in conflict. Pastoralists, through their associations or indigenous institutions, have to develop both the skills to operate in their ever-changing environment and the necessary "leverage" to ensure that improved knowledge and understanding are actually used to improve policy and legislation in support of pastoralism as a livelihood system (Hesse and Thebaud 2006, 22).

As noted earlier, the creation of borders during the colonial era contributed to the tension among pastoral communities in East Africa. Understanding this fact is vital to the management of pastoralist conflicts because of their regional and international dimensions, including arms flows to both Kenya and Uganda (Mkutu 2008, 23). The regional challenges to tackling the proliferation of small arms and light weapons are undoubtedly great. It is important to destroy any arms that have been collected in order to reduce the likelihood they will reenter the communities (Mkutu 2006). Working closely with communities in the design and implementation of weapons collection programs is also crucial (Eavis 2002, 258–59). Former combatants should be assisted by both their governments and communities in order to be reintegrated fully, reducing the possibility of their rejoining in the arms trade and thus exacerbating instability in the region. Initiatives should also be made to create community awareness of the dangers of small arms, provide security, and reduce the demands for these weapons.

The governments of both Kenya and Uganda have failed to facilitate equitable development among pastoralist communities, leaving them marginalized and insulated by the top-down ways of managing conflicts over resources (Mkutu 2008, 23), which has often resulted in violent armed conflicts. Governments' failure to invest in developing and protecting livelihoods in drought-prone areas constitutes a political choice that undermines pastoralism as an effective method of coping in arid and semiarid areas (Birch and Grahn 2007, 4). However, human security cannot be separated from state operations (Barnett and Adger 2007, 646). Providing measures to protect people when their livelihoods suddenly contract is a vital role of the state. Giving more attention to cultural values and the hierarchical structure within pastoralist communities, their conflict-resolving institutions, and their resource-management and resource-sharing practices, is crucial for peacebuilding in the region. To facilitate this, an "elicitive" approach should be used whereby the "local knowledge" informs "experts" in designing interventions into problems pertaining to resources and constraints within a specific context (Jabs 2007, 1516). Access rights are constantly renegotiated between different groups at different times of the year, in response to the seasonal and interannual availability of resources (Hesse and Thebaud 2006, 16). In many cases, violent conflicts are contained because of the "social capital" developed by pastoral communities among themselves and with other communities who share common interests and common resources in a social, cultural, and economic symbiosis (Thebaud and Batterbury 2001, 76). People within and across communities possess their own means of handling disputes over natural resources. This situation reflects the fact that resource management and conflict management are interlinked processes that aim to bring consistency, order, and accountability to situations of competition and conflicting interests. The main techniques used by communities to handle conflicts include negotiation, mediation, and arbitration (Castro 2007, 347).

Early warning systems must also be invested to protect pastoral communities from impending calamities, safeguard their livelihood assets, and increase their resilience (Birch and Grahn 2007, 3). Early warning systems help to increase preparedness for drought and other climatic risks. Interventions such as purchasing power during droughts, and community-based water development (wells, rain water harvesting, and dams), should be instituted. Microfinance services can also be used to widen pastoralists' options before, during, and after risk events in order to reduce their vulnerability. Access to credit and savings schemes can help pastoralists to purchase veterinary medicines (Fratkin and Mearns 2003, 119–20) to reduce the risk of vast herds being decimated by disease.

Finally, we must further stress the vital and unique feature of pastoralist groups—their ability to adapt to their ever-changing harsh environment. Effective strategies should be logically underpinned by a commitment to strengthening pastoralists' existing adaptive capacities and to put in place the kind of enabling environment within which they can exercise them. This commitment would involve the protection of migration routes and investment in infrastructure such as roads and markets (Birch and Grahn 2007, 8).

In this chapter we have argued that social, economic, and institutional factors have contributed to the destabilization of pastoralist communities as much as environmental ones did. Factors like erratic rainfall and periodic drought have always been a part of pastoralist life, to which groups like the Karimojong, Turkana, and Pokot have adapted over the years. Many social, economic, and even political factors have also contributed to the inauspicious situation of pastoralists by destabilizing herd sizes and neglecting the needs of communities. These factors include restrictions on movement, access to water and grazing land, disregard by the state, and the proliferation of small arms and light weapons. Various strategies for peacebuilding have been explored by researchers, and we believe that the most important strategy to employ among pastoral communities will be the human needs and rights-based approach, which, if implemented at the grassroots level, can create a positive transformation for pastoral communities in conflict.

References

Barnett, Jon, and Neil W. Adger. 2007. "Climate Change, Human Security and Violent Conflict." *Journal of Political Geography* 26, no. 6: 639–55.

Birch, Isobel, and Richard Grahn. 2007. *Pastoralism—Managing Multiple Stressors and the Threat of Climate Variability and Change*. Human Development Report 2007/2008. Accessed 12 October 2012. Retrieved from United Nations Development Program website, http://hdr.undp.org/en/reports/global/hdr2007-2008/papers/birch_isobel%20 and%20grahn_richard.pdf..

Brauch, H. Günter, et al. 2002. *Climate Change and Conflicts*. Adelphi Research. Accessed 15 October 2012. http://www.afes-press.de/pdf/Brauch_ClimateChange_BMU.pdf.

Carius, Alexander, and Kerstin Imbusch. 1999. "Environment and Security in International Politics: An Introduction." In *Environmental Change and Security: A European Perspective*, edited by A. Carius and K. M. Lietzmann, 7–30. Berlin: Springer.

Castro, Peter. 2007. "Communities and Natural Resource Conflicts in Africa: Reflections on Conflict Management Options for Peacebuilding in Darfur." In *Environment and Conflict in Africa: Reflections on Darfur*, edited by Marcel Leroy, 341–54. Addis Ababa, Ethiopia: University for Peace.

Daily Monitor. 2011. "Karimojong Leaders Slam Government Support for Massive Farming." *Daily Monitor*, 12 November.

Eavis, Paul. 2002. "SALW in the Horn of Africa and the Great Lakes Region: Challenges and Ways Forward." *Brown Journal of World Affairs* 9, no. 1: 251–60.

Fratkin, Elliot, and Robin Mearns. 2003. "Sustainability and Pastoral Livelihoods: Lessons from East African Maasai and Mongolia." *Human Organization* 62, no. 2: 112–22.

Hagmann, Tobias, and Alemmaya Mulugeta. 2008. "Pastoral Conflicts and State-Building in the Ethiopian Lowlands." *Afrika Spectrum* 43, no. 1: 19–37.

Hesse, Ced, and Brigitte Thebaud. 2006. "Will Pastoral Legislation Disempower Pastoralists in the Sahel?" *Indigenous Affairs* 1, no. 6: 14–23.

Homer-Dixon, Thomas. 1999. *Environment, Scarcity and Violence*. Princeton, NJ: Princeton University Press.

IPCC. 2001. *Climate Change 2001: Impacts, Adaptation and Vulnerability*. Contribution of Working Group II to the Third Assessment Report of IPCC. Cambridge: Cambridge University Press.

Jabs, Lorelle. 2007. "Where Two Elephants Meet, the Grass Suffers: A Case Study of Intractable Conflict in Karamoja, Uganda." *American Behavioral Scientist* 50, no. 11: 1498–1519.

Knaute, David, and Sacha Kagan, eds. 2009. *Sustainability in Karamoja? Rethinking the Terms of Global Sustainability in a Crisis Region of Africa*. Cologne: Rüdiger Koppe.

Kopel, David, Joanne D. Eisen, and Paul Gallant. 2003. "Gun Ownership and Human Rights." *Brown Journal of World Affairs* 9, no. 2: 3–13.

Leroy, Marcel, ed. 2007. *Environment and Conflict in Africa: Reflections on Darfur*. Addis Ababa, Ethiopia: University for Peace.
Markakis, John. 2007. "Conflict in the Horn of Africa." In *Environment and Conflict in Africa: Reflections on Darfur*, edited by Marcel Leroy, 54–59. Ethiopia: University for Peace.
Mkutu, Kennedy A. 2006. "Small Arms and Light Weapons among Pastoral Groups in the Kenya-Uganda Border Area." *African Affairs* 106, no. 422: 47–70.
———. 2008. *Guns and Governance in the Rift Valley: Pastoralist Conflict and Small Arms*. Bloomington: Indiana University Press.
Moyini, Yakobo. 2004. "Impact of Environmental Change on Human Vulnerability in Karamoja, North-eastern Uganda." In *Africa Environmental Outlook: Case Studies on Human Vulnerability to Environmental Change*. Nairobi: United Nations Environment Program (UNEP).
Mulugeta, Alemmaya, and Tobias Hagmann. 2008. "Governing Violence in Pastoralist Space: Karrayu and State Notions of Cattle Raiding in the Ethiopian Awash Valley." *Afrika Focus* 21, no. 2: 71–87.
Nordås, Ragnhild, and N. Peter Gleditsch. 2007. "Climate Change and Conflict." *Political Geography* 22, no. 6: 627–38.
Osman-Elasha, Balgis, and El-Amin Sanjak. 2007. "Global Climate Changes: Impacts on Water Resources and Human Security in Africa." In *Environment and Conflict in Africa: Reflections on Darfur*, edited by Marcel Leroy, 27–43. Addis Ababa, Ethiopia: University for Peace.
Osterle, Matthias. 2007. "Armed Economies, Militarized Identities, Excessive Violence: Automatic Rifles and the Transformation of Nomadic Pastoralism in Northwestern Kenya." *Colloquium Africanum*. Accessed 16 October 2012. http://www.academia.edu/1507971/From_Raiders_to_Rustlers_The_Filial_Disaffection_of_a_Turkana_Age-Set.
Raleigh, Clionadh. 2007. "New Directions in Climate Change-Conflict Literature." In *Environment and Conflict in Africa: Reflections on Darfur*, edited by Marcel Leroy, 63–72. Addis Ababa, Ethiopia: University for Peace.
Reuveny, Rafael. 2007. "Climate Change-Induced Migration and Violent Conflict." *Journal of Political Geography* 26, no. 6: 656–73.
Schwartz, Daniel M. 2002. "The Environment and Violent Conflict." In *Encyclopedia of Global Environmental Change*, edited by Ted Munn, 137–49. Vol. 5. Chichester, UK: John Wiley.
Timmerman, Peter, ed. 2002. *Social and Economic Dimensions of Global Environmental Change*. 137–49. Chichester, UK: John Wiley.
Stites, Elizabeth, and Darlington Akabwai. 2009. "Changing Roles, Shifting Risks: Livelihood Impacts of Disarmament in Karamoja, Uganda." Feinstein International Center. Accessed 16 October 2012. http://www.scribd.com/doc/17497055/Changing-Roles-Shifting-Risks-Livelihood-Impacts-of-Disarmament-in-Karamoja-Uganda.
Tänzler, Dennis, Alexander Carius, and Sebastian Oberthür. 2002. "Climate Change and Conflict Prevention: The Relevance for the International Process on Climate Change—Background Paper." Report of the Special Event on Climate Change and Conflict Prevention, 16th Meeting of the Subsidiary Bodies to the UNFCCC, Bonn, 10 June 2002. Berlin: Federal Ministry for the Environment, Nature Conservation and Nuclear Safety.
Terekegn, B. 2007. "Pastoralism and Adaptation to Climate Change." In *Environment and Conflict in Africa: Reflections on Darfur*, edited by Marcel Leroy, 170–80. Addis Ababa, Ethiopia: University for Peace.

Thebaud, B., and Simon Batterbury. 2001. "Sahel Pastoralists: Opportunism, Struggle, Conflict and Negotiation. A Case Study from Eastern Niger." *Global Environmental Change* 11, no. 1: 69–78.

Vadala, Alexander A. 2003. "Major Geopolitical Explanations of Conflict in the Horn of Africa." *NORD-SUD Aktuell* 27, no. 4: 627–34.

PART III
Social and Cultural Dimensions of Conflict and Peacebuilding in the Great Lakes

8 Media Sustainability in a Postconflict Environment

Radio Broadcasting in the DRC, Burundi, and Rwanda

Marie-Soleil Frère

THIS CHAPTER INTERROGATES the capacity of radio stations in three countries of the African Great Lakes region (Democratic Republic of Congo, Burundi, and Rwanda) to act as influential independent stakeholders in the postconflict public debate. The three countries are all former Belgian colonies and have been historically, economically, and culturally interconnected for decades. During the past twenty years, Burundi, Rwanda, and the DRC have experienced varying degrees of liberalization of the political space as well as the media landscape after decades of single-party rule and state monopoly on the media. Moreover, these three countries have also undergone armed conflicts in which some journalists and media agencies have been key players. Radio stations especially have experienced significant growth in recent years and radio broadcasting in these postconflict environments is clearly superseding print and television media, both of which are perceived as elitist and urban-based.

I first present an overview of the radio broadcasting landscape in the three countries. After examining the obstacles that radio stations face in that environment, I then analyze a peculiar dynamic that has spread in recent years among radio stations in the three countries, known as "media synergy." These initiatives, aimed at sharing human and material resources between media outlets and at producing joint contents, were established during elections as the stations were trying to overcome the obstacles they faced. Finally, I interrogate the sustainability and professional autonomy of some of the main local radio stations in the three Great Lakes countries, which have become financially dependent on Western donors.

An Overview of the Radio Broadcasting Landscape

Radio remains the leading news media in the DRC, Burundi, and Rwanda. A survey by the International Telecommunications Union (ITU 2008) shows that 88 percent of Burundian households possess a transistor (while only 23 percent own a TV set) and that 97 percent of Kinshasa households and 85 percent of rural households in the DRC have a radio (while only 30 percent have access to television, except for Kinshasa where the percentage is much higher). With regard to Rwandan households, more than half own a radio. Being the most popular media with people in both urban and rural areas, radio broadcasting is the most likely media that apparently can contribute most effectively to public debate, information dissemination, and the political education of citizens.

In the DRC, the radio broadcasting landscape was first liberalized in the 1990s and this was followed by a huge increase in the number of radio stations in the country (Frère 2009a). In 2011, some four hundred mostly local stations operated in the DRC, notably community-based stations, faith-based denominational stations, and profit-oriented private outlets. Nevertheless, this large number of stations has not necessarily meant a huge diversity of choice for the Congolese audience.

Except for Kinshasa where almost forty stations are available, most local audiences only have access to very few stations, as radios broadcast on a limited wavelength with a range of between fifty and one hundred kilometers. Only two stations tend to offer national coverage. On the one hand, the government-owned national broadcaster RTNC (Radio Télévision Nationale du Congo), based in Kinshasa, maintains a subsidiary broadcasting studio and newsroom in each of the other ten provinces. The subsidiary studios are supposed to receive and broadcast the programs from Kinshasa and also to complement broadcasting schedules with local productions, but most of them are experiencing major technical problems. Radio Okapi, an international radio station established by the UN Peacekeeping Mission in the Congo (MONUC, renamed MONUSCO in 2010) and managed by the Swiss Foundation Hirondelle (Swallow), was set up in 2002 with the aim of reinforcing peace through proactive broadcasting and sensitization of the public. Radio Okapi, which covers 85 percent of the territory, has become the nation's most widely developed station.

Established when the country was still split among different armed groups, Radio Okapi has done a remarkable job in restoring the Congolese social fabric nationwide, enabling the inhabitants from the different areas to share their views again after years of alienation. Broadcasting in French and in the four national languages (Lingala, Kikongo, Tshiluba, and Kiswahili), it has progressively set up a newsroom with over 120 journalists and has distinguished itself as the most credible and professional journalistic outlet in the country.

Besides these two, the forty other Kinshasa-based radio stations are either commercial or denominational, with about half belonging to Pentecostal "Awakening" (or

"Revival") Churches. Eighteen of them are related with a twin-sister television station. Out of Kinshasa, most denominational stations are either mainstream Christian (Catholic or Pentecostal) or Kimbanguist (mainly in Western Congo)—an indigenous Christian sect with a distinct African theological fervor. Some are involved in civic education, development, and current-events reporting. Such is the case for Radio Elikya (Catholic) and Radio Sango Malamu (Protestant) in Kinshasa, Radio Amani (belonging to the Archdiocese) in Kisangani, Radio Maria (Catholic) and Radio Sauti ya Rehema (Protestant) in Bukavu, RATELKI (Radio Télévision Kimbanguiste) in the Lower Congo, Radio Fraternité Buena Muntu (Catholic) in Mbuji Mayi, RTDM (Radio Télévision du Diocèse de Matadi), and Radio Tomisa (Catholic) in Kikwit.

In the countryside, community-based stations are the most prevalent. The war has generated precarious and insecure operating conditions for these stations, but has also made them popular among the communities to which they are giving a voice. For instance, Radio Maendeleo in Bukavu, Radio Communautaire du Katanga in Lubumbashi and Radio Communautaire Mwangaza in Kisangani play an important role in local communities, which no longer expect that solutions to their problems will come from Kinshasa. Run by local associations, these stations are nevertheless often under pressure from local authorities that try to use them as their political instrument.

Besides denominational and community-based stations, private commercial radio stations were also created in Congolese towns, especially before the 2006 and the 2011 polls. Several candidates (running for the National Parliament or the Provincial Assembly) established a radio station in their hometown to use it as a personal promotion tool. For instance, in 2006, Jean-Pierre Bemba extended the network of his Réseau Liberté stations throughout the Equator province (his electoral stronghold). At the same time, Digital Congo, owned by Joseph Kabila's sister, Jaynet, also enlarged its broadcasting capacities, establishing transmitters in all major towns of each province.

Moreover, several international broadcasters are established in FM in Kinshasa: the BBC (British Broadcasting Corporation), RFI (Radio France Internationale), Africa no.1 and RTBF (Belgian francophone public broadcaster). RFI, which has transmitters in six other towns in the Congo, is especially popular, far ahead of the BBC (IMMAR 2008a). The popularity of RFI is so important that it is often seen as a key player in the local political sphere.

The Burundian radio landscape developed in the late 1990s and within a peculiar historical context (Ntiyanogeye 2008). Indeed, Burundi experienced at the beginning of the civil war in 1993–94 a real "hate media."[*] The country was also shaken by the terrible experience of Radio Télévision libre des Mille Collines (RTLM) in neighboring Rwanda. Burundi then turned into a kind of laboratory for radio and peacebuilding. In 1995, the American nongovernmental organization (NGO) Search for Common Ground (SFCG) established a studio in Bujumbura called Studio Ijambo ("wise words" in Kirundi), with the specific aim of producing radio programs that could help reconciliation among local communities.

In the following years, private radio stations were created with the support of foreign NGOs and donors, which put an end to the monopoly of state radio and helped broadcast SFCG's programs: CCIB-FM (radio of the Chamber of Commerce in Burundi) was established in 1995, Radio Umwizera (which would become Radio Sans Frontières Bonesha FM) in 1996, Radio Culture in 1998, Radio Publique Africaine (RPA) in 2001, Radio Isanganiro in 2002, and Radio Renaissance in 2004. These stations all stated that their aim was to provide balanced and neutral information, promote peace initiatives, and try to bring together the Burundian people, building bridges between the Hutu and the Tutsi (Frère 2007, 20–22).

These new private broadcasters have transformed the former journalistic practices and media programming, as exercised previously by the national broadcaster RTNB (Radio Télévision Nationale du Burundi), which had benefited from a monopoly on the airwaves since its creation in 1960. Rejecting "government-oriented" information, the new private stations opened up their airwaves to both the armed rebels and the local populations so they could voice their claims and concerns. They organized and aired public debates on the major national issues, criticized the bad governance of many leaders, and discussed all the taboos from the violent history of Burundi. Often confronting the government, and subject to many attacks and press-freedom violations, the private Burundian radio stations have developed a strong professional solidarity, responding collectively each time their rights were threatened.

Their solidarity has been facilitated by the fact that they were independent of political parties (more so than in the neighboring DRC) and their staff was multiethnic. Their strength also came from the fact that they have received important support from foreign donors, allowing them to enjoy the minimal material and financial conditions necessary to work professionally.

In 2011, some fourteen stations are operational in Burundi, including some denominational stations: Radio Ivyzigiro (Pentecostal) in Bujumbura and Radio Maria Burundi (Catholic) in Gitega.[2] Three international broadcasters are also established in Bujumbura: RFI since 1998, the BBC since 2000, and VOA since 2003; the latter two broadcasts in Kirundi (roughly the same language as Kinyarwanda) for an hour every day.

In recent years, the Burundian radio sector has experienced two major trends: politicization and decentralization. On the one hand, new radio stations have been established that are close to the ruling party CNDD-FDD (National Council for the Defense of Democracy—Forces for the Defense of Democracy) that won the 2005 and 2010 elections. Created in 2008, Rema FM stands out from other stations in Bujumbura, using a politically engaged and sometimes accusatory tone that has raised some concern among international press-freedom organizations.[3] On the other hand, new community stations have been set up outside Bujumbura. Some of them are also suspected of being close to President Nkurunziza's political party, such as Umuco FM in Ngozi and Star FM in the Kayogoro, both managed by individuals with close ties to the CNDD-FDD.

Rwanda has been the last to open up the radio sector to private initiatives. Indeed, following the tragedy of the first private radio station in Rwandan history, RTLM, created in 1993, there was a huge distrust towards the broadcasting media on the side of the authorities and of the audience (Thompson 2007, Frère 2007). It was only ten years later, and after a public regulatory authority was established, that new private radio stations were again authorized, in 2004. In 2011, more than twenty of them were allowed to broadcast.

Rwandan radio stations are either private and profit-oriented (Contact FM, Radio 10, City Radio, Radio Flash, and Isango Star in Kigali), community-based (Radio Salus from the School of Journalism and Communication at the National University of Rwanda in Butare, and Radio Izuba in Kibungo), or denominational (Radio Mariya, Radio Ijwi Ry'ibyiringiro, Radio Restore, and Radio Umucyo). Radio Rwanda is the national broadcaster, established within ORINFOR (Rwandan Office for Information), and it has recently set up local regional stations in Rubavu, Huye, and Musanze. It claims to cover 95 percent of the territory. Four foreign stations (RFI, BBC, VOA, and DW [Deutsche Welle]) broadcast on FM in Kigali, including two (the British and the American) scheduling an hour-long daily program in Kinyarwanda. RFI has been interrupted several times, following the "ups and downs" of diplomatic relations between France and Rwanda.

Since the country is small, some of those stations cover a reasonable portion of the territory. Nevertheless, they still have limited capacities, especially regarding human resources, in a country where the genocide of the Tutsi and massive killings of the Hutu opponents decimated the intellectual elite. For instance, Contact FM, by far the more professional of the private radio stations, has a team of twelve journalists in its newsroom, including three Kenyans and two Burundians, in order to have presenters with the required linguistic skills for the English and French news broadcasts. Most other stations mainly broadcast music, entertainment, sports, commercials, religious preaching, or open-mic programs devoted to the youth. As the information sector is watched closely by the government, many stations do not discuss political or economic issues (Frère 2007).

Challenges for Radio Stations in Postconflict Central Africa

Radio pluralism is thus a reality in these three countries. Nevertheless, radio stations face several obstacles that prevent consolidation and professionalization. A first obstacle lies in the economic frailty of these media outlets. Although some of the major stations enjoy decent budgets (US$40,000 a month for Contact FM in Rwanda; US$42,000 for Radio Isanganiro in Burundi; US$33,000 for Radio Maendeleo in the DRC), staff and equipment remain limited. Most of the smaller stations must manage with very little money (e.g., Radio Sauti Ya Mkaji in Kasongo, in the eastern Congo, has a yearly budget of US$10,000), and largely survive due to the commitment of volunteers.

The local economic fabric has been affected by war, making it difficult for the stations to generate money from advertising or from the public's direct contributions. Their audience is impoverished and destitute, a fact that benefits neither media consumption nor the development of an advertising market. Material work conditions are difficult and radio stations must operate despite power cuts, for which not all media outlets can compensate by purchasing a generator. The absence of any motorized means of transport often limits journalists to the newsroom or to the boundaries of the city where the media is located.

Moreover, journalists are often underpaid, leading them to do "something else" besides journalism, whether through their media or outside of it. The poor salary conditions push journalists and presenters to the widespread practice of "advertorial news," called *coupage* in the DRC, *per diem* in Burundi, or *giti* in Rwanda. This is a practice whereby journalists receive money from their source of information: widespread in the Congo, these forms of rewarded journalism are also expanding in Burundi and Rwanda. They are forbidden by the professional codes of ethics adopted in the three countries, but seem unavoidable in a context where, in the DRC for instance, the monthly wage of a radio presenter ranges from US$30 to US$80 and is not even paid regularly.

Therefore, the stations that can provide better material and financial working conditions for their staff are those supported by the international community or foreign donors. For instance, journalists with Radio Isanganiro earn from US$150 a month, and those with Radio Okapi start with a minimum monthly salary of US$800. These more substantial wages can help avoid "rewarded journalism" practices, but the implication is that the stations are surviving due largely to foreign donors' support. This financial dependence sometimes has an impact on media content, since the stations will try to satisfy the donor and its priorities rather than their own audiences' expectations. For instance, a 2005 study within the Burundian radio stations showed that broadcasting schedules were mainly occupied by programs either produced by international agencies (which bought airtime on the stations to broadcast them) or by the radio station itself but on topics suggested by the donors. Programs on issues such as children's rights, the demobilization of armed groups, transitional justice, or the prevention of HIV/AIDS followed one another, giving the stations "a rather boring and monotonous tone" (Burton 2006). It is also for the purpose of survival that some stations, mainly in the DRC, seek the financial support and protection of local political authorities, which are the only ones able to provide electricity, information, or security guarantees.

Political insecurity is the second obstacle faced by radio stations in the three countries and it is mainly associated with the preponderant press-freedom violations that occur in a postconflict environment. Although the freedom of the press is inscribed in the constitution and guaranteed by the Press Law (adopted in 1996 in the DRC, in 2003 in Burundi, and in 2002—reformed in 2009—in Rwanda), journalists are often threatened, more or less openly, by military or public officials. These threats can either be explicit—journalists in all three countries are regularly the target of physical violence and are often imprisoned—but they can also be more insidious when discrete pressure from the authorities or zealous civil servants encourages self-censorship. As a consequence, journalists are often afraid and must, as a Rwandan journalist remarked, "be prudent without being cowardly" (Ruremesha, quoted in Frère 2007, 106).

In the DRC, the press-freedom organization Journaliste en danger (JED) publishes a yearly census of all the attacks on the press witnessed nationwide.[4] Assassination, jail terms, threats of many kinds, economic or judiciary pressure, and administrative sanctions are all unfortunate realities facing journalists. Even journalists with Radio Okapi, who are supposed to be better protected as staff members of a UN media outlet, have been targeted, and two of them were shot dead in Bukavu in 2007 and 2008. In Burundi, several radio journalists (with Radio Isanganiro and RPA) were jailed for months in 2006 in connection with a story they published about an alleged coup plot that had resulted in the arrest of the former president.[5] Directors of the major private radio stations in Bujumbura have been harassed, threatened, and made victims of daily summons and cautions for the past two years.

In Rwanda, self-censorship is a widespread practice: "Editors and reporters walk a tightrope," the Media High Council acknowledged in 2008, "cautious not to degenerate into any kind of journalism that may fan divisionism or publish stories not in consonance with rigid editorial lines. This affects journalistic creativity" (MHC 2008, 34). If Rwandan journalists sometimes act in spite of journalism ethics or even the legal framework, the prosecutions and sanctions are often disproportionate to the offense itself. On 26 July 2010, one week before the presidential election (already criticized for its lack of pluralism), thirty media outlets were threatened with suspension because they had failed to respect administrative requirements included in the 2009 Press Law. As the French organization Reporters sans Frontières declared: "The Media High Council's measures, coming just a few days before the election, are highly suspect. The aim is to clamp down on the press and prevent journalists from doing their job as independent and impartial observers of the election process." One month earlier, the editor of a Rwandan private newspaper had been gunned down in front of his house.

Besides economic sustainability and attacks against journalists, a third obstacle to radio development is the lack of professional education and training. Although journalism education is now available in the three countries, many radio professionals have been trained "on the spot." In Burundi, it was only in 2010 that a new master's degree in journalism was created at the University of Bujumbura. Until then, Burundian journalists were trained within their newsrooms or by attending short-term training sessions at the Burundi Press House (Maison de la Presse du Burundi). In Rwanda, although the School of Journalism and Communication was set up in 1996 at the National University of Rwanda, the Media High Council observed in 2008 that, of the 427 journalists working in Rwandan media, only 27 percent held a degree either in journalism or communications. In the DRC, besides the journalism school of Kinshasa created in 1973, called IFASIC (Institut Facultaire des Sciences de l'Information et de la Communication), many public and private universities have opened new communication sciences departments. Nevertheless, of the 4,000 media workers identified by the National Union of the Congolese Press (UNPC), the overwhelming majority has never had any kind of journalism education or training.

Moreover, the common trend in the three countries is that the best-educated journalists do not remain in the newsrooms. They seek better-paid jobs in the PR departments of large NGOs or institutions, or become communications advisers for political parties or politicians. Journalism is therefore seen as the first step to access to better opportunities. The consequence is a high turnover in many newsrooms, which makes it difficult for the media to consolidate.

A potential fourth obstacle to the development of a pluralist radio landscape lies in the appropriation by the government of the national broadcaster. Although attempts have been made to give these stations a "public service" status and content, they remain the government's mouthpiece. In countries emerging from authoritarian regimes and conflicts, state media have been used for decades to broadcast propaganda instead of information. Access to the public media by the opposition remains problematic. Instead of opening the airwaves to all components of society, national broadcasters remain strictly government-oriented and are unwilling to give voice to civil society. This situation has contributed, in Burundi and the DRC, for instance, to the radicalization of private media. The confiscation of the national broadcaster has generated closer ties between private stations and the political opposition and civil society, leading those stations to being called "the voice of the opposition."

In Burundi, the RTNB, which has two radio channels, moved between 2004 and 2006 towards more pluralism in its content, benefiting at the same time from an important support from Belgian foreign aid (€3 million over three years). This project aimed to help the RTNB integrate digital technologies and "reinforce its public-service mission." The strategic plan adopted by the RTNB board in 2003 stated that: "The airwaves belong to everybody and every citizen has the right to know the main points of view at stake about any issue of importance for Burundian society." Nevertheless, after winning the 2005 election, the ruling party seized back the national broadcaster, firing and appointing staff members to ensure the media would follow its master's voice. Programs have become less pluralist, and seem to revert to the era of one-party rule.

The RTNC in the DRC is on the same track. It is altogether strictly controlled by the Ministry of Media and Communications, and completely neglected by the authorities. Once the pride of the Mobutu regime, the national broadcaster is now a deteriorated "white elephant." Budgets are allocated to private media or programs whose producers are faithful to the ruling party, the PPRD, or to the communication teams of officials. These produce news items that are then sent to the national media in order to be aired in the news or magazine broadcasts, although they were not initiated by the impoverished RTNC's newsrooms.

In Rwanda, several media-monitoring projects (around the 2003, 2008, and 2010 elections) have demonstrated that the national radio station was blatantly imbalanced in its coverage of the RPF and its candidates. In 2003, for instance, while Kagame benefited from 60 percent of the total airtime spent on the four presidential candidates, he was also systematically presented in a positive light, in contrast to his main challenger, Faustin Twagiramungu, widely accused of "divisionism" in the media. In 2008, for the parliamentary elections, candidates who did not belong to the ruling RPF did not have the means to make their way to the regional public radios and only used small portions of their allocated time (MHC 2008b). The impact of the national broadcaster's "monotonous" tone should not be neglected since, as stated before, other private media generally have a smaller coverage. The population outside the major urban areas therefore has a privileged access to the national radio, totally dominated by the ruling party.

Media Synergies and Collective Dynamics

To overcome these obstacles, some radio stations in the three Great Lakes countries decided to set up collective projects, aimed at doing together what they could not achieve individually. The first example is the "media synergy" that took place in Burundi during the 2005 elections. Some months before the polls, acknowledging both their responsibilities and their limited capacities, the main radio stations of Bujumbura decided to cover the election together. Backed by SFCG, they organized a joint newsroom in which they pooled their human resources to create a network of correspondents, which would be likely to cover the elections nationwide. Moreover, the creation of a joint editorial board would enable donors to support a single collegial body, instead of having to support each one individually (Frère 2011).[6]

During the constitutional referendum, seven media took part in the synergy, including the main private radio stations and the national Burundi Press Agency (ABP). A total of sixty-five journalists were mobilized and some fifty were dispatched into the field, first and foremost into those communities where political tension risked being important. The fifteen remaining journalists formed a joint editorial team in Bujumbura. The "synergy" produced sixteen radio news programs broadcast simultaneously on the airwaves of the participating radio stations.

This experience was so much appreciated by the participating media and by the audience that, during the following communal and legislative elections, 120 journalists from eleven Burundian media took part in the project. The national RTNB and two Congolese media from Bukavu joined the team. More than twenty special editions of radio news broadcasts were produced for each poll. Thanks to Radio Isanganiro's Internet website, the programs were also accessible to the Burundian diaspora.[7] Nestor Nkurunziza, a Burundian journalist living in the DRC, remarked that, "broadcast over the Internet, the synergy made it possible for Burundians in the diaspora to know what was happening.

The diaspora was able to have access to information in real time, whereas what is happening inside the country is often reported by foreign radios which deform reality."[8]

The synergy also proved to be very useful to the electoral administration, facilitating communications between the CENI (National Independent Electoral Commission) and its local staff in the field. The CENI made use of the synergy to convey its instructions or put an end to certain irregularities (EU-EOM 2005, 47). During the communal elections, for instance, the president of the CENI used the synergy broadcast to inform his colleagues that the closing of the polls would be delayed by a few hours to allow farmers, who had gone to their fields to farm the land after a rainy night, to come and cast their vote. It is also thanks to an investigative report by the synergy on proxy trafficking that the CENI banned voting by proxy on the eve of the polls. The synergy's correspondents also revealed other dysfunctions, such as the lack of indelible ink, the absence of some parties' ballot papers in some polling stations, and the deliberate removal of some lists in other places.

For many Burundians, the synergy "made it possible to reduce the risk of fraud by virtue of the fact that the unfolding of the election was reported live and throughout the country" (Ntiyanogeye 2008, 95). Some observers believe that the project also had an impact within the profession, as public and private media worked together: "It proved the capacity of most Burundian journalists to move away from the leaden years of journalism and overcome their own prejudices" (Bastin 2005). Lastly, the synergy improved information quality. As its main organizer claimed: "it made it possible to fill in the shortage of human resources of each media, and also to better check the contents of the broadcast information given that there were various news sources and several people to control this information."[9]

However, the synergy also generated some criticism, especially from one of the major radio stations, RPA, which had refused to take part. "We couldn't all speak with a single voice. There had to be some diversity," said Alexis Sinduhije, director of the RPA.[10] In his view, such a project also weakens information since citizens no longer have access to a plurality of voices. The RPA's refusal to participate was also motivated by the fact that the initiative stemmed from SFCG. Indeed, "the RPA does not wish to be under the umbrella of SFCG, thereby giving credit to donors for the successful media coverage of the election" (quoted in Palmans 2008, 163).

Nevertheless, the initiative was so successful that the Burundian stations decided to pursue it beyond the elections and even the RPA joined the network. Regularly—and especially when the freedom of the press is threatened—the stations simultaneously broadcast programs created together. During the 2010 elections, the synergy, gathering fifteen media outlets, once again provided complete, balanced, and unbiased coverage in a very tense context, as the political opposition decided to withdraw from the electoral process after the first stage of the communal polls.

The success of the Burundian synergy went beyond its borders and inspired similar initiatives abroad. In the DRC, where a national synergy is practically impossible given the vast area of the country, some community-based stations tried to set up local synergies during the 2006 polls. While "radio warfare" (Frère 2011) was starting between stations belonging to the main challengers of the presidential and legislative elections, some stations pooled their forces in Mbuji Mayi, Bukavu, Kisangani, and Lubumbashi to create joint editorial teams, share information, and diffuse it simultaneously. In Sud-Kivu, participating journalists were sent to the various towns and reported to a central newsroom set up in Radio Maendeleo. "For four days," the director of Radio Maendeleo, Kizito Mushizi, explained, "listeners were able to follow not only the unfolding of the election, but also the atmosphere reigning in Sud-Kivu." A listener from Bukavu claimed: "If journalists work like this throughout the country during the elections, politicians who are used to bribing the media risk being ridiculed. It will be very difficult to bribe or threaten such a network" (quoted in Chirhalwirwa 2006, 2).

In Katanga, eight stations joined forces, each delegating two journalists to a centralized newsroom hosted by the Katanga community radio (RCK). Every Saturday throughout the electoral period, the synergy produced a one-hour program in Swahili and in French, relayed by all member radios. Then, for the five days surrounding the election, the joint editorial staff prepared and broadcast thirty-six joint radio newscasts in Lingala, Kiswahili and French. The commercial director of Radio Phoenix Université acknowledged that: "The synergy enabled journalists and even their various directors to consolidate their relations and create a harmonious atmosphere. Harmony has been achieved because these radios used to be at war with one another, but now they exchange programs, files and broadcasts. Solidarity at work is now a reality."[11] Several participating journalists also insisted on the formative aspect of such an experiment, which enabled staff to discover new work methods and submit them to collective and constructive criticism from other colleagues.

The Congolese synergies also drove local listeners to tune in to local stations rather than Radio Okapi. For the first time, local stations could compete with the UN station, as they would broadcast detailed local news, while Radio Okapi's correspondents gave a more general overview of the situation. A listener in Bukavu simply cried out that "this time, we did not have to wait for RFI to learn how the elections were unfolding in Sud-Kivu" (quoted by JED 2006, 22). Thus, Congolese synergies have probably helped strengthen the credibility and popularity of local stations while reinforcing professional solidarity in a highly competitive and politicized media environment. As in Burundi, media synergies continued beyond the election period, operating regularly on special occasions, around issues of general interest (e.g., World Press-Freedom Day, International Day of Women or of HIV/AIDS). In 2011, for the second democratic polls in the DRC after the war, five radio synergies were established, involving more than sixty journalists and, for the first time, these local networks were connected to a joint central newsroom based in the RTGA station in Kinshasa, which disseminated the information nationwide. For seventy-two hours before, during, and after the polls, joint newscasts in French and in the four national languages were broadcast through these synergies, reaching hundreds of thousands listeners.

In Rwanda, too, a radio synergy was set up during the 2008 parliamentary election, with the support of the Media High Council. The aim was not to prepare joint news broadcasts, but to send correspondents from various private and public radios into the country's main towns. Each radio received the contact details of some twenty journalists mobilized within the country and from whom they could obtain information.

Also inspired by the synergies, Contact FM, together with Flash FM and City Radio, initiated in 2007 a debate program entitled *Political Space* on political issues in the country. It was broadcast simultaneously by the three stations and on Contact FM's website.[12] Together with Radio Salus, Contact FM also participated in the production of several "regional synergies" aimed at facilitating the flow of information between the media and the audiences of the three countries. *Génération Grands Lacs* (Great Lakes Generation), initiated by SFCG, is a weekly participatory program produced and broadcast simultaneously by these two Rwandan stations, and by Radio Maendeleo in Bukavu and Radio Isanganiro in Bujumbura. The program aims to show that the youth of the three countries share common concerns and interests, despite the gap that the war has created between them.

Regards croisés sur la région des Grands Lacs (Different perspectives on the Great Lakes region), a program supported by the Institut Panos Paris (IPP) that ended in 2009, also associated these four stations. Every month, one of the partner radios organized, produced, and broadcast jointly thematic debates on issues related to the future of the region: security, cross-border business, justice and impunity, good governance and democracy, and regional integration. This program aimed to improve the flow of information and points of view among the various stations and to give the audience of each country access to the views of other citizens and journalists living across the border. The program was interrupted because of a lack of funding to support a rather costly technical device, but also because of disagreements between the Congolese and Rwandan radio stations.

If national or local synergies encourage professional solidarity, these regional experiments have also started to dismantle the wall of suspicion and distrust that the war raised between neighboring communities in the region. In a recent study (Nindorera 2009), listeners have underlined how much these programs can contribute to fueling a sense of belonging to a shared space, where the main hope of each citizen is peace and security. "The countries of this region are like communicating vessels which demand unified solutions," a listener claimed, while another argued that such programs were "a part of the path out of our conflicts" (quoted in Nindorera 2009, 12).

These regional collaborations have also led to the establishment of an online recording agency, Echos des Grands Lacs, a digital platform through which twelve radio stations in the region can share sounds and news items on a daily basis.[13] Also supported by the IPP, the project increases the credibility and reputation of local stations. As a Congolese community radio manager points out: "Our audience appreciates the fact that we have correspondents in Kigali and Bujumbura. They are very impressed that we can provide them with news items from abroad. It has made us even more popular."[14]

Sustainability, Financial and Editorial Independence

As I have shown, media synergies and regional collaborations provide good opportunities to overcome the lack of technical means and human resources while reinforcing professional solidarity. When national broadcasters are part of these dynamics (as was the case in Burundi and in some of the Congolese synergies), these projects can also help bring some pluralism to the "public service" media content. Synergies can also contribute to strengthening the defense of the freedom of the press. Nevertheless, these projects have so far, and to a large extent, been financially supported by foreign donors. They often cease not because they are meaningless or because journalists are not sufficiently committed, but because the funding comes to an end. This unveils a reality that has become problematic for many stations in the countries this study focuses on: media sustainability is dependent on foreign donors, which encourages a form of subordination of the local dynamics to the strategies and priorities of Western partners.

In the DRC, some stations are entirely dependent on foreign funding. In 2009, Radio Okapi had a yearly budget of US$13 million, fully provided by the UN and other foreign donors. Under no circumstances could such a cost be supported by local resources from the Congolese advertising market. As Bill Orme (2010) remarked in a report on the "exit strategies" for the radio stations created in the context of the UN peacekeeping missions, this budget might only be a feather in the huge cost of the MONUSCO (estimated at US$1.3 billion in 2009), but it is disproportionate to the local media's operating budget. Indeed, Radio Okapi's budget weighs only about one percent of the annual cost of the MONUSCO, but it is twenty six times above that of the most famous community radio station in Sud-Kivu, Radio Maendeleo. Therefore, Radio Okapi could never, in its current state, survive if the MONUSCO withdrew.

But neither could Radio Maendeleo's yearly budget of US$400,000 be supported locally and it, too, is provided by foreign donors. Of course, all four hundred Congolese radio stations are not funded directly by international NGOs or church networks, but many of them do benefit from other types of support, for instance receiving free magazines, being paid to broadcast ready-made educational programs, or selling airtime to foreign-backed "development" projects.

Since the end of the war, the Congolese media have benefited massively from foreign goodwill. Between 2004 and 2008, more than €43 million from bi- or multilateral sources have been injected in the information sector in the DRC (Frère 2009b). And although there is an impressive number of local media, it is always the same "credible" and "efficient" ones that receive support, and sometimes even the same individual journalists, identified as more professional, who benefit from all training opportunities.

In neighboring Burundi, the donors' generosity has also kept the radio sector alive for over ten years. For instance, the budget of Radio Isanganiro reached US$480,768 in 2008, mainly supported by the EU, Oxfam, the Belgian Embassy, and Swiss Foreign Aid. Advertising revenue only contributed seven percent of the budget. The other two major private stations in Bujumbura, Radio Bonesha and RPA, were also established thanks to international governmental or nongovernmental organizations, and in 2006, advertising revenue generated only 12.5 percent and 20 percent of their budgets, respectively (Fyon 2007, 18).

On a smaller scale, the community radio Ijwi ry'umukenyezi in Giheta, with only three permanent staff members, had a yearly budget of around US$48,000, consisting entirely of donations from foreign partners. The station closed down in 2011, being unable to secure this limited budget. Even the only quality independent newspaper, *Iwacu*, was created thanks to funding from the Belgian Ministry of Foreign Affairs. After three years of operation, it has reached a circulation of 2,000 copies and is probably the most appreciated newspaper in the country. But its founder and director, Antoine Kaburahe, has no illusions: "When foreign support ceases, we'll shut down" (quoted in Nyundiko 2010, 12).

Private radio stations in Rwanda operate on an entirely different economic model, inspired by the Anglo-American commercial broadcasting strategy, probably under the influence of neighboring Uganda. For instance, Contact FM also has a monthly budget of some US$40,000, but most of its funding comes from advertising or partnerships with the business sector. It has chosen to broadcast popular entertainment rather than educational programs, and uses four languages (Kinyarwanda, French, English, and Swahili) in the hope of extending its scope to neighboring Uganda, Tanzania, Eastern Congo, and Burundi. Contrary to their Burundian and Congolese counterparts, Contact FM and Radio 10 have had access to bank loans, allowing them some corporate flexibility. Nevertheless, community stations in Rwanda are also dependent on foreign money. Radio Salus, for instance, is backed by UNESCO and the European Union, besides receiving money from the University of Rwanda.

The financial dependence of many radio stations in the three countries generates major constraints. Firstly, donor support is often short-lived and must be renegotiated yearly. Radio Okapi went through a high level of anxiety in 2008 when the Canadian government (which had provided more than US$3 million the previous year) suddenly decided to stop funding the station. Eventually, a special donation from the Belgian government helped fill the gap.

It is generally the most powerful and efficient media (Radio Okapi and Radio Maendeleo in the DRC, Radio Isanganiro in Burundi) that are also the least able to generate locally the funding they need to operate. Professional journalism is costly, and therefore the media that are most efficient in providing reliable and well-presented information are also those whose budgets are disproportionate to the capacities of the local market. The citizens have indeed access to professional, cross-checked, and verified news, but these journalistic products would be far above their purchasing power if they had to support their real cost. Therefore, these quality media are a luxury for the local population and would disappear if donors withheld their support. The fact that donors can either leave or turn to other priorities is a constant threat and a source of anxiety for the managers and the audiences of these stations.

Nevertheless, other experiences in Africa show that alternative scenarios are possible. Of the fourteen stations created by the UN within their peacekeeping missions, five shut down when the UN left while another seven currently still broadcast (six in Africa and one in Haiti).[15] But two other stations have succeeded in converting themselves into local media outlets.

In Sierra Leone, the UN radio station, established in 1999, had been operating for ten years, and was highly appreciated for its neutrality and endorsement of "public service" missions. In 2008, when the Blue Helmets withdrew definitively, the UN, for the first time in history, allowed the station to remain and to keep broadcasting. In late 2009, the Sierra Leone parliament established a new Sierra Leone Public Broadcasting Corporation (SLPBC), integrating the former UN station. The SLPBC is now a national "public service" media, led by a board on which civil society is widely represented. The UN agreed to continue to provide some funding to the new media until it can be fully sustainable with public funding and commercial advertising revenue.

A second example of a successful durability strategy is that of Radio Ndeke Luka (Bird of Chance) in the Central African Republic. The station was created in 1998 within the UN peacekeeping mission MINURCA and operated for two years before being shut down. As the radio was the only independent broadcaster in a particularly landlocked and underinformed country, the Swiss Fondation Hirondelle agreed with the UN to put it back on air. Since then, the aim of the Fondation Hirondelle has been to find ways to turn Radio Ndeke Luka into a local independent radio station. This objective was reached after ten years and Radio Ndeke Luka has become, in 2010, a fully Central African private commercial broadcaster. Its brand-new marketing department and advertising sales house are so dynamic that by August 2010, they were already generating more than 30 percent of the station's yearly budget.

These two success stories are a source of hope, even though it is only in a few years that one will be able to conclude whether the SLPBC has retained its independence from government or whether Radio Ndeke Luka has become fully self-supporting. They suggest that there is a real chance that the local media in postconflict countries can fully reappropriate their own public sphere.

But financial dependence is not only an issue for sustainability. It can also lead to the subordination of local players to the priorities of foreign partners, and thus to a lack of autonomy in the definition, by local stations, of their own future. In the case of the DRC, the major donors (France, UK, EU, and soon USAID), now use "calls for proposals" to allocate their budgets to local media.[16] But this system often requires a high level of technical skills, a solid financial background, and good managing capacities to deal with large amounts of money. So Western NGOs end up being the ones introducing proposals aimed at supporting local radio stations. For these international NGOs, local stations are the necessary local partners or beneficiaries that will give credibility to their proposal. When such calls for proposals are launched, local stations in the DRC as well as in Burundi often have to choose between several international NGOs courting them for partnership. The choice may be highly sensitive for the local stations, because signing with the right partner (the one that is more likely to win the bid) can be crucial to their own existence in the future. In such cases, radio stations, if they want to survive, are forced to work with Western NGOs, which act as the compulsory middlemen between the local stations and the donors' money. Radio stations are therefore sometimes strategically forced into projects they neither want nor believe in. This has already created much frustration for local radio stations and sometimes trapped them into broadcasting programs not always matching their editorial line.

This is not to say that international NGOs specializing in media support in the Great Lakes region are not skilled or do not bring any added value to local stations. But the support system must be questioned as it is based on mechanisms that are (for technical and financial reasons) beyond the reach of those media they are supposed to sustain.

In the DRC, Rwanda and Burundi, broadcasting plurality is an undeniable reality. A total regression, back to a state monopoly, seems unlikely. Nevertheless, some radio stations among the most efficient, professional, and appreciated ones currently have major sustainability concerns.

On the one hand, foreign donors who paid much attention to media players in the postconflict era might turn to other priorities now that peace has come and the ghost of the "hate media" seems to have faded away. Moreover, donors have started setting up support mechanisms that are less flexible than those established in haste during the postconflict or transition period. The procedures are often complex, leading local radio stations to rely on Western NGOs to apply for, and ultimately manage, projects and budgets.

On the other hand, sustainability problems have led some stations to trade their independence for material and financial support from politicians and businessmen. Editorial lines become inconsistent, sometimes also because individual journalists, unsatisfied with their salary, attempt to come by other revenue by developing side strategies: they tend to practice another job simultaneously, work as a freelancer for international media, try to integrate international organizations, or turn to "rewarded" journalism.

Solidarity among radio stations, nationally and internationally, might be a good way out of this dead end: not only to share the limited resources around synergy operations or to build a more powerful front to face attacks against the freedom of the press, but also to have a voice and participate fully in the debates and projects elaborated to strengthen peace and state-building in the region. For, in any case, radio broadcasting remains the main tool to reach the citizens, and there will be no democracy in the Great Lakes without informed citizens and independent media.

Notes

1. The expression "hate media" was first used in 1993 by the French press-freedom organization Reporters sans Frontières to describe the Burundian press (Barnabé 2005, 56–73).
2. Two denominational stations (Radio Ijwi ry'Amahoro and Radio Ijwi ry'Umukenyezi) closed down in 2011 because of a lack of funding, recalling the unsustainability of the Burundian media outlets and their dependency on foreign donors.
3. In 2010, the EU election-monitoring mission has noted that the tone of Rema FM broadcasts has become "increasingly aggressive." Amadou Ousmane, spokesman for the UN mission in Burundi, has even compared the station to the Rwandan RTLM.
4. See the annual reports on the website: www.jed-afrique.org. Accessed January 2011.
5. Jean-Claude Kavumbagu, the director of the Netpress agency, spent ten months in jail (from July 2010 to May 2011) for alleged treason after publishing a dispatch questioning whether the Burundian security forces could deal with an attack like the one that hit Uganda in early July 2010.
6. The project was backed by PADCO (Planning and Development Collaborative International, an international development consultancy firm financed by USAID/OTI), French development aid, UNESCO, the nonprofit Belgian organization Kabondo, the National Independent Electoral Commission (CENI), and even a commercial sponsor, Barudi (Burundian Breweries).
7. See www.isanganiro.org. Accessed January 2011.
8. Nestor Nkurunziza, a journalist with the Lokole Centre, one o'clock radio news, *Synergy*, dated 25 September 2005.
9. Adrien Sindayigaya, director of Studio Ijambo, personal interview, Bujumbura, Sept. 2009.
10. Alexis Sinduhije, personal interview, Bujumbura, Dec. 2009.
11. Dimitri Musampule, executive secretary of Remack, commercial manager of Radio Phoenix Université, quoted by IPP (2008, 15).
12. See www.contactfm.rw. Accessed January 2011.
13. See www.echos-grandslacs.info. Accessed January 2011.
14. Quoted by Pierre Martinot, IPP staff member, personal interview, Kinshasa, May 2009.
15. These stations were created in Cambodia (1992–93), Somalia (1993–94), Rwanda (1994–96), Croatia (1996–97), the Central African Republic (1998–2000), and East Timor (1999–2002). They are still operating in Sierra Leone (2000–), the DRC (2001–), Côte d'Ivoire (2004–), Liberia (2003–), the Sudan (2006–), Darfur (2009–), Chad (2008–), and Haiti (2007–). See Orme (2010).
16. In April 2010, United States Aid for International Development (USAID) launched a call for proposals in order to allocate a budget of US$15 million to support the Congolese media over the following three to five years.

References

Barnabé, Jean-François. 2005. "Les médias assassins au Burundi." In *Les médias de la haine*, edited by Renaud de la Brosse, 56–73. Paris: La Découverte.
Bastin, Jen-François. 2005. "Note de synthèse sur la synergie des médias." Bujumbura: Kabondo ASBL, Unpublished Document.
Burton, Charline. 2006. *Débat autour du concept de journalisme de paix. Approche critique de l'opérationnalité concrète des médias dits pour la paix.* Master's thesis, Department of Information and Communication Sciences, University of Brussels.

Chirhalwirwa, Pascal. 2006. "Rapport interne sur la synergie électorale." Paris: Institut Panos Paris, Unpublished Document.
European Union-Electoral Observation Mission (EU-EOM). 2005. "Burundi, elections législatives 2005." Bujumbura, Burundi: European Union.
Frère, Marie-Soleil. 2007. *The Media and Conflicts in Central Africa*. Boulder, CO: Lynne Rienner.
———. 2009a. *Le paysage médiatique congolais. État des lieux, enjeux et défis*. Kinshasa, DRC: FCI.
———. 2009b. "Appui au secteur des médias: quel bilan pour quel avenir?" In *Réforme au Congo (RDC). Attentes et désillusions*, edited by Theodore Trefon, 191–210. Cahiers Africains. Tervueren/Paris: Musée Royal de l'Afrique Centrale/L'Harmattan.
———. 2011. *Elections and the Media in Post-conflict Africa: Votes and Voices for Peace?* London: Zed Books.
Fyon, Jean-Claude. 2007. "Médias du Burundi: Enquête de terrain et orientations pour un renforcement économique du secteur." Bujumbura, Burundi: Institut Panos Paris.
IMMAR. 2008. "Étude d'audience des médias Congolais." (Annual Audience Survey for Radio Okapi). Unpublished Document. http://www.mediathequepanosparis.org/IMG/pdf/Etude_IMMAR_1.pdf.
Institut Panos Paris (IPP). 2008. "Rapport final du projet SPOT." Kinshasa, DRC: Institut Panos Paris.
International Telecommunications Union (ITU). 2008. *African Telecommunication / ICT Indicators 2008: At a Crossroads*. Geneva, Switzerland: ITU.
Journaliste en Danger (JED). 2006. *La liberté de presse en période électorale. Assassinats, agressions, menaces, expulsions, destructions, propagandes, procès bidons et dérapages dans les médias*. Kinshasa, DRC: Journaliste en Danger.
Media High Council (MHC). 2008a. *State of the Media Report 2008*. Kigali: MHC.
———. 2008b. *Media Monitoring Report on the Allocation of Airtime and Space in the Public Media to Political Parties and Independent Candidates*. Kigali, Rwanda: MHC.
Nindorera, Willy. 2009. *Rapport global d'évaluation de l'émission regards croisés sur les Grands Lacs*, Paris-Bujumbura: Institut Panos Paris.
Ntiyanogeye, Athenase. 2008. *Le paysage médiatique du Burundi des origines au lendemain des élections de 2005*. Bujumbura, Burundi: R.P.P.
Nyundiko, Désiré. 2010. "L'intervention des bailleurs de fonds dans les budgets des médias privés au Burundi." Master's thesis, School of Journalism, National University of Burundi.
Orme, Bill. 2010. *Broadcasting in UN Blue: The Unexamined Past and Uncertain Future of UN Broadcasting*. Washington, DC: CIMA (Center for International Media Assistance).
Palmans, Eva. 2008. *Médias et politique en situation de crise: le cas du Burundi*. PhD diss., University of Antwerp.
Thompson, Alan. 2007. *The Media and the Rwanda Genocide*. London: Pluto.

9 Youth in Transition

The Arts and Cultural Resonance in Postconflict Northern Uganda

Lindsay McClain Opiyo
and Tricia Redeker Hepner

THREE DECADES AGO, art therapist and scholar Harriet Wadeson (1980, 3) stated, "Life, Meaning, Creativity, Art. In the largest sense, they are all one." In a different yet contemporaneous vein, sociocultural anthropologists began ethnographically documenting and theorizing, through diverse cross-cultural case studies, that "there is nothing innate in human nature that constitutes a barrier to perpetual peace, except willful ignorance" (Montagu 1994, xii; see also Howell and Willis 1989; Sponsel and Gregor 1994). In yet a third and related development, anthropologists interested in human rights and social justice linked elements of an emergent anthropology of peace with longstanding disciplinary interests in violence, conflict and aggression to develop a rich and critical body of scholarship analyzing the flexible appropriation of the "universal" notions of human rights and justice among societies coping with the impact of domination, poverty, war, and political conflict (see Preis 1996; Merry 2006a; Wilson 1997). This chapter weaves together elements of these intellectual strands to critically examine how the creative arts have played a central role in the formulation and dissemination of ideas and practices associated with peace, reconciliation, and human rights among the Acholi—notably the youth—in contemporary postconflict northern Uganda.

For over two decades, the people of northern Uganda have suffered from severe persecution and marginalization both at the hands of the government of Uganda and through the violence of rebel insurgencies: namely, the Lord's Resistance Army, or LRA (see Opongo, this volume; Ochen, this volume). Since independence in 1962, nearly every corner of the country has undergone some period of violence resulting from rebellion, state intimidation, or regional and tribal division—an unfortunate remnant of Britain's "divide-and-rule" colonial tactics. However, the systematic discrimination against northerners has been particularly acute since the mid-1980s. When President Yoweri Kaguta Museveni came to power in 1986 through protracted guerrilla warfare, a series of chain reactions rippled throughout the north. Several groups, fearing reprisal from the new regime, took up arms against the state, including the LRA. In a tragic twist of events, both the rebels and the government began violently targeting civilians, leaving much truth to the African proverb that when two elephants fight, it is the grass that gets trampled.

The consequences of this instability in northern Uganda are staggering. Millions were displaced by the violence, and an estimated 60,000 people were abducted by rebels (Anwar 2007; see also Finnström 2008). As a result, northern Uganda is thought to have some of the highest levels of posttraumatic stress disorder (PTSD) and depression recorded anywhere, with an estimated 54 percent of the population suffering from PTSD (Roberts et al. 2008, 4). Numerous ethnic groups suffered from this violence, but the Acholi were located at the heart of the conflict in northern Uganda and were therefore especially affected. For example, an estimated 90 percent of Acholi were relocated to the more than fifty internally displaced persons (IDP) camps in Acholiland. Extensive research has been done to document indigenous concepts of justice and reconciliation given the severe scope and magnitude of the conflict (see Baines 2005). Relatedly, since the conflict formally ended in 2006, northern Uganda has witnessed the exponential growth of both indigenous and foreign nongovernmental organizations (NGOs) and special programs intended to foster peace, social and individual healing, and reconciliation. Many of these explicitly target young people and utilize the arts as media of expression. In her research on creative expression and the refugee experience, Margaret Mills identified a general "lack of attention ... to the areas of cultural expression and artistic experience," and found that many aid workers and service providers framed refugees as passive victims with their culture in disarray, instead of supporting channels for creative expression (Mills 1990). The plethora of cultural and arts-based NGO interventions in northern Uganda today suggests a shift in the last two decades, in which aid programming increasingly values creative and cultural expression. With respect to scholarship, however, something of the reverse has happened: Little or no academic attention has been paid to the meaning and impact of creative and cultural expression in the northern Ugandan context. Our chapter aims to begin breaking this silence.

In seeking to understand how the performing and plastic arts—including dance, drama, poetry, music, painting, drawing, and sculpture—may play a role in addressing individual and social trauma and contribute to postconflict reconstruction in Acholiland, we draw on two years of original ethnographic research in northern Uganda, as well as current research and debates within art therapy and anthropology. An especially fruitful point of convergence for our analysis is the issue of cross-cultural applicability of key concepts such as suffering, trauma, and mental health on the one hand, as well as human rights, justice, and dignity on the other, in the pursuit of peace and reconciliation. As scholars in both art therapy and anthropology have pointed out, the core concepts associated with both posttraumatic stress and "universal" human rights originated in primarily Western settings and embed experiences of trauma, as well as notions of rights and dignity, within the individual, generating a vigorous debate about cross-cultural applicability (e.g., Roy 1999; Chilcote 2007; Das et al. 2001). However, anthropologists and others have amassed a considerable body of ethnographic research that demonstrates the extent to which "universalizing" discourses of both mental health and human rights become richly contextualized, adapted, and culturally appropriated across diverse contexts (Dosamantes-Beaudry 1999; Merry 2006a, b; Weiss and Marmar 1997), and how peace, justice, and reconciliation can be effected through cultural practices (Howell and Willis 1989; Montagu 1978; Sponsel and Gregor 1994) and the arts (Byers 1996; Giddings 2009; Kalmanowitz and Lloyd 1999). Similarly, analyses of postconflict situations have demonstrated that perspectives on justice can vary significantly within a single social or cultural context, reflecting the diversity of experiences and emotions associated with violent episodes and their resolution (Justice and Reconciliation Project 2008). That reconciliation has emerged as a dominant approach in northern Uganda over and above other possible approaches to justice has implications for the cultural expression of associated ideas like peace and the securing of human rights and dignity.

Rather than viewing local cultural forms as an obstacle to realizing rights or as reified entities that are broken, fragmented, destroyed, or distorted by conflict, anthropologists have pointed to the processes by which people marshal cultural resources, and often remake practices or institutions, as strategies for seeking justice, building peace, achieving reconciliation, and defining human rights. The processes by which peace, justice, and human rights become articulated "in the vernacular" (Merry 2006b) have therefore moved the debate away from a stale (and stalemated) discussion of Western versus non-Western, or whole versus fragmented forms and discourses, to one in which culture is conceptualized as open, dynamic, internally contested, creative, and transformative (Cowan et al. 2001; Goodale 2009; Preis 1996). At the same time, An-Na'im's (1992) now-classic observation that "universal" concepts such as human rights and, perhaps even peace and reconciliation, are most meaningful and effective when they resonate with—indeed, emerge from—existing cultural values and experiences, remains highly relevant (see also Kymlicka 1996), especially in disciplines where such a critical and process-oriented anthropological approach to culture is less firmly rooted.

Our analysis is based on original ethnographic data gathered by Lindsay McClain Opiyo in 2007–2009 over four separate trips to Gulu, Uganda, and ongoing observations gleaned by both authors in subsequent visits or periods of residency.[1] In addition to participant observation in a Gulu youth center, attending music and dance performances, and implementing an art journal project in conjunction with the youth center's art teacher, informal interviews with leading figures engaged in regional peace talks, politicians, religious leaders, teachers, returnees, artists, child-mothers, aid workers, and musicians were conducted. Attending concerts, performances, radio interviews, and workshops provided further insight into how art and music were recruited as tools for addressing trauma and promoting concepts and practices associated with reconciliation, peacebuilding, and human rights. In addition, qualitative interviews with thirty-nine primary school students and the administration of the Impact of Events Scale-Revised (Weiss and Marmar 1997) to measure subjective distress related to specific life events further illuminated elements of the postconflict problems that artistic approaches were explicitly intended to address.

Indeed, there exists in northern Uganda a wide variety of programs and individuals using the creative arts as tools for peacebuilding, reconciliation, and human rights consciousness, with the latter encompassing everything from civil and political freedoms to domestic violence and development. These programs were therefore key sites in which to analyze the discursive form and cultural expression of the interrelated concepts of peace, reconciliation, justice, and human rights, as both northern Ugandans and international actors sought to give specific shape to them. While unique in regards to their specific target audience, creative media, and project implementation, all of these programs sought to foster self-expression among individuals and/or communities in Acholiland, and in turn, represent sources for community-building, and for personal and collective healing in the wake of conflict, displacement, and human rights abuses.

Our analysis focuses on evaluating and comparing several different creative arts programs in northern Uganda and their differential appeal among people of different genders, ages, and locations of residence. Following Merry (2006b), we distinguish among three types of programs and approaches: those that are indigenous and locally driven; those that represent hybridizations of Acholi and non-Acholi (typically Western) forms; and transplanted initiatives or approaches to peacebuilding that were formulated and led by foreigners, but instituted in Acholiland.

Our findings indicate that those approaches that are more intimately linked to communities through their own initiation and leadership, and those that accommodate or resonate with existing cultural patterns and preferences, tend to be most successful in engaging Acholi youth in artistic expression and contributing to community building and collective healing. At the same time, the introduction of new forms of expression have provided fertile ground for creatively engaging concepts of peace, reconciliation, and human rights, while also revealing important variations in how people of different ages, genders, and locations of residence understand and express such concepts through the arts. The implications of these findings are twofold. Consistent with the arguments advanced in the anthropological literature on peace and human rights, we demonstrate that taking cultural patterns and internal variation within communities seriously can benefit and enrich peacebuilding, reconciliation, and human rights consciousness in postconflict settings. Secondly, we suggest that those initiatives whose design and implementation are integrated into the social fabric and norms of the communities they intend to aid are more sustainable and, ultimately, effective in reaching their goals.

Initiatives for Creative Expression in Acholiland

Art interventions that aim to foster peace and reconciliation in Acholiland and contribute to the development of human rights consciousness vary in their degree of cultural resonance depending on their articulation with longstanding patterns of expression. In what follows, we examine the cultural relevance of different types of creative expression in northern Uganda by exploring and comparing the three types of initiatives we have outlined above. While there is some overlap among these three types of initiatives, we find the distinctions useful for interpreting the differential appeal of forms of creative expression among Acholi youth of different genders, ages, and areas of residence.

In her ethnographic analysis of the global dissemination and local development of programs and discourses of women's rights in Hawai'i, Fiji, India, and Hong Kong, Merry (2006b) noted the central role played by NGOs and programs that contributed to the cultural adaptation and vernacularization of rights concepts. The range of outcomes in diverse settings suggested a distinction between forms of vernacularization that were replications of forms initiated in (predominantly) Western or Northern contexts like the United States and were only "thinly adapted to local circumstances," versus those that were hybrids and drew "more extensively on local institutions, knowledge, idioms, and practices" (2006b: 48) to genuinely transform otherwise Western-originated concepts and practices. Merry argued that women's rights programs that resonated with local patterns but also introduced hybridized or novel practices and ideas were often the most engaging and transformative. In further analyses of the global dissemination of women's human rights, Merry (2006a) concluded that the "cultural work" performed by these initiatives was vitally important in and of itself, regardless of whether they were always successful in their legal and political challenges to abuses of women's rights in specific settings.

That is, by encouraging the development and articulation of rights consciousness, such programs and initiatives contributed to shifting cultural patterns in ways that helped align them more explicitly with human rights norms and provided people with alternative possibilities for thinking about the present and future of gendered sociopolitical relations. Such findings are significant in light of arguments that human rights concepts are inherently alien to African settings (Mutua 2002) and other critical approaches demonstrating that people realize and challenge concepts like human rights *through* culture (An Na'im 1992; Cowan et al. 2001; Preis 1996), as well as locate resources for peacebuilding and reconciliation through existing cultural norms and patterns (Howell and Willis 1989; Sponsel and Gregor 1994; see also Nagengast 1994). Our analysis of programs that harnessed the creative arts for the purposes of peacebuilding, reconciliation, and human rights consciousness in Acholiland adapts and expands Merry's model of vernacularization to suggest three types of initiatives: indigenous, hybrid, and transplanted.

Indigenous Initiatives

For the purpose of this study, indigenous initiatives are defined as any creative expression that is locally driven and based on art forms associated with longstanding patterns of expression in northern Uganda. Among the Acholi, these indigenous initiatives often involve music and dance. Across the greater north, music, dance, and drama groups perform Acholi dances and songs for community events. At times, they participate in competitions at local, regional, and national levels. Primary school competitions may involve traditional dances such as the *bwola* and *dingi-dingi*, wedding processions often include dancing and singing, and musical performances in IDP camps incorporate instruments made out of local materials and foreign-aid canisters. Performances involve both males and females close in age. In primary school, children begin learning how to craft the instruments, play them, and dance the routines, although there is a generation of men and women who came of age during the war and missed the opportunity to learn these indigenous performance arts due to insecurity, instability, and protracted displacement. The indigenous creative initiatives most commonly practiced today in northern Uganda are communal in nature and powerfully join people together.

Although not as prevalent today as music and dance, poetry is a prewar form of indigenous expression that gained the Acholi worldwide recognition. In the 1960s and '70s, Acholi poet and anthropologist Okot p'Bitek gained global fame for poems on African rural life and Westernization. His best-known poems, *Song of Lawino* and *Song of Ocol*, written first from the perspective of the wife (Lawino) and later rebutted by her husband (Ocol), articulate the conflict in Acholi society between traditions of the past and present-day Western influences. In our experience, however, today it is women who most commonly carry on this tradition of poetry. In one IDP camp, Opiyo met a formerly abducted woman who wrote poetry in the form of song to convey her sentiments towards conflict resolution. "This world will stop the fight. Forgiveness is good. This world will stop the fight. The goodness of forgiveness, if you see, will stop the fight. Let us first start," she sang in Luo. Composed in the local style, this song reflects a longstanding oral tradition in Acholiland used to comment and advise on social situations and problems.

Hybrid Initiatives

Hybrid initiatives can be defined as organized forms of creative expression that are locally driven and run, but articulated with international, contemporary forms of art. Oftentimes, these forms are inspired by Western popular culture. For example,

Acholi vocalists have adopted a reggae, rap, and rhythm and blues (R&B) fusion style. They were inspired by American rappers of the 1990s like the Notorious B.I.G. and Tupac Shakur, as well as "freedom fighters" and liberation artists like South Africa's Lucky Dube and Jamaica's Bob Marley. When this music is fused with Acholi beats, the result is often a high energy dance hall genre with lyrics discussing social issues directly related to the impact of the LRA insurgency and the war, including the stigma of abduction and child soldiering, children's rights, justice, reconciliation, and "defilement," or the sexual abuse of young people by the LRA or government soldiers. During the latter years of the war, this music had the unique opportunity to reach vast audiences in northern Ugandan society through the radio, namely, station Mega FM. Through strategic programming, people in the IDP camps enjoyed the same music as the rebels in the bush and the government soldiers. This contemporary Acholi music had the effect of creating a common creative referent among groups that were otherwise engaged in conflict with one another, and as such, represents one current source for reconciliation.

In a country with a history of media censorship, two northern artists, Jahria Okwera and Jeff Korondo, exemplify the ability to communicate serious messages safely through the use of music. One of Okwera's songs, "Dwog Paco" (Come Back Home), urges rebels to accept the government's offer of amnesty, and was the theme song to a popular radio talk show on Mega FM by the same name. During this particular show, returnees were brought on-air to share their experiences in the bush, and upon return, urged others to come home as well. Sings Okwera:

> Boys, come back home please
> The world is also calling for you
> Do not think you are wrong-doers
> We have now forgiven you
> Come back and organize your clan so that peace returns to the north
> Listen to us
> Return home[2]

In another popular song titled simply "ICC," Jeff Korondo explores the debate and controversy surrounding the indictment of top LRA commanders by the International Criminal Court (ICC). In the chorus he asks,

> Why have you brought the ICC?
> How is the ICC going to help us?
> Hey Government, we ask you why
> How is the ICC going to help us?[3]

Korondo urges leaders to remember to consider the needs of the victims and questions how the court will help those who survived the conflict. The lyrics reflect the developing popular consciousness in northern Uganda about international human rights institutions like the ICC, and provide a forum for public debate about their meaning, relevance, and possible impact on postconflict reconciliation.

In another song, entitled "Wan Lutino" (We the Children), Korondo speaks to yet another debate among northern Ugandans, this time regarding children's rights. Korondo's song—performed in Luo and blending Acholi styles with rap and reggae—responds to a public debate regarding the applicability of the Convention on the Rights of the Child (CRC) in a period of postconflict reconstruction. The lyrics at once demonstrate the ambivalence many northern Ugandans feel about this dimension of human rights discourse, and at the same time provide a culturally resonant frame of reference through which to realize the meaning of internationally constructed children's rights. Verses one and two are worth quoting at length:

> Every day when they talk about children's rights, many people think they spoil the children, but I really think that is not true.
> These are basic needs for the little child.
> Basic needs are these:
> Letting your child grow with happiness,
> Giving your child a chance to play,
> Listening to the ideas and problems of the child,
> Fulfilling the basic needs for appropriate growth.
> When we provide these basic needs, then that is what we call children's rights!
> The children too have their roles that they have to play.
> Taking goats for pasture—Your role!
> Sweeping the compound—Your role!
> Washing dishes—Your role!
> Fetching some water—Your role!
> But most important is to study hard, study hard our children!
> When given a little task, finish it well, and finish it well![4]

It is important to note that Korondo's song was written in 2005 for a campaign initiated by Save the Children in Uganda (SCiU). The following year, he was commissioned to write another song, "Otam pi Lutino" (Think about the Children), for SCiU and the Uganda Parliamentary Forum for Children in anticipation of the 2006 national elections. The local branches of the international NGO had authored a "Children's Manifesto" spelling out these rights, and candidates for the elections were asked to sign pledges to uphold children's rights. The tripartite pledge included free and mandatory education for all children; prevention and punishment of all forms of child abuse; and an end to the long conflict in the north. As a popular musician with the capacity to reach large numbers of people through this music, Jeff Korondo was given some of the highlights of the campaign and asked to write "Otam pi Lutino" about the issues.

Although the link between the "Children's Manifesto" and the Convention on the Rights of the Child is not clearly noted in the song, we view this as an example of how the international rights spelled out in the CRC were adapted to the northern Ugandan context, in which popular music played a key role. Korondo's songs demonstrate how northern Ugandans are making internationally constructed concepts of children's rights meaningful while the very existence of the song itself acknowledges the internal cultural debate at work. Speaking of the content of basic children's rights, Korondo is simultaneously helping to provide a human rights frame through which former child soldiers, abductees, children displaced in camps, and their parents and elders can understand how the conflict violated those basic rights and how peace can help restore them. However, the restoration and realization of those rights are not primarily to be found in the abstract definitions provided by human rights conventions, but in the everyday activities that children do and the ways they contribute to the community and family. Moreover, by exhibiting a hybrid of Acholi music with rap and reggae, the songs appeal to diverse audiences and manifest the artistic dynamism of Acholi culture itself.

Another hybrid form of expression that has picked up momentum in recent months is break dancing. A group of male youth based in central Uganda formed a group called Breakdance Project Uganda that travels around the country and teaches vulnerable youth how to break dance for social change (their efforts are portrayed in the popular film *Bouncing Cats*). The group uses dance and performance art to communicate messages of peace and reconciliation while providing a safe space for youth to interact with one another, share their ideas and problems, and just have a good time. Like the contemporary Acholi music, break dancing allows people to participate in a Western style of expression that is so popular among the youth in Uganda, while attaching positive messages to what in the West is (ironically) often attributed to a violent, crime-ridden subculture.

These new styles in northern Uganda have both individualistic and communal qualities. Even though singing typically features a single performer composing the songs and performing on stage, he or she nonetheless excites the crowd during the show and creates a communal setting where everyone is engaged with the music simultaneously, achieving a kind of "communitas" in the midst of otherwise imperfect solidarity and social cleavages (Turner 1968). These styles are different than local, Acholi styles of dance and music because they offer performers more flexibility to create new routines and write lyrics with messages relevant to contemporary issues. For example, indigenous Acholi dance styles typically utilize the routines that are largely predetermined. They follow a series of scenes and beats that characterize the dance as belonging to a particular, uniquely Acholi style. However, with a style as improvisational as break dancing, the dancer has the freedom to move any way he or she wishes, and develop a routine that reflects inner thoughts and feelings at that very moment.

Transplanted Initiatives

Transplanted initiatives are based on non-Acholi customs and traditions. They are introduced and run by Westerners often hoping to help foster reconciliation and healing after the war. More frequently, these initiatives involve the visual arts. While there are certainly some Acholi people who paint, draw, and sculpt, it is not generally a very common form of art in the region. According to informal interviews conducted with youth in a primary school and at a youth center, visual art requires a certain "God-given talent," and if youth feel as though they do not possess the talent for it, they do not try to improve. This is coupled by the fact that materials for making visual art are expensive and inaccessible to most young people. In 2008, Opiyo co-designed a small art journal program for children at a Gulu youth center and witnessed the students experience considerable difficulty using unfamiliar materials such as paint, crayons, and glue. Although, in addition to dance and music programs, the center did run a small visual arts program staffed by Acholi individuals, most of the students had little exposure to the materials introduced for the journals. Similar observations were made between June and August of 2009 during an art therapy study at a primary school in Gulu.[5] This school also had an art department with Acholi staff, but it was reserved for students with a demonstrated natural ability in visual art, and most of the participants in the art therapy study had never before used the materials presented to them.

Furthermore, transplanted initiatives sometimes lack necessary sensitivity to societal norms of coping with trauma and war. For example, in the West, a drawing of a violent encounter in war, or perhaps life as a child soldier, quickly and effectively resonates with an audience otherwise unfamiliar with such circumstances because of the focus on the individual and the way in which this taps into powerful imaginaries of conflict in Africa. The drawing also holds added emotional appeal, having been done by a child. However, it is potentially insensitive to *expect* a person to share a traumatic experience just because a pen or pencil is in front of him or her. Accordingly, transplanted visual art initiatives are most likely to breach Acholi norms pertaining to expression, especially of traumatic events, and prematurely request and expect visual depictions of such events. According to an in-depth analysis on Acholi indigenous justice, norms of expression pertaining to wrongdoing are historically oral and require both trust and a voluntary process (Baines 2005). Completing visual art with a stranger potentially violates both of these norms.

Despite the predominance of visual arts in transplanted programs, there are also foreign initiated programs that focus on performance art. For example, in 2008, the National Theatre in Uganda's capital of Kampala presented a play entitled *Butterflies of Uganda*. The production was written and developed by Westerners and first performed in California. The plot centered on the conflict in the north and one young girl's experience as an abducted child soldier. The cast was Ugandan, although there were very few performers native to the north. While moderately successful in Kampala and the United States, the play was not performed elsewhere in Uganda.

Variations in Resonance and Appeal

The activities in these three categories of creative expression appeal differently to people in northern Uganda. Although there are no absolutes, this analysis provides some general insight into the appeal of forms of creative expression according to gender, age, and residential location in the north. These findings are significant beyond indicating internal variations in preferences for forms of artistic expression because they also indicate the extent to which Acholi culture itself is dynamic and contested, especially during a postconflict period when explicit efforts are being made to redefine cultural norms and patterns. By and large, we find that older people, females, and those who live in the rural regions find indigenous styles most appealing and resonant, while younger people in the towns, and especially young males, gravitate towards hybridized forms. Transplanted initiatives that do not lend themselves to adaptation with existing cultural and social norms, or that introduce completely alien concepts and forms of expression, seem to be the least successful among all groups.

Gender

Gender-based interest in various methods of creative expression does not follow easily determinable patterns, although there are certainly forms of art that have widespread appeal among both males and females. For example, longstanding forms of Acholi dance seem to be enjoyed equally among males and females, whereas observations in schools and youth centers showed that boys are more apt to demonstrate an interest in drawing than girls. During the aforementioned art therapy study in Gulu, the girls expressed much more enthusiasm for drama and skits enacting northern folktales, and requested more activities involving drama. The boys also seemed to enjoy drama but had a much longer attention span for activities involving drawing and painting than did the girls. Both boys and girls enjoyed a break dancing workshop, and both showed relatively equal levels of frustration when they could not get the steps.

The art journal project at a Gulu youth center revealed similar trends regarding interest in visual art. The group started with an equal number of boys and girls, but it was only the boys who continued with the voluntary program until the end and showed genuine enjoyment during the activities. In both the art therapy and the art journal projects, the girls participating often became discouraged and abandoned the directives, drawing flowers and other items of their own choosing instead.

Preferences for forms of expression do not reflect innate differences between boys and girls, of course. Rather, they emerge from the way in which gendered differences are institutionalized and embedded in the structural realities of Ugandan society. While both sexes may appreciate a particular form of expression, one may dominate the profession. For example, in Acholi music, there are fewer female performers than male performers, and it is readily acknowledged that professional music is a male-dominated industry. During personal communication with Ugandan youth, no girls were encountered who aspired to be well-known performing artists, whereas it was common for boys to think of top performers as their role models and aspire to perform and record albums like them. However, at performances, relatively equal numbers of males and females composed the audiences. Both men and women listen to the radio programs as well, although it is often men and boys in the camps who have the most time to gather around a radio while the women and girls engage in domestic labor.

While extensive research has been done by Annan et al. (2008) on the status of women after the war, there has been little to no mention of how Acholi social norms affect girls' behavior (but see Ochen, this volume). However, gendered social norms clearly play a role in shaping artistic expression and preferences. Acholi women and young girls are often encouraged—and sometimes forced—to assume roles as wives and mothers at a young age at the expense of a career or vocation, and may view a career in the arts as interfering with domestic duties. In addition, it is often the boys who are encouraged in the arts at school. Like math and science, visual art is a male-dominated field in Uganda. Girls' affinity to drama can possibly be traced to long-standing Acholi patterns of storytelling, in which elders were responsible for teaching folktales to children. This practice has been disrupted, however, due to war and mass displacement. Rediscovering it is therefore an important component in postwar peacebuilding and reconciliation as realized through existing cultural resources.

Age

In addition to gender affecting preferences of creative expression in northern Uganda, age also plays an important role. As might be expected, elders tend to hold fast to older, indigenous forms of dance and music, while youth embrace and fuel artistic movements attuned to external influences. Efforts such as Breakdance Project Uganda have faced some criticism for encouraging youth to pursue this new dance style, fearing that it will be learned at the expense of indigenous dances. Such anxiety about cultural transformation is clearly a legacy of the prolonged conflict that wracked Acholiland, disrupted the generational transmission of indigenous Acholi forms of knowledge, and resulted in the disproportionate deaths of older people.

In addition, camp life also altered Acholi patterns of expression, many of which involved the arts, like storytelling, mentioned above. Historically, elders would gather extended family members about a central fireplace where they would share stories and proverbs with younger generations. Because of camp curfews, general instability, and the death of many elders, this practice was largely unable to continue during the war (see Carlson and Mazurana 2010). Now with the accessibility and appeal of Western-style art and music, both through media and the multitude of foreign aid workers present in the major towns, urban youth are exposed to preexisting Acholi forms alongside those derived from foreign sources. For example, the same youth center in Gulu where the break dancers from the capital come to teach also offers children lessons in Acholi styles of dance and music.

Residence

In Acholi society, one's physical location or locality also factors into one's choice of creative expression. In the rural areas, there is less exposure to foreign-originated styles and less influence by foreign programs and aid workers. However, radio stations can now reach everyone, even in the most remote of locations, and radio features contemporary Acholi music, as well as indigenous Acholi styles. In contrast, most performances of the contemporary and hybridized styles of expression are limited to Gulu, Lira, and Kitgum towns.

Christian churches are another haven for creative expression in northern Uganda, and unlike the dance halls of the towns, churches are found in all communities, both rural and urban. Church groups were very active in the peace process and have been devoted proponents of indigenous justice mechanisms, namely, *mato oput*, or "drinking of the bitter herb," an Acholi ceremony that reconciles two groups after a murder (see Baines 2005). Several youth and women interviewees reported that "church is a place to go and forget about the past," particularly through music and dance. In Uganda, the worship portion of the service, complete with music, dance, and song, is often very emotional and animated. Some churches offer multiple services to accommodate both the local language and English. At Christ Church in Gulu, the English service is more subdued and features hymns. The local language service and the Christ Church Luo Choir offer a more colorful worship experience by incorporating northern instruments and Acholi-style songs. Ethnographic observations have shown that churches are therefore important community-based institutions that also provide a venue for self-expression. Given their historical rootedness in colonial missions, as well as their incorporation of indigenous expression in worship, churches represent some of the most successful hybridized initiatives.

Sustainability and Transformation: Further Implications for Peacebuilding, Reconciliation, and Human Rights Consciousness

The funding sources of these projects affect their short- and long-term sustainability. In recent years, northern Uganda has received an outpouring of foreign assistance and financial aid from both governments and NGOs. More recently, with the worldwide economic crisis and the international community's short attention span for African conflicts and wars, emergency relief and humanitarian efforts in northern Uganda have been downsized or terminated altogether. The sustainability of postconflict arts programs varies, and the withdrawal of foreign funding forces a discontinuation of many initiatives.

While the local initiatives and some hybrid ones may lack the large financial backing of the foreign projects, their programs often have the highest degree of ownership and resonance within the communities, as we have demonstrated. Even if every foreign organization and funding source leaves tomorrow, the Acholi will still be dancing and singing songs handed down through generations. The artists singing in contemporary genres will continue performing and the break dancers breaking, although if they lose funding from the NGOs to perform at events or go on tours around the community, their effectiveness as vehicles for peacebuilding, reconciliation, and human rights consciousness in the community will certainly change. Northern artists in recent months have lamented their lack of income after many NGOs have discounted programs that take them to the field for community performances. However, transplanted initiatives that generally lack strong community backing and legitimacy stand little chance of sustainability over the long term.

With little or no operating budget, as is the case of many local initiatives, the indigenous arts often operate in more localized ways than transplanted or even hybrid programs. Transplanted and hybrid initiatives often put on large competitions, exhibitions, or shows, for which local initiatives do not have the funding. (An exception is school music, dance, and drama competitions that attract students from across the regions.) However, because the indigenous arts are so ingrained into Acholi patterns of expression, and because hybrid initiatives both appeal to young people and provide unique opportunities to address the most contemporary debates with respect to postconflict reconciliation, peacebuilding, and human rights, there is little reason to believe they will not continue, at least at the micro-level.

Two dynamics are therefore at work regarding sustainability. The first is the financial support granted to foreign or transplanted initiatives, and the fact that many such initiatives vanish when the international community decides to withdraw support or redirect funds elsewhere. Further, because of their funding, transplanted initiatives have the ability to branch out across communities and towns and reach more people. This funding offers a form of sustainability that many of the Ugandan initiatives do not have. Lacking comparable financial resources, the indigenous and even hybrid initiatives cannot expand at the same rate as the transplanted programs, despite their greater cultural resonance. Second, community ownership of the form of expression affects its ability to persevere even without funding or when the foreign implementers abandon the programs and leave the region. While there are indigenous organizations that receive grants from foreign sources, as a whole, transplanted programs have greater resonance with foreign funders and, therefore, indigenous initiatives are less likely to receive the large sums that transplanted programs receive. Hybrid programs seem to straddle this divide: while having greater appeal and popularity among northern Ugandans than transplanted initiatives, their very hybridity means that they also resonate with foreign funders, making them more appealing to the international community than indigenous initiatives. This seems to suggest that hybrid initiatives may in fact represent the most promising venue for the art of peacebuilding in northern Uganda.

Our findings, based on sustained ethnographic research and framed primarily in terms of contemporary critical analyses in anthropology, point up several broader implications for comparable situations in the Great Lakes region and African continent. First and foremost, longstanding, indigenous norms and patterns of communication and expression influence all facets of life. The point may seem so obvious as to remain unstated, but is too often overlooked by many well-intentioned non-Ugandan individuals and organizations seeking to participate in postconflict reconstruction and peacebuilding. Without understanding the historical and political experiences, sociocultural norms and values, and patterns of expression among a particular people, it is difficult to understand the impact that a specific form will have on healing and reconciliation of the community and of individuals. Organizations and foreign funders should therefore take issues of cultural resonance into primary consideration when implementing programs or designing peacebuilding interventions. This can be done by involving community members in project development, by conducting assessments, or by hiring community members for program implementation. Some may consider this suggestion trite, but many transplanted initiatives have been observed implementing programs with little to no regard for Acholi norms of expression or leadership input.

Relatedly, sensitivity is paramount with respect to trauma as well. Creative expression can induce dialogue on conflict and reconciliation, but respect for a society's method of coping with war and violence should also be considered. In northern Uganda, people are often instructed to "forget and forgive" by local counselors. Because this has been a widespread approach to peacebuilding, one cannot expect people to immediately and openly express their feelings about the past, whether through the medium of the arts or otherwise.

Our findings also suggest that the appropriateness of a particular intervention can be measured by identifying a target audience and doing sufficient research on what appeals to them and what best achieves the goals of the initiative. This can be as simple as interviewing potential participants to see what creative forms interest them the most. This research demonstrated that age, gender, and location affect the resonance of a particular art form. In northern Uganda, older people, as well as rural populations have historically had more exposure to indigenous creative expression than those in the towns. Although this is not to say that more contemporary or hybridized forms are irrelevant to rural populations, one must remember that rural areas may not have had the same level of exposure to outside influence as towns and, therefore, initiatives unfamiliar to existing patterns of expression may not resonate as much. At the same time, the increasing popularity of hybrid music aired via radio throughout all regions of northern Uganda indicates that rural populations find much to be enjoyed in the musical styles of artists who blend Acholi and other forms. Moreover, as evidenced by the popularity of both break dance and *bwola* dance among young people, projects that include both foreign-originated forms of expression and Acholi styles can have a wide appeal. However, it is worth noting again that in northern Uganda, performance arts—whether in the form of music, dance, or drama—have much more resonance than the visual arts. In other societies, where the legacy of visual arts or crafts is richer, this may not be the same.

Each of the circumstances of reconciliation and peacebuilding are different, as are the specific patterns of expression and communication in any location. While we must not hold universal assumptions about the specifics of creative expression as a force for peacebuilding, our analysis has shown how the arts—and especially artistic initiatives that resonate with but also challenge existing cultural forms in positive ways—can be highly effective vehicles for the advancement of peace and reconciliation and the vernacularization of human rights. In northern Uganda, as in other locations around the world, longstanding patterns of expression come into contact with foreign-originated forms of art and create new dynamics for creative expression. In conflict and postconflict situations, understanding and noting these dynamics can result in better-equipped and more successful interventions and initiatives. It is also worthwhile to pay closer attention to how music and the arts provide a wellspring of resources for peace and reconciliation.

Notes

1. Opiyo's research was funded primarily by the University of Tennessee. She also served as an intern on an art therapy study funded by the US National Institutes of Health, Minority Health International Research Training Program (MHIRT) of Christian Brothers University. Her former position in the Justice and Reconciliation Project (JRP) in Gulu provides further insight into the dynamics of peacebuilding.
2. Lyrics translated from Luo by Jeff Korondo. Courtesy of Jahria Okwera.
3. Lyrics translated from Luo by Jeff Korondo. Courtesy of Jeff Korondo.
4. Lyrics translated from Luo by Jeff Korondo. Courtesy of Jeff Korondo.
5. This project, a component of the Minority Health International Research Training (MHIRT) Program at Christian Brothers University, was supported by Grant Number T37MD0011378 from the National Institute On Minority Health and Health Disparities. The content is solely the responsibility of the authors and does not necessarily represent the official views of the National Institutes of Health.

References

An-Na'im, Abdullahi Ahmed. 1992. "Toward a Cross-Cultural Approach to Defining International Standards of Human Rights: The Meaning of Cruel, Inhuman, or Degrading Treatment or Punishment." In *Human Rights in Cross-Cultural Perspectives: A Quest for Consensus*, edited by Abdullahi Ahmed An-Na'im, 19–43. Philadelphia: University of Pennsylvania Press.
Annan, Jeannie, Christopher Blattman, Khristopher Carlson, and Dyan Mazurana. 2008. *The State of Female Youth in Northern Uganda: Findings from the Survey for War Affected Youth (SWAY): Phase II*. Medford, MA: Tufts University.
Anwar, Yasmin. 2007. "Damning Report on Uganda War Crimes." *University of California-Berkeley News*, June 15. http://berkeley.edu/news/media/releases/2007/06/15_LRA.shtml.
Baines, Erin. 2005. *Roco Wat I Acoli: Restoring Relationships in Acholi-land: Traditional Approaches to Justice and Reintegration*. Kampala: Liu Institute for Global Issues, Gulu District NGO Forum, and Ker Kwaro Acholi.
Byers, Julia Gentleman. 1996. "Children of the Stones: Art Therapy Interventions in the West Bank." *Art Therapy: Journal of the American Art Therapy Association* 13, no. 4: 238–43.
Carlson, Khristopher, and Dyan Mazurana. 2010. "Accountability for Sexual and Gender-Based Crimes by the Lord's Resistance Army." In *Children and Transitional Justice:*

Truth-Telling, Accountability, and Reconciliation, edited by Sharanjeet Parmar, Mindy Jane Roseman, Saudamini Siegrist, and Theo Sowa, 235–66. Cambridge, MA: Harvard University Press.
Chilcote, Rebekah. 2007. "Art Therapy with Child Tsunami Survivors in Sri Lanka." *Art Therapy: American Art Therapy Association* 24, no. 4: 156–62.
Cowan, Jane K., Marie-Bénédicte Dembour, and Richard A. Wilson, eds. 2001. *Culture and Rights: Anthropological Perspectives.* Cambridge: Cambridge University Press.
Cowan, Jane K. 2006. "Culture and Rights after Culture and Rights." *American Anthropologist* 108, no. 1: 9–24.
Das, Veena, Arthur Kleinman, Margaret Lock, Mamphela Ramphele, and Pamela Reynolds, eds. 2001. *Remaking a World: Violence, Social Suffering, and Recovery.* Berkeley: University of California Press.
Dosamantes-Beaudry, Irma. 1999. "Divergent Cultural Self Construals: Implications for the Practice of Dance/Movement Therapy." *The Arts in Psychotherapy* 26, no. 4: 225–31.
Finnström, Sverker. 2008. *Living with Bad Surroundings: War, History, and Everyday Moments in Northern Uganda.* Durham, NC: Duke University Press.
Giddings, Joshua D. B. 2009. "Music, Peacebuilding, and Conflict Transformation in Post-war Liberia." In *War to Peace Transition: Conflict Intervention and Peacebuilding in Liberia,* edited by Kenneth Omeje, 153–70. Lanham, MD: University Press of America.
Goodale, Mark. 2009. *Surrendering to Utopia: An Anthropology of Human Rights.* Stanford, CA: Stanford University Press.
Howell, Signe, and Roy Willis, eds. 1989. *Societies at Peace: Anthropological Perspectives.* New York: Routledge.
Justice and Reconciliation Project. 2008. *Complicating Victims and Perpetrators in Uganda: On Dominic Ongwen.* Kampala: Justice and Reconciliation Project, Liu Institute for Global Issues, and Gulu District NGO Forum.
Kalmanowitz, Debra, and Bobby Lloyd. 1999. "Fragments of Art at Work: Art Therapy in the former Yugoslavia." *The Arts in Psychotherapy* 26, no. 1: 15–25.
Kymlicka, Will. 1996. *Multicultural Citizenship: A Liberal Theory of Minority Rights.* New York: Oxford University Press.
Merry, Sally Engle. 2006a. *Human Rights and Gender Violence: Translating International Law into Local Justice.* Chicago: University of Chicago Press.
Merry, Sally Engle. 2006b. "Transnational Human Rights and Local Activism: Mapping the Middle." *American Anthropologist* 108, no. 1: 38–51.
Mills, Margaret Ann. 1990. "Creative Expression and the Refugee Experience." In *Reimaging America: The Arts of Social Change,* edited by Mark O'Brien and Craig Little, 45–59. Philadelphia: New Society.
Montagu, Ashley. 1978. *Learning Non-Aggression: The Experience of Non-Literate Societies.* New York: Oxford University Press.
Montagu, Ashley. 1994. Foreword to *The Anthropology of Peace and Nonviolence,* edited by Leslie Sponsel and Thomas Gregor, ix–xiv. Boulder, CO: Lynne Rienner.
Mutua, Makau. 2002. *Human Rights: A Political and Cultural Critique.* Philadelphia: University of Pennsylvania Press.
Nagengast, Carole. 1994. "Violence, Terror and the Crisis of the State." *Annual Review of Anthropology* 23: 109–36.
Preis, Ann-Belinda. 1996. "Human Rights as Cultural Practice: An Anthropological Critique." *Human Rights Quarterly* 18: 286–315.

Roberts, Bayard, Kaducu F. Ocaka, John Browne, Thomas Oyok, and Egbert Sondorp. 2008. "Factors Associated with Post-traumatic Stress Disorder and Depression amongst Internally Displaced Persons in Northern Uganda." *BMC Psychiatry* 8: 38. doi:10.1186/1471-244X-8-38.

Roy, Ranju. 1999. "Culturally Sensitive Therapy: Accents, Approaches and Tools." In *Art Therapy, Race and Culture*, edited by Jean Campbell, Marian Liebmann, Frederica Brooks, Jenny Jones, and Cathy Ward, 117–32. London: Jessica Kingsley.

Sponsel, Leslie, and Thomas Gregor. 1994. *The Anthropology of Peace and Nonviolence*. Boulder, CO: Lynne Rienner.

Wadeson, Harriet. 1980. *Art Psychotherapy*. New York: John Wiley & Sons.

Weiss, Daniel, and Charles Marmar. 1997. "The Impact of Event Scale—Revised." In *Assessing Psychological Trauma and PTSD*, edited by John P. Wilson and Terence M. Keane, 399–411. New York: Guilford.

Wilson, Richard A., ed. 1997. *Human Rights, Culture and Context: Anthropological Perspectives*. London: Pluto.

10 Gender Issues in Reintegration

A Feminist and Rights-Based Analysis of the Experiences of Formerly Abducted Child-Mothers in Northern Uganda

Eric Awich Ochen

THIS STUDY SEEKS to contextualize the experiences of formerly abducted child-mothers in northern Uganda within a feminist and rights-based perspective, paying particular attention to those aspects that imply gendered power relations and examining the extent to which gendered injustices are inherent in the experiences of formerly abducted child-mothers (see Haralambos and Holborn 2008; McLaughlin 2003; Saul 2003; Ramazanoglu and Holland 2002; Nicholson 1990). In exploring reintegration, I argue that a feminist perspective enables one to tease out political, socioeconomic, and cultural issues from the point of view of northern Ugandan girls and young women affected by armed conflict, abduction, and sexual abuse, and provides a theoretical location for analyzing their subjective experiences of the reintegration process.

In line with studies that have noted gendered power imbalances in the political economy, as well as in the socioeconomic and cultural circumstances of most communities affected by armed conflict (Frerks et al. 2005; DeBerry 2004; McKay and Mazurana 2004), I explore how the sociocultural structures, norms, and practices in "the bush" mirror—but also markedly differ from—what obtains in Acholi society both before and after the Lord's Resistance Army (LRA) conflict. While elements of patriarchy pervade both rebel and "normal" or peacetime societies, the patriarchal dynamics in times of peace are experienced differently by most women and girls than in times of violence. Violence, force, and arbitrary violations of sociocultural values overwhelmingly define rebel society. In "normal" society, however, while the social structure is also regulative, gendered, and hierarchical, there is more room for freedom and choice.

This approach differs from dominant studies of Acholi sociocultural organization that tend to portray patriarchy as inherently oppressive to females (Okello and Hovil 2007; El-Bushra and Sahl 2005). I suggest that there is a need to reexamine patriarchy and traditional conceptualizations of women's and children's rights based on the way formerly abducted child-mothers make sense of the similarities and differences between rebel society and "normal" society. Despite the deeply traumatic experiences and rights violations that the formerly abducted child-mothers underwent, their resilience, fortitude, and agency stand out strongly. Examples of agency and initiative are observable in their efforts to secure available livelihood opportunities that enable them to support their children born in captivity, and restore their dignity as members of peacetime society.

Situating the Analysis

Northern Uganda has experienced incessant insecurity over the last twenty-three years, a situation arising from the confrontation between the Lord's Resistance Army (LRA) rebels and the Ugandan government. Displacement has been especially widespread in the Acholi subregion (covering the districts of Gulu, Amuru, Kitgum, and Pader), where some 25 percent of people remain in internally displaced persons (IDP) camps, although the majority (75 percent) has returned home (Norwegian Refugee Council 2010). As with other contemporary conflicts, such as in Sierra Leone, Angola, and Mozambique, one key element of the northern Ugandan conflict has been widespread child abduction. Since the beginnings of the conflict, up to 30,000 children are reported to have been abducted, of which 30 percent are estimated to be girls (Human Rights Watch 2006; McKay and Mazurana 2004). Since 2006, however, a hiatus in the conflict allowed many displaced persons to return to their original homes (International Crisis Group 2007). With the return, escape, and rescue of children, concerns drifted towards how they can be supported for effective reintegration within their communities. This chapter is based on original fieldwork on the reintegration challenges of the young girls who became mothers during the period of abduction and, subsequently, returned with their children.

The study was carried out between July 2009 and March 2010 in the Gulu and Amuru districts. The research was qualitative in nature and involved nineteen young women, aged 17–25, who had been abducted as young children, had given birth to children in the bush, and subsequently returned to their communities. In addition, seven focus groups and nine key informant interviews were also conducted to elicit the perspectives of other stakeholders and those who interacted directly with former abductees. The study used a triangulated design, and combined both a snapshot and retrospective perspective. The latter applied mainly to the formerly abducted child-mothers, as they explored their experiences from the time in the bush through their resettlement process in the community, while the former design mainly captured the perspectives of the members of the community (Flick 2006). A narrative approach elicited through in-depth interviews was the primary method for data gathering from the study participants.

Gender Issues in Armed Conflict

The abduction and recruitment of children (including girls) into armed forces has become a defining characteristic of most contemporary intrastate conflicts (Achvarina et al. 2008). Within the last two decades there has been increased interest in the effects of armed conflict on girls and women (see Mazurana et al. 2008; Annan et al. 2007; Frerks et al. 2005; McKay and Mazurana 2004; UNFA 2002). In almost all civil conflict in developing countries, women and girls have suffered either directly or indirectly; they have been targeted by fighting forces to be used as cooks, domestic servants, sex slaves, porters, and in some cases as fighters (McKay 2004; McKay and Mazurana 2004).

Commenting on the scale of exploitation of women and young girls in Teso, eastern Uganda, De Berry (2004) writes that girls were at risk of sexual exploitation by both rebels and government forces. De Berry identifies a number of factors that increase vulnerability for girls, including militarization, displacement, soldiers dictating movements within the camps, and commodification of sex (De Berry 2004, 52).[1] She also suggests that many girls in situations of war forgo their own sexual protection in the quest for survival, thus exposing themselves to the risks of HIV/AIDS and social ostracism. Her study also identifies some of the supportive factors for girls coping with sexual abuse and exploitation during and after war, including "affective ties" between the young person and the family, as well as availability and accessibility of business opportunities for girls and women. She concludes that the girls in Teso were both victims of adversity and "active resilient survivors" (De Berry 2004, 58), noting that their agency was visible in how they took advantage of various opportunities within the camps to ensure their own and their dependants' survival. Analysis of the data emerging from my own research in northern Uganda also points out the resilience, agency, and fortitude of formerly abducted child-mothers who are actively involved in shaping their own future, despite facing substantial socioeconomic and psychosocial challenges.

Children's Rights Discourse

Because most former abductees were so young when they were taken by the rebels, and subsequently returned from the bush with children of their own, children's rights discourse has emerged as especially important in postconflict northern Uganda. Indeed, the concept of children's rights and human rights discourse in general have been at the forefront of policy interventions for children. Globally, the United Nations has been championing the protection of the rights of children. However, there are both proponents and critics of the dominant discourse on rights. Wald (2004) observes that while there has been historically a movement since the latter part of the 1850s to provide children with rights, the notion of children's rights is a controversial one. Wald notes that some of the issues embedded in rights should actually be framed as a moral obligation of parents towards their children, and questions heavy state proscriptions and interventions in regard to some of the rights promoted for children.

The 1989 Convention on the Rights of the Child (CRC) effectively replaced the earlier declarations and has been ratified by all countries except the United States and Somalia (Gadda 2008). Lachman et al. (2002) argue that while substantial progress has been made in the developed countries, children in the developing world often find themselves disadvantaged by structures that do not guarantee effective protection. These structures include child protection policies and legislation, presence of implementing institutions such as the police, and department of probation services and other quasi-government agencies. While these structures exist, they are often not well facilitated and resourced. Both the African Charter on the Rights and Welfare of the Child (ACRWC) and the CRC make a case for strong family and community involvement in child protection. However, in countries affected by armed conflict, social support inherent within extended families has also been eroded. This is, however, not to deny the fact that some African cultural practices also harm children, such as female genital cutting (Skaine 2005; Ladjali et al. 1993).

The Machel study (1996) on the protection of children affected by armed conflict makes a number of observations, arguing for culturally specific interventions to protect children's rights.[2] However, the study was also critiqued for its universalist prescriptions. Boyden (1994) opines that care should be taken to avoid a universalist interpretation of children's experiences of conflict, and suggests that children's resilience be considered. Significantly, while the Machel study was cognizant of the uniqueness of contexts in most parts of the world, it proposed universalist solutions. It should be pointed out, however, that interventions that are culturally acceptable in one context might not be equally acceptable in another context. At the same time, it is recognized that developing culturally sensitive interventions would enhance the acceptability of "universal" children rights.

Recent studies in northern Uganda indicate that emphasizing rights as a concept foreign to the local culture, rather than integral to it, could cause communities to misinterpret the message of children's rights (Abola et al. 2009; Ochen 2009). When children's rights are presented as something new that requires a realignment of sociocultural organization, this could bring about alienation of children from the sociocultural framework and affect family and community cohesion. In working with young people in postconflict Sierra Leone, Shepler (2005, 2) developed a model for supporting a reintegration process "informed by the global human rights regime but created in everyday practice at the intersection of the global and the local." This kind of approach contextualizes children's rights within local sociocultural situations (see Opiyo and Hepner, this volume).

Despite its limitations, the CRC, and the discourse on children's rights to which it has given rise, provide a very useful framework for understanding child protection interventions, and thus form part of the framework for the analysis of the data on which this chapter is based. Coming from a children's rights programming background, I argue that the formerly abducted child-mothers are rights holders who are not only victims of their experiences but resilient actors whose rights have been violated as children—and, more specifically, as girls subjected to situations that abused them on the basis of their gender. It is imperative to appreciate their experiences within a rights discourse as well as relative to the sociocultural contexts of both rebel and "normal" Acholi society. This will enable interventions to be directed towards meeting formerly abducted child-mothers' developmental rights instead of just meeting their needs.

The Implications of Feminist Perspectives for Researching Children in Armed Conflict

The social organization of the Acholi is heavily gendered in terms of social expectations of women/girls compared to men/boys. The man is the head of the household, although in most families, there is always a patriarch who is the overall head of the bigger extended family. Within the household, women are generally taken as homemakers, with control over food and household assets. The control of animals, land, and other cash crops, however, always rests with the male household head. Decision making about strategic family and household issues and resources also rests with the male head, although—theoretically—women are consulted. Children and women are naturally expected to submit and be obedient to the male family head.

Now, as in the past, the Acholi family is mainly polygamous in nature, with possession of several wives and children viewed as a source of pride. Different huts/houses were built for the wives within the same homestead. The socialization process provided for an arrangement whereby the women would prepare girls to take up responsibility within the homes and, similarly, male relatives would prepare the boys for their own roles within the community. Responsibilities for girls/young women include domestic chores, childcare, cooking, and farming. Women are also expected to participate in other communal and social activities aimed not only at ensuring a community's food security but also at creating social cohesion and harmony. These roles were distinct and socially constructed by the institutions and norms of the society. The social institutions presupposed and regulated an individual's interests and behaviors. Generally, women performed roles that were lighter in weight but more engaging or longer lasting compared to what men performed.[3]

It is imperative to point out that while this description of Acholi social organization suggests an ordered society imbued with social harmony and gendered coexistence, a more nuanced analysis might suggest avenues and instances of rights violations and gendered domination, as I show later in this chapter. Even though systems were in place to ensure women's and children's participation in family and community affairs, these were controlled by male-headed institutions, in which women had limited if any supervisory roles. Such powers are susceptible to abuse by those that wield them. While the perspectives of elders indicate a positive bias towards the wider social interest, vested male and patriarchal power might still be at play. Moreover, Acholi society today is much different from twenty-five years ago when the conflict began; changes induced both by the conflict and other dynamics broadened the scope of interaction between the Acholi and others, providing considerable avenues for empowerment to women and children.

Considering that the formerly abducted child-mothers were young women interacting in complex, gendered relationships from rebel captivity to reintegration within communities, a feminist analytical lens is appropriate. It is probable that the gendered power imbalances inherent in Acholi social organization reflected themselves in the dependency of women and girls on male-orchestrated decisions, and influenced their exploitation in the conflict situation (Okello and Hovil 2007). Although male children have been equally the target of exploitation by fighting forces (Okeny 2009), the experiences of girls and young women in the context of the war merit special attention. It is imperative that women's experience of conflict and the reintegration process is subjected to an analytical lens that appreciates the underlying cultural nuances and other factors that are often not considered, such as the gendered social organization that underpins "normal" society. For example, studies from eastern Uganda, Sierra Leone, Angola, and Mozambique all suggest that the subjugation and exploitation of female children in conflict situations interacts with power imbalances at play in the community's existing protection systems (Mazurana and Carlson 2006; El-Bushra and Sahl 2005; Mazurana and McKay 2004). This, in turn, may further alienate women and girls from the needed psychosocial and socioeconomic support, and constrain reintegration initiatives (UNICEF 2005, 203).

While some studies of northern Uganda recognize the violations of the rights of children, and emphasize women and children's experiences of conflict, in most cases such analysis is not cast within a sociocultural context. Also neglected is a critical analysis of the social institutions that regulate social interactions, and the ways in which such institutions are affected by conflict. Certain positions are thus presented incorrectly as entrenched and sanctioned cultural practices when, in reality, these are dynamic and contested. Moreover, some of the literature focuses on the intra- or postconflict periods without a critical analysis of the preconflict factors that actually promote the respect for the rights of women and children. By reflecting on gender and children's rights issues relative to Acholi society in preconflict, intraconflict, and postconflict phases, we gain a more contextualized understanding of how girls and women have been affected.

Reintegration of Female Excombatants

The literature seems to present a mixed situation regarding issues affecting the reintegration of female excombatants. Frerks et al. (2005) suggest that sociocultural expectations push women to embrace the same gender identity and roles as in the preabduction situation, yet other structural issues such as legal restrictions on land and property inheritance put female excombatants and abductees in a far worse situation than their male counterparts. In most cases, these roles (and behavioral expectations) differ significantly from what the returned child-mothers were used to during periods in the bush with the rebels.

It has also been suggested that the reintegrated girls have at times resisted or violated the social values and norms practiced by the communities from which they were originally plucked. This is exemplified in their reported display of high levels of aggressive behavior, such as being quarrelsome, rebellious, and abusive to those around them (see also Frerks et al. 2005; McKay 2004, 25). These behaviors are interpreted by the community as a violation of acceptable gender norms and social values, further alienating the child-mothers.

It is important to point out that Acholi society expects women to be submissive. Some commentators have argued that formerly abducted child-mothers are not deliberately flouting the conventions and norms of their society; rather, that these values may have been partly or wholly forgotten during their years in the bush (McKay 2004, 25). But as Swaine and Feeny (2004, 67) note, the disruption of family and community support networks significantly undermines a girl's ability to make sense of events and experiences, therefore compromising her coping abilities.[4] It is also clear that young women who returned with children found more challenges reintegrating than those without children. In some cases, formerly abducted young women have been labeled "prostitutes," as they attempt to move on from one failed relationship to the next, in pursuit of long-term companionship (McKay 2004; Chitalia and Odeh 2004). In a cultural context in which marriage is a key cornerstone of family and community life, failure to find a marriage partner appears to be one of the greatest hindrances to social reintegration. I return to these issues in subsequent sections of this chapter.

Abduction and Exploitation

Most of the girls in this study had been abducted either from home or on their way to school. Abduction thus took place either at night or during broad daylight. Discussion with community leaders and key informants indicated that the vulnerability of girls was partly explained by the rebel strategy of abducting young children who are more easily convinced to implement the rebels' objectives. The study also indicated that the abduction of young girls was apparently the rebels' way of furthering their "lineage" through procreation with the girls.[5] The young women themselves felt that the rebels' decision to abduct young girls who were barely able to understand sexual matters was apparently predicated on the latter's presumed freedom from HIV/AIDS (see also Shefer and Foster 2009; Tallis 2008).

Abduction of children contrasts significantly with the conception in normal Acholi society that war is an adult affair, and children traditionally were not involved in war. The direct involvement of children (including girls) in war was therefore unprecedented. The very social institutions that had protected children from rights violations were thus broken and bypassed in this case. Interviews with traditional leaders suggest that child sexual abuse and gender-based violence of any nature is abhorred by Acholi traditional values. This includes physical, sexual, mental, and emotional violence. Acholi norms and practices encourage harmony within the home; while women were expected to submit to their husbands, a man was required to respect his wife and children, and involve them in family decisions. Furthermore, sexual abuse and misconduct were heavily penalized. A man who abused a woman would have to pay compensation to the community or clan, and cleanse the woman with certain rituals and practices, such as slaughtering a goat. A habitual offender would be disowned and disbanded from the community or clan. Despite the presence of these sanctions, however, gender-based violence did occur in Acholi preconflict society, although this was eclipsed by the intraconflict situation and current postconflict period.

Efforts were also made to ensure the welfare of children. Abduction of children, perpetrated mainly by male rebel soldiers, could be viewed as an extension of patriarchal hegemony that prevails in "normal" society. However, while patriarchal powers were reportedly used to advance communal and social interests under normal or peacetime conditions, these same powers in the bush were used to abuse and violate the rights of the girls.[6] The former observation is, nonetheless, a contested one.

"Wifely" Expectations in the Bush

Upon abduction by the rebels, the girls were allocated to men who were expected to become "husbands" to the girls. In addition to their roles as fighters, girls were expected to perform "wifely duties," which included bearing and rearing children, cooking, and washing. A situation therefore arose wherein child-wives were supposed to be taking care of (their) children and "husbands" in a highly precarious environment. This contrasts significantly with the role played by Acholi girls in normal society, where child rearing was a preserve of adults. For girls who became pregnant while very young, a whole range of clan members and other support systems existed. Moreover, before a girl reached eighteen, the age of majority, she would have undergone the most significant motherhood training activities by female relatives. This support system was absent in the bush and the environment under which the girls were exercising such roles was very far from "normal." The childhood of the children born to the rebels was a disturbed and distorted one, and thus very different from what obtains in a normal prewar Acholi society where children were protected through social, political and economic structures.

It is imperative to point out that for most of the child-mothers, understanding adult responsibility and complying with these roles was difficult. The multiplicity of roles of the child-mothers in the bush reflects what other young women go through in "normal" society, but the difference lies in the context, the severity of the tasks, and the room for dissent, which was not present in the bush. Furthermore, while roles and obligations outside the bush are allocated based on age, physical maturity and social expectations, this does not appear to be the case in the bush, where young girls were violently forced into early sex, motherhood, and wifely roles. Anena described in detail her experiences in the bush:[7]

> One day Otiti [rebel commander] called me to go inside his house but I refused. He wanted me and another girl called Amony to go with him to Nisitu. From there, he called me to go and sleep with him but I refused; he called Amony and she also refused to go. He called one girl called Anek, and asked if there was water and ordered her to bring it. That water was poured on our bodies until we were completely wet. He ordered us to stand throughout the night, which we did.
>
> After three days he came back from Nisitu, he asked, 'are my prisoners around'? Aciro said yes, he came at around 7:00 pm with one girl called Lanyero from Nisitu. They brought some water, poured on us again, that day we stood inside the house, wet, and he called Lanyero and he started having sex with her in front of us (Amony and I). He said as we have refused to come and sleep with him, we should now watch him. . . . The following day again water was poured on us, my legs were swollen for standing for the second time. . . . and for the third day again, we stood for the whole night.

Flarena added:

> For me when I refused to accept the sexual advances of the man. . . . I was taken to the commander who was heading that battalion. He said 'you are just leaving this lady [treating her with kid gloves] why don't you just beat her with a machete?' So that night he called me again in the night and I refused. Later he called me during the day again and I refused. . . . He waited when all the ladies had gone to the well and he told me not to go to the well, and so I did not go. Then he told me to go to his house, I went and stayed in his house and then he asked me to go with him to bed but I refused. Then he picked a wire lock and hit me with it. . . . he picked a gun and started cocking it, saying 'have you ever seen a person who has been killed? If not, then in the evening I am calling you back here, let me wait and see if you are going to refuse, then you may have to choose between death and life.' He then asked: 'what do you choose between death and life?' And I told him that I choose life. So it was that night that I felt what it was for a man to sleep with a woman and it instilled a lot of fear in me because I felt a lot of pain and I felt so bad about myself.

As presented above, the resistance put up by the girls against sexual exploitation was not a one-off struggle. For some of the girls it happened over several weeks and even months, and they submitted only when threatened with death. This is consistent with Allen's (2005) observation, and shows the extent to which some girls resisted unwanted, exploitative relationships.

The agency of abducted girls was also clearly visible in how they coped with their motherhood and parental responsibilities in the bush. Once the child-mothers came to accept their children and their motherhood roles, they tried in very difficult circumstances to ensure that they and their children stayed alive. One of the child-mothers, Harriet, noted that, "I realized that my own childhood was already lost. The only way through which I can redeem this lost childhood is by ensuring that my children survive the turbulence in the bush and return with me home alive, perhaps they are the ones who would also take care of me in the future." Harriet actually left the bush on her own despite the fact that she was a senior officer. Her main motivation for returning home was the protection and safety of her three children.

Further findings suggest that abductees' desire to regain control over their lives and assure a better future for their children was another key motivation for escape. This too demonstrated agency as it involved initiative and thoughtful actions:

> When we reached an area near my home that I knew very well I decided to escape. While people were still sleeping I got up and carried my child. As I knew how everyone was sleeping, I decided to pick my steps carefully so that they don't find me. So I started walking back to where we came from and I went and sat at some water point and waited for the rebels to leave before continuing on my journey home. When I reached Gira-gira, I got some people in the garden so I sneaked into a cassava plantation because I was hungry. So I reached and asked for cassava but you could even see from my appearance that I had been part of the rebels. (Harriet)
>
> The reason why I thought of that [escape] was one day when we were in Ayago there was some commander who had a small radio and he had put it on.... I heard the voices of some of the girls who were with us in the bush. So I started thinking that even if I don't go through the government [local authorities] once I reach home... I will manage to live. So that was the time I thought of escaping, otherwise I was afraid that if I escape I might be killed. (Aber)

"Relay" of Wives

One way in which the girls and child-mothers were subjugated and their rights violated was exhibited in how they were treated on the death or defection of their allocated "husbands." In such situations, the child-mothers were reallocated to another man. According to one of the child-mothers whose "husband" had been killed by the rebels for apparent dissent:

> One day, a Tata lorry came and they put us on the vehicle and drove back to Nisitu. That is when they wanted to kill him [her then allocated husband]. We just heard from the people that Otiti was killed.... We stayed in his home but one day the nine of us [wives of the executed husband] were sent to different homes. I was taken to Kony's place; from there he changed me to become his wife and in 2000 I gave birth (Lamaro).

The "distribution" of the young women did not consider their feelings or that of their children. The latter were expected to naturally develop affection for their new "fathers." The "relay" of wives was therefore another humiliating experience for the girls that had an overall bearing on their dignity. They were used as objects for the satisfaction of the dominant male powers who were in physical, sexual, and psychological control over their lives (Shefer and Foster 2009; El-Bushra and Sahl 2005). This phenomenon could also partly explain the propensity of formerly abducted child-mothers to change spouses in the postresettlement or reintegration period. In such situations, adapting to "normal" life and social relationships became a challenge. It is my view that the practice of the relay of wives made the young women open to the possibility of having multiple and sequential relationships. It is also possible that the practice of relaying wives, especially where relationships with subsequent rebel husbands were more abusive, led to a higher degree of distrust for men in general and could have therefore sown seeds of negativity about long-term relationships for some of these young women.

Oppression by Senior "Wives"

The arrangements for allocating wives in the bush indicate that the rebels, especially the commanders, had harems of wives. When new batches of girl abductees were brought, they were apportioned to the various rebel officers as future wives, although initially placed under a senior wife. Interviews indicated that when girls were abducted at a tender age, they were made to stay with a senior wife until they started menstruating, and then were taken over as wives themselves, with the man demanding sex from them. Some of the senior wives would take advantage of their privileged positions to physically and socially abuse the new arrivals in their homesteads:

> From Jabulen I was taken to Nono's home. In his home there were seven girls and I was the eighth, from there if you are still young they called you ting ting. I got one of his wives called Agnes who was very rude and arrogant. If she wanted to take her bath, first you have to scrub/brush her leg, clean it with a towel before taking her bathing water in the bath shelter. After bathing she will leave the basin, the knickers for you to go and wash it, day in and day out. (Lamaro)

So, in addition to the gendered power dynamics that pitted powerless abducted girls against powerful male rebel commanders and soldiers (El-Bushra and Sahl 2005; McKay 2004), the girls were subjected to oppression at the hands of the powerful and influential figure of the senior "wife," an older woman put in charge of all the other younger "wives" within a particular rebel household. The gender dynamics were therefore such that power and dominance was meted out not only by males but by other females in a higher social status and position of power. This suggests a hierarchy of leadership and organization that is not only gendered but is also subject to culturally determined social positioning based on age and seniority. While reflective of "normal" Acholi society, including how the confrontational behavior of senior rebel wives reflects certain tendencies among women in polygamous homes, it is also critically different in the amount and degree of violence and coercion. The space for exercise of power and dominance was much more pronounced in the rebel household than would obtain in a normal social arrangement. In the latter, the other wives in the home would have some power themselves and avenues for redress within the wider extended family. This did not seem to be the case in the bush. It is also possible that powerful senior wives might be venting their anger at society's failure to protect them in the first place. It is thus arguable that while violence might not be a male domain, the behavior of the senior wives depicts an extreme survival mechanism under broader conditions of violence.

Loss of Childhood and Other Forms of Control

Most of the girls in this study were abducted around the age of eleven. While the conflict had a significant impact on the experience of childhood in northern Uganda generally and the insecure environment in which all children were living, those who were not abducted still had some restricted space in which to exercise their identity as children. However, for abductees, the life in the rebel camp significantly affected their childhood. At once they were thrown into a world that did not afford them the protection normally provided to children. For example, one of the girls, Flo, was shocked that all at once she was viewed as a woman and expected to have sexual relations with a man she regarded in the outer society as a father figure. To abducted girls this was an attack on their innocence and a denial of an opportunity to just be children. In this case, the construction of womanhood in the bush with the rebels differed greatly from wider Acholi society, where sociocultural and legal instruments provided protection for underage girls and determined the age of maturity for girls. In this way, the patriarchal and cultural arrangements protected rather than undermined the girls' childhood and womanhood, illustrating how culture, rights, and gender intersect to enhance protection and promotion of the welfare of the children (see also Shepler 2005). Sexual violence and rape of underage girls were socially sanctioned and punished. The norms regulating sexual practices among the Acholi were broken by the rebel establishment.

The social organization of the rebels described by the returning abductees is a complex one, with its own rules and normative arrangements that had some similarities but also marked differences from the wider Acholi society. Whereas girls were distributed and redistributed—"inherited"—by rebels, the advent of HIV/AIDS did away with the practice of wife inheritance in Acholi society generally, although isolated cases might still exist. Among the rebels, sexual submission was based on fear and coercion, whereas in the outer society relationships were based on mutual feeling and agreement. Moreover, deviance from the rebel-prescribed rules and regulations often elicited heavy punishment, and in many cases summary executions. While patriarchal domination in the bush reflected the general tendency in Acholi society that favors men as the main decision makers, it did not offer the young women the social safety nets and protections that are embedded in a normal sociocultural environment. This is because the nature of the rebel society was tyrannical with little opportunity for redress other than punishment. Normal Acholi society on the other hand provides avenues for expression of grievances within the extended family system.

Gender and Reintegration

Psychosocial Support at Reception and Rehabilitation Centers

Reception and rehabilitation centers were established by nongovernmental organizations to respond to the immediate and psychosocial needs of children and other former abductees coming out of rebel captivity, prior to their reunion with the community. The reception center supported and prepared former abductees for life in "normal" society, which was itself significantly transformed as a result of the war. While displacement and sociocultural degeneration had affected society for a substantial amount of time, more choice, freedom, and support were available than in the bush. Support activities in the reception centers ranged from individual counseling sessions and group therapy to other structured activities, such as basic education to prepare former abductees to return to school or join vocational institutions. Individual counseling was aimed at enabling returnees to come to terms with their bush experience as well as to help social workers to arrange a support plan. Group therapy was utilized through play and activities like dance and storytelling to help the returnees open up and to promote psychosocial healing. Follow-up reports suggest that formerly abducted children (including child-mothers) who passed through reception centers were reintegrating better in the community and had a wider support base compared to those that did not (see also Bainomugisha 2011; Allen and Schomerus 2006). However, psychosocial support agencies have also been critiqued for placing formerly abducted children into a context that did not offer effective protection from reabduction, nor provide enough opportunities for effective resettlement and reintegration (see Allen and Schomerus 2006).

Dilemmas of the Family: Reunion with Former Abductees

While many families of formerly abducted child-mothers were happy for their return, some of the families were confused by the dilemma. As explained by one parent in Bungatira subcounty, Gulu district: "although we were happy for our children's return, we were not sure what to do with them. A lot of time had passed and some of us did not even know our own children anymore." This statement is understandable given the children were quite young at abduction and returned when they were older, with their own children. The cultural construction of childhood is inherently paradoxical: normally childbirth (by a girl) marks the end of childhood and the beginning of adulthood. Indeed the concept of "child-mothers" is foreign to the local cultural conceptualization. For some families, the ambivalence towards formerly abducted child-mothers is exacerbated by the fact that the latter participated in serious atrocities while with the rebels. One of the girls, Maggie, recounted her disappointment with her father's attitude on her return:

> He said where am I going with my children? If possible I should leave those children in GUSCO [an agency] or give them to the government and I join the army. He said

that I should join the government army because there is no place for me at home. So this really broke my heart.... but my sister refused my father's idea.

The inability of the people closest to formerly abducted child-mothers to offer unequivocal support is therefore a critical issue with which these young women have to contend. This is exacerbated by the fact that they cannot call on the support of the families of the biological father(s) of their children, as in most of the cases they were simply not known to them. Doing so may also mean legitimizing the brutality the young women suffered.

Analysis of the data suggests that families' and communities' resentment and fear of returned abductees has lingered. This fear is exhibited in subtle ways, however. For some family members, their fear seems to come from the attitudes of the community and perceptions that stigmatize the families of former abductees. Some families were also reluctant to shoulder the additional burden of feeding the returned abductees and their children. Two dimensions of rights-based concerns thus come to the fore: on the one hand, some of the child-mothers (who were legally children, or below age eighteen at the time they returned to the community) also required support and respect for their rights as children. On the other hand, their children born in captivity also needed to be nurtured and protected from rights violations within the community.

Relationships with Potential Suitors

Many formerly abducted child-mothers also experienced difficulty with issues pertaining to marital and sexual relationships. As aptly put by one of the child-mothers, "These people are only interested in our bodies and what we have to offer yet they cannot accept and look after us and our children." Being young and desirous of meaningful relationships with men, as well as social acceptance, when one relationship fails, the young women try another: "At times he just surprises you and tells you he is no longer interested in staying with you ... with insults such as 'you are demon possessed.' So being young, you would still think that if you get another person there might be a difference" (Anena). Because this situation has repeated itself over and over again in the lives of many formerly abducted young women, society has now labeled them "men hoppers." Further interrogation of the "men hopper" phenomenon among young women who were former abductees indicated that there are two dimensions to this issue. First is the negative public opinion of the returned abductees, sometimes held by people close to their suitors:

> It was from his mother, she said that she does not want formerly abducted women, and that women who were formerly abducted, first of all they are wicked, secondly they like butchering people with machetes. He added that there was a time a formerly abducted woman 'butchered' her co-wife with a machete. 'So I don't want any dirty characters in my home,' she said, and that her son should find another woman. This disrupted our relationship and I am now living alone. (Alobo)

The argument here is that some men who enter relationships with formerly abducted young women may wish to maintain such relationships but the negative public opinion presents significant challenges. This appears to be one of the greatest hindrances to social reintegration of the young women as they have felt rejected and dehumanized.

The second dimension of the problem relates to the inability of former abductees to follow the cultural prescriptions that require women to be submissive to their husbands. As noted earlier, one cultural expectation of a young woman among the Acholi community is that she will unequivocally submit to her husband. The perceptions among community members in northern Uganda are also that formerly abducted young women exhibit some aggression in their relationships with other people, including potential suitors (see also Frerks et al. 2005; McKay 2004). This aggression could in fact be a response by the young women to a judgmental context that puts excessive demands on them to show their "goodness." It is also possible that the young women's experiences of subjugation and domination while in the bush could have awakened a strong will to resist patriarchal norms and male domination prevailing in "normal" society. Interviews with child-mothers indicated that many of them chose to stay with their own children rather than abandoning them for marital purposes. As Rose stated:

> When I returned home from the reception center, I met a man who expressed interest in me. I told him about my experiences and that I had two children whom I will have to take with me if I married him. He initially told me he would look after me and the children. But when I accepted his proposal he started telling me that I should leave my children somewhere else. I decided to let go of that relationship and concentrate on utilizing my tailoring skills to access money to support my children. I have been living alone for several years now and I am self-reliant and even help my brother's children.

It is possible that as survivors of abduction, brutality, and both male and female domination, these young women question cultural expectations of submissiveness upon reintegration. Furthermore, removal from their communities at the very time at which they would be inculcated into the sociocultural requirements for passage to womanhood means that they have missed out on crucial socializing influences; this, too, may have a bearing on their postreturn lives.

The abandonment of formerly abducted child-mothers by their postbush partners appears to make it very difficult for some of them to cope emotionally. A number of the young women have withdrawn from social interactions beyond their circle of close family and fellow former abductees. In discussions, the young women exhibited anger at their social stigmatization and the lack of support they felt when conflicts arose with other community members. The resultant effect is further seclusion and isolation. This raises questions about whether genuine reconciliation and reintegration can be fully achieved.

It appears that self-perceptions of worth and dignity among formerly abducted child-mothers are severely constrained by their rejection from certain sectors of society, be it their suitors or other people. The desperation and feelings of hopelessness were demonstrated by one formerly abducted child-mother, Flo, when she stated that: "If I knew life was going to be so hard out here, I should have left these children in the bush. It is very difficult trying to raise these children alone without support from anyone." Flo displaced a lot of aggression towards the children; whenever they erred she would mete out disproportionately heavy punishment on them. This seemed largely due to her perceived feelings of inadequate social support and societal rejection.

Social Capital and Formerly Abducted Child-Mothers

Social capital has played a key role in the reintegration process of formerly abducted child-mothers. The term "social capital" refers to the informal networks, associations and relations that people can rely on to enhance social functioning. For some former abductees, social support groups (such as churches and their own networks) helped them cope with the challenges of life in the postreturn community. One of the former abductees narrated how she decided to settle close by other former abductees within the vicinity of Gulu municipality so they could provide emotional, physical, and socioeconomic support for each other. The following statement by Filda illustrates how former abductees have created a "sub-community" in response to the difficulties they experienced with reintegration:

> We always try to encourage each other because right now like in Kabedo-opong where we are, you cannot go ask for something from someone else. . . . So we always ask for things amongst ourselves as we are close to each other. This is because other people do not think well about the problems that we went through. Even if you ask for something you will not be given. So we always encourage each other, share ideas and advice each other.

This kind of behavior may also be motivated by desire to avoid confrontations with people in the community. In an effort to proactively avoid problems, the formerly abducted child-mothers decided to utilize their own social capital and resources based on their specific historical and circumstantial situation: mainly, common experiences of abduction and motherhood in the bush, as well as friendships forged at the reception and rehabilitation centers. An interesting feature of this gendered social support network is that the former abductees mainly drew upon other women and did not rely on male former abductees. This form of supportive collaboration was present among both the child-mothers who resettled within the Gulu town vicinity and in the rural areas. While this network is protective of the dignity of the young women and helps them to avoid problems with the established community, there are inadequacies. This was evident in the fact that, in situations where all members lack an item that one of them wanted to use, they may not access the item at all. It is important to note, however, that the formerly abducted young women who created their own networks of support did not close out the other members of society completely. Many of the former abductees are members of other social groups like churches.

The argument developed in this chapter is that the gendered exploitation and subjugation of abducted girls who become child-mothers did not start at their point of abduction but is a reflection of preexisting patriarchal systems that afford women less power compared to men. However, a nuanced analysis also suggests that while certain behavior within the bush reflects a wider Acholi sociocultural positioning, there are also significant differences. Indeed, many of the oppressive activities among the rebels are not culturally prescribed. The behavior of the rebels cannot thus be referred to as an "expression" of Acholi culture as they have abrogated and flouted these conventions and institutions in a number of cases, as shown in the discussion. While the experience of abduction, brutality, and sexual commodification at the hands of the rebels are extreme forms of gendered-based exploitation, this should not be seen in isolation from cultural positioning of women in society more generally. This explains why women themselves are implicated in the oppression of other women and why even on reintegration, women who were formerly abducted continue to undergo difficulties. In addition, I have argued that the gendered experience of subjugation in the bush meant that young girls experienced much deeper challenges compared to boys, especially as they now face significant social rejection on account of their past and motherhood in the bush.

While on the surface it may appear as if some formerly abducted child-mothers are doing well economically and meeting the needs of their children, analysis suggests that they clearly struggle emotionally and continue to face stigmatization. Meaningful reintegration should encompass interventions that openly address this subjugation and stigmatization of formerly abducted young women. Interventions for reintegration should consider the inherent power structures that might be at play in the community's protection systems and structures, which might in turn further alienate women and girls from the needed psychosocial support, thereby constraining reintegration programs (UNICEF 2005, 203). It is suggested that in planning interventions for these young women, a focus on the intersection of their abduction experiences, self-identity perceptions and identities ascribed by the outer community, Acholi gender constructions, and cultural norms should be kept in clear focus. Such an approach is possible only if the intersectionality of the experiences of these young women is taken into consideration. Methodologically, a feminist analysis prioritizes such an approach.

This study also suggests that reintegration interventions should not only look at the physical and socioeconomic needs of the former abductees but also their relationships with people in the community. It is my view that the quality of relationships formerly abducted young women build with their communities will determine the success of reintegration. Addressing relationships is incomplete without tackling the gender issues affecting such relationships and the stigma associated with sexual abuse in the bush. Rights-based interventions supporting the formerly abducted child-mothers should also be cognizant of cultural issues, expectations, and demands; "rights" should not be seen as decontextualized from sociocultural institutions. Furthermore, intervention programming should consider the agency, strengths, and aspirations of formerly abducted young women themselves and take a long-term approach that also addresses broader development issues within community.

Notes

1. At the height of the insurgency in Teso, the camps were under a virtual curfew with regulations of movements of people controlled by the army.

2. This was a seminal study on the effects of armed conflict on children, commissioned by the United Nations to provide more in-depth information on the magnitude of the effects of armed conflict on children and thereby support the development of concrete mitigation agendas.

3. Interviews with members of the Ker Kwaro Acholi traditional cultural institution.

4. In contrast, Corbin (2008, 330) argues that her study did not indicate more difficult experiences for the girls/young women compared to male counterparts; in fact, boys argued that girls often marry off and have an easier life. This finding, however, seems to differ significantly from most other studies (such as McKay 2004; McKay and Mazurana 2004; Frerks et al. 2005).

5. Interviews with key informants, Gulu district.

6. Interviews with elders of the traditional cultural institution, Ker Kwaro Acholi, which is the custodian of Acholi cultural values. According to the elders, the vesting of leadership powers in men was to ensure social order but not to mistreat other people (including women and children).

7. Pseudonyms of research participants are used in all parts of this analysis.

References

Abola, Charles, Paul Omach, Eric Awich Ochen, Catherine Anena, and Ateenyi Barongo. 2009. *Evaluation of Norwegian Development Cooperation through Norwegian Non-governmental Organisations in Northern Uganda (2003–2008)*. Oslo: The Norwegian Agency for International Development (NORAD).

Achvarina, Vera, Ragnhild Nordås, Gudrun Ostby, and Siri A. Rustard. 2008. "A Subnational Study of Child Soldier Recruitment in African Regions." PRIO Conference Paper, PVS special issue 2009. Accessed 23 September 2009. http://www.prio.no/Research-and-Publications/Publication/?oid=186766.

Allen, T. (2005) *War and Justice in Northern Uganda: An Assessment of the International Criminal Court's Intervention*. An independent report by Crisis States Research Centre, Development Studies Institute; London School of Economics. Accessed 18 October 2012. http://www.dfid.gov.uk/r4d/Output/173656/Default.aspx.

Annan, Jeannie, Christopher Blattman, Khristopher Carlson, and Dyan Mazurana. 2007. *Making Reintegration Work for Youth in Northern Uganda: Findings from Two Phases of the Survey of War Affected Youth*. Accessed 1 December 2008. http://www.sway-uganda.org/SWAY.Reintegration.pdf.

Bainomugisha, Arthur. 2011. "Child Soldiers in Northern Uganda: Examining Opportunities and Challenges for Reintegration." PhD diss., University of Bradford.

Boyden, Jo. 1994. "Children's Experiences of Conflict Related Emergencies: Some Implications for Relief Policy and Practice." *Disasters* 18, no. 3: 254–67.

Chitalia, Ami, and Michael Odeh. 2004. "Children in Armed Conflict: How Girl Soldiers Are Punished by Their Past." Youth Advocate Program International Resource Paper. Accessed 1 October 2012. http://www.yapi.org/rpgirlsoldiers.pdf.

Corbin, Joanne. 2008. "Returning Home: Resettlement of Formerly Abducted Children in Northern Uganda." *Disasters* 32, no. 2: 316–35.

De Berry, Joanna. 2004. "The Sexual Vulnerability of Adolescent Girls during Civil War in Teso, Uganda." In *Children and Youth on the Frontline: Ethnography, Armed Conflict and Displacement*, edited by Jo Boyden and Joanna De Berry, 45–62. New York: Berghahn.

El-Bushra, Judy, and Ibrahim Sahl. 2005. *Cycle of Violence: Gender Issues in Armed Conflict*. London: Agency for Cooperation and Research in Development (ACORD).

Flick, Uwe. 2006. *An Introduction to Qualitative Research*. 3rd ed. London: Sage.

Frerks, Georg, Tsjeard Bouta, and Ian Bannon. 2005. *Gender Conflict and Development*. Washington, DC: The World Bank.

Gadda, Andressa. 2008. "Rights, Foucault and Power: A Critical Analysis of the United Nations' Convention on the Rights of the Child." Edinburgh Working Paper in Sociology No 31, University of Edinburgh.

Haralambos, Michael, and Martin Holborn. 2008. *Sociology: Themes and Perspectives*. London: Harper Collins.

Human Rights Watch. 2006. *Abducted and Abused: Renewed Conflict in Northern Uganda*. New York: Human Rights Watch.

International Crisis Group. 2007. "Northern Uganda: Seizing the Opportunity for Peace." Brussels: Africa Report No. 124 (April).

Lachman, Peter, Ximena Poblete, Peter Ebigbo, Sally Nyandiya-Bundy, Robert Bundy, Bev Killian, and Jaap Doek. 2002. "Challenges Facing Child Protection." *Child Abuse and Neglect* 26: 587–617.

Ladjali, Malika, Tracey Rattray, and Rupert Walder. 1993. "Female Genital Mutilation: Both the Problem and the Solution Rest with Women." *British Medical Journal* 307: 406.

Machel, Graca. 1996. *Promotion and Protection of the Rights of Children: Impact of Armed Conflict on Children*. UNICEF. Accessed 6 June 2009. www.unicef.org/graca/a51–306_en.pdf.

Mazurana, Dyan, and Khristopher Carlson. 2006. "The Girl Child and Armed Conflict: Recognizing and Addressing Grave Violations of Girls' Human Rights." Paper prepared for the meeting of the UN Division for the Advancement of Women (DAW) in collaboration with UNICEF Expert Group Meeting on the elimination of all forms of discrimination against the girl child. Florence, Italy 25–28 September 2006. Accessed 30 October 2009. http://www.un.org/womenwatch/daw/egm/elim-disc-viol-girlchild/ExpertPapers/EP.12%20Mazurana.pdf.

Mazurana, Dyan, Khristopher Carlson, Christopher Blattman, and Jeannie Annan. 2008. *A Way Forward for Assisting Women and Girls in Northern Uganda: Findings from Phase II of the Survey for War-Affected Youth*. Accessed 9 March 2009. http://www.sway-uganda.org/SWAY.

McKay, Susan. 2004. "Reconstructing Fragile Lives: Girls Social Reintegration in Northern Uganda and Sierra Leone." *Gender and Development* 12, no. 3: 19–30.

McKay, Susan, and Dyan Mazurana. 2004. *Where Are the Girls? Girls in Fighting Forces in Northern Uganda, Sierra Leone and Mozambique: Their Lives during and after War*. Montreal: Rights and Democracy.

McLaughlin, Janice. 2003. *Feminist Social and Political Theories*. Basingstoke, UK: Palgrave Macmillan.

Nicholson, Linda. 1990. *Feminism/Postmodernism*. New York: Routledge.

Norwegian Refugee Council. 2010. "Peace, Recovery and Development: Challenges in Northern Uganda." Accessed 30 November 2010. http://www.internal-displacement.org/8025708F004CE90B/(httpDocuments)/D15CF62D20C90469C12576FE002EEFA4/$file/Uganda+briefing+paper+-+March+2010.pdf.

Ochen, Eric Awich. 2009. "Evaluation of Save the Children in Uganda's Child-Protection Strategy in Northern Uganda." A Consultancy Report submitted to Save the Children's country office. Kampala.

Okello, Moses Chrispus, and Lucy Hovil. 2007. "Confronting the Reality of Gender-Based Violence in Northern Uganda." *International Journal of Transitional Justice* 1: 433–43.

Okeny, Robert. 2009. "Reintegration of Formerly Abducted Persons in Gulu, Northern Uganda: A Case Study of Gulu Support the Children Organization in Uganda." Research paper submitted to the Institute of Social Studies, The Hague, Netherlands.

Ramazanoglu, Caroline, and Janet Holland. 2002. *Feminist Methodology: Challenges and Choices*. London: Sage.

Saul, Jennifer Mather. 2003. *Feminism: Issues and Arguments*. Oxford: Oxford University Press.

Shefer, Tamara, and Don Foster. 2009. "Heterosex among Young South Africans: Research Reflections." In *The Prize and the Price: Shaping Sexualities in South Africa*, edited by Melissa Steyn and Mikki Van Zyl, 267–89. Cape Town: Human Sciences Research Council.

Shepler, Susan. 2005. "The Rites of the Child: Global Discourse of Youth and Reintegrating Child Soldiers in Sierra Leone." *Journal of Human Rights* 4: 197–211.

Skaine, Rosemarie. 2005. *Female Genital Mutilation: Legal, Cultural and Medical Issues*; Jefferson, NC: McFarland.

Tallis, Vicci Anne. 2008. *Feminisms, HIV and AIDS: Addressing Power to Reduce Women's Vulnerability*. PhD diss., School of Development Studies, University of Kwazulu Natal.

UNFPA. 2002. *The Impact of Conflict on Women and Girls: A UNFPA Strategy for Gender Mainstreaming in Areas of Conflict and Reconstruction*. Proceedings of a conference in Bratislava, Slovakia, 13–15 November 2002. Accessed 5 November 2009. http://www.unfpa.org/upload/lib_pub_file/46_filename_armedconflict_women.pdf.

UNICEF. 2005. "Report on the Situation of Children and Women in the Republic of Uganda." Kampala: United Nations Children Funds.

Wald, Michael. 2004. "Children Rights: Cultural Concerns." *International Encyclopedia of the Social and Behavioral Sciences*, 1720–1725.

11 The "Ambivalence of the Sacred"

Christianity, Genocide, and Reconciliation in Rwanda

Janine Natalya Clark

For three months in 1994, the Christian churches of Rwanda served as the country's killing fields.
Timothy Longman (2001, 163)

Concepts of forgiveness and reconciliation are at the core of Christian teaching.
Hubert G. Locke (2004, 34)

SINCE THE TERRORIST attacks on the World Trade Center and the Pentagon on September 11, 2001, "the religious dimension of conflict has been the focus of increasing attention" (Ganiel and Dixon 2008, 419). To fixate only on the negative aspects of religion, however, is to overlook the quintessential "ambivalence of the sacred" (Appleby 2000); that is to say, that religion can serve both as a source of conflict and as a vehicle for peace. The example of Rwanda exemplifies these two faces of religion. In 1994, as genocide engulfed the country, it was not only the international community that largely stood by and watched (Dallaire 2004). So too did Rwanda's Christian churches. As Christians massacred fellow Christians,[1] places of worship became places of slaughter and indeed some clergymen took an active part in the killings. The churches thus bear significant responsibility for the genocide. To cite Longman (2010, 306), "churches played an important role in helping to make participation in the killing morally acceptable, whatever the individual reasons for participation."

The primary concern of this chapter is not with the churches' culpability during the genocide, however, but rather with their role as peacebuilders in postgenocide Rwanda. According to Paris (2004, 236), "Making peacebuilding more effective is... an essential first step in countering the broader problem of civil conflict in the post–Cold War era." My central argument is that one way to improve the effectiveness of peacebuilding is to involve a wider range of actors—and in particular, religious actors. As "people who have been formed by a religious community and who are acting with the intent to uphold, extend or defend its values and precepts" (Appleby 2000, 9), religious actors play a critical role in peacebuilding, "a dynamic process with the twin objectives of consolidating peace (building positive peace) and averting a relapse into conflict (preserving negative peace)" (Mani 2007, 15). In critically examining the role of churches and religious actors during and after the Rwandan genocide, I demonstrate the importance for postconflict societies of what I call "peacebuilding from within."

The Case for Religious Peacebuilding

According to Appleby (2000, 211–12), "At the heart of peacebuilding is conflict transformation, the replacement of violent with nonviolent means of settling disputes." The critical question is how to induce this conflict transformation. Existing literature on peacebuilding and postconflict societies focuses heavily on the notion of liberal peacebuilding and the idea that political and economic liberalization ensures stable and lasting peace after conflict (see, for example, Paris 2004). Liberal peacebuilding is an inherently top-down approach that entails the external imposition of peace, and for this reason it is deeply problematic. To cite Mani (2007, 14), "Peacebuilding needs to be domestically rooted and 'owned' by the local population and not imported or imposed." Peacebuilding is a holistic process in which entire communities should be involved. In the absence of such involvement, ordinary people may feel disconnected from the peace process (Mac Ginty 2008, 187), which potentially impacts the stability and durability of the peace achieved. Due to its focus on the macro level, liberal peacebuilding is also a very generic, broadbrush approach that does not address the specific needs and requirements of individual postconflict societies. In effect, "The liberal democratic peace model encourages a template or conveyor belt approach to peacemaking in which similar peacemaking methods are employed in different locations" (Mac Ginty 2008, 187).

Liberal peacebuilding can be contrasted with peacebuilding from below, the aim of which is to empower local communities from the bottom up. In peacebuilding from below, "solutions are derived and built from local resources" (Ramsbotham, Woodhouse, and Miall 2005, 222). The approach adopted in this chapter is both a variation on peacebuilding from below and a middle ground between the latter and liberal peacebuilding. Based on the premise that there is significant peacebuilding potential inside communities themselves (Curle 1994, 96), I am specifically concerned with "peacebuilding from within." My approach diverges from peacebuilding from below, however, by focusing on the role of "middle-level leaders" (Lederach 1997)—notably religious actors—as potential peacebuilders within their communities.

Peacebuilding from Within and the Potential of Religious Actors

Proceeding from Appleby's (2000, 212) definition of religious peacebuilding as "the various phases, levels and types of activity, by religious actors and others that strengthen religion's role in creating tolerant and nonviolent societies," there are five main reasons why religion constitutes a potentially valuable peacebuilding resource. First, reconciliation is a critical component of any peacebuilding process (Lederach 1997, 24; Hamber and Kelly 2005), and is often conceptually imbued with deep religious undertones. According to Lederach (1999, 26), for example, reconciliation is "a journey, an encounter and a place. God calls on us to set out on this journey. It is a journey through conflict, marked by places where we see the face of God, the face of the enemy, and the face of our own self." Hence, if reconciliation is understood as the restoration of relationships not only between individuals but also "between God and persons" (Amstutz 2006, 154), it is a process that can begin and flourish within religious institutions themselves. This is especially true if reconciliation is understood as requiring some degree of forgiveness. In the words of the late Martin Luther King: "He who is devoid of the power to forgive is devoid of the power to love. Forgiveness is a catalyst creating the atmosphere necessary for a fresh start and a new beginning" (quoted in Wells 2006, 194). Although the process of forgiveness is inherently personal and individual, the principle of forgiveness is deeply embedded in many religious traditions and hence religious actors are in a position to encourage forgiveness and reconciliation through religious teachings, spiritual guidance, and support.

Secondly, in situations of conflict and mass violence, morality breaks down, neighbors turn on neighbors, and hatred and prejudice replace friendship and respect. In postconflict societies such as Rwanda, therefore, part of the restoration of law and order involves the restoration of fundamental norms that are necessary for the peaceful functioning of society, and this is where religion can serve as a vital moral compass. To cite Harpviken and Røislien (2008, 353), "Religious faiths enshrine dogmas that constitute normative systems" and it is through these normative systems that religious actors can play a significant peacebuilding role. To do so, they simply have to remain *religious actors* (Appleby 2000, 16); to promote and respect cardinal religious values and to lead by example. In short, "Religious leaders ... serve peace best by first recalling and emphasizing the principles and virtues professed by all the world's major religions—particularly the values of tolerance and nonviolence" (Carter and Smith 2004, 294).

The third argument in favor of religious peacebuilding is that in situations of violent ethnic conflict, multilayered identities undergo a major process of reductionism, with the result that people's ethnic identity often becomes their primary identity. Ethnicity in turn becomes the basis for "us/them" distinctions and the vilification of the out-group. A critical element of peacebuilding, therefore, is the reconnection of people through the creation of a unifying identity, and religious actors can aid this process. As Harpviken and Røislien (2008, 354) underline, "Religious belief systems have a particular identity-forming potential. Religion is not just *individual*; it is also *social*, offering each believer a sense of belonging to a community of fellow believers." Instead of focusing on the differences between people, religious actors are well placed to emphasize shared characteristics and common humanity (Kriesberg and Millar 2009, 26), and ultimately to facilitate the creation of a consolidating meta-identity that encourages individuals to see themselves first and foremost as children of God.

Religion should also be taken seriously in peacebuilding processes because it relates to the issue of trust. In postconflict societies that have experienced war crimes and widespread human rights violations, trust is likely to be in short supply, particularly at an interpersonal and community level. Trust building is a difficult and sensitive process and one in which religious actors have a potentially very significant role to play. A distinction can be drawn between vertical trust (trust in institutions) and horizontal trust (interpersonal trust), and the former significantly influences the latter (Eek and Rothstein 2005, 6). Hence, in order for people to begin trusting each other again, their trust in institutions must first be restored, and religious actors can serve as a catalyst for this process. They are above politics, at least in theory, and "by virtue of the organization and normative system they represent, religious authorities may have a credibility that is difficult for a nonreligious peace broker to acquire" (Harpviken and Røislien 2008, 365).

The fifth and final reason why religious peacebuilding matters is that in conflicts entailing significant religious involvement, it is essential that the peace process does not marginalize and alienate religious actors. The latter should not be allowed to become "spoilers" (Stedman 1997) and to destabilize the fragile peace process. It is important, therefore, that religious actors are given an opportunity to play a constructive peacebuilding role in postconflict societies.

To advocate religious peacebuilding without exploring the darker side of religion, however, is necessarily problematic. In order to make a convincing and credible case for religious engagement in peace processes, it is imperative to acknowledge and to address both the destructive and the constructive potential of religion. The role of Rwanda's Christian churches and religious actors during and after the 1994 genocide illustrates these two dimensions of religion.

Rwanda's Christian Churches and the 1994 Genocide

To comprehensively examine and assess the role and responsibility of Rwanda's Christian churches during the 1994 genocide, it is not sufficient to focus only on the early 1990s. Rather, it is also essential to consider the wider historical context. While the colonial powers, first Germany and later Belgium, are widely accused of politicizing and entrenching the ethnic divisions that ultimately paved the way for genocide in Rwanda (see, for example, Straus 2006, 20; 2007, 124; Omeje, this volume), what is frequently overlooked is that the churches themselves greatly encouraged and fostered Hutu/Tutsi divides. Hence, the culpability of the churches is not limited to their actions and omissions during the genocide itself but also extends to their broader, historical role in contributing to the underlying causes of the genocide, not least through their endorsement of the so-called Hamitic thesis.

The Historical Background

In aligning themselves with the Tutsis, the colonial powers were strongly influenced by the Hamitic thesis, a quintessentially racist concept based upon the assumed superiority of white European races. Upon their arrival in Rwanda, therefore, the colonial powers viewed the generally lightest-skinned group, the Tutsis, as inherently more sophisticated than either the Hutus or the Twa, and thus chose to indirectly rule Rwanda through these "Hamites." What is often underplayed is that the churches similarly embraced and institutionalized the Hamitic thesis (Bjørnlund et al. 2004, 149, 159; Katongole 2005, 79–80). To cite Mamdani (2001, 98), "when it came to breathe institutional life into the Hamitic hypothesis, the colonial church acted as both the brains and hands of the colonial state." Hence, rather than condemning and publicly rejecting institutional discrimination against the Hutus, instead the churches condoned and helped to legitimize it. Longman (2001, 169), for example, notes that "both because they saw Tutsi as the established elite who needed to be appeased and because they believed in the natural superiority of Tutsi, missionaries initially offered educational and employment opportunities overwhelmingly to Tutsi."

This policy of favoring the Tutsis created growing resentment and anger among the Hutus, whose increasing calls for greater power were most clearly articulated in the 1957 Hutu Manifesto. Hutu frustrations boiled over in 1959, which marked the beginning of the Hutu Revolt. The Belgians responded by switching allegiance from the Tutsis to the Hutus and so too did the churches, thus highlighting that "the colonial and clerical establishments worked as one" (Kinzer 2008, 27). It was, for example, a Catholic press in northern Rwanda that printed copies of the aforementioned Hutu Manifesto, and some of the Manifesto's authors—like Grégoire Kayibanda—had close links to the Bishop of Kabgayi, André Perraudin. Kayibanda, the head of the rabidly anti-Tutsi PARMEHUTU party (Party for the Emancipation of the Hutus), which formed in 1957, was Perraudin's private secretary and the former editor of a Catholic newspaper. He went on to become Rwanda's first president in 1962. The responsibility, therefore, for the ethnic violence that engulfed Rwanda between 1959 and 1962 lies not only with Hutu extremists and the colonial powers.[2] Some of the responsibility also lies with the churches themselves.

By embracing the Hamitic thesis, the churches not only helped to encourage and legitimize ethnic divides, but also to institutionalize them through their continued engagement in ethnic politics. After the Catholic Church transferred its loyalty from the Tutsis to the Hutus, for example, the majority of leadership positions within the church went to Hutus; "the last Tutsi bishop, Jean-Baptiste Gahamanyi, was appointed in 1961. Thereafter, and until the genocide, all appointments were Hutu" (Cantrell 2007, 335). That they had become so heavily enmeshed in ethnic politics, moreover, meant that when the genocide began in April 1994, the churches were more a part of the problem than the solution. It is in the soil of Rwanda's colonial and postcolonial history, therefore, that we find the roots of the churches' passive and active culpability during the genocide. In the words of one *génocidaire*: "The white priests took off at the first skirmishes. The black priests joined the killers or the killed. God kept silent and the churches stank from abandoned bodies" (quoted in Hatzfield 2005, 134).

The Complicity of the Churches

Rwanda's Christian churches, in particular the Catholic Church, have been widely criticized for inaction during the genocide (see, for example, Smith 2004, 2; Ugirashebuja 2004, 55). Not only were an estimated 11 percent of victims slain in places of worship (Smith and Rittner 2004, 181) but the churches generally refrained from condemning the violence, although there were exceptions. By thus failing to call for an end to the bloodshed, "church authorities left the way clear for officials, politicians, and propagandists to assert that the slaughter actually met with God's favour" (Des Forges 1999, 246).

Virulent anti-Tutsi propaganda played a critical role in facilitating Rwanda's descent into genocide. President Habyarimana's regime, and in particular the state-run radio station Radio Télévision des Milles Collines (RTLM), repeatedly exhorted the country's Hutus to round up and exterminate the Tutsi *inyenzi* (cockroaches). Hence, "no one could escape the image of the Tutsi as the ultimate threat to Hutu. For this message was repeatedly and consistently promoted over a period of four years, not only through media, but also at political lettings and rallies, and at every level of the administrative chain" (Fujii 2004, 106). During this time, it was incumbent upon the churches to use their powerful influence within society to offer an alternative message appealing for calm, tolerance, and peace. Yet in the main this did not happen. Rather than seeking, through the promotion of transcendent Christian spiritual and moral values, to heal the ethnic divides that they themselves had helped to entrench, the churches overwhelmingly continued to accept and to rationalize those divides. Hence, as one analyst argues, "Rwanda's Christian churches were implicated in the violence not simply because they failed to prevent it or even because they legitimized the regime that carried out the genocide. Instead, the churches helped make genocide possible by making ethnic violence understandable and acceptable to the population" (Longman 2001, 166).

The culpability of Rwanda's churches during the genocide, however, was not only or primarily passive and limited to omissions (Longman 2010, 5–6). In 2001, for example, a court in Belgium convicted two Benedictine nuns from the Sovu monastery in Rwanda, Sister Kizito (Julienne Mukabutera) and Sister Gertrude (Consolata Mukangango), of genocide. It sentenced them to prison terms of thirteen and fifteen years respectively. Two years later, in 2003, the International Criminal Tribunal for Rwanda (ICTR) sentenced Elizaphan Ntakirutimana, a leading Seventh Day Adventist pastor, to ten years' imprisonment for aiding and abetting genocide. In other words, there were members of the clergy who openly supported the violence (Smith 2004,

2; Kinzer 2008, 160), and others who actively helped to make that violence possible. To cite Bishop Rucyahana (2007, 77): "In a truly macabre and sacrilegious twist, the genocide planners convinced numerous pastors and religious leaders to join their plot. The clergymen were to encourage Tutsi to seek sanctuary in their churches; they would then notify the government death squads to perform their slaughter."

In December 2006, for example, the ICTR sentenced Father Athanase Seromba, a Catholic priest in the parish of Nyange, Kibuye prefecture, to fifteen years' imprisonment for genocide and crimes against humanity. After President Habyarimana's plane was shot down over Kigali on April 6, 1994, thereby igniting one hundred days of mass carnage, Tutsis began arriving at Seromba's church seeking refuge. From 12 April 1994, the church was surrounded by *Interahamwe* and other Hutu extremist militias; and on 16 April, the church was razed using a bulldozer, resulting in the deaths of at least 1,500 Tutsi refugees. While the ICTR rejected the prosecution's claim that Seromba himself had personally given the order for the church to be destroyed, it found that, "the Prosecution has proved beyond a reasonable doubt that Athanase Seromba was informed by the authorities of their decision to destroy the church and that he accepted the decision" (ICTR 2006, para. 268). It further accepted the prosecution's contention that Seromba had encouraged the bulldozer driver to destroy the church (ICTR 2006, para. 269). During the genocide, people had naturally sought refuge in Rwanda's churches, believing that they would be safe there. Indeed, RTLM advised them to do so. Yet as examples such as Nyange and Nyamata highlight, many churches became places of slaughter rather than sanctuary.[3]

It is important to acknowledge that there were individual acts of bravery and kindness during the genocide. In *Left to Tell*, her powerful and inspiring account of how she survived the Rwandan genocide, Immaculée Ilibagiza, a young woman from the village of Mataba in Kibuye, describes how a Protestant pastor hid her and five (later seven) other Tutsis in his bathroom. Her feelings toward the pastor are often ambiguous and fluctuate from respect to disdain and fear. After one month in hiding, Ilibagiza (2007, 123) writes, "We could tell that he no longer saw us as his neighbors who were in danger and in need of help. Now he viewed us the way the killers did: as nonhumans, cockroaches that were destined to be exterminated before the war was over." She portrays the pastor as naïve and too easily susceptible to the media's toxic anti-Tutsi propaganda, despite being an educated man. Ultimately, however, she softens towards him, recognizing that, "he had risked everything for us, and he had saved our lives" (Ilibagiza 2007, 170).

Some religious figures, moreover, did denounce violence and call for an end to the bloodshed, like the late Andre Sibomana, a Rwandan Catholic priest. A vocal critic of the Catholic Church's failure to fulfill its moral responsibility during the genocide, he insisted that, "The church did not plan the genocide on an ideological level, but there is no doubt that, as among the politicians, the military, and the United Nations, the weakness of the church's reactions to daily violence prepared people psychologically to accept violence as something normal" (Sibomana 1999). The late Pope John Paul II himself issued several statements appealing for the massacres to stop (see, for example, Roth 2004, 25). Overall, however, the negative examples outweigh the positive. It can thus be argued that, "although there were many admirable acts of courage by individual Christians, the church hierarchies were at best useless and at worst accomplices in the genocide" (Rucyahana 2007, 105).

Nevertheless, religious support for and complicity in the genocide is not the end of the story. While the culpability of Rwanda's churches has been well documented, too often the analysis stops there without examining the role of religion in postgenocide Rwanda. An actor's endorsement of and participation in violence does not preclude them from subsequently assuming a constructive peacebuilding role, as highlighted, for example, by the involvement of former paramilitaries and prisoners in conflict transformation work in Northern Ireland (Shirlow and McEvoy 2008). In Rwanda today, religious actors are clearly involved in peacebuilding work.

Religious Peacebuilding in Postgenocide Rwanda

A host of faith-based domestic organizations and charities are doing invaluable work to aid peacebuilding and reconciliation in postgenocide Rwanda, such as the Friends Peace House.[4] Founded in December 2000 by the Evangelical Friends Church of Rwanda, its mission statement declares, among other things, that "our vision is a unified Rwandan society which has a vibrant culture of peace, which respects the human rights of all its members, and which promotes human development."[5] Among its various activities, the Friends Peace House provides aid to vulnerable groups such as widows and recently released prisoners, and organizes seminars and trainings on, inter alia, conflict resolution, human rights, the healing of trauma, and reconciliation. In 2004, it set up a project called Alternatives to Violence, which provided training to over 1,000 village-level judges in conflict resolution and listening skills, and its Women in Dialogue project brings together Hutu and Tutsi women to meet, to discuss their experiences, and to participate in seminars and trainings.

With a similar focus, the Solace Ministries[6] were set up to lend support to genocide survivors, particularly widows and orphans. This nongovernmental organization (NGO) offers counselling and trauma healing, listens to survivors, and gives them an opportunity to share their stories. The Solace Ministries aim to assist genocide survivors not only emotionally and psychologically, however, but also practically. Their activities include, for example, helping orphans to gain access to education and setting up demonstration farms to allow survivors to grow crops, earn an income, and receive training in animal rearing and the creation of small businesses.

The work of MOUCECORE (Mouvement Chrétien pour l'Evangélisation, le Counselling et la Réconciliation) places a strong emphasis on forgiveness; "the heart of MOUCECORE teaching is to help people to see the results of bitterness and the need to root it out ... They look at the consequences of letting bitterness take root: anger, division and, above all, a desire for revenge" (Guillebaud 2005, 176). MOUCECORE thus encourages people to transfer their pain to Jesus Christ and thereby liberate themselves from suffering, so that they may move forward. Its work is very diverse and targets a range of different social groups. It has a training center in Kigali that offers two-week seminars for Christian leaders in issues such as conflict transformation, healing and reconciliation, and community holistic development. It also provides training for Sunday school teachers. Vulnerable groups, however, are a key focus of its activities. For example, MOUCECORE organizes youth camps and Bible classes for young people; it provides legal aid for the poor and marginalized; it mobilizes Christian community groups to offer care and support to those who require it, irrespective of faith; and it supports small projects, particularly in agriculture and animal husbandry, which generate an income for widows and others in need.

Christian Action for Reconciliation and Social Assistance (CARSA)[7] was established in 2002 "with the objective of promoting reconciliation, reconstruction, and consolidation of a peaceful society with a culture of peace, dialogue, solidarity, and social welfare" (CARSA 2005). It focuses primarily though not exclusively on Rwanda's youth and places a particular emphasis on reconciliation and the promotion of a culture of peace. One of its key activities is the provision of seminars on trauma healing and reconciliation. CARSA also organizes "crusades" on topics such as how to combat genocide ideology and the role of youth in reconciliation.

Like CARSA, the Christian charity Ubaku u Rwanda[8] (To Build Rwanda) concentrates particularly on the young generation. Its mission statement claims inter alia: "We are building Rwanda's future by building up these young people."[9] It thus offers shelter, education, and guidance to orphans and street children, in order to help facilitate their reintegration back into society and to enable them to live independent lives away from Rwanda's streets. In addition to providing accommodation for thirty young boys and men, the Ubaku u Rwanda Centre in Kigali offers emotional support in the form of "drop-in" days, skills-based training, and Christian spiritual growth through Bible study and group prayer. It also works with families in conflict and seeks to prevent and alleviate poverty in Rwanda. Through these various activities, it aims "to advance the Christian faith for the benefit of the public in accordance with the statement, *the love of Christ compels us.*"[10]

Within Rwanda's Christian churches themselves, the Anglican Church in particular has strongly embraced a peacebuilding role. According to one commentator, for example, "it was the only Church to do a bit of honest soul-searching and try to understand what had happened, questioning its type of evangelization, its relationship with the regime, and its weaknesses on the ethnic question" (Prunier 2009, 6). Archbishop Emmanuel Mbona Kolini has been especially vocal and has openly recognized the church's own failures during the genocide. In 2004, Kolini declared that "the failure of the church in the genocide is an opportunity for the church to cleanse itself and ask for forgiveness" (quoted in Cantrell 2007, 348); and at a meeting of the Anglican Peace and Justice Network in Kigali, in September 2007, he stressed that "the Church must confess its sins first. Hope begins there."[11] Such acknowledgements constitute a critical step in the peacebuilding process; the churches cannot preach reconciliation until they repent of their own sins (Ndahiro 2004, 244).

While Anglican leaders like Kolini are saying all the right words, the church's peacebuilding is not confined simply to the declarative level. The church, for example, is actively seeking to aid peacebuilding through the use of *palaver*, a cultural, social-political institution with its roots in precolonial Rwanda. Settimba (2009, 285) notes that, "the aim of palaver is a reconciliation of views to provide, or attain, a uniform perception of a dispute.... According to tradition, a successful palaver is one in which a perception is reoriented so that it is shared by all." While palaver is very similar to *gacaca*, a traditional dispute resolution mechanism resurrected by the Rwandan government in 2000 to deal with a backlog of cases resulting from the genocide (Waldorf 2010), palaver primarily focuses on the background to the conflict rather than on issues of responsibility.

Beyond palaver, there are many more positive examples of Anglican "peacebuilding from within." In the Shyira diocese in Ruhengeri, as one illustration, Bishop John Rucyahana has organized a range of activities and projects specifically designed to bring people together, reflecting his conviction that "the key to reconciliation is to find where you come together—what unites us—your common source" (Rucyahana 2007, 167). In addition to setting up reconciliation conferences, he has helped to establish a mixed-faith Prison Fellowship that seeks to prepare prisoners for life outside of their cell walls and to encourage them to face their crimes and repent. Rucyahana's church, through the Prison Fellowship, is also involved in the *Umuvumu* Tree Project, which was created in 2002 to allow prisoners and genocide survivors to meet. Such projects aim not only to enable and facilitate contact between perpetrators and victims but also to allow them to constructively work together. The Prison Fellowship's "Towards Forgiveness" housing program, for example, provides a way for released prisoners and survivors to engage together in building projects. According to one former prisoner, "the cooperation we experienced during the construction of the houses really helped to close the gap between us and the survivors of the genocide. We used the time we spent together to talk about many things that helped reconcile us. When an old lady would pick up a brick, there would be an ex-convict to help her" (quoted in Rucyahana 2007, 187).

In 2002, Rucyahana himself established the Sunrise Elementary School, a boarding school attended mainly by children whose parents were killed in the genocide but also by those whose families took part in the killings. In keeping with the ethos of Ubaku u Rwanda, Sunrise views Rwanda's children as the key to rebuilding the country in every sense of the word. As Rucyahana (2007, 214) explains: "By having children from all walks of life, we establish reconciliation and then spread it back into the community at large. These children come home with changed behaviour, with good thinking, with a witness for life, and they share their bright hope with others."

As the above examples highlight, religious peacebuilding *is* occurring in postgenocide Rwanda. It is a practice and not simply a possibility, which in turn underscores that religion and faith have a crucial part to play in the country's reconciliation and healing process. At the same time, however, there are legitimate grounds for questioning whether Christianity can fulfil its peacebuilding potential in today's Rwanda.

Ongoing Problems and Challenges

There are two fundamental issues that threaten to compromise and undermine the churches' role as peacebuilders in Rwanda: namely, persistent denial within the Catholic Church and the continuing politicization of religion.

Denial and the Catholic Church

To aid reconciliation, Rwanda's Christian churches "need to first acknowledge their own role in fostering and contributing to injustice and conflict" (Cilliers 2002, 49). In the case of the Catholic Church, however, such acknowledgement has generally been lacking (Longman 2010, 7). Instead, the church has frequently taken refuge in denial, and more specifically in interpretative denial (Cohen 2001).[12] In 1994, for example, from their exile in Zaire (now the Democratic Republic of Congo), a group of Catholic priests wrote to the Vatican insisting that: "To speak of genocide and to insinuate that only Hutus killed Tutsis is to be ignorant [of the fact] that Hutus and Tutsis have been each other's executioners. We dare even to confirm that the number of Hutu civilians killed by the army of the RPF [Rwandan Patriotic Front] exceeds by far the number of Tutsi victims of the ethnic troubles" (quoted in African Rights 1995, 906). A member of the Roman Catholic order of the Sisters of the Assumption, for her part, insists that "in general, the [religious] communities and pastors tried to do all that was in their power to save the people, but faced with a band of armed people, priests and brothers, whose hands were empty, who were without weapons or any means of defense, were powerless" (Mukarwego 2004, 121).

The church has further engaged in denial by supporting its members who participated in the genocide. The Catholic Church in Italy, for example, protected the aforementioned Father Athanase Seromba; and a Roman Catholic priest has emphatically argued that Sisters Kizito and Gertrude, the two Benedictine nuns found guilty of genocide by a court in Belgium, "were judged less for what they were unable to do to help the victims than for being representatives of the genocide who could finally be tried in Belgium. In addition, they were members of the Church" (Neyt 2004, 256). In response to the conviction of the two nuns in 2001, the late Pope John Paul II issued the following statement: "The Church . . . cannot be held responsible for the guilt of its members who have acted against the law of the Gospel; they themselves will be called to give account for their actions" (quoted in Rucyahana 2007, 106). Yet while thus denying any institutional blame, the Vatican has "paid legal fees for its clergy suspected of being involved in the genocide" (Rucyahana 2007, 106). Furthermore, while

Pope Benedict formally apologized in March 2010 to Irish Catholic victims of sexual abuse, the Vatican to date has offered no official apology to survivors of the Rwandan genocide. For one commentator: "The silence of the Vatican is contempt. Its failure to fully examine its central place in the Rwandan genocide can only mean that it is fully aware that it will not be threatened if it buries its head in the sand" (Kimani 2010).

If the Catholic Church continues to persist in denial and to refrain from condemning its members who participated in the genocide, it will not have the requisite moral authority and credibility to play a constructive peacebuilding role in Rwanda. It cannot truly inspire and encourage forgiveness without first recognizing that it too must ask for forgiveness. According to Locke (2004, 34), "too often, the Church finds itself caught up in the language and processes of forgiveness and reconciliation without having taken the harder, first steps of remorse and penance." If, moreover, the church continues to engage in denial, its members are likely to follow its lead.[13] Yet denial is a fundamental obstacle to reconciliation; as a critical first step the latter requires acknowledgement of guilt and "the acceptance of responsibility for atrocities or other events symbolizing intercommunal and interpersonal relations" (Jeong 2005, 156).

The Politicization of Religion

Rwanda's Christian churches have historically been closely aligned to political power, from the colonial period through to the regimes of Grégoire Kayibanda and Juvénal Habyarimana. This politicization compromised both their integrity as spiritual institutions and their ability to speak out against the genocide. The churches' potential as peacebuilders cannot be fully harnessed, therefore, without a "return to religion" and a process of depoliticization. In the words of Bartoli (2004, 150), "Christianity seems especially to become an obstacle to peacebuilding when it aligns itself too closely with secular power." Unfortunately, however, it seems that the churches are continuing to thus align themselves, in particular the Anglican Church.

After ethnic violence erupted in Rwanda in 1959, thousands of Tutsi refugees fled to neighbouring Uganda. Determined to eventually return to their homeland, the children of these refugees subsequently formed the Rwandan Patriotic Front (RPF), and on October 1, 1990 the RPF launched a military attack on northern Rwanda. This was the start of a three-year civil war between the RPF and the Rwandan Army (FAR), which ended on August 4, 1993 with the signing of the Arusha Accords. One provision of these accords was that all refugees who had been forced to flee Rwanda during and after 1959 would now be free to return to the country. Determined, however, to block and prevent the implementation of this peace agreement, which they viewed as a fundamental threat to their own positions and power, Hutu extremists within Habyarimana's regime—like Colonel Théoneste Bagosora and his Comité pour la Défense de la République (CDR)—set into motion their genocidal plans. One hundred days of mass carnage ensued. The genocide ended in July 1994 when the RPF took control of the country, and a new government was inaugurated on July 19, 1994. Seeking to respect the terms of the Arusha Accords, the incoming government encouraged the Tutsi diaspora to return to Rwanda, which they did in vast numbers; "roughly the same numbers came back (around 700,000) as had been killed (800,000)" (Prunier 2009, 5).

Anglican clergymen were among those who returned to Rwanda from neighboring Uganda. These clergymen had spent all of their lives in Uganda and therefore spoke English rather than Kinyarwanda and French. Yet while the Anglican Church is now playing an important peacebuilding role, one commentator maintains that "the Ugandan origins of the Anglican hierarchy present several barriers to the church being an effective mouthpiece for reconciliation and political inclusiveness" (Cantrell 2007, 340). Rwanda's president, Paul Kagame, was the military commander of the mainly Tutsi-based RPF, and during his presidency there has been a gradual "Tutsization" and "RPF-ization" of power (Reyntjens 2004, 188). While Kagame's regime is officially promoting a national unity and reconciliation policy that negates ethnic identities and emphasizes people's Banyarwanda (Rwandan) identity, unofficially ethnicity remains highly significant in Rwanda. By 2000, for example, "out of a total of 169 of the most important office-holders, 135 (or about 80 percent) were RPF/RPA [Rwandan Patriotic Army] and 119 (or roughly 70 percent) were Tutsi" (Reyntjens 2004, 188). Furthermore, it is no coincidence that crimes committed by the RPF remain unpunished.[14] Like Kagame's regime, the Anglican Church is similarly propagating the message that ethnicity is a defunct category in Rwanda and that Hutu/Tutsi distinctions are no longer of relevance. The problem, however, according to Cantrell's research, is that "while church leaders and pastors repeatedly refer to themselves as Rwandan," their Ugandan origins and consequent close links with the ruling RPF regime mean that "the Hutu populace, still poor and without access to power, continue to see the ruling classes, in both church and state, as Tutsi" (Cantrell 2007, 340).

Finally, peacebuilding and reconciliation are processes that require an honest and open engagement with the past, and this cannot fully happen as long as ethnicity is treated as irrelevant (Clark 2010a). Even if ethnic identities are constructed and a legacy of the colonial period, as Kagame insists (2008, xxiii; see also Omeje, this volume), the critical point is that ethnicity was a core element of the genocide. If, therefore, the church continues to advocate the policies of the Kagame regime and to negate the significance of ethnicity, it will not only remain politicized but will struggle to achieve its full peacebuilding potential. In the very poignant words of one genocide survivor, "Without speaking the truth about what hurts us, reconciliation is impossible. There are many church leaders in Rwanda who sing and praise the Lord with loud voices, but don't touch the truth about what happened" (Uwibereyeho King 2002).

According to Brewer, Higgins and Teeney (2010, 1012), "If not portrayed as a benign irrelevance, religion is depicted as a malign force." The Rwandan case shows that religion can indeed be a deeply malign force. By embracing the Hamitic thesis, helping to define ethnic identities, encouraging ethnic divisions, and accepting discrimination first against the Hutus and later against the Tutsis, Rwanda's Christian churches assisted in creating the preconditions for wide-scale bloodshed. Later, when the genocide began, the churches broadly turned the other way. As one commentator observes, "the most important contribution religions can make to peace is to recognize that when conflict emerges, they have the responsibility to speak out against violence and persecution" (Schneier 2002, 112). Not only did the churches largely refrain from doing this but there were clergymen, priests, and nuns who actively encouraged or participated in the killings.

Underlining the fundamental "ambiguity of the sacred" (Appleby 2000), however, this chapter has also shown that religion need not be a malign force. But it is also not of benign irrelevance. Through critical analysis of religious actors and churches in Rwanda, I have argued for the importance of involving religious actors in peacebuilding processes "from within." While there has been much scholarly debate on whether "justice"—dispensed through the ICTR, Rwanda's domestic courts, and its *gacaca* courts—can aid reconciliation (see, for example, Sarkin 2001; Humphrey 2003; Longman, Pham and Weinstein 2004), the important issue of whether and to what extent religion itself can facilitate the process has received far less attention. Hence, in contrast to the churches' involvement and culpability during the genocide, the part that they are playing in postgenocide Rwanda is relatively underresearched. In addressing this gap, and in theorizing religious actors and churches as representing a form of peacebuilding from within, I have shown the significance and vitality of religious peacebuilding in Rwanda today. Nevertheless, denial within the Catholic Church and the continued politicization of religion threaten to undermine the churches' ability to realize their full potential as religious peacebuilders. The Rwandan case has thus underscored the imperative of a "return to religion." As Appleby (2000, 16) stresses, "religious actors make a difference when they remain *religious* actors." Moreover, given that "the space for religion ... in peacebuilding is theoretically expansive yet hardly explored" (Carter and Smith 2004, 280), scholars and practitioners alike need to examine and understand the impact that religious peacebuilding is having on the ground and from within postconflict societies like Rwanda.

Notes

1. According to Rwanda's 1991 census, 90 percent of the population declared themselves as Christians (Bowen 2004, 37).

2. During this period, approximately 10,000 Tutsis were killed while a further 120,000 were forced to flee to neighboring countries such as Burundi and Uganda.

3. In mid-April 1994, 5,000 people were massacred in the church in Nyamata.

4. http://www.friendspeacehouse.rw. Accessed 15 August 2011. There are also a variety of international Christian organizations working in Rwanda, like the Scottish Catholic International Aid Fund (SCIAF) and Catholic Relief Services. Their many activities include HIV/AIDS prevention, food aid, emergency assistance, micro-finance programs, and peacebuilding.

5. http://www.friendspeacehouse.rw/about.html. Accessed 15 August 2011.

6. http://www.solacem.org/. Accessed 15 August 2011.

7. http://carsa.org. Accessed 17 August 2011.
8. http://www.ubakurwanda.org.uk. Accessed 17 August 2011.
9. http://www.ubakurwanda.org.uk/Home. Accessed 23 August 2011.
10. http://www.ubakurwanda.org.uk/Home. Accessed 25 August 2011.
11. http://www.anglicancommunion.org/acns/digest/index.cfm/2007/10/4/Conflict-transformation-focus-of-nineday-gathering. Accessed 27 August 2011.

12. According to Cohen (2001, 7), in cases of interpretative denial, "it is not the raw facts (something happened) that are being denied but they are given a different meaning from what seems obvious to others."

13. In Bosnia-Herzegovina, for example, denial within the Serbian Orthodox Church has encouraged denial among ordinary Serbs (see Clark 2010b).

14. Reinforcing their observation that "impunity remains the rule for crimes committed by the RPF within and outside of Rwanda," Lemarchand and Niwese (2007, 183) maintain that "of all the obstacles in the way of national reconciliation, the application of double standards in meting out punishment for crimes of genocide is not the least problematic."

References

African Rights. 1995. *Rwanda: Death, Despair and Defiance*. Rev. ed. London: African Rights.

Amstutz, Mark R. 2006. "Restorative Justice, Political Forgiveness, and the Possibility of Political Reconciliation." In *The Politics of Past Evil: Religion, Reconciliation, and the Dilemmas of Transitional Justice*, edited by Daniel Philpott, 151–88. South Bend, IN: University of Notre Dame Press.

Appleby, R. Scott. 2000. *The Ambivalence of the Sacred: Religion, Violence, and Reconciliation*. Lanham, MD: Rowman & Littlefield.

Bartoli, Andrea. 2004. "Christianity and Peacebuilding." In *Religion and Peacebuilding*, edited by Howard Coward and Gordon S. Smith, 147–66. Albany: State University of New York Press.

Bjørnlund, Matthias, Eric Markusen, Peter Steenberg, and Rafiki Ubaldo. 2004. "The Christian Churches and the Construction of a Genocidal Mentality in Rwanda." In *Genocide in Rwanda: Complicity of the Churches*, edited by Carol Rittner, John K. Roth, and Wendy Whitworth, 141–67. St. Paul, MN: Paragon House.

Bowen, Roger W. 2004. "Genocide in Rwanda 1994: An Anglican Perspective." In *Genocide in Rwanda: Complicity of the Churches*, edited by Carol Rittner, John K. Roth, and Wendy Whitworth, 37–48. St. Paul, MN: Paragon House.

Brewer, John D., Gareth I. Higgins, and Francis Teeney. 2010. "Religion and Peacemaking: A Conceptualization." *Sociology* 44, no. 6: 1019–1037.

Cantrell, Phillip A. 2007. "The Anglican Church of Rwanda: Domestic Agendas and International Linkages." *Journal of Modern African Studies* 45, no. 3: 333–54.

Carter, Judy, and Gordon S. Smith. 2004. "Religious Peacebuilding: From Potential to Action." In *Religion and Peacebuilding*, edited by Howard Coward and Gordon S. Smith, 279–301. Albany: State University of New York Press.

Christian Action for Reconciliation and Social Assistance (CARSA). 2005. "Annual Report 2005." Accessed 10 August 2011. www.carsa.org.rw/CARSA's%20REPORT%202005.pdf.

Cilliers, Jaco. 2002. "Building Bridges for Interfaith Dialogue." In *Interfaith Dialogue and Peacebuilding*, edited by David R. Smock, 47–60. Washington, DC: United States Institute of Peace Press.

Clark, Janine N. 2010a. "National Unity and Reconciliation in Rwanda: A Flawed Approach." *Journal of Contemporary African Studies* 28, no. 2: 137–54.

———. 2010b. "Religion and Reconciliation in Bosnia and Hercegovina: Are Religious Actors Doing Enough?" *Europe-Asia Studies* 62, no. 4: 671–94.
Cohen, Stanley. 2001. *States of Denial: Knowing about Atrocities and Suffering.* Cambridge: Polity.
Curle, Adam. 1994. "New Challenges for Citizen Peacemaking." *Medicine and War* 10, no. 2: 96–105.
Dallaire, Roméo. 2004. *Shake Hands with the Devil: The Failure of Humanity in Rwanda.* London: Arrow.
Des Forges, Alison. 1999. *Leave None to Tell the Story: Genocide in Rwanda.* New York: Human Rights Watch.
Eek, Daniel, and Bo Rothstein. 2005. "Exploring a Causal Relationship between Vertical and Horizontal Trust." QOG Working Paper 4 (2005). Göteborg, Sweden: Quality of Government Institute, University of Göteborg.
Fujii, Lee Ann. 2004. "Transforming the Moral Landscape: The Diffusion of a Genocidal Norm in Rwanda." *Journal of Genocide Research* 6, no. 1: 99–114.
Ganiel, Gladys, and Paul Dixon. 2008. "Religion, Pragmatic Fundamentalism, and the Transformation of the Northern Ireland Conflict." *Journal of Peace Research* 45, no. 3: 419–36.
Guillebaud, Meg. 2005. *After the Locusts: How Costly Forgiveness Is Restoring Rwanda's Stolen Years.* Oxford: Monarch.
Hamber, Brandon, and Gráinne Kelly. 2005. "A Place for Reconciliation? Conflict and Locality in Northern Ireland." Accessed 5 August 2011. http://cain.ulst.ac.uk/dd/report18/ddreport18.pdf.
Harpviken, Kristian, and Hanne Eggen Røislien. 2008. "Faithful Brokers? Potentials and Pitfalls of Religion in Peacemaking." *Conflict Resolution Quarterly* 25, no. 3: 351–73.
Hatzfield, Jean. 2005. *A Time for Machetes: The Rwandan Genocide. The Killers Speak.* London: Farrar, Straus and Giroux.
Humphrey, Michael. 2003. "International Intervention, Justice, and National Reconciliation: The Role of the ICTY and ICTR in Bosnia and Rwanda." *Journal of Human Rights* 2, no. 4: 494–505.
Ilibagiza, Immaculée. 2007. *Left to Tell: One Woman's Story of Surviving the Rwandan Holocaust.* London: Hay House.
International Criminal Tribunal for Rwanda (ICTR). 2006. "The Prosecutor vs. Athanase Seromba." *ICTR-2001-66-I*, Trial Chamber Judgment, 13 December.
Jeong, Ho-Won. 2005. *Peacebuilding in Postconflict Societies: Strategy and Process.* Boulder, CO: Lynne Rienner.
Kagame, Paul. 2008. "Preface." In *After Genocide: Transitional Justice, Post-conflict Reconstruction and Reconciliation in Rwanda and Beyond*, edited by Phil Clark and Zachary D. Kaufman, xxi–xxvi. London: Hurst.
Katongole, Emmanuel M. 2005. "Christianity, Tribalism, and the Rwandan Genocide: A Catholic Reassessment of Christian Social Responsibility." *Logos* 8, no. 3: 67–93.
Kimani, Martin. 2010. "For Rwandans, the Pope's Apology Must Be Unbearable." Accessed 10 August 2011. http://www.guardian.co.uk/commentisfree/belief/2010/mar/29/pope-catholics-rwanda-genocide-church.
King, Régine Uwibereyeho. 2002. "Trauma, Healing and Reconciliation in Rwanda." Accessed 8 August 2011. http://www.ijdcr.ca/VOL01_03_CAN/articles/king.shtml.

Kinzer, Stephen. 2008. *A Thousand Hills: Rwanda's Rebirth and the Man Who Dreamed It.* Hoboken, NJ: John Wiley & Sons.
Kriesberg, Louis, and Gearoid Millar. 2009. "Protagonist Strategies That Help End Violence." In *Conflict Transformation and Peacebuilding: Moving from Violence to Sustainable Peace*, edited by Bruce W. Dayton and Louis Kriesberg, 13–29. London: Routledge.
Lederach, John Paul. 1997. *Building Peace: Sustainable Reconciliation in Divided Societies.* Washington, DC: United States Institute of Peace Press.
———. 1999. *The Journey toward Reconciliation.* Scottsdale, PA: Herald.
Lemarchand, René, and Maurice Niwese. 2007. "Mass Murder, the Politics of Memory and Post-genocide Reconstruction: The Cases of Rwanda and Burundi." In *After Mass Crime: Rebuilding States and Communities*, edited by Béatrice Pouligny, Simon Chesterman, and Albrecht Schnabel, 165–89. Tokyo: United Nations University Press.
Locke, Hubert G. 2004. "Religion and the Rwandan Genocide: Some Preliminary Considerations." In *Genocide in Rwanda: Complicity of the Churches*, edited by Carol Rittner, John K. Roth, and Wendy Whitworth, 27–35. St. Paul, MN: Paragon House.
Longman, Timothy. 2001. "Church, Politics and the Genocide in Rwanda." *Journal of Religion in Africa* 31, no. 2: 163–86.
Longman, Timothy. 2010. *Christianity and Genocide in Rwanda.* New York: Cambridge University Press.
Longman, Timothy, Phuong Pham, and Harvey M. Weinstein. 2004. "Connecting Justice to Human Experience: Attitudes towards Accountability and Reconciliation in Rwanda." In *My Neighbor, My Enemy: Justice and Community in the Aftermath of Mass Atrocity*, edited by Eric Stover and Harvey M. Weinstein, 206–25. Cambridge: Cambridge University Press.
Mac Ginty, Roger. 2008. *No War, No Peace: The Rejuvenation of Stalled Peace Processes and Peace Accords.* Basingstoke, UK: Palgrave Macmillan.
Mamdani, M. 2001. *When Victims Become Killers: Colonialism, Nativism and the Genocide in Rwanda.* Kampala: Fountain Publishers.
Mani, Rama. 2007. *Beyond Retribution: Seeking Justice in the Shadows of War.* Cambridge: Polity.
Mukarwego, Marie C. 2004. "The Church and the Rwandan Tragedy of 1994: A Personal View." In *Genocide in Rwanda: Complicity of the Churches*, edited by Carol Rittner, John K. Roth, and Wendy Whitworth, 117–25. St. Paul, MN: Paragon House.
Ndahiro, Tom. 2004. "The Church's Blind Eye to Genocide in Rwanda." In *Genocide in Rwanda: Complicity of the Churches*, edited by Carol Rittner, John K. Roth, and Wendy Whitworth, 229–49. St. Paul, MN: Paragon House.
Neyt, Martin. 2004. "Two Convicted Rwandan Nuns." In *Genocide in Rwanda: Complicity of the Churches*, edited by Carol Rittner, John K. Roth, and Wendy Whitworth, 251–58. St. Paul, MN: Paragon House.
Paris, Roland. 2004. *At War's End: Building Peace after Civil Conflict.* Cambridge: Cambridge University Press.
Prunier, Gérard. 2009. *From Genocide to Continental War: The "Congolese" Conflict and the Crisis of Contemporary Africa.* London: Hurst.
Ramsbotham, Oliver, Tom Woodhouse, and Hugh Miall. 2005. *Contemporary Conflict Resolution: The Prevention, Management and Transformation of Deadly Conflicts.* 2nd ed. Cambridge: Polity.

Reyntjens, Filip. 2004. "Rwanda Ten Years On: From Genocide to Dictatorship." *African Affairs* 103: 177–210.

Roth, John K. 2004. "Part I: The Church and Power—Raising Voices." In *Genocide in Rwanda: Complicity of the Churches*, edited by Carol Rittner, John K. Roth, and Wendy Whitworth, 25–26. St. Paul, MN: Paragon House.

Rucyahana, John. 2007. *The Bishop of Rwanda: Finding Forgiveness amidst a Pile of Bones*. Nashville, TN: Thomas Nelson.

Sarkin, Jeremy. 2001. "The Tension between Justice and Reconciliation in Rwanda: Politics, Human Rights, Due Process, and the Role of the *Gacaca* Courts in Dealing with the Genocide." *Journal of African Law* 45, no. 2: 143–72.

Schneier, Arthur. 2002. "Religion and Interfaith Conflict: Appeal of Conscience Foundation." In *Interfaith Dialogue and Peacebuilding*, edited by David R. Smock, 105–14. Washington, DC: United States Institute of Peace Press.

Settimba, Henry. 2009. *The Anglican Church Role in the Process of Reconciliation in Rwanda*. Cambridge: Perfect Publishers.

Shirlow, Peter, and Kieran McEvoy. 2008. *Beyond the Wire: Former Prisoners and Conflict Transformation in Northern Ireland*. London: Pluto.

Sibomana, André. 1999. "Never Again? The Church and Genocide in Rwanda: Excerpt." Accessed 9 August 2011. http://findarticles.com/p/articles/mi_m1252/is_19_126/ai_57884848/?tag=content;col1.

Smith, Stephen D. 2004. "Introduction." In *Genocide in Rwanda: Complicity of the Churches*, edited by Carol Rittner, John K. Roth, and Wendy Whitworth, 1–3. St. Paul, MN: Paragon House.

Smith, James M., and Carol Rittner. 2004. "Churches as Memorial Sites: A Photo Essay." In *Genocide in Rwanda: Complicity of the Churches*, edited by Carol Rittner, John K. Roth, and Wendy Whitworth, 181–205. St. Paul, MN: Paragon House.

Stedman, Stephen J. 1997. "Spoiler Problems in Peace Processes." *International Security* 22, no. 2: 5–53.

Straus, Scott. 2006. *The Order of Genocide: Race, Power, and War in Rwanda*. Ithaca, NY: Cornell University Press.

———. 2007. "Origins and Aftermaths: The Dynamics of Genocide in Rwanda and Their Post-genocide Implications." In *After Mass Crime: Rebuilding States and Communities*, edited by Béatrice Pouligny, Simon Chesterman, and Albrecht Schnabel, 122–41. Tokyo: United Nations University Press.

Ugirashebuja, Octave. 2004. "The Church and the Genocide in Rwanda." In *Genocide in Rwanda: Complicity of the Churches*, edited by Carol Rittner, John K. Roth, and Wendy Whitworth, 49–63. St. Paul, MN: Paragon House.

Waldorf, Lars. 2010. "'Like Jews Waiting for Jesus': Posthumous Justice in Post-genocide Rwanda." In *Localizing Transitional Justice: Interventions and Priorities after Mass Violence*, edited by Rosalind Shaw and Lars Waldorf, 183–202. Stanford, CA: Stanford University Press.

Wells, Ronald A. 2006. "Northern Ireland: A Study of Friendship, Forgiveness, and Reconciliation." In *The Politics of Past Evil: Religion, Reconciliation, and the Dilemmas of Transitional Justice*, edited by Daniel Philpott, 189–222. South Bend, IN: University of Notre Dame Press.

Index

abductees: escape of, 206; and human rights, 187, 199; reintegration of, 18, 203, 209–11; sense of self, 18; and social capital, 212–13; as wives, 207–8, 210, 211

abduction: of children, 198, 199, 203–4; by LRA, 87, 185; penalties for, 125; return from, 209, 212, 213; of women and girls, 2, 197–98, 203–8, 211, 213. *See also* reabduction

abuse: child, 185–86, 201; human rights, 61, 95, 125–27, 182; sexual, 185, 197, 199, 201, 204, 213; of women, 183, 201, 204, 207

accountability: and justice, 122–23, 126–28, 135, 137; in politics, 112–13, 115–17, 131, 138, 153; and reform, 97, 107, 137–39

Acholi ethnic group, 17–18, 85–92, 98–99, 179–214; normal society of the, 18, 201, 203, 207, 208

Acholiland, Uganda, 90, 98, 180, 182–84, 190

adaptation: to climate, 42, 146; cultural, 42, 189; of human rights discourse, 17, 183

African Union (AU), 3, 74, 94–5

Afro-pessimist, 8

age, 189–93, 205, 207–8. *See also* youth

agency, 4, 6, 18, 198–99, 205–6, 214

aid workers, 180, 182, 190–91

Amin Dada, Idi, 56–57, 91, 147

Amnesty Act of 2000, 95, 97–98

amnesty, 97–98, 127, 132–33, 185

Anglican Church, 19, 225–26, 228–29. *See also* Christianity; religion

Angola, 10, 43, 120, 198, 202

Annan, Kofi, 14, 33, 106, 120, 136; mediation by, 124, 134; and peacebuilding models, 14, 106, 120, 136

anthropology, 8, 179–81, 192

Arabs, 34, 49, 88

arms. *See* weapons

arts, the: performance art, 184, 187–88, 193–94 (*see also* music; dance); and reconciliation, 16, 182–83; visual, 187–90, 193. *See also* therapy: art

Arusha, city of, 42, 55, 58, 60, 74; significant treaties, 34, 39–40, 42, 228–29

Baganda Kingdom, 27, 29, 32, 89, 91

Bahutu. *See* Hutu

Bahutu–Batutsi conflict, 11, 35

Bantu-speaking ethnic groups, 35–36, 87–88, 92

Banyamulenge ethnic group, 42–43, 60

Banyarwanda ethnic group, 29, 50, 92, 229

Banyoro government, 88, 90, 101

bataka, 89

batongole, 89

Batutsi. *See* Tutsi

breakdance. *See* dance

British East Africa, 51, 65, 71

broadcasting, 17–18, 161–65, 176–77; development of, 165–69; independence of, 173–76; and synergy, 169–73. *See also* radio

Buganda, Kingdom of, 49, 53, 88–90

Bukavu, DRC, 163, 167, 169, 171–72

bush, the: child mothers in, 18, 198–201, 203–7, 212–14; experience in, 97, 185; rebels, 185, 203–4; return from, 185, 202, 209–12; society, 18, 197, 203; war, 39, 92

bwola, 184, 193. *See also* dance

Catholic Church, the, 19, 163–64, 221, 222–23, 227–28. *See also* Christianity; religion

cattle: economy, 36, 50, 92, 141, 146–49; and land use, 27, 153, 155; rustling, 57, 92–93, 147, 149–50; warlordism, 150

Central African Republic (CAR), 2, 10, 94, 175, 177n15

Central province, Kenya, 29, 123

child soldiers, 2, 185, 187–88. *See also* formerly abducted child mothers

childhood, 204, 206, 208–9

children: born in captivity, 198, 205–6, 210–11; protection of, 18, 209, 199–202, 206, 208–9; rights of (*see* rights: child)

Christianity, 19, 217; involvement in genocide, 217, 220–21, 222–24; and peacebuilding, 218, 220, 224–27. *See also* religion

climate change, 13, 15, 27, 123; and conflict, 141, 143–44, 151–53 (*see also* eco-conflicts); and pastoralism, 141–43, 144–47, 153–56

Cold War, the: and the post-independence period, 12, 55, 57, 72; and regionalization, 66, 72

colonial: administration districts, 26, 30, 37, 50, 58, 90; governance, 13, 28–29, 37, 44, 90–93, 107; warrant chiefs, 30

Commission of Inquiry into Postelection Violence, 119, 127

235

Committee of Eminent African Personalities, 106, 124, 128
common market, 54–55, 65, 71, 74, 78
community ownership of expression, 192
conflict, armed: in genocide, 5, 7; gender and youth issues in, 199–202; justice after, 138; lessening of, 11, 128; over resources, 154; sexual abuse during, 197. *See also* violence
conflict: architecture, 4–5; epicentre, 11, 25, 34–35; hiatus in conflict, 198; preconflict factors, 202, 204; postconflict period, 16–18, 179–82, 189, 202–4
consociationalism, 42
constitutional referendum, 106, 111, 119, 169
constitutionalism, 60, 62
Contact FM, 165, 172, 174
Convention on the Rights of the Child (CRC), 186, 200–201
coping: with environmental changes, 15, 142, 146–47, 149, 154; with trauma, 179, 188, 193, 199, 203
corruption: neopatrimonial, 30, 32; political, 102, 115–16, 119, 123, 127, 132; prebendal, 42
counseling, 193, 209, 224. *See also* therapy: art
coupage, 166
creative arts. *See* arts, the
cultural resonance, 183, 192–93
customs union, 50, 70, 74, 77–78

dance, 17, 180–81, 184–85, 187–93, 209; breakdance, 187, 190, 191, 193
decolonization, 28, 30–31, 37, 53, 107
demilitarization, 97, 101
demobilization, demilitarization, and reintegration (DDR), 97
diamonds, 30, 43, 101n1
diaspora, 59, 169, 229
diktats, 5, 77
dingi-dingi, 184. *See also* dance
disarmament, 93, 95, 148, 153–54
displacement: by climate, 145; colonial, 27; during conflict, 38, 182, 184, 190, 198–99; internal, 129 (*see also* internally displaced persons); and reconciliation, 129, 190, 209
divide-and-rule and discriminatory policy, 28–30, 180

East African Civil Society Organizations Forum (EACSOF), 76–77, 79
East African Common Market, 12, 54–55, 65, 71
East African Common Services Organization, (EACSO), 53, 71
East African Community (EAC): collapse of, 56, 58–59, 62, 66, 72, 78–79; criticism of, 11, 72, 76; and development plans, 47, 70; establishment of, 12, 55; intervention by, 3, 58–59; and nonstate actors, 74–77; and Observer Status, 75
East African Community Treaty (EACT), 74–77, 79
East African Federation, 12, 51, 53, 65–66, 71
East African High Commission (EAHC), 52, 65
eco-conflicts, 15, 141, 151–52. *See also* climate change
economic partnership agreement (EPA), 76–78
education: basic, 58, 186, 209, 221, 224–25; civic, 163; politicized, 89, 162; privilege in, 37; professional, 167–68
elders: and folklore, 190; loss of power of, 150; as proponents of reconciliation, 98, 134, 187; and the social order, 202, 214n6
elections: disputes, 14, 33, 106–9, 115–20, 136, 167; and the media, 167–71; postelection violence, 13–14, 32–33, 44, 107, 112–15, 119, 122–30; as a sign of change, 38, 42, 95, 109, 114
Electoral Commission of Kenya (ECK), 32, 106–8, 111, 115–16, 136, 170
emotional violence. *See* violence: emotional
environmental scarcity, 143–44
Eritrea, 2, 10
Ethiopia, 2, 10, 29
ethnocide, 4–5. *See also* genocide
ethnonationalism. *See* nationalism
European Union (EU), the, 32, 76–77, 152, 174
excombatants, 97, 202–3. *See also* returnees
experiences, intersectionality of, 213

family: decisions about, 204; extended, 201, 208; and government, 108, 200; justice of, 86, 137; land, 37; rights, 187; togetherness, 190, 199, 201, 203, 209–11
Federation of East Africa, 50, 65
feminism, 7, 18, 197–98, 201–2, 213
folktales, 189–90. *See also* storytelling
foreign policy, 54, 57, 67
formerly abducted child mothers, 18, 184, 197–99, 201–3, 207–14
Front for Democracy in Burundi (FRODEBU), 39, 41
functionalism, 68–70, 73; Eurofunctionalism, 12, 78; neofunctionalism, 68–69, 75

gacaca courts, 119, 226, 230
ganwa, 38
gender: and arts, 182–83, 189–90, 193; injustice, 197, 201, 213; and politics, 114; power imbalance of, 197, 20–23, 207; support programs, 209, 212; and violence, 199, 204
génocidaires, 42

genocide: 2–3, 5, 19; aftermath of, 40, 165, 218, 224–27; and the church, 217, 220–24, 226–28, 230; and displacement, 42; and ethnicity, 29, 39, 229; heroics, 223; inaction during, 40–41, 217, 222–23; and sex 7, 44
geo-demographic issues, 25, 27, 34
German East Africa, 26, 65, 71
giti, 166
Government of Uganda (GOU), 85, 97, 179
grievances, expressions of, 28, 51, 93–94, 100–101, 123, 208
gucupira, 50
Gulu Peace Accord, 96
Gulu, Uganda, 92, 181, 188–91, 198, 209, 212

Habyarimana, Juvénal, 38, 228
Hamitic thesis, the, 35–36, 220–21, 229
healing: collective, 17, 182; national, 115, 135; and reconciliation, 97, 124, 127, 131, 139, 224–25; and rehabilitation, 209; role of religion in, 224; through art, 180, 187, 193
HIV/AIDS, 78, 166, 181, 199, 203, 208
Holy Spirit Mobile Force (HSMF), 86
Holy Spirit Movement (HSM), 86–87, 92, 96
Horn of Africa, the, 29, 51
human rights: abuses, 61, 98, 107, 182; Commission, 95, 97–98, 129–30, 133–34; consciousness, 17, 179–83, 191–92; in the courts, 130–33, 138, 186; protection of, 3, 59, 62, 119, 125–26, 132, 224; vernacularization of, 17, 181–82, 194; violations, 110, 130–31, 220
humanitarian intervention, 26, 107, 191; crises, 3, 14, 85–87, 112; international law, 127
Hutu ethnic group, 28–31, 35–42, 49–50, 220–24, 227–29
Hutu Force for the Defense of Democracy (FDD), 41
Hutu Manifesto, the, 221
Hutu Revolt, the, 221

Impact of Events Scale-Revised, the, 182
Implementation and Management Mechanisms (IMM), 97
Impuzamugambi, 40
independence: and integration, 53; post-independence period, 29–34, 55–57, 62, 78, 86, 89–91, 100, 107–8; the struggle for, 28–29, 32–33, 37–38, 107
Independent Electoral and Boundaries Commission (IEBC), 114–6
initiatives: community based, 3, 72, 155; grassroots, 13–14, 28, 61–62, 156; hybrid, 184–87, 192; indigenous, 184, 192; peacebuilding, 3, 11, 87, 95–98, 164, 182–84; transplanted, 182, 184, 187–89, 192–93

integration: and civil society, 48, 172; and economics, 54; and politics, 60, 66–71, 77; regional, 10–12
Interahamwe, 40, 42, 223
interdependence, 67, 73
internally displaced persons (IDPs), 2, 33, 37, 98–99, 129; camps, 180, 184–85, 198; resettlement of, 14, 99, 107, 112
International Criminal Court (ICC), 85–87, 99–100, 122, 127–28, 130–31, 135–37; critique of, 185–86
International Criminal Tribunal for Rwanda (ICTR), 19, 222–23, 230
international governmental organizations (IGOs), 74
international justice. *See* justice
international law, 125, 131
inyenzi (cockroaches), 222
Isango Star, 165
Iteso ethnic group, 88, 142
Iwacu, 174

Joint Liaison Group (JIG), 97
journalism, 161–173; independent, 173–6. *See also* media; radio
Juba Peace Talks, 96, 100
Judicial Service Commission, 116–8
justice: economic, 3, 9; mechanisms of transitional, 14, 99, 125–30, 135–37; and reconciliation, 19, 122–39, 180–81; restorative, 14, 85–86, 99–100, 122, 125; transitional, 13–15, 55, 99–100, 122–36, 137–39

kabaka, 88–9
Kalenjin ethnic group, 28–29, 32–33, 122–23, 129, 136–37
Kampala, Uganda, 54–55, 87, 188
Karamoja, 57, 92, 142, 147–50, 152–53
Karamojong ethnic group, 29, 88, 91, 93, 106
Katanga, DRC, 31, 49, 163, 171
Katikiro ethnic group, 31, 49, 163, 171
katikiro, 89
Kayibanda, Grégoire, 37, 221, 228
Kenya African Democratic Union (KADU), 32, 53
Kenya African National Union (KANU), 32, 53, 108–11
Kenya National Dialogue and Reconciliation (KNDR), 127–28, 131–32
Kenyatta, Jomo, 28, 32, 53, 56
Kikuyu ethnic group, 28–29, 32–33, 49, 122–23, 129, 136–37
kimbugwe, 89
Kinyarwanda language, 29, 50, 164–65, 174, 229
Kirundi language, 163–64
Kisangani, DRC, 43, 163, 171

Kisii ethnic group, 33, 123
Kiswahili language, 9, 162, 171–72
Kitgum, Uganda, 191, 198
Kofi Annan Foundation, 128
Korondo, Jeff, 185–87, 194n2-4
Kriegler Commission, 115
kwihutura, 50

Lagos Plan of Action (LPA), 58, 238
Land Act, 97–98
land-grabbing policy, 27
Legislative Assembly, 52, 71, 78
Legislative Councils, 52, 89
Lingala language, 162, 171
livelihood, and earning potential, 92, 110, 144–49, 151–55, 198
Lord's Resistance Army (LRA): agenda of, 87, 92, 94; insurgency, 86–87; and the International Criminal Court, 13, 99–100; tactics, 87, 92, 94; victims of, 2, 18, 92, 180, 185, 198
LRA Disarmament and Northern Uganda Recovery Act, 95
LRA-GOU peace negotiation, 85–87, 91–92, 94–96, 100–101
Lubumbashi, DRC, 163, 171
Lugbara ethnic group, 88, 90
Luhya ethnic group, 32–33, 123
lukiiko, 89
Lule, Yusufu, 57, 91
Luo ethnic group/language, 29, 32–33, 88, 123, 184–86, 191

Maasai ethnic group, 27–29, 32, 49, 142
magendo, 57
Mahdi ethnic group, 88, 90, 91
Marxism/Leninism, 34
Mataba, Kibuye, Rwanda, 223
Matheniko ethnic group, 147
mato-oput, 99, 191
Matuga constituency, 119
Mau Mau liberation war, 28–29
Mbuji Mayi, DRC, 163, 171
media, the, 9, 16, 19, 162–65, 176–77, 190; antagonism by, 55, 163; challenges to, 165–69; monitoring, 169; state involvement with, 110, 185; sustainability, 173–76; synergy, 161, 169–73
Media High Council, 167, 172
militarism, 5–7, 40, 86, 93–94, 149, 199
Military Commission, the, 91
Ministry of Justice, 138
Ministry of Media and Communications, 168
Mobutu Sese Seko, Joseph, 31, 42–43, 168

Moi, Daniel Arap, 28, 32–33, 57, 59–60, 118, 134
Mombasa, Kenya, 57, 59
moral economy, 6
moral ethnicity, 6
motherhood. *See* formerly abducted child mothers
Mouvement Chrétien pour l'Evangelisation, le Counselling et la Réconciliation (MOUCECORE), 224–25
Muhutu. *See* Hutu
multinational corporations (MNCs), 56, 67
Mungiki, 119, 123
Museveni, Yoweri: and Arusha Accord, 60; and the LRA insurgency, 86–87, 92, 95–96, 99; relationship with Paul Kagame, 39, 43; rise to power, 91–92, 96, 180
music, 16–17, 165, 180–83, 194; appeal of, 188–91; pop 184–87. *See also* performance art
Mutesa I, Kabaka, 49, 89
Mututsi. *See* Tutsi
Mwai Kibaki, 32–33, 106, 132, 136
mwami, 36

National Council for the Defense of Democracy (CNDD), 41, 164
National Resistance Army (NRA), 92, 96, 147
National Resistance Movement (NRM), 61, 86–87, 92, 95–96
national unity, 33, 41, 101, 102n2, 229
National University of Rwanda, 165, 167
nationalism: ethnonationalism, 13, 86–87, 92, 94, 100–101; and independence, 28, 31–34; and regionalization, 60, 78, 87; and war propaganda, 40–41
nation-state, the, 1, 10, 14
natural resources, 4, 43, 143, 151, 153, 155
neopatrimonialism: corruption, 30, 32; in government, 6, 28, 33–34; politics of, 12, 28; and the state, 8, 76, 79. *See also* patrimonialism
new barbarism thesis, the, 8
New Regionalism Theory (NRT), 73–74
Nilotic-speaking ethnic group, 27, 36, 87–88, 92
nongovernmental organization (NGO): and arts and culture, 180; environmental rehabilitation by, 152; peace building, 100; and justice, 85, 186; and reconciliation, 163, 174, 209, 224; regionalization, 72; UN-ECOSOC statute for, 74
North Kivu region, DRC, 29, 42
northeastern Uganda, 15, 141–2
Ntaryamira, Cyprien, 39–41
Nyerere, Julius, 12, 33–34, 53, 56–59, 65, 67

Observer Status, 12, 75–76, 79
Ocampo Six, the, 130

Odinga, Oginga, 32
Odinga, Raila, 32–33, 136
Okwera, Jahria, 185, 194n2
Operation Iron Fist, 94
Operation Lightning Thunder, 94
Orange Democratic Movement (ODM), 32–33, 111–12, 118, 124, 128–29, 136
Organization of African Unity (OAU), 39, 58

p'Bitek, Okot, 90, 184
palaver, 226
pan-Africanism, 12, 53, 58, 67–68, 102n2
parastatal company, 48
parliament, members of (MPs), 113, 115, 130
Party of National Unity (PNU), 32–33, 111–12, 123–24, 128, 136
Party of the Movement of Hutu Emancipation (PARMEHUTU), 31, 37, 221
pastoralism: adaptation of, 146–47, 151–55; and cattle, 149–50; and climate change, 141–42, 144–46, 152; and violence, 15–16, 27, 143–44, 147–49, 152
patriarchy: by the state, 18; in wartime, 197–98, 201–4; after wartime, 211–13
patrimonialism, 6, 79, 108. See also neopatrimonialism
peacebuilding. See justice; reconciliation
peacekeeping mission. See United Nations: conflict intervention
performance art. See art; performance
Permanent Tripartite Commission, 50, 75. See also East African Community; Observer Status
poetry, 180, 184
Pokot ethnic group, 15, 141–42, 144, 147–50, 152, 155
political clientelism, 6, 38
political tribalism, 6
posttraumatic stress disorder (PTSD), 180
power, personalization of, 123, 131
prebendal, 6, 7, 42. See also corruption
progovernment militias, 40
prosecution, criminal, 15, 97, 122–25, 128–30, 133, 136–38
protectorate, 88, 90
psychosocial support, 86, 93, 199, 212, 209, 223

radio, 17, 161–69, 171–77, 185, 191–93, 222
Radio Bonesha, 164, 174
Radio Isanganiro, 165–67, 169, 171–72, 174
Radio Maendeleo, 163, 165, 171–74
Radio Maria, 163, 164
Radio Okapi, 17, 162, 166–67, 171, 173–74
Radio Salus, 165, 172, 174
Radio Sauti ya Rehema, 163

Radio Télévision libre des Mille Collines (RTLM), 163, 165, 177n3, 222–23
Radio Télévision Nationale du Congo (RTNC), 162, 168–69
railways, 30, 48, 52, 57, 71
reabduction, 209. See also abduction
rebels: in Burundi, 42, 164; in DRC, 2, 42–43; society of, 197–98, 201, 208; in Sudan, 94; in Uganda (*see* Lord's Resistance Army); weapons, 93; and wives, 203–7
reception and rehabilitation center, 209, 211–12
reconciliation; 3, 17; local concepts of, 148, 180–82, 184–88, 211; and peacebuilding, 191–94; policies of, 97–100, 128–32; and religion, 9, 19, 217–19, 224–28; versus justice, 15, 122–23, 127, 135–39
regionalism, 11–13, 47, 65–66, 71–73, 79
regionalization, 12, 65–66, 70–75, 77–79
rehabilitation, 85, 152, 209, 212
reintegration, 197–99, 202–3, 209–13
religion, 3, 5, 6, 9, 16, 217–18; Anglican, 19, 225–26, 228–29; Catholic, 19, 32, 38, 163, 164, 221–22, 223, 227, 228–30; and peacebuilding, 19, 218–20, 229–30; Pentecostal 162–64; politicization of, 19, 228–30; Protestant, 13, 162, 223; Seventh Day Adventist, 222
resettlement: of colonial populations, 27, 29; of formerly abducted child soldiers, 198, 207, 209; of IDPs, 14, 99, 112
resilience, 18, 147, 155, 198–200
returnees, 98, 182, 185, 209
Rift Valley, 27–29, 123, 129, 142
rights violation. See human rights
rights: children's, 166, 185–87, 198, 199–201; women's, 183
rights-based perspective, 15, 18, 152, 197, 210, 214
Rwandan Patriotic Front (RPF), 39–42, 169, 227–29, 231n14
rwodi, 88

sabataka, 89
Search for Common Ground (SFCG), 163–64, 160–70, 172
Serena Process. See KNDR
sex: commodification of, 199, 213; slavery, 2, 199
sexual: abuse, 185, 197, 199, 204, 213 (*see also* abuse); exploitation, 199, 204–5, 207–8; protection, 209; violence (*see* violence: sexual)
shadow governments, 124
small arms and light weapons (SALW), 2, 86, 93, 101, 147–50, 154
social acceptance, 18, 210
social capital, 155, 212–14

social norms, 15–19, 72–73, 147. 152–54, 188–90, 201–4
socialism, 56; Fabian, 34; *Ujamaa*, 34
socialization, 18, 201
Somalia, 2, 10, 48, 93, 148, 200
Southern Sudan, 2, 10, 29, 36, 96
state-centric model, 12
statism, 59, 60
stigmatization, 211–13
storytelling, 190, 209. *See also* folklore
subjugation, 202, 206, 211, 213
submissiveness, 201, 203–5, 211
suffering, 17–18, 41, 61, 97, 135, 179–80
support network, social, 203, 212
sustainability, 101, 153, 167, 173–76, 191–92
Swahili language, 49, 171, 174
synergy, 161, 169–72, 176

Ten Point Program, 95, 102n2
Teso, 88, 142, 199, 214n1
therapy, 209; art, 180–81, 188–89, 194n1
trade, 30, 49, 53–57, 70, 77–78; preferential trade agreements, 76
transnationalism, 59, 67
trauma, 148, 198; and PTSD, 181; social, 17–18, 180, 188; treatment of, 182, 188, 193, 224–25
Truth, Justice and Reconciliation Commission (TJRC), 14–15; Act of 2008, 132; critique of, 122, 127, 130, 134, 137–39; establishment of, 124, 127, 131–33; versus prosecution, 128, 130–31, 135
Turkana: ethnic group, 15, 32, 57, 142, 147–48, 152–55; Lake, 9
Tutsi ethnic group, 28–31, 35–41, 164–65, 220–24, 227–30
Twa ethnic group, 31, 35–37, 41, 221

Ubaku u Rwanda, 225–26
Uganda Constitutional Commission (UCC), 95–96
Uganda Human Rights Commission (UHRC), 92, 98
Uganda National Liberation Army (UNLA), 91, 102n3, 147
Uganda People's Defense Force (UPDF), 87, 148, 153
Uganda Peoples Democratic Movement/Army (UPDM/A), 86, 96

Uganda's north-south conflict, 13, 85, 91–93, 96
Ujamaa socialism in Tanzania, 34
UN Peacekeeping Mission in the Congo (MONUC, renamed MONUSCO in 2010), 17, 162, 173
Union for National Progress (UPRONA), 31, 38–39, 41
United Nations (UN): conflict intervention, 13, 43, 162, 173; criticism of, 41; humanitarian projects, 39, 74, 133, 191, 199; mediation, 33, 39, 95, 134
United Nations Assistance Mission for Rwanda (UNAMIR), 39, 41
United Nations Secretary General, 14, 33, 96, 106, 134, 147. *See also* Kofi Annan

victims: justice, 129, 131–32, 134–35, 137, 226–27; of genocide, 19, 41, 222, 226–27; of the LRA, 18, 92, 185, 199, 201; of other mass violence, 124–26
violence: and climate change, 141–46; coping with, 193; emotional, 204; ethnic, 2, 5, 37–38, 109, 221, 228; gender-based, 44, 204, 207–8; mass, 124–25, 219; normalizing, 223–24; postelection (*see* election: postelection violence); sexual, 43–44, 208; structural, 3–16
visual art. *See* art: visual
vulnerability: of governments, 67, 143, 152; of individuals, 92, 150, 187, 199, 203, 224–25; of populations, 100, 145, 148, 153, 224–25

weapons, 15; culture of, 148; proliferation of, 86, 93, 147–54; trade of, 19, 30, 147, 150–54; violence as a, 44, 205. *See also* disarmament; small arms and light weapons
West African Civil Society Forum (WACSOF), 77
Western Europe, 26, 68
Westphalia system, 66
Wives: co-, 201, 207, 210; expectations of, 204–6; perspectives of, 184; "relay" of, 206–7; senior, 207–8; young girls as, 190, 204, 207
womanhood, 208, 211
women's rights. *See* rights: women's

youth: activists, 39, 172, 187; and artistic expression, 17, 165, 179, 181–83, 188–91; disillusionment of, 32, 106; as soldiers, 40, 119, 122, 124, 129, 136. *See also* child soldiers

Contributors

Doreen Alusa is an International Relations lecturer in the School of Humanities and Social Sciences at the United States International University (USIU) in Kenya. She is on the steering committee of the UK government-funded Development Partnership in Higher Education (DELPHE) project at USIU and is currently finalizing her PhD in International Politics at the University of South Africa. She has various publications in the areas of East African foreign policy, food security, and regionalism including: "Regional Integration and Food Security in East Africa" (2008) and *GMO Politics: Implications for Africa's Food Export Commodities* (2010).

Alfred Anangwe, a sociologist by training, is the Research Coordinator at Arid Lands Institute, Nairobi, Kenya. Arid Lands Institute is a research and advocacy NGO working with pastoralists in Eastern Africa. He has participated in various research projects in collaboration with some accomplished Kenyan scholars and has published in the *African Journal of International Affairs*, *Encyclopedia of African Folklore*, and *Governing African Health Systems*, an edited book project under the CODESRIA Textbook Series. His current research interests include political conflict and democracy in Africa, terrorism in Eastern Africa, health sector reforms in Kenya, and the relevance of African culture in development. He has presented papers in a number of international conferences.

Harriet K. Bibangambah is the Research Officer at Greenwatch, an environmental advocacy NGO in Uganda. She is involved in research, capacity building, and advisory work around policy influencing strategies; engaging in advocacy for respect of the rule of law and for the right to public participation and involvement in environmental matters; drafting research reports, monitoring, and evaluation, analysis of data, networking and the use of social media and online communications. She holds an MA in Management Studies from Uganda Management Institute, focusing on Public Administration and Management, and a BA in Social Sciences from Makerere University. She has worked on a wide range of research projects, employing a range of different methodologies, specializing in public administration, decentralization, governance, and community work and organizational management.

Janine Natalya Clark is a lecturer in the Politics Department at the University of Sheffield, UK. She has also taught at Queen's University in Belfast and at the University of York, and was a Postdoctoral Research Fellow in the International Politics Department at Aberystwyth University from 2006 to 2009. Her research interests include postconflict societies, particularly in the former Yugoslavia and the African Great

Lakes; war crimes; transitional justice; the relationship between criminal trials and interethnic reconciliation; and religious peacebuilding. Clark is the author of *Serbia in the Shadow of Milošević: The Legacy of Conflict in the Balkans* (2008). Her other recent work includes articles in the *Journal of International Peacekeeping*; *Ethnopolitics*; the *Journal of International Criminal Justice*; and the *International Criminal Law Review*.

Marie-Soleil Frère is a Research Associate at the National Fund for Scientific Research in Belgium and teaches at the Department of Information and Communication Sciences at the University of Brussels, where she is also the director of the Research Center in Information and Communication. Her research focuses on African media, and particularly on the role of the media in the political evolution of Francophone Africa. She is the author of *Elections and the Media in Post-conflict Africa* (2011), *The Media and Conflicts in Central Africa* (2007), *Medias et Communications sociales au Burkina Faso* (2003), and *Presse et Democratie en Afrique Francophone* (2000).

Tricia Redeker Hepner is an Associate Professor of Anthropology and Vice Chair of Africana Studies at the University of Tennessee. Her research and teaching interests focus on forced migration, transnationalism, political conflict, peacebuilding, and human rights activism in the Horn of Africa and the Great Lakes region and their diasporas. Her recent publications include *Soldiers, Martyrs, Traitors, and Exiles: Political Conflict in Eritrea and the Diaspora* (2009), and *Biopolitics, Militarism, and Development: Eritrea in the Twenty-First Century* (coedited with David O'Kane, 2009). She is also a founding co-editor of the *African Conflict and Peacebuilding Review* journal. Her research has been funded by the National Science Foundation, Social Science Research Council, and the Wenner-Gren Foundation, among others. She received a PhD from Michigan State University in 2004 and a certificate in Forced Migration and Refugee Issues from York University in 2009. At the University of Tennessee she is chair of the Migration and Refugee Studies division of the Center for the Study of Social Justice, a core faculty member of the program in Disasters, Displacement and Human Rights, and co-director of the Gulu Study and Service Abroad Program, in partnership with Gulu University, Institute for Peace and Strategic Studies, Uganda.

Julaina A. Obika is a lecturer and researcher at the Institute of Peace and Strategic Studies (IPSS) at Gulu University, northern Uganda. She has a background in Gender and Development Studies from Makerere University in Kampala and a master's degree in Conflict Transformation and Management from The Nelson Mandela Metropolitan University (NMMU) in Port Elizabeth, South Africa. Julaina has been involved in a number of consultancies and research studies, both at local and international levels. She has consulted for organizations like CARE international, World Vision, Save the Children in Uganda, and World Food Program. Her areas of research interest include peacebuilding, conflict resolution and women studies. She is also the Secretary for the Development Partnerships for Higher Learning (DelPHE) project at Gulu University and coordinates the Gulu Study and Service Abroad Program (GSSAP) with Dr. Tricia Redeker Hepner.

Eric Awich Ochen lectures at the Makerere University's Department of Social Work and Social Administration within the College of Humanities and Social Sciences. He completed his doctoral studies at the Centre for Applied Childhood Studies in the School of Human and Health Sciences, University of Huddersfield in November, 2011. He holds an MSc in Development and Project Planning (with Distinction) from the University of Bradford (2002) and a BA degree in Social Work and Social Administration from Makerere University in Uganda (1999). Eric has previously worked with Save the Children Denmark, Gulu Support the Children Organization (GUSCO), and Community Development Resource Network. He has also supported several development agencies as an evaluation and project development consultant. Eric's present professional interest is in planning of intervention programs to meet the needs and rights of children in Uganda, a country emerging from prolonged conflict. His doctoral research explores the narratives of young women's experiences of the conflict and reintegration process in Northern Uganda. He is also the author of several articles or chapters on children in conflict situations, published in the *Journal of Community Practice*; *Reflection: Social Work Innovations in Africa*; and *Aspects of Social Development and Local Governance in Uganda*, edited by Nicholas Awortwi and Auma Okwany.

Hannington Ochwada is an Assistant Professor in the Department of History at Missouri State University in Springfield, Missouri. He holds an MA degree in Education from Kenyatta University in Nairobi, and a PhD degree in History and Gender Studies from Indiana University in Bloomington, Indiana. Hannington has taught history at Kenyatta University in Nairobi, Marquette University in Milwaukee, Wisconsin, and Center College in Danville, Kentucky. He has published in *Africa Development*; *Afrika Zamani: A Journal of African History*; *Transafrican Journal of History*; *Journal of Eastern African Research and Development*, *Discovery and Innovation*; *Urban Affairs Review*, and other professional journals. He has contributed chapters and entries in edited books and encyclopedias and is co-author of *A Grammatical Sketch of the Lusaamia Verb* (2006). He currently conducts research on gender, biography, and security issues with specific reference to Africa.

Ozonnia Ojielo is the Coordinator for Conflict Prevention and Recovery, Bureau of Crisis Prevention and Recovery, United Nations Development Programme, New York. He was previously the Senior Peace and Development Advisor to the UN Resident and Humanitarian Coordinator in Kenya and Chief of the Peacebuilding Programme of UNDP Kenya, and the former Chief of Operations and subsequently Officer-in-Charge at the Sierra Leone Truth and Reconciliation Commission. He has first and advanced degrees in History, an LLB in Law, MBA in Strategic and Project Management and a PhD in Peace and Conflict Studies. He was formerly a human rights lawyer in Nigeria

(1990–2002), university academic (University of Nigeria, Enugu Campus and at the Enugu State University of Science and Technology, Enugu, Nigeria, 1992–2001) and president of the research and advocacy organization, Centre for Peace in Africa, Lagos, Nigeria (1993–2002). He is the author of two books: *Alternative Dispute Resolution* (2001); *Managing Organisational Disputes: A Systems Approach* (2002) and editor of *Rethinking Peace and Security in Africa* (2002), and *ADR: Options for an Economy in Transition* (2003), as well as journal articles and book chapters.

Kenneth Omeje is Professor of International Relations at the United States International University (USIU) in Nairobi, Kenya. He holds a PhD in Peace Studies from the University of Bradford and an MA degree in Peace and Conflict Studies from the European Peace University in Stadt-Schlaining, Austria. He has previously held the position of Lecturer / Research Fellow in African Peace and Conflict Studies at the Department of Peace Studies, University of Bradford, and in the Institute for Development Studies, Department of Political Science, University of Nigeria, Nsukka. He has held visiting research fellowship positions at the Center for African Studies, University of Florida, Gainesville, USA (1992); Institute of Higher Education, Comprehensive University of Kassel, Germany (Summer 2000); the Law Department, Keele University, UK (Spring 2000); and Department of International Politics, University of Wales, Aberystwyth (2001). Kenneth is the author of *High Stakes and Stakeholders: Oil Conflict & Security in Nigeria* (2006); and editor of *Extractive Economies and Conflicts in the Global South: Multi-regional Perspective on Rentier Politics* (2008); *State–Society Relations in Nigeria: Democratic Consolidation, Conflicts and Reforms* (2007); and *War to Peace Transition: Conflict Intervention and Peacebuilding in Liberia* (2009). He has more than seventy publications, including contributions to international encyclopedias and articles in major peer-reviewed journals.

Lindsay McClain Opiyo is a master's student at the Kroc Institute for International Peace Studies at the University of Notre Dame. She holds a bachelor's degree from the College Scholars Program at the University of Tennessee, where she studied the role of the arts in peacebuilding and development in Africa. Lindsay was recently employed by the Justice and Reconciliation Project in Gulu, Uganda, where she worked with grassroots, war-affected communities on issues of accountability and reconciliation. She is a founding member of the Jazz for Justice Project and Music for Peace.

Elias Omondi Opongo is a lecturer at Hekima Institute of Peace Studies and International Relations (Hekima College), Catholic University of Eastern Africa, Nairobi, Kenya, and a Jesuit priest. He holds a PhD in Peace Studies from University of Bradford, UK; an MA degree in International Peace Studies from the J. B. Kroc Institute, University of Notre Dame, Indiana; and Licentiate degree in Theology with a specialization in Social Ethics from Weston Jesuit School of Theology, Cambridge, Massachusetts. He is a conflict analyst and peace practitioner, and former Director of Jesuit

Hakimani Centre in Nairobi, Kenya and has taught courses in peace and conflict studies at universities in the United States and Eastern Africa. Elias has conducted peace and reconciliation workshops/trainings in different parts of Africa, and has also worked as a peacebuilding consultant for UNESCO-PEER (Horn of Africa); Jesuit Refugee Service Eastern Africa, and many other organizations. He was formerly Director of the Department of Social Justice for Jesuits of Africa and Madagascar, and Project Director of Jesuit Refugee Service, Ngara, Tanzania. His book publications include: *Peace Weavers: Methodologies of Peace Building in Africa* (2008); *Faith Doing Justice: A Manual for Social Analysis, Catholic Social Teachings and Social Justice* (2007), and *Making Choices for Peace: Aid Agencies in Field Diplomacy*, coauthored with A. E. Orobator (2006).

www.ingramcontent.com/pod-product-compliance
Lightning Source LLC
Chambersburg PA
CBHW021806220426
43662CB00006B/205